NEW ENGLISH KEY NOTES

Series Editor: Tony Lake

MENTOR BOOKS

Published in 2008 by

Mentor Books

43 Furze Road

Sandyford Industrial Estate

Dublin 18

Tel: 01–2952 112 / 3

Fax: 01–2952 114

Website: www.mentorbooks.ie

email: admin@mentorbooks.ie

Design: Kathryn O'Sullivan

Layout & Edited by: Nicola Sedgwick

ISBN: 978-1-906623-24-1

Printed in Ireland by ColourBooks Ltd.

, 1 3 5 7 9 10 8 6 4 2

Contents

Note to Students

The purpose of *New English Key Notes* is to offer some practical assistance and advice to students preparing for Leaving Certificate Higher Level English – Paper 2. The notes presented here explain and analyse the three elements of the literature syllabus:

• Single Text (*King Lear*) • Comparative Study • Poetry.

New English Key Notes aims to promote a clear-minded, analytical approach to the exam. The range of aspects considered in these notes is not intended to be either exhaustive or prescriptive. Essential phrases are in **bold type**.

Single Text: This sections includes a Scene-by-Scene Summary and Commentary on *King Lear*. Key Points are listed at the end of each scene, stressing the most important aspects in relation to plot development, characterisation, themes, style, etc. Following Exam Guidelines, a variety of Exam Topics are addressed. Finally, The Characters of the play are also examined in terms of their traits and dramatic function. Key Adjectives are listed at the end of each section to highlight each character's most striking qualities.

Comparative Study: This section examines three popular, accessible texts: *Lies of Silence*, *Dancing at Lughnasa* and *Il Postino* in terms of the three prescribed comparative modes:

    A. Cultural Context

    B. General Vision and Viewpoint

    C. Literary Genre.

Key Points of Comparison / Contrast are listed at the end of each section. With such a wide range of texts from which to choose, the aim here is to encourage a coherent comparative approach to the three texts chosen. Finally there are Guidelines for Answering Exam Questions as well as Sample Answers for each mode of comparison.

Poetry: This section discusses the poems of eight poets individually. Key Points are listed at the end of each poem. The Sample Answers given here are considerably longer than the responses expected of students in the exam itself (most responses are three to four A4 pages). The lengthy answers given here are designed to suggest a wide range of areas of possible discussion and to discourage rote learning of such answers. The emphasis throughout this section is on the central importance of personal engagement grounded in the text. Finally there are extensive Guidelines on Answering Exam Questions.

The last section explains **Key Literary Terms**.

King Lear

Introduction

King Lear is believed to have been written around 1605. While the opening scenes of the play suggest a fairytale-like plot with its extremes of good and evil, it is soon apparent that *King Lear* is one of the darkest and most tragic of Shakespeare's tragedies. The vision of the play is, in many respects, extremely pessimistic.

Similar to all of Shakespeare's tragedies, *King Lear* portrays the downfall of a once-great man. Like all of the other tragic heroes, Lear's downfall is caused by a fatal flaw. While Macbeth is ambitious, Othello jealous and Hamlet indecisive, Lear is rash. This rashness is immediately apparent in the opening scene where Lear declares his intention of dividing up his kingdom. His decision to abdicate the throne seems to be motivated by a sense of weariness with the 'cares and business' of kingship. He claims that in dividing the kingdom at this point, he wishes to prevent 'future strife', but, ironically, this is precisely and inevitably what his selfish decision to renounce the throne causes. Seeming to decide the manner in which he will divide the kingdom on a whim ('Which of us shall we say doth love us most?'), Lear compounds the dangerous foolishness of his decision to step down from the throne. The flattery his 'love test' invites immediately flows from both Goneril and Regan, whose desire to out-do each other in their declarations of 'love' prefigures the deadly rivalry that will later consume and destroy them both. Cordelia, the only daughter that genuinely loves Lear, refuses to massage her father's ego such is her disgust at the contrived nature of her sisters' expressions of love. An outraged Lear impetuously disowns and disinherits his one true daughter, dividing his kingdom between Goneril and Regan.

Lear pays an extremely high price for his foolishness. Having given Goneril and Regan power and authority over him, Lear is now at their mercy and neither love nor compassion feature among their qualities. The callous sisters coldly strip Lear of his remaining power and dignity and their unnatural ingratitude ultimately drives Lear to insanity. On the positive side, Lear grows through his suffering, paradoxically acquiring 'reason in madness' and gradually becoming a better and wiser man. While he is eventually reconciled with Cordelia, the play ends in a heartbreakingly tragic manner with Lear carrying the body of the lifeless Cordelia onto the stage.

The play explores such universal themes as the parent-child relationship, love, ingratitude, the abuse of power, growth through suffering and redemption. The universality of these themes is underscored by the fact that the sub-plot (the story of Gloucester and his sons) reflects and reinforces the key themes in the play.

Scene-by-Scene Summary and Commentary

ACT 1 Scene 1

The opening scene introduces us to most of the characters in the play. It is dominated by Lear's abdication (i.e. his resignation from the throne) and by the artificial love-test which will decide the manner in which the kingdom is divided. As king, Lear was seen as God's representative on earth and was not expected to surrender (give up) his power and authority. While Lear believed that he would ensure future peace and harmony by dividing the kingdom at this point (. . . that future strife may be prevented now'), this unwise decision would ironically ensure the opposite since it would inevitably lead to rivalry and conflict in the future. Furthermore, the ridiculous manner in which he sets out to divide the kingdom is a recipe for disaster. The love-test reflects Lear's foolishness and egotism (self-centred nature) – he believes that he can measure love in words and demands that his daughters express their love for him in a very public manner. Lear's foolishness will plunge the kingdom into chaos, in the process causing unimaginable suffering both for Lear himself and for a range of other characters. While Lear must inevitably pay the price for his faults and failings, the price he ultimately pays is strikingly out of proportion to his initial blunder.

When Lear asks which of his daughters loves him most, he inevitably invites flattery and both Goneril and Regan are happy to pander to his ego (flatter him) in order to advance themselves. Goneril hypocritically proclaims that she loves her father 'more than words can wield the matter'. There is an obvious irony in Regan's observation that she is 'made of the self metal' as Goneril since both sisters love power far more than they love Lear. From the outset, we see the sibling rivalry between these equally false sisters when Regan immediately tries to outdo her sister in her profession of love for Lear: 'In my true heart I find she names my very deed of love, only she comes too short . . .' While these expressions of love are exaggerated and insincere, the sentimental old king is easily duped (fooled). **Goneril and Regan are each awarded a third of the kingdom following their artificial professions of love for Lear.**

Lear has already decided that Cordelia, his favourite daughter, will get the best share of the kingdom. However, when he asks her what she can say 'to draw a third more opulent' than her sisters, he is stunned by her simple response: 'Nothing'. Disgusted by her sisters' hypocrisy, Cordelia refuses to flatter Lear: 'I cannot heave my heart into my mouth. I love your majesty according to my bond: nor more, nor less'. She goes on to logically ask: 'Why have my sisters husbands if they say they love you all?' Cordelia's refusal to indulge Lear sets in motion a series of disastrous events. While it is true that the whole tragedy might have been avoided had Cordelia simply humoured the whimsical (impulsive) Lear, she has high personal standards and will not stoop to using 'the glib and oily art' of flattery to secure her share of the kingdom. She may also have inherited some of her father's pride and obstinacy (stubborness). While Cordelia's expression of love sounds cold and unfeeling, she, unlike her sisters, truly loves her father as a daughter should. **Her refusal to take part in Lear's foolish game reflects her spirit and courage.**

In refusing to flatter Lear, Cordelia inevitably incurs his wrath (provokes his anger). We see Lear's rash and fiery nature when he disowns the daughter he always loved most: 'Here I disclaim all my paternal care, propinquity and property of love.' Furthermore, he jeopardises (endangers) her marital prospects by also disinheriting her. Lear's response to Cordelia's plain speaking is harsh, extreme and wildly disproportionate to the perceived wrong that has been done to him. Lear's misjudgement of Cordelia is one of the root causes of the tragedy, and will haunt him for much of the painful personal journey he will shortly be forced to undertake.

Lear's foolishness is again cast into sharp relief (brought into clear focus) by his stated determination to 'retain the name and all the additions to a king' even after he has given up the crown. He naively believes that he can keep the title and trappings of kingship after he has walked away from the responsibilities of leadership – this, of course, is utterly unrealistic on Lear's part.

It is at this point that we see Kent's remarkable loyalty, bluntness and moral courage. Kent idolises Lear, regarding him as his king, father, master and patron. However, he is unwilling to remain silent in the face of Lear's shocking rashness and bravely comes to Cordelia's defence. We see how unreal Lear's self-image is when he warns Kent not to come 'between the dragon and his wrath'. Lear sees himself as an all-powerful being, before whom everyone should quake. Lear is spiritually blind at the start of the play, unable to see himself or others in a true light. Kent is the only person in the court brave enough to stand up to Lear, bluntly telling him that he is 'mad' and that he is bowing to flattery. He rightly believes that his unmannerly behaviour

towards his king is, in the circumstances, justified. Kent begs Lear to 'check this hideous rashness', reminding him that he has only ever regarded his own life as 'a pawn' to wage against Lear's enemies. Aware of Lear's spiritual blindness, Kent pleads with him to 'see better', before plainly telling him: 'I'll tell thee thou dost evil.'

Kent is one of the most admirable characters in the play, consistently speaking his mind regardless of the personal consequences. Like Cordelia, he too pays a high price for daring to challenge Lear. Accustomed to a lifetime of unquestioning obedience, Lear is enraged by Kent's intervention and banishes him. In a few dramatic minutes, Lear seems to cut himself off from those who love him most. Before leaving the court, Kent expresses the hope that the gods will watch over Cordelia and that Goneril and Regan's actions will match their words of love. He is a good judge of character and, in contrast to the gullible Lear, does not accept flowery declarations of love at face value.

Lear now turns to address Cordelia's suitors. Pointing out that she is now without a dowry and is the object of his 'hate', he asks Burgundy and France if they will 'take her, or leave her'. It is difficult to believe that Lear is talking about his own flesh and blood here, such is his heartless tone. Burgundy and France are sharply contrasting characters. Burgundy is practical and mercenary-minded and has no interest in marrying Cordelia without the promised dowry. However, France is more sensitive to Cordelia's plight, pointedly asking how Lear's favourite daughter ('your best object') can possibly have fallen from favour in such a dramatic manner. We see Cordelia's nobility and spirit when, acknowledging that she lacks the 'glib and oily art' of flattery, she asks Lear to explain that she has not lost favour because of any dishonourable act on her part. **France is very impressed with Cordelia's personal qualities and is prepared to marry her despite her lack of a dowry. He tells Burgundy that 'she is herself a dowry'.** In his eyes, love has nothing to do with money or territory: 'Love's not love when it is mingled with regards that stand aloof from the entire point'. Addressing her as 'Fairest Cordelia', France declares that she is 'most rich, being poor'. **France's love for Cordelia is sincere, and sharply contrasts with the 'love' of Burgundy, which is entirely based on material considerations.**

While Cordelia impresses us with her honesty, courage and composure, we also admire her judgement. She sees through her sisters' hypocrisy and tells them so as she leaves the court: 'I know you what you are . . .' Remarkably, despite Lear's dreadful treatment of her, she remains concerned for him: 'I would prefer him to a better place.' She shrewdly predicts that Goneril and Regan's true intentions will be revealed in time: 'Time shall unfold what plaited cunning hides.'

After Cordelia and France leave, Goneril and Regan reflect on the dramatic events that have occurred. They are genuinely taken aback (shocked) by Lear's poor judgement and rashness. Goneril states that Lear 'always loved our sister most; and with what poor judgement he hath now cast her off appears too grossly'. She points out that Lear

has always been fiery and impulsive: 'The best and soundest of his time hath been but rash'. Reflecting on Lear's lack of self-knowledge, Regan tells her sister that 'he hath ever but slenderly known himself'. Goneril and Regan's observations are obviously not rooted in any loving concern for Lear, but in their fear that his rash and fiery nature may cause difficulties for them in the future. **Here we learn that Lear's flaws – his rashness and lack of self-knowledge – are deeply ingrained in his character.**

By the close of the opening scene, Goneril and Regan are already conspiring (secretly plotting) against Lear. Goneril appears to be the dominant sister: 'Pray you, let us hit together.' Having used cunning and flattery to gain their share of the kingdom, they immediately plan to take Lear's remaining power from him. They see no good in their own father and intend to 'do something' about him quickly. Goneril and Regan are particularly unappealing characters because they are utterly ungrateful and callous (unfeeling). While Lear was cruel to Cordelia, he acted on the spur of the moment. In contrast to Lear's unthinking cruelty, Goneril and Regan's evil actions are coldly pre-meditated. **Of course, Lear's tragedy is that he has cut himself off from his one loving daughter and given his two scheming daughters power and authority over him.**

KEY POINTS

- Lear is a deeply flawed character – he is gullible, arrogant, morally blind and rash.
- The love-test invites flattery, and Goneril and Regan do not hesitate to tell Lear what he wants to hear, their artificial expressions of love ensuring them of their share of the kingdom.
- We see Lear at his worst when he disowns and disinherits the loving Cordelia and when he banishes the loyal Kent.
- Cordelia is honest, noble and courageous.
- Kent is loyal, blunt and courageous.
- France displays true love for Cordelia, being prepared to marry her without a dowry.
- Goneril and Regan are cunning, hypocritical and ungrateful – by the close of the opening scene they have formed an alliance and are already plotting against Lear.

ACT 1 Scene 2

This scene opens with a soliloquy from Edmund (A soliloquy is basically a speech in which a character is thinking aloud to him/herself – its value lies in the insights it offers into the character's innermost thoughts.). **This soliloquy helps us to better understand Edmund's character and motivation, revealing him to be proud, ambitious, defiant and ruthless.** We learn of Edmund's devious plan to trick his father, Gloucester, into giving him Edgar's inheritance: 'Legitimate Edgar, I must have your land.' Edmund believes in the law of the jungle, the survival of the fittest: 'Thou, Nature, art my goddess . . .' He is as cold and calculating as Goneril and Regan. He does not feel bound by any moral code or natural law, and will achieve his goals by whatever means are necessary. In that sense, **Edmund is a Machiavellian character, believing that the end justifies the means.** We see his pride when he defiantly rejects the label that

society has attached to him because he was born outside of wedlock: 'Why bastard? Wherefore base? When my dimensions are as well compact, my mind as generous and my shape as true as honest madam's issue'. It is difficult not to feel a grudging admiration for Edmund's determination to succeed in life and so rise above his lowly status in society. Edmund is a clever schemer and – at this point in the play – a likeable villain.

As the play develops, we see the obvious similarities and parallels between the main plot (the story of Lear and his children) and the sub-plot (the story of Gloucester and his children). Just as Edmund is as unscrupulous as Goneril and Regan, so is Gloucester as gullible as Lear. Gloucester also shares Lear's rashness and moral blindness. Edmund exploits Gloucester's superstitious and credulous (gullible/unsuspecting) nature. His plan is simple – he arouses his father's interest in a letter he is reading by pretending to hide it.

Edmund then uses this letter to destroy his brother, Edgar's, reputation. The letter seems to suggest that Edgar is plotting to murder his aged father because he is impatient to inherit his estate, and that he is looking for Edmund's assistance. Rash like Lear, Gloucester never stops to think and ponder the authenticity (genuineness) of this letter. He immediately condemns Edgar: 'Abhorred villain! Unnatural, detested, brutish villain!' Gloucester's inability to see the truth about his sons is an indication of his moral/spiritual blindness. By pretending to defend Edgar, Edmund simply further convinces Gloucester of Edgar's guilt. Edmund manipulates his father with consummate (expert) skill, convincing him to eavesdrop on a conversation between Edgar and himself. Gloucester agrees in order to find out about Edgar's true intentions.

Gloucester is a superstitious character and blames all kinds of problems in the world of men on the stars: 'These late eclipses in the sun and moon portend no good to us.' Edmund laughs at his father's superstitious nature. For Edmund the idea of blaming various problems on the stars is simply ridiculous ('the excellent foppery of the world'). He believes that life is shaped not by the stars, but by people themselves. Edmund believes in the power of his own will – he believes that his destiny lies in his own hands.

The success of Edmund's scheming has much to do with the gullibility of both Gloucester and Edgar. Edgar is presented as a noble, but credulous character. When Edmund tells Edgar that Gloucester is angry with him, Edgar rightly concludes that someone has tarnished his reputation ('Some villain hath done me wrong'), but never suspects that his good name has been destroyed by his brother's lies. At the close of this scene Edmund delights in the ease with which he has manipulated both Gloucester and Edgar. He exploits his father's gullibility and his brother's nobility in order to advance his own selfish plans: 'A credulous father and a brother noble . . . on whose foolish honesty my practices ride easy'. Edmund may have been unfortunate in terms of the circumstances of his birth, but is determined to achieve his goals through his scheming: 'Let me, if not by birth, have lands by wit'. He has no scruples (conscience) and will do whatever is necessary to bring about his own advancement: 'All with me's meet that I can fashion fit.'

KEY POINTS

- Edmund is ambitious, scheming and unscrupulous (without conscience).
- He manipulates both Gloucester and Edgar with expert ease.
- Gloucester shares certain characteristics with Lear, being both gullible and rash.
- Edgar is noble, but rather credulous.
- From the beginning there are clear similarities between the sub-plot and the main plot.

ACT 1 Scene 3

It is not long before Goneril reveals her true nature. With her share of the kingdom secured, she has no need to flatter or indulge Lear any longer. **This scene introduces us to the key theme of filial ingratitude** (the ingratitude of the child towards the parent). Goneril had earlier agreed to provide hospitality for her father and his followers, but has no intention of honouring this agreement. She encourages her servant Oswald to be disrespectful towards Lear: 'Put on what weary negligence you please'. She wants to provoke a confrontation with Lear so that she can assert her authority over him. Goneril resents the fact that Lear still behaves as if he were king despite having given away all of his power, and cannot disguise her contempt for him: 'idle old man that still would manage those authorities that he hath given away.' The hypocrisy of her declaration of love for Lear in the opening scene is underlined by her disdainful remark: 'Old fools are babes again'. She speaks of her father with a total lack of love and respect. Lear is about to start paying the price for his earlier foolishness. Goneril is the dominant sister and sends a message to Regan, urging her to follow her lead in relation to Lear: 'I'll write straight to my sister to hold my very course'.

KEY POINTS

- Goneril's filial ingratitude quickly becomes apparent.
- She encourages her servants to neglect Lear in order to provoke a confrontation with him.
- Goneril ensures that Regan treats Lear as she has done – she is the more enterprising, more dominant sister.

ACT 1 Scene 4

Kent returns in disguise to help Lear. He is so devoted to Lear that he is prepared to serve him as a lowly servant despite Lear having treated him so harshly: '. . . thy master, whom thou lovest, shall find thee full of labours.' Lear still acts as if he were king, demanding that his dinner be served without delay. However, Goneril's servants have been ordered to make Lear and his followers feel less welcome and one of Lear's knights clearly perceives the changed atmosphere: 'Your highness is not entertained with that ceremonious affection as you were wont.' He speaks of 'a great abatement (lessening) of kindness'. Oswald is deliberately disrespectful towards Lear when he describes him as 'My lady's father'. **The idea that his status in life is now defined in relation to his daughter infuriates Lear.** Angered by Oswald's insulting attitude towards Lear, Kent trips up the disrespectful servant.

The Fool plays an important role in Lear's personal development by relentlessly reminding him of his foolishness. Lear calls him 'a bitter fool' because he speaks the bitter truth. Kent recognises the Fool's wisdom when he remarks: 'This is not altogether fool, my Lord'. The Fool bluntly tells Lear that he was foolish to give up his crown: 'Thou hadst little wit in thy bald crown, when thou gavest thou golden one away'. He rightly points out that Lear has given his daughters power and authority over him: 'Thou madest thy daughters thy mother.' Goneril angrily speaks of the 'all-licensed fool' because he seems to have a licence to say whatever he likes.

When Goneril appears, she takes Lear to task (scolds him) for the rowdy (noisy and disorderly) behaviour of his knights ('men so disorder'd, so debosh'd and bold') She demands that Lear control his men and reduce their number. **Lear's knights are the last reminder of his royal power and Goneril is determined to strip her father of his remaining power and authority.** Moreover, Lear's knights might, in certain circumstances, pose a military threat to the new regime (government). Goneril later dismisses fifty of these knights 'at a clap'.

Goneril's bitter attack stuns Lear: 'Are you our daughter?' Not only does Lear struggle to recognise Goneril, he struggles with his own identity: 'Who is it that can tell me who I am?' Accustomed to automatic respect and unquestioning obedience, Lear had always seen himself as an almost superhuman figure. Now that he is being treated with undisguised contempt, he is shaken to the very core of his being. This incident marks the beginning of Lear's battle to retain his sanity. Lear dismisses Goneril as a 'degenerate bastard', foolishly believing that Regan will treat him better: 'Yet have I left a daughter.' He describes Goneril's ingratitude as a 'marble-hearted fiend' and uses animal imagery ('detested kite', 'wolvish visage') to highlight her lack of humanity. **Lear now sees**

Cordelia's 'sin' as a 'most minor fault' – the first sign that he is growing through suffering.

Albany arrives on the scene and urges Lear to be patient. However, Albany seems to be a weak, ineffectual character, who has neither been consulted nor informed about Goneril's plans for Lear: 'My lord, I am guiltless, as I am ignorant of what hath moved you.' While Albany appears to be sympathetic towards Lear, his attempted protest on the latter's behalf is ignored by Goneril, who despises her husband's 'milky gentleness'.

Lear is furious with himself when he realises his earlier foolishness: 'O Lear, Lear, Lear! Beat at this gate that let thy folly in and thy dear judgement out!' However, we once again see Lear's rash and fiery nature when he curses Goneril with sterility: 'Into her womb convey sterility! Dry up in her the organs of increase, and from her derogate body never spring a babe to honour her!' If she is to have a child, Lear hopes that it will be an unnatural, thankless child so that she too will feel the pain of filial ingratitude, which he describes as being 'sharper than a serpent's tooth'. Lear is filled with shame that his daughter can treat him with visible contempt, but realises that he is to blame for his present predicament, having given her the power to belittle him. Lear laments his moral blindness: 'Old fond eyes, beweep this cause again, I'll pluck ye out, and cast you with the waters that you lose, to temper clay.'

KEY POINTS

- The ever-loyal Kent returns in disguise to serve Lear as a lowly servant.
- The Fool continues to relentlessly remind Lear of his foolishness and wrongdoing.
- Goneril openly criticises Lear's knights, demanding that Lear control their behaviour and reduce their number. She wishes to strip him of the remnants of his power, authority and kingly dignity. She goes on to dismiss fifty of Lear's knights 'at a clap'.
- Lear is so profoundly shocked by Goneril's humiliating scolding that he struggles to recognise her ('Are you our daughter?') and indeed struggles to recognise himself ('Who is it that can tell me who I am?'). This is the first step in Lear's mental disintegration.
- We again see the rash and fiery side to Lear in the manner in which he curses Goneril with sterility.
- Albany appears to be a well-intentioned, but weak and powerless character.

ACT 1 Scene 5

Lear sends Kent ahead to Regan's castle with a letter announcing his imminent arrival. He is unaware that Goneril has already sent a letter to Regan, urging her to follow her course of action in relation to Lear. After Kent departs, Lear reflects on the injustice he has done Cordelia: 'I did her wrong.' Here we see Lear taking another step on the road to self-knowledge. Helping him along this road is the Fool, who continues to be unrelenting in his efforts to make Lear more self-aware. **While Lear foolishly believes that Regan will treat him better than Goneril, the Fool perceives that both sisters are fundamentally alike:** 'She will taste as like this as a crab does to a crab.' We see the Fool's caustic (biting/sarcastic) wit when he reminds Lear of the error of his ways in abdicating and leaving himself without a home and at the mercy of his daughters. He tells Lear that even the humble snail has a house 'to put his head in; not to give it away to his daughters, and leave his horns without a case'. He informs Lear that he has grown old without growing wise: 'Thou shouldst not have been old till thou hadst been wise.' Lear is now painfully aware of the depth of Goneril's unnatural thanklessness: 'Monster ingratitude!'

By the close of this scene, Lear can sense the insanity rising within him, pleading with the heavens to keep him sane: 'O let me not be mad, not mad, sweet heaven! Keep me in temper: I would not be mad!'

KEY POINTS

- Kent is sent to Regan's castle with a letter informing her of Lear's imminent arrival.
- The Fool continues to remind Lear of his foolishness so that he may become more self-aware.
- Lear displays further signs of personal growth when, reflecting on Cordelia, he acknowledges, 'I did her wrong'.
- Sensing his incipient (the beginning of) insanity, Lear pleads with the heavens to keep him sane.

ACT 2 Scene 1

The opening lines of this act underline the foolishness of Lear's decision to divide the kingdom, with Curan asking Edmund if he is aware of the growing rivalry between Cornwall and Albany: 'Have you heard of no likely wars toward, 'twixt the Dukes of Cornwall and Albany?' **This scene brings Edmund's cunning nature into clear focus.** Meeting Edgar, Edmund insists that his brother is in real danger and is not safe in their father's castle. Tricking the unsuspecting Edgar into participating in a fake sword fight, Edmund inflicts a wound on himself to dupe the malleable (easily influenced), credulous Gloucester into seeing him as loyal and loving, and Edgar as treacherous and unnatural. Shouting aloud to attract his father's attention, Edmund draws attention to his injury, before going on to paint an utterly dark picture of Edgar, claiming that he had tried to enlist his assistance in murdering Gloucester. Pretending that he reminded Edgar of how 'strong a bond the child was bound to the father', and that he wanted nothing to do with his brother's 'unnatural purpose", Edmund easily convinces Gloucester of Edgar's villainy. Gloucester immediately concludes that Edgar is a

'murderous coward' who must be hunted down and brought to justice: 'Let him fly far: Not in this land shall he remain uncaught, and found – dispatch.' **The similarity between Lear and Gloucester is immediately apparent – both are easily manipulated and rash.** Just as Lear makes an exile of Cordelia, his one true daughter, Gloucester makes a fugitive of Edgar, his loyal and loving son. In another rash act, Gloucester disinherits Edgar as Lear had disinherited Cordelia, telling Edmund that he is now his heir: '. . . of my land, loyal and natural boy, I'll work the means to make thee capable.' **Both Lear and Gloucester foolishly give children, who prove to be thankless and cruel, power and authority over them.**

Edmund is a quick-thinking opportunist, turning every situation to his own advantage. When Regan asks if Edgar (Lear's godson) was consorting (keeping company) with Lear's disorderly knights, Edmund immediately replies that he was indeed accompanying them. Edmund avails of every opportunity to further tarnish (blacken) his brother's reputation. At this point we learn that Regan will extend no welcome to Lear, telling Cornwall that she will 'not be there' if he and his knights look to stay with her. **As plot and**

sub-plot converge, we see clear lines of division emerging as Edmund wins his way into the service of the Duke of Cornwall and becomes aligned with the other evil characters. Impressed by the 'child-like office' Edmund has displayed in defence of his father, and by his 'virtue and obedience', Cornwall declares: 'Natures of such deep trust we shall much need: You we first seize on.'

KEY POINTS

- The foolishness of Lear's decision to divide the kingdom is underlined by the rumour of a possible war between Cornwall and Albany.
- Edmund's opportunism and quick thinking are clearly visible in this scene.
- This scene sees plot and sub-plot converge, leaving the forces of evil combined when Cornwall invites Edmund to enter his service.
- Similarities between plot and sub-plot are very evident in this scene.

ACT 2 Scene 2

When Kent meets Oswald at Gloucester's castle, he cannot disguise his contempt for him and gives him a tongue-lashing before drawing his sword. Kent's hatred of Oswald is intensified by his knowledge of the letter that he carries from Goneril to Regan, urging her sister to treat Lear as she has done: 'Draw, you rascal; you come with letters against the king; and take Vanity the puppet's part against the royalty of her father.' When Kent starts beating him with the flat of his sword, the cowardly Oswald cries out for help, attracting the attention of Cornwall, Regan, Edmund and Gloucester.

Kent's fierce loyalty to Lear and his determination to protect the king's honour at all costs underlie his blunt responses to Cornwall, which inevitably incur the latter's wrath. Bluntness is a striking feature of Kent's character: 'Sir, 'tis my occupation to be plain.' It is his bluntness and 'saucy roughness' that results in Kent enduring the humiliation of being placed in the stocks (normally a punishment for common criminals).While Cornwall is a brutal character, his wife Regan is even more cruel. When Cornwall declares that Kent will remain in the stocks, 'till noon', the vengeful Regan overrules him, demanding that he remain stocked 'till night . . . and all night too'. **Unconcerned for himself, Kent points out that, in placing the king's messenger in the stocks, Cornwall and Regan are disrespecting Lear's royalty:** 'You shall do small respect, show too bold malice against the grace and person of my master, stocking his messenger.' Gloucester remonstrates with Cornwall: 'Let me beseech your grace not to do so.' He goes on to echo Kent's earlier observation about the stocking of his messenger being grossly disrespectful to Lear: '. . . the king must take it ill that he is so slightly valued in his messenger.' While Gloucester's intervention is weak and ineffectual, it is at least a protest. In registering his disapproval of Cornwall and Regan's actions, we see that Gloucester is essentially a decent, well-intentioned character with a sense of justice. He tells Kent, 'I am sorry for thee, friend' and promises him: 'I'll entreat for thee' (plead on his behalf).

At the close of this scene we see Kent in a reflective mood in the stocks. We learn that Cordelia has made contact with him and is aware of Lear's plight. Kent plans to co-operate with Cordelia in restoring the kingdom to its previous state of order. Kent is a philosophical character who looks forward to the wheel of fortune turning full circle: 'Fortune, good night: smile once more; turn thy wheel.'

KEY POINTS

- Kent insults and abuses Oswald, knowing that he brings letters intended to further undermine respect for Lear.
- Cornwall is a brutal character who orders that Kent be placed in the stocks.
- Regan is the dominant partner in this marriage, overruling Cornwall, and insisting that Kent be left in the stocks for a much longer period. These characters are well-matched as both are fundamentally evil and cruel.
- Kent is a strong character who is devoid of (without) self-pity. When placed in the stocks his primary concern is that his stocking represents a gross insult to Lear's royalty.
- While Gloucester's protest against the stocking of Kent is weak and ineffectual, he is a decent character with a sense of justice.
- Cordelia has made contact with Kent who intends to co-operate with her in her planned efforts to restore the kingdom to a state of order.

ACT 2 Scene 3

In this brief scene we see that Edgar has been forced to adopt the disguise of a mad Bedlam beggar in order to avoid arrest: 'I will preserve myself; and am bethought to take the basest and most poorest shape.' His father's unjust treatment of him has reduced Edgar to the level of a hunted fugitive who cannot escape from the country because the ports are heavily guarded: 'Poor Turlygood! Poor Tom! That's something yet: Edgar I nothing am.'

KEY POINTS

- In this scene we see that Gloucester's rash and foolish behaviour has reduced Edgar to the level of an outlaw who is forced to adopt the disguise of a mad Bedlam beggar in order to avoid arrest.
- Edgar seems to be a resilient character, capable of taking the vicissitudes (varying fortunes/ups and downs) of life in his stride.

ACT 2 Scene 4

In this dramatic scene, Lear is pushed to the very brink of insanity by the ingratitude of his daughters. He is deeply shaken when he arrives at Gloucester's castle to find his messenger, Kent, in the stocks. Lear struggles to come to terms with this public display of disrespect towards him: 'They durst not do it; they could not, would not do't; 'tis worse than murder to do upon respect such violent outrage.' The Fool takes this opportunity to once again remind Lear of the depth of his foolishness: 'Fathers that wear rags do make their children blind, but fathers that bear bags shall see their children kind.' When Kent details the treatment he received at the hands of Regan and Cornwall, Lear struggles to retain his mental and emotional balance: 'O how this mother swells up towards my heart! *Hysterica passio*, down, thou climbing sorrow, thy element's below!' While the Fool fears for Lear, his loyalty to his master is unwavering: 'But I will tarry; the fool will stay.' **When Lear is informed that neither Regan nor Cornwall will come to greet him, he is enraged, but can only rant powerlessly:** 'Vengeance! Plague! Death! Confusion!' Seeming to realise his powerlessness, Lear pathetically makes excuses for Regan and Cornwall and adopts a more conciliatory approach: 'The king would speak with Cornwall; the dear father would with his daughter speak. At this point he again senses and struggles to resist his rising insanity: 'O me, my heart, my rising heart! But down!'

When Regan and Cornwall finally appear, Lear complains to Regan about how Goneril has treated him, using animal imagery to again convey the unnaturalness of her ingratitude: 'O Regan, she hath tied sharp-tooth'd unkindness, like a vulture, here.' **Lear is shocked when Regan tells him to return to Goneril and apologise for his behaviour. What follows is quite pathetic as Lear kneels before Regan, pleading with her to take him in:** 'On my knees I beg that you'll vouchsafe me rainment, bed and food.' When Lear explains how Goneril has cut his retinue by half, he cannot contain his rage and again curses Goneril: 'All the stored vengeance of heaven fall on her ingrateful top!' When Regan suggests that Lear will curse her in a similar manner when 'the rash mood' is on him, he immediately rejects the idea of such a possibility: 'No, Regan, thou shalt never have my curse.' **Naively, he tells her that she is more aware of the natural bond that links parent and child and of the debt of gratitude she owes him:** '. . . thou better know'st the offices of nature, bond of childhood, effects of courtesy, dues of gratitude.'

All of Lear's delusions are shattered when Goneril arrives and Regan, in a public display of unity, takes her by the hand. When Cornwall tells Lear that it was he who put Kent in the stocks, Regan cuts short any further questions on the matter with a particularly callous remark: 'I pray you, father, being weak, seem so.' She again suggests that Lear should return to Goneril with his reduced retinue. The prospect of returning to Goneril nudges Lear ever closer to insanity. Describing Goneril as 'a disease that's in my flesh', Lear declares that he can stay with Regan, 'I and my hundred knights'. Regan quickly interposes, asking Lear why he needs so many knights and telling him that she will welcome no more than twenty-five of his followers. When Lear pathetically remarks, 'I gave you all –', Regan callously replies: 'And in good time you gave it.' **The two sisters now combine to humiliate Lear and strip him of his remaining shreds of dignity by whittling down the number of knights he is to be allowed.**

What follows clearly indicates that Lear's personal growth will be a lengthy, uneven process. Having attempted to measure love in terms of words in the opening scene of the play, Lear now attempts to measure it in terms of the number of knights each sister will allow him to retain. Addressing Goneril, Lear foolishly declares: 'Thy fifty yet doth double five-and-twenty, and thou art twice her love.' When Regan asks why he needs even a single knight, Lear's response is rational and clearly argued as he emphasises the importance of human dignity: . . . our basest beggars are in the poorest thing superfluous: allow not nature more than nature needs, man's life is cheap as beast's.' Now fully aware of the depth of his daughters' ingratitude ('unnatural hags'), Lear strives not to break down mentally and emotionally. He raves about the revenges he will have, but is, of course, powerless. He begs the gods to touch him with 'noble anger' so that he does not break down in tears. Lear knows he is now very close to losing his mental equilibrium: 'O fool, I shall go mad!'

Feeling that he has no option but to leave Gloucester's castle, Lear and his remaining followers move towards the gates of the castle. Regan makes no attempt to stop her aged father leaving the relative comfort of the castle as he faces out into the stormy, exposed moors. When Gloucester announces that Lear is 'in high rage' and points out the extremely harsh conditions that await him on the moors, Regan coldly replies: 'O, sir, to wilful men, the injuries they themselves procure must be their schoolmasters', before declaring: 'Shut up your doors.' We again see that Regan and Cornwall are well matched when the latter remarks, 'My Regan counsels well'.

KEY POINTS

- Lear is horrified and incredulous at the sight of his messenger (Kent) in the stocks – this action constitutes a gross and open insult to his royalty.
- The Fool continues to remind Lear of his foolishness. However, the Fool is unwaveringly loyal to Lear. Even though he fears for his master, he declares that he will remain with him.
- Lear is further shocked when Regan and Cornwall refuse to greet him when he arrives at Gloucester's castle. Initially enraged, he adopts a quieter approach when he seems to realise his powerlessness.
- Lear foolishly believes that Regan will treat him better than Goneril, but his delusions are quickly shattered when Goneril arrives and Regan takes her by the hand. Lear now realises that both sisters have been acting as one against him.
- The anguish he feels as a result of his daughters' filial ingratitude pushes Lear to the very brink of insanity.
- Lear senses and strives to resist the insanity rising within him.
- Lear leaves Gloucester's castle in a state of high dudgeon (in anger).

ACT 3 Scene 1

This scene opens with Kent asking a gentleman (who seems to be a supporter of the king) about the whereabouts of Lear. The gentleman informs Kent that Lear is out in the middle of the storm, raving at the elements and trying to outdo them in their fury. The gentleman reports that Lear 'strives in his little world of man to out-scorn the to-and-fro conflicting wind and rain'. **The outer, physical storm mirrors the inner storm that is raging in Lear's mind. Through the gentleman we learn of the Fool's unswerving loyalty to Lear. The Fool endures the harshness of the storm alongside his master, trying to distract him from 'his heart-struck injuries'.** Kent speaks of a division between Albany and Cornwall, although at this point this division is not yet out in the open ('. . . the face of it be cover'd with mutual cunning'). **Kent has many important roles in the play, one of which is maintaining the link between Cordelia and Lear.** It is Kent who informs the gentleman (and the audience) that the King of France is aware (through his spies) of Lear's plight. He also tells us of the French force that has landed in Dover for the purpose of rescuing Lear. '. . . from France there comes a power into this scattered kingdom'. Kent asks the gentleman to make his way to Dover as quickly as possible and tell Cordelia of Lear's 'unnatural and bemadding sorrow'. Kent ensures that Cordelia will know the message he carries comes from him by giving the gentleman a ring that Cordelia will recognise to be his. This scene ends with Kent going off to search for Lear.

KEY POINTS

- The gentleman informs Kent of how Lear is raving at the elements, trying to outdo them in their fury.
- The ever-loyal Fool remains with Lear through the worst of the storm, trying to cheer him up and distract him from his anguish.
- Through Kent we learn of a growing rift between Albany and Cornwall and of a French force that has landed in England for the purpose of rescuing Lear.
- Kent acts as a link between Lear and Cordelia, keeping the latter updated on her father's situation.
- The counter-movement against the forces of evil has begun.

ACT 3 Scene 2

Lear is out on the moors in the eye of the storm, raving at the elements and urging them to destroy the universe that has created his ungrateful daughters: '. . . strike flat the thick rotundity of the world! Crack nature's moulds, all germens spill at once that make ingrateful man!' Here we see that Lear remains as egocentric (self-centred) as ever, calling out for the universal destruction because of his own intense pain. Concerned for his master, the Fool urges Lear to seek shelter from the storm, even if that means asking his daughters to forgive him: 'Here's a night pities neither wise men nor fools.' **Lear feels that the elements have joined forces**

with his 'two pernicious daughters' to inflict further suffering on him. Yet there are signs that he is growing through his suffering as he now sees himself as 'a poor, infirm, weak and despised old man' – a self-image far removed from that in the opening scene when he arrogantly saw himself as an all-powerful dragon to be feared by all. Lear seems to sense that he is close to losing the balance of his mind, and tries to remain patient: 'No, I will be the pattern of all patience, I will say nothing.'

When Kent enters the scene, he underlines the unparalleled ferocity of this storm: 'Since I was a man such sheets of fire, such bursts of horrid thunder, such groans of roaring wind and rain I never remember to have heard.' **This violent tempest reflects both the storm in Lear's mind and the chaos in wider society. As he reflects on his** situation, it is difficult to disagree with Lear's assessment of himself as 'a man more sinned against than sinning'. That Lear has done wrong is incontrovertible (undeniable), but the punishment meted out to him is disproportionate to his wrongdoing. Lear is very conscious of his changing mental state: 'My wits begin to turn.' **He is now on the verge of insanity. Yet there are further indications of his personal growth in his compassion for the Fool:** 'Poor fool and knave, I have one part in my heart that's sorry yet for thee.' Kent's humanity and sympathy for Lear are evident when he guides him to a hovel in which he can shelter. This scene concludes with the Fool predicting that great disorder is coming to England: 'Then shall the realm of Albion come to great confusion.'

KEY POINTS

- The storm on the moor reflects both the tempest in Lear's mind and the chaos in wider society. Disorder in the world of man is mirrored by disorder in the world of nature.
- Lear's egocentric nature is still to be seen in his appeal to the elements to destroy the universe that created his 'pernicious daughters'.
- There are signs that Lear is growing through suffering in his vision of himself as 'a poor, weak, infirm and despised old man' and in his compassion for the Fool.
- The Fool remains with Lear through his darkest hours, trying to cheer him up. His concern for his master is genuine, and his unwavering loyalty very admirable.
- Kent's observations on the storm highlight its unequalled ferocity and, by extension, the inhuman callousness of Lear's unnatural daughters who have closed their doors against their aged father on the night of the worst storm in living memory.
- Kent's sympathy for Lear is to be seen as he guides him to shelter.

ACT 3 Scene 3

This scene opens with Gloucester expressing his disquiet (unease) at the manner in which Lear is being treated by his daughters and sons-in-law: 'I like not this unnatural dealing.' This is obviously very ironic because Gloucester is utterly unaware of the 'unnatural dealing' of his own son, Edmund, to whom he is expressing his concerns. Edmund's falseness and hypocrisy are strikingly evident in his response: 'Most savage, and unnatural!' When Gloucester asks his guests if he can go to assist Lear, they take control of his house, warning him of the dire consequences that would follow any attempt he might make to support Lear in any way.

Gloucester goes on to confide in Edmund all that he knows about the developing military situation. He tells him about the rift between the dukes and, more importantly, about a letter he has received informing him of the French landing: 'These injuries the king now bears will be revenged home; there's part of a power already footed . . .' Despite the threats hanging over him, Gloucester departs to help Lear: **'If I die for it, as no less is threatened me, the king, my old master, must be relieved.'** Up to this point Gloucester has been a weak, foolish, ineffectual character – unlike Kent he did not have the courage to speak out against Lear's cruel, unjust treatment of Cordelia in the opening scene. **But now Gloucester displays a new strength of character, risking his life to help Lear.**

No sooner has Gloucester confided all in Edmund than the latter instantly decides to tell Cornwall everything. He does this in the hope of being rewarded for his 'loyalty' and in the full knowledge that his father will face death as a result of his callous, unnatural betrayal of him. **Edmund's ruthless philosophy is summed up in his declaration at the close of this scene: 'The younger rises when the old doth fall.'**

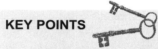

KEY POINTS

- Gloucester expresses his concern at the manner in which Lear is being treated, and is threatened with death if he attempts to assist the king.
- Gloucester confides in Edmund, telling him all that he knows about the counter-action against the new regime, as outlined in a letter informing him of the French landing at Dover.
- This scene sees a dramatic development in Gloucester's character – a man who was foolish and ineffectual in the early stages of the play now displays strength and courage in his determination to assist Lear.
- Edmund's utterly callous character is apparent in his decision to betray his father to Cornwall in order to advance himself.

ACT 3 Scene 4

This scene opens with Kent guiding Lear into a hovel. Kent's deep affection for Lear is evident in his response to Lear asking him if he will break his heart: 'I'd rather break mine own.' **In his state of mental and emotional torment, Lear is barely aware of his physical discomfort:** '. . . the tempest in my mind doth from my senses take all feeling else save what beats there. Filial ingratitude!' **When Lear reflects on the ingratitude of his daughters to whom his 'frank heart gave all', he realises that this is the cause of his insanity:** 'O that way madness lies; let me shun that; no more of that.' **We see further evidence of Lear's new sense of humanity as he ushers the Fool into the hovel ahead of him:** 'In boy, go first.' **Lear's personal growth is also to be seen in his new awareness of the poor whom, as king, he had neglected.** As he reflects on the plight of the 'poor naked wretches' that surround him, Lear reproaches (blames) himself for neglecting these, most needy of people: 'I have ta'en too little care of this!' **Most remarkably, Lear now preaches the doctrine of social justice**, suggesting that the wealthy should share some of their riches with the poor: 'Expose thyself to feel what wretches feel, that thou mayest shake the superflux to them and show the heavens more just.'

When Edgar, disguised as a madman enters the hovel, it is clear that Lear has now lost his sanity as he sees Poor Tom's destitution (poverty) and misery entirely in terms of his own experience: 'Hast thou given all to thy daughters? And art thou come to this?' When Kent respectfully explains that Poor Tom has no daughters, the old, fiery Lear is again to be seen: 'Death, traitor! Nothing could have subdued nature to such a lowness but his unkind daughters.' Lear can only see himself in Edgar and the pity he feels for

Edgar, he also feels for himself. This scene offers the audience a contrast between Edgar's feigned (pretended) madness and Lear's genuine insanity, which is again to be seen when he calls Poor Tom 'a noble philosopher'. Lear once more uses animal imagery to convey the inhuman behaviour of his daughters, but now sees that he was partly responsible for making them what they have become: 'Judicious punishment! 'Twas this flesh begot these pelican daughters.'

With Lear once again displaying his ingrained flaws of egocentricity and rashness, we see that his personal growth is gradual and uneven – just as he seems to develop on a personal level, we see his old faults surface again. But the uneven nature of Lear's development adds to the realism of the play - while people can certainly learn from experience and become better and wiser individuals, it would be unrealistic to suggest that someone who is rash by nature could develop into a model of self-restraint and composure. Paradoxically, it is when Lear loses his sanity that he acquires true wisdom. Looking at the half-naked Edgar, Lear sees man reduced to his essence: '. . . unaccommodated man is no more but such a poor, bare, forked animal as thou art'. Wishing to reduce himself to the basic level of Poor Tom and the poor that surround them, Lear starts to tear off his clothes, symbols of material wealth and possessions that are now meaningless to him. The Fool remains with Lear, still endeavouring to boost his master's spirits as he encourages him to take shelter from the raging storm: 'Prithee nuncle, be contented; 'tis a naughty night to swim in.' However, the Fool has patently (clearly) become more serious in this scene as he seems to be filled with foreboding (anxiety).

When Gloucester arrives in the hovel to assist Lear, he condemns ungrateful children who mistreat their fathers: 'Our flesh and blood, my Lord, is grown so vile that it doth hate what gets it.' **Gloucester's loyalty to Lear is very admirable because, in attempting to assist his king, he puts his own life at serious risk:** '. . . my duty cannot suffer to obey in all your daughters' hard commands.' Kent perceives that Lear is drawing ever closer to complete insanity: 'His wits begin to unsettle.' Gloucester identifies with Lear's torment in that he too has been deeply pained by filial ingratitude: 'Thou say'st the king grows mad; I'll tell thee, friend, I am almost mad myself.' Of course, Gloucester is still blind to his misjudgement of his own sons, and of the grave injustice he has done Edgar.

KEY POINTS

- Lear welcomes the storm as a distraction from his inner suffering ('This tempest will not give me leave to ponder on things would hurt me more').
- Lear recognises that it is his daughters' ingratitude that lies at the root of his present mental problems, and strives not to think about their thanklessness ('O that way madness lies; let me shun that; no more of that').
- This scene provides us with much evidence of Lear's personal growth – we see his humanity in his kindness towards the Fool, whom he ushers into the hovel ahead of him, and in his newly developed social conscience which is apparent in his acknowledgement that, as king, he neglected the poor. Most dramatically, Lear now declares that the rich should share some of their wealth with the poor.
- When Edgar, disguised as Poor Tom, enters the hovel, Lear's flaws remain very much in evidence – he sees Edgar's plight entirely in relation to his own situation, asserting that only the new arrival's 'unkind daughters' could have reduced him to such a level of misery. In this scene it is apparent that Lear's growth to self-awareness will be gradual and uneven.
- Kent's concern and affection for Lear are immediately evident as he guides his master to a place of shelter and tells him that he would rather break his own heart than cause Lear any additional suffering.
- Gloucester demonstrates admirable loyalty to Lear, risking his own life to assist his king.
- The Fool remains with Lear, but is noticeably more serious as he seems to be very fearful for the future.

ACT 3 Scene 5

Edmund has already supplanted (displaced) Edgar as heir to his father's earldom, but is now impatient for his inheritance. We see the full extent of Edmund's ruthlessness in this scene when he betrays his father in the full knowledge that Gloucester will face severe punishment for his support for the king. The scene opens with Cornwall clearly intent on exacting revenge on Gloucester: 'I will have my revenge 'ere I depart his house.' Edmund hypocritically claims that it pains him to reveal his father's 'treason': 'O heavens! That this treason were not, or not I the detector!' In reality, Edmund does not hesitate to tell Cornwall of the letter implicating Gloucester in the French landing. In an aside, Edmund expresses his hope that Gloucester will be found comforting Lear, so that he will appear even more treacherous in Cornwall's eyes. His hypocrisy is again evident when he tells Cornwall: 'I will persevere in my course of loyalty, though the conflict be sore between that and my blood'.'

KEY POINTS

- This scene highlights Edmund's ruthlessness and hypocrisy as he continues with his unscrupulous, immoral pursuit of wealth and power.
- Cornwall appears to be as gullible as he is vengeful, being easily manipulated by the cunning Edmund.

ACT 3 Scene 6

Early in this scene, Kent states that Lear is now completely mad: 'All the power of his wits have given way to his impatience.' This scene is intriguing in the sense that it brings the three 'madmen' of the play together: Lear, who is genuinely insane, Edgar who has been forced to assume the disguise of a madman in order to avoid arrest and the Fool, the 'official madman' of the play whose verbal contributions combine the meaningless and the insightful. In his madness, Lear announces that, as king, he is going to put the 'she foxes' that are his daughters on trial: 'Arraign her first; 'tis Goneril . . . she kicked the poor king, her father.' He sees Edgar, in rags, as a 'robed man of justice', declaring that he, along with the Fool and Kent will sit in judgement of his cruel daughters. Both Kent and Edgar are deeply moved by the sight of this once-great king now reduced to the level of a madman. The concerned Kent urges Lear to be patient, clearly perceiving that anger exacerbates (worsens) his mental condition: 'O pity! Sir, where is the patience now, that you so oft have boasted to retain?' For his part, Edgar struggles to maintain his disguise as his tears flow in sympathy for the tormented old king: 'My tears begin to take his part so much, they'll mar my counterfeiting.' Lear cannot begin to understand his daughters' inhumanity, declaring that Regan is to be dissected in an attempt to see what 'makes these hard hearts'.

When the loyal Gloucester enters the scene, he tells Kent of a plot to kill the king, and instructs him to take the king to Dover, where he will find 'welcome and

protection'. Gloucester stresses the urgency of the situation, urging Kent to take Lear to Dover immediately, and warning that a half an hour's delay would cost all of them their lives. As he reflects on Lear's suffering, the admirably philosophical Edgar concludes that his own pain pales into insignificance when compared to that of the king: 'How light and portable my pain seems now when that which makes me bend

makes the king bow.'

The Fool says little in this, the final scene in which he plays a part. There is no room for the Fool's witticisms in this dark scene and, having done his best to help make Lear more self-aware, his dramatic function is fulfilled, and he is neither seen nor spoken of again.

KEY POINTS

- Lear is now completely insane – a fact twice confirmed by Kent ('All the power of his wits have given way to his impatience', '. . . his wits are gone').
- This scene brings the three 'madmen' of the play together in a scene which powerfully conveys the depth of Lear's torment.
- In his insanity, Lear puts his cruel daughters on trial.
- Both Kent and Edgar are deeply moved by Lear's intense suffering.
- The loyal Gloucester arrives to assist his king, informing Kent of a plot to kill Lear.
- Edgar dismisses his own pain when he sees the depth of Lear's anguish, showing himself to be a strong, philosophical character devoid of (without) self-pity.
- With Cordelia's forces gathered in Dover, the country is on the brink of war.

ACT 3 Scene 7

This is one of the most dramatic scenes in the play, indeed in any of the Shakespearian tragedies. It is memorable for the unspeakable savagery that sees Gloucester's eyes being cut from his head in an act of barbaric retribution (revenge) following Edmund's betrayal of his father. When Gloucester returns to his castle, he finds his enemies awaiting him, impatient to exact vengeance on him. Regan sets the tone for the appalling cruelty that follows when she declares: 'Hang him instantly!' Goneril prefers the idea of Gloucester experiencing more

protracted (prolonged) suffering: 'Pluck out his eyes.' Cornwall urges Edmund to leave since '. . . the revenges we are bound to take upon your traitorous father are not fit for your beholding'. When he addresses Edmund as 'my lord of Gloucester', we learn how Edmund has been rewarded for betraying his own father.

Gloucester reminds his vengeful enemies that they are his guests, but his pleading is in vain. Since Goneril and Regan have no respect for the natural bond that ordinarily connects parent and child (Regan callously refers to Lear as 'the lunatic king'), they (along with Cornwall) are unlikely to be influenced by the natural bond that should link a host and his guests. Gloucester addresses Regan as 'Unmerciful lady', which only prompts her to pluck his beard – a gesture expressing her disrespect for him. Bound to a chair, Gloucester courageously resigns himself to his fate: 'I am tied to the stake and I must stand the course.' When Regan questions him as to why he brought Lear to Dover, Gloucester's response is (in the light of what happens shortly after this exchange) charged with irony: 'Because I would not see thy cruel nails pluck out his poor old eyes, nor thy fierce fangs in his anointed flesh stick boarish fangs.' Here animal imagery is once again employed to highlight the inhumanity of Lear's unnatural daughters.

Gloucester believes in the idea of divine justice, declaring that he will see 'the winged vengeance overtake such children'. At this point, Cornwall, in an act of unimaginable barbarity, cuts one of Gloucester's eyes from his head. Anxious to outdo her husband in her cruelty, Regan demands that the second eye also be gouged out since 'one side will mock another; the other too'. However, one of Cornwall's servants now feels compelled to

intervene, and draws his sword. As the servant and Cornwall fight, Regan stabs the servant in the back – but not before he has inflicted a mortal wound on Cornwall, whose visible pleasure in his sadistic torture of the helpless Gloucester is sickening: 'Out, vile jelly! Where is thy luster now?' In his darkness and pain, Gloucester calls out for Edmund, prompting Regan to heap mental torment onto his physical agony by delightedly informing him that it was Edmund who betrayed him: 'Thou call'st on him that hates thee; it was he that made the overtures of thy treason to us, who is too good to pity thee.' **It is hugely ironic that Gloucester acquires moral vision at the very moment that he loses his physical vision: 'O my follies! Then Edgar was abused. Kind gods, forgive me that, and prosper him!'** In a final act of cruelty, Regan orders the blind Gloucester to be thrown out at the gates, from where he can 'smell his way to Dover'.

The way in which the servants care for Gloucester's wounds, along with the courageous intervention of the servant who gave his life in an attempt to protect Gloucester, serve as reminders of man's humanity and better qualities.

KEY POINTS

- Gloucester's eyes are gouged out by Cornwall in an act of monstrous savagery.
- Edmund's villainy is now exposed and out in the open.
- The brave intervention of one of Cornwall's servants serves as a ray of light, a reminder of man's finer instincts in a particularly dark scene.
- It is one of the great ironies of the play that Gloucester acquires moral vision at the very moment that he loses his physical sight.

ACT 4 Scene 1

The opening lines of this scene reflect Edgar's optimism and lack of self-pity: 'The worst returns to laughter.' However, within seconds of this very positive observation, Edgar is horrified to see his blinded father being led by an old man. Gloucester's concern for the old man reflects his growing concern for others: 'Thy comforts can do me no good at all; thee they may hurt.' His burgeoning (rapidly growing) self-awareness is accompanied by a profound sense of despair: 'I have no way and therefore want no eyes; I stumbled when I saw . . .' Gloucester longs only to see his son Edgar again: 'Might I but live to see thee in my touch, I'd say I had my eyes again!' Ironically, the son he loves is within touching distance, but cannot yet reveal his true identity to the world at large. Gloucester now has a very dark view of the gods, believing that they kill men for their amusement: 'As flies to wanton boys, are we to the gods; they kill us for their sport.' He asks the disguised Edgar to guide him to Dover, but first requests the old man to 'bring some covering for this naked soul' (the disguised Edgar), another indication of his new sense of compassion and awareness of the needs of others. Gloucester is keenly aware of the strange times in which they live 'when madmen lead the blind'. Edgar finds it increasingly difficult to maintain his disguise because he is so deeply moved by his father's suffering: 'I cannot daub it further.' Like Cordelia, Edgar bears no ill feeling towards the father who wronged him.

One of the most interesting developments in Gloucester's character is his new sense of social justice which prompts him, as it did Lear, to call for the redistribution of wealth: 'So distribution should undo excess, and each man have enough.' In this scene, Gloucester is so overwhelmed by despondency that all he wants is to be brought to the cliffs of Dover, where he intends to take his own life.

KEY POINTS

- While Edgar is a resilient (strong) and optimistic character, he is deeply shocked to see his blinded father being guided by an old man.
- We see considerable evidence of Gloucester's personal growth in his concern for the old man and in his desire to see wealth redistributed more fairly.
- Gloucester, overwhelmed by despair, sees no point to his life and only wants to reach Dover so that he can commit suicide by throwing himself from the cliffs.

ACT 4 Scene 2

The most striking aspect of this scene is Albany's dramatic personal transformation. He is so changed from the weak and ineffectual character we encountered earlier in the play as to be virtually unrecognisable. No sooner has Goneril mentioned 'our mild husband' than Oswald brings her attention to the 'new' Albany: '. . . never man so changed. I told him of the army that was landed; he smiled at it.' According to Oswald, Albany's loyalties appear to have totally changed: 'What most he should dislike seems pleasant to him; what like offensive.' **For all her bad points (and they are many), Goneril is a strong character, possessed of spirit and determination.** The French have landed, and she immediately takes control of the situation. Dismissing her husband's 'cowish terror', Goneril herself takes up arms in preparation for the imminent battle, sending Edmund ahead to help Cornwall organise his forces. After Edmund (now the Earl of Gloucester) leaves, Goneril admits to her love for him, contrasting him with the husband she despises: 'O the difference of man and man! To thee a woman's services are due.'

When Albany enters the scene, it is immediately clear that he is no longer the feeble character who was seemingly content to live in his wife's shadow. He tells Goneril exactly what he thinks of her, making no attempt to hide the feelings of contempt she inspires in him: 'O Goneril, you are not worth the dust that the rude wind blows in your face.' Albany declares that Goneril's unnatural behaviour (towards Lear, her father) will earn its own appropriate reward: 'She that herself will sliver and disbranch from her material sap, perforce must wither and come to deadly use.' Like Lear, Albany uses animal imagery to highlight the utterly unnatural behaviour of both Goneril and Regan, describing them as 'tigers, not daughters'. Goneril still refuses to accept that she is now dealing with a very different man to the one that she had dominated and controlled for so long: 'Milk-liver'd man!' Albany's hatred of his wife is so intense that he declares that he could physically tear her limb from limb: 'Were it my fitness to let these hands obey my blood, they are apt enough to dislocate and tear thy flesh and bones . . .' He describes her as 'a fiend' in 'woman's shape'. When Albany learns that Cornwall has been killed, he sees his death as an example of divine justice at work: 'This shows you are above you justicers, that these our nether crimes so speedily can venge!'

Goneril is not, in one sense, pleased with the news of Cornwall's death because, with her husband dead, Regan could emerge as her rival for Edmund's affections. Having learnt of Edmund's betrayal of his father and of his leaving his father's castle so that Cornwall and Regan could more freely torture him for his act of 'treason', Albany dedicates himself to avenging Gloucester's eyes: 'Gloucester, I live to thank thee for the love thou show'dst the king and to revenge thine eyes.' **This scene sees the forces of good gaining an unlikely ally in the shape of the dramatically transformed Albany.**

KEY POINTS

- In this scene Albany has clearly undergone a dramatic personal transformation – he is now an utterly different character from the feeble, subservient character we saw earlier in the play.
- Albany dedicates himself to avenging Gloucester's eyes.
- Like Gloucester, Albany believes in the concept of divine justice.
- Goneril now views Edmund as a suitable, indeed desirable, partner, but anticipates competition from Regan.
- The death of Cornwall, along with the dramatic transformation of Albany's character, are positive developments in terms of the battle the forces of good, led by Cordelia, will shortly face against the forces of evil.

ACT 4 Scene 3

This scene is set in the French camp at Dover. Kent asks the gentleman who had brought his message to Cordelia about her reaction to his report. The language and imagery used to describe Cordelia suggests that she is a royal, saintly figure: 'It seem'd she was a queen over her passion . . .', 'There she shook the holy figure from her heavenly eyes'. Kent again expresses his belief in the power of fate: 'It is the stars, the stars above us, govern our conditions.' Kent updates the audience on Lear's condition. It seems that, in the midst of his bewilderment, Lear has moments of clarity: '. . . sometimes in his better tune remembers what we are come about.' Kent explains that Lear feels too ashamed of his cruel mistreatment of Cordelia to approach her: '. . . burning shame detains him from Cordelia.' On the positive side, the fact that Lear is guilt-ridden over the wrongs he did his one true daughter is another indication of his personal growth.

KEY POINTS

- Cordelia is depicted as the personification of love, goodness and forgiveness in her response to Kent's report on Lear's condition.
- Kent once again displays his philosophical disposition as he restates his belief in the stars.
- Lear's shame at his grossly unjust treatment of Cordelia is another sign of his personal growth.

ACT 4 Scene 4

This scene vividly highlights Cordelia's loving, forgiving nature, while also revealing a steely side to her character as she prepares to lead her forces against the evil powers that now rule the kingdom. In Cordelia's words, Lear is now 'as mad as the vex'd sea'. He is wandering about, covered in flowers (a sign of insanity in all Shakespearian dramas) and singing aloud. Cordelia is again seen as the epitome (personification/embodiment) of loving forgiveness, declaring that she would give all of her 'outward worth' to the person who could help Lear to regain the balance of his mind. She understands her father's nature and orders

that he be found before his 'ungoverned nature' prompts him to take his own life. Cordelia also impresses us with her composure and determination as she faces into a critical battle. When she is told that the British forces are marching towards them, she remains calm and unruffled, pointing out that her army stands ready: ''Tis known before; our preparation stands in expectation of them.' **At the close of this scene, Cordelia insists that her presence in England is not motivated by ambition for conquest or power, but by concern for her aged father and his rights: 'No blown ambition doth our arms incite, but love, dear love and our aged father's right.'**

KEY POINTS

- This scene showcases Cordelia's kind, loving and forgiving nature.
- Cordelia also shows a new side to her character – a real determination to rescue her father from her evil sisters, who even now are plotting to kill Lear.
- Cordelia declares that she is not in England for any ambitious reason, but only out of concern for her aged father.

ACT 4 Scene 5

This scene sees Regan in conversation with Oswald, Goneril's personal servant and messenger. When Regan enquires about Albany's forces, Oswald, ever loyal to his evil mistress, replies that Goneril is the more capable military leader: 'Your sister is the better soldier.' **While the previous scene highlighted Cordelia's forgiving nature and the power of love, this scene reflects Regan's callous nature and the power of evil and jealousy. Regan regrets the fact that Gloucester was not killed earlier because, in his blinded state, he turns**

people against the present regime: 'It was great ignorance Gloucester's eyes being out to let him live.'

This scene brings the growing rivalry between Goneril and Regan into clear focus. The evil sisters are now locked in what will prove to be a deadly conflict for Edmund's affections. It is rather ironic that sisters driven primarily by hatred and ruthless ambition should now find themselves at loggerheads over their love for the one man. Regan tells Oswald that she knows that Goneril 'does not love her husband', before going on reveal her jealous streak when she says that she has seen Goneril flirting with Edmund: 'She gave strange oeillades and most speaking looks to noble Edmund.' Utterly unprincipled, Regan pleads with Oswald to show her Goneril's letter, before going on to openly declare her love interest in Edmund: 'My lord is dead; Edmund and I have talked; and more convenient is he for my hand than for your lady's.' She asks Oswald to deliver a note from her to Edmund, while also requesting that he inform Goneril of what she has just said. Regan's cruelty is again to be seen at the close of this scene when she tells Oswald that he will be rewarded if he kills Gloucester: 'If you do chance to hear of that blind traitor, preferment falls on him that cuts him off.' The cowardly Oswald agrees to do what Regan asks, untroubled by the idea of serving two mistresses.

KEY POINTS

- This scene highlights the growing rivalry between Goneril and Regan over Edmund.
- Regan's unscrupulous nature is to be seen in her attempts to persuade Oswald to show her Goneril's letter.
- Her cruelty is again evident in her regret at having let Gloucester live, and in her instruction to Oswald to kill him if he encounters him.
- Oswald, a minor character, is as unscrupulous as the evil sisters he serves.

ACT 4 Scene 6

This is a very significant scene in a variety of ways. Firstly we see how Edgar restores his suicidal father's will to live by tricking him into believing that he has jumped from the cliffs of Dover and has survived because the gods wished him to live. While Edmund had deceived Gloucester early in the play, his actions were motivated by selfish ambition. In total contrast, Edgar's deception of Gloucester in this scene is motivated by loving concern.

Edgar tricks Gloucester into believing that he is on the very edge of the cliff, vividly describing his dizziness as he looks at the sheer drop from the top of the cliff, depicting the fishermen on the beach as being no bigger than mice, and even speaking of 'the murmuring surge' of the sea below. Taking his father by the hand, Edgar tells Gloucester that he is now within a foot of the edge. While Gloucester remains as credulous as ever, Edgar feels a little guilty at his deception, but justifies it on the basis that it is for the worthy cause of ridding his father of his despair: 'Why I do trifle thus with his despair is done to cure it.' When Gloucester falls forward, Edgar adopts the voice of a different persona – a man on the beach who witnessed Gloucester's 'fall' – and declares to the disoriented old man, 'Thy life's a miracle', before going on to claim that 'the clearest gods, who make them honours of men's impossibilities, have preserved thee'. (It is interesting, but not entirely surprising given his innate optimism, that Edgar retains his belief in the miraculous capabilities of 'the clearest gods'). Gloucester believes this explanation of his 'survival' and announces that from this moment on he will 'bear affliction' and endure life's sorrows and difficulties until the gods decide it is his time to die.

The second major episode in this scene is the meeting of Lear and Gloucester. In his insanity, Lear continues to show signs of personal growth. Speaking of Goneril and Regan, Lear observes, 'They flattered me like a dog . . . they are not man o' their words: they told me I was everything; 'tis a lie, I am not ague-proof'. **The uneven nature of Lear's personal development is again to be seen in an outburst typical of the old, arrogant Lear:** 'Ay! Every inch a king: When I do stare, see how the subject quakes.' **What is particularly striking about this scene is the sense that the mad Lear sometimes makes.** He wisely tells the blind Gloucester, 'A man may see how this world goes with no eyes', before going on to deliver some sharp insights into the double standards and corruption that lie at the heart of the justice system: 'Through tattered clothes small vices do appear: Robes and furred gowns hide all. Plate sin with gold, and the strong lance of justice hurtless breaks; arm it in rags, a pigmy's straw doth pierce it.' He is also very sharp in his insights into the falseness of politicians: 'Get thee glass eyes; and like a scurvy politician, seem to see the things thou dost not.' **Edgar aptly sums up the wisdom that Lear, in his insanity, displays when he speaks of Lear's 'reason in madness!'** Lear even reveals a philosophical capacity when he reflects, 'When we are born, we cry that we are come to this great stage of fools.' Lear then lapses into nonsensical ramblings, prompting Gloucester to express his deep sympathy for the tormented old king: 'A sight most pitiful in the meanest wretch, past speaking of in a king.'

He now sees his own suffering as insignificant compared to Lear's and reiterates his willingness to let the gods decide when he is to die, praying that he will never again be tempted to take his own life: 'You ever-gentle gods, take my breath from me; let not my worser spirit tempt me again to die before you please!' Gloucester also reflects that Lear has one daughter who redeems nature 'from the general curse which twain (the two evil, unnatural sisters) have brought her to'.

Having already saved his father's life once, Edgar is now called upon to save it a second time when the cowardly Oswald enters the scene, proclaiming to Gloucester: 'That eyeless head of this was first framed flesh to raise my fortunes.' As the despicable Oswald draws his sword, Edgar intervenes and, following a brief skirmish, kills the man he calls 'a serviceable villain', well-suited to serving his villainous mistress. **The letter that Goneril had written to Edmund is now in Edgar's hands. Edgar is horrified when he reads that Goneril wants Edmund to kill her husband ('You have many opportunities to cut him off'). The fact that she refers to 'our reciprocal vows' indicates that the unscrupulous, deceitful Edmund has won the hearts of both sisters and will use this to his advantage as he continues his relentless, ruthless pursuit of power.** Edgar struggles to come to terms with the depth of Goneril's evil: 'A plot upon her virtuous husband's life!'

At the close of this scene Gloucester envies the king his madness – he would prefer to be insane so that he would not be conscious of his own deep sorrow: 'Better I were distract, so should my thoughts be severed from my griefs.'

KEY POINTS

- Edgar deceives his father in order to restore his will to live.
- This scene brings the main plot and subplot together, with the insane Lear meeting the blind Gloucester.
- Lear displays considerable insight in his insanity – Edgar describes this phenomenon as 'reason in madness'.
- Goneril's callous, ruthless nature is reflected in the letter she sends Edmund, requesting him to kill Albany, her husband.
- Regan is equally evil, regretting that Gloucester was allowed to live, and ordering Oswald to kill him if he encounters him.
- The rivalry between the evil sisters over Edmund continues to grow in intensity.
- Edgar saves his father's life a second time when he kills his would-be assassin, the cowardly Oswald.
- While Gloucester is no longer suicidal, his torment is such that he envies Lear his insanity because, in his distracted state, he is unaware of his anguish.

ACT 4 Scene 7

This scene opens with Cordelia thanking Kent for his loyalty and devotion to Lear. She is sincerely thankful to Lear's most loyal subject for all that he has done for her father, despite Lear's mistreatment of him: 'O thou good Kent, how shall I live and work to match thy goodness?' Ever humble, Kent responds that to be acknowledged is to be 'o'er-paid.' This is a very moving scene, with Cordelia's forgiveness of her 'child-changed father' reinforcing our image of her as the very embodiment of love. **In total contrast to the evil that pervaded the previous scene, this scene is full of positive emotions, with Cordelia not hesitating to forgive her father and doing everything possible to restore his sanity.** She prays to the gods to 'cure this breach in his (Lear's) abused nature'. **Like Edgar, Cordelia is a healing agent, whispering to the sleeping Lear:**

'Restoration hang thy medicine on my lips; and let this kiss repair those violent harms that my two sisters have in thy reverence made!' She struggles to comprehend the depth of her sisters' cruelty. As she reflects on Lear being locked out to face the worst storm in living memory, she sadly remarks, 'Mine enemy's dog, though he had bit me, should have stood that night against my fire.'

When Lear awakens, he is confused, believing himself to be dead and Cordelia an angel: 'You do me wrong to take me out of the grave; thou art a soul in bliss; but I am bound upon a wheel of fire, that mine own tears do scald like molten lead.' **The wheel of fire image suggests Lear's torment, while his tears are prompted by his feelings of guilt at his cruel mistreatment of Cordelia.** As he gradually comes to his senses, he sees Cordelia, not as an angel, but as his loving daughter who is now asking for his blessing. Lear pleads with her not to mock him, describing himself as 'a very foolish fond old man' and acknowledging his mental difficulties: 'I fear I am not in my perfect mind.' **In this lucid moment Lear shows how much he has grown on a personal level through his intense suffering. His feelings of guilt and shame are so strong that he declares himself willing to take his own life:** 'If you have poison for me, I will drink it. I know you do not love me, for your sisters have, as I remember, done me wrong:

You have some cause, they have not.' Cordelia's response shows her to be the epitome (embodiment) of tenderness and forgiveness: 'No cause, no cause.' As before, Cordelia does not express her feelings in any kind of effusive (gushing) manner, but there is no doubting the heartfelt sincerity of what she says to her aged and anguished father. **Lear's new sense of personal awareness is again evident as he humbly asks for Cordelia's forgiveness: '. . . pray you now, forget and forgive: I am old and foolish.'**

KEY POINTS

- In this very moving scene, Lear is reconciled with his one true daughter, Cordelia.
- Cordelia is portrayed as the personification of love, compassion and gentleness.
- Lear's lucid (clear-minded) moments show how much he has grown on a personal level through his deep personal suffering. In this scene he displays admirable self-knowledge and humility.

ACT 5 Scene 1

In this scene the critical battle between the forces of good and evil is imminent. Edmund is still not sure of Albany's support, describing him as being 'full of alteration and self-reproving'. Albany finds himself in a difficult situation – his sympathies lie with Lear and Cordelia, but his primary duty is to repel the French force that has landed at Dover and, in order to do this, he needs the military assistance of people he now despises. The rivalry between Goneril and Regan continues to intensify, threatening the unity of the English force. Regan asks Edmund directly if he loves her sister. His reply ('In honour'd love') in no way placates

(appeases/calms) her. Regan is now consumed by jealousy: 'I shall never endure her: dear my lord, be not familiar with her.' Goneril is similarly obsessed by Edmund, declaring that she would sooner lose the battle than lose Edmund to Regan. However, her practical side quickly reasserts itself, as she demands unity in the face of the French, pointing out that all other matters can be addressed later.

Just before the battle commences, Edgar (still in disguise) arrives and gives Albany the letter from Goneril to Edmund which proves their treachery. He also tells Albany that, if he achieves victory, to sound the trumpet and he will produce a champion who will confirm the truth of the letter's contents.

Edmund's soliloquy at the close of this scene reinforces our image of him as a callous, immoral character. He delights in his deception and cynical manipulation of Goneril and Regan: 'To both these sisters have I sworn my love; each jealous of the other as the stung are of the adder.' He wonders which he shall take, knowing that 'neither can be enjoyed if both remain alive'. Edmund reflects on his need of Albany for the battle ahead, but wants him dead after the battle. While Goneril had earlier expressed her desire for Edmund to kill Albany, Edmund believes that it is Goneril who should arrange for her husband to be killed: 'Let her who would be rid of him arrange his speedy taking-off.' Edmund's total ruthlessness is further underlined by his decision to have both Cordelia and Lear executed after the battle, despite Albany having already stated his intention of sparing their lives. **While Edmund has nothing against either Lear or Cordelia on a personal level, anyone whom he perceives to be a potential threat in his quest for ultimate power is to be eliminated: '. . . for my state stands on me to defend, not to debate.'**

KEY POINTS

- Edmund's uncertainty regarding Albany's intentions points to the latter's dilemma – while his sympathies lie with Lear and Cordelia, his primary duty is to repel the French force that is now on English soil.
- The rivalry between Goneril and Regan in relation to Edmund has grown so intense and bitter that it now threatens the unity of the English force.
- Edgar gives Albany the letter proving Goneril's treachery, before going on to tell him that, after the battle, he can produce a champion who will defend the truth of the letter's contents.
- Edmund's ruthless ambition is reflected in his soliloquy at the close of this scene – he wants Albany, Cordelia and Lear to be killed because they are potential threats to his pursuit of power.

ACT 5 Scene 2

This brief scene is set on the battlefield. Edgar ensures that his father is safe and comfortable before leaving to join the battle. He returns almost immediately, with the grim news that Cordelia's forces have been defeated, and that Lear and Cordelia have been taken prisoner. While Gloucester is plunged into black despair ('No farther sir: a man may rot even here'), Edgar remains resilient, philosophically accepting life's varying fortunes: 'Men must endure their going hence, even as their coming hither: Ripeness is all . . .' In Edgar's view, death, like birth, is part of life, and what is most important is being prepared for and accepting of both.

KEY POINTS

- Defeat in battle is a major setback for the forces of good.
- The capture of both Lear and Cordelia is a particularly gloomy development, leaving Gloucester deeply depressed.
- Edgar remains as resilient as ever, determined to accept the vicissitudes (varying fortunes/ups and downs) of life.

ACT 5 Scene 3

With Lear and Cordelia now the prisoners of Edmund, their lives are clearly in great danger. Edmund has already stated his intention of killing them both in defiance of Albany's plan to pardon them. Cordelia remains as devoted as ever to Lear, telling him that she is sad only for him: 'For thee oppressed king am I cast down; myself could else out-frown false fortune's frown.' In his insanity, Lear looks forward to spending time in prison with Cordelia, where they will philosophise about the nature of life ('the mystery of things'). When Edmund orders that they be taken away, we again see the old fiery Lear: 'He that parts us shall bring a brand from heaven.' Without spelling out exactly what he wants done with them, Edmund leaves the captain who takes them away in no doubt as to what he expects of him: '. . . to be tender-minded does not become a sword.'

There appears to be some hope for Lear and Cordelia when Albany enters the scene, and asks that they be handed over to him. When Edmund replies that both have been imprisoned because of their potential ability to win popular support ('. . . to pluck the common bosom on his side'), he speaks to Albany as if he were his equal ('The question of Cordelia and her father requires a fitter time'). Angered by the content and tone of Edmund's remarks, Albany immediately asserts his authority over him: 'Sir, by your patience, I hold you but a subject of this war, not a brother.' When Goneril and Regan spring to Edmund's defence, they inevitably and immediately begin to quarrel. **The jealousy between the two evil sisters reaches a dramatic climax in this final scene. When Regan publicly declares Edmund to be her 'lord and master', she has already been poisoned by Goneril. Albany now arrests both Edmund and Goneril ('this gilded serpent') on charges of treason,** the proof for which is to be found in Goneril's letter to Edmund. Acting on the instructions of the disguised Edgar, Albany now asks that the trumpet be sounded. If no champion appears to defend the truth of his accusations, Albany declares that he will himself engage Edmund in trial by combat and throws down a glove. However, this does not prove necessary. After Albany orders the trumpet to sound, Edgar (still in disguise) enters.

Edgar now accuses Edmund of treachery: '. . . thou art a traitor, false to thy gods, thy brother, and thy father, conspirant against this high illustrious prince.' While the rules of knighthood allow Edmund to ignore a challenge from an unknown warrior, he immediately accepts the challenge: 'What safe and nicely I might well delay by rule of knighthood, I disdain and spurn: Back do I toss these treasons to thy head.' The fight is brief, with Edgar quickly inflicting a mortal blow on Edmund. When Goneril tells Edmund that he was not obliged 'to answer an unknown opposite', Albany contemptuously dismisses her: 'Shut your mouth, dame.' Albany then shows Edmund the letter Edgar had given him, confirming his and Goneril's treachery.

Edmund redeems himself to some extent in the final scene. He makes no attempt to deny the truth of the letter's contents: 'What you have charged me with, that have I done; and more, much more; the time will bring it out . . .' **Edmund then forgives the man who has killed him., prompting a generous response from Edgar who now, in turn, forgives the brother who had brought such chaos and pain into his world**: 'Let's exchange charity.' The manner in which events have developed reinforces Edgar's belief in the idea of divine justice: 'The gods are just, and of our pleasant vices make instruments to plague us.' **Edmund accepts his fate in a philosophical manner: 'The wheel is come full circle.'** Edgar now gives a lengthy account of his life since he had to adopt a new identity, culminating in the news that Gloucester had died between 'two extremes of passion, joy and guilt' when Edgar revealed his true identity to him. **The high drama that characterises the closing scene continues with news of other dramatic incidents: Goneril is dead after committing suicide, as is Regan, who was poisoned by her sister. It is very ironic that these callous sisters died as a result of their shared love for Edmund, who derives some grim satisfaction from the fact that he was loved by two women:** 'Yet Edmund was beloved: the one the other poisoned for my sake, and after slew herself.' **Remarkably, it is Edmund who draws everyone's attention back to Lear and Cordelia, revealing a further hint of humanity before he dies:** '. . . some good I mean to do, despite of mine own nature.' Announcing that he has already signed Lear and Cordelia's death warrants, he asks that someone go to the castle where they are imprisoned with the utmost haste. Tragically, no sooner has Edgar departed for the castle than Lear arrives, carrying Cordelia's lifeless body in his arms. **Lear's suffering and sense of loss are so intense as to be almost beyond description.** He cannot comprehend how everyone else is not as devastated as he is: 'Howl! howl! howl! howl! O, you are men of stones . . .' We again see the old, fiery Lear as he rages against the world: 'A plague upon you, murderers, traitors all!' Despite his advanced age, Lear killed the man that hanged Cordelia. Interestingly, Lear finally recognises Kent ('Are you not Kent?'), who goes on to explain that he was Caius, his servant who, from the start, had followed Lear's 'sad steps'. Kent aptly sums up the grim and desolate mood at the close of the play when he observes that 'all's cheerless, dark and deadly'.

When an officer enters with news of Edmund's death, Albany dismisses it as 'but a trifle here', before going on to describe how things would be in the kingdom under the new regime: 'All friends shall taste the wages of their virtue, and all foes the cup of their deservings.' By now the heartbroken Lear, unable to understand why 'a dog, a horse, a rat have life', and Cordelia 'no breath at all' is close to death himself. **As Lear slips into his final sleep, an attempt is made to revive him, but Kent immediately intervenes. Ever protective of his royal master, Kent points out that Lear has suffered enough: 'Vex not his ghost: O let him pass! He hates him that would upon the rack of this tough world stretch him out longer.'** The rack image (like the earlier 'wheel of fire' image) dramatically highlights the extent of Lear's torment.

In the closing lines of the play, Albany (assuming the role of kingmaker) addresses Kent and Edgar as 'friends of my soul', before stating that they both should rule in the kingdom from now on, 'and the gored state sustain'. However, Kent's primary duty is to Lear, and death is no barrier to his loyalty and devotion to his master: 'I have a journey, sir, shortly to go: my master calls me, I must not say no.' Kent plans to take his own life so that he can continue to serve Lear in the next life, leaving Albany and Edgar to restore the 'gored state' to health.

KEY POINTS

- The closing scene is filled with dramatic incidents, becoming increasingly grimmer with each new revelation.
- Lear and Cordelia are arrested. Edmund's intention is to have both executed because both have the ability to attract popular support and consequently may pose a threat to his political ambitions.
- When Edmund addresses Albany as if he were his equal, the latter puts him firmly in his place, pointing out that he is his 'subject', not his 'brother'.
- Albany arrests both Goneril and Edmund on charges of 'capital treason'.
- Edgar comes forward as Albany's champion to defend the authenticity (truthfulness) of Goneril's letter to Edmund (the document that proves their treason).
- After Edgar deals a fatal blow to Edmund, he reveals his true identity and the two are reconciled.
- Edmund redeems himself to some extent in the final scene by admitting to his crimes and by making a belated effort to do some good before he dies by revealing that he has signed Lear and Cordelia's death warrants.
- When Lear arrives, carrying his beloved Cordelia's lifeless body, his grief knows no bounds.
- Gloucester dies between two extremes of passion, joy and grief, after Edgar reveals his true identity to him.
- The love rivalry between Goneril and Regan over Edmund reaches a dramatic climax in this scene, with Goneril poisoning Regan, before dying by her own hand after her treachery has been revealed.
- Kent remains unwaveringly loyal to Lear, insisting that there be no attempt to revive him as he nears death because he has already suffered enough 'upon the rack of this tough world'. Kent's loyalty to Lear extends beyond the physical world – he intends to take his own life so that he may serve his master in the next world.
- It will fall to Albany and Edgar to restore the kingdom to a state of order and health.

Guidelines for Answering Exam Questions

Structure your Answer

1   A brief plan – this should be no more than key words or phrases.

2   An introduction – this should outline your general response to the question.

3   Aim for a points-based answer, avoiding excessive narrative.

4   Make one main point per paragraph.

5   Points should be discussed in a logical order.

6   The opening sentence in each paragraph (the paragraph sentence) should state the main point of the paragraph.

7   Maintain focus on, and refer back to, the terms of the question.

8   Support your points by close reference to, and quotation from, the text.

9   A brief conclusion.

Main Areas for Exam

1   The manner in which characters are portrayed.

2   The importance / role / dramatic function of particular characters.

3   Themes.

4   Key scenes.

5   Soliloquys.

6   Language, imagery and symbolism.

7   Your personal response to the play.

Exam Topics

'Despite his serious flaws, the audience remains sympathetic towards Lear.'

If the play is to work as a tragedy, we must retain a degree of sympathy for the protagonist (central character), **King Lear** through to the end of the play. While Lear is a deeply flawed character who is the architect of his own downfall, we ultimately see him as 'a man more sinned against than sinning'. While Lear clearly does wrong, the greater wrongs are done to him. He earns our sympathy because he is pained to the point of insanity by the unnatural behaviour of his 'pelican daughters' and elicits our admiration because he demonstrates a capacity to grow through his intense personal suffering. It is also significant that Shakespeare encourages us to see Lear in the same positive light as those characters in the play that we admire.

The dramatic opening scene brings Lear's serious and related flaws into sharp focus. We see the very harmful effects of his arrogance, his moral blindness, his gullibility and, particularly, his rashness. The love test dramatically underscores (underlines) Lear's foolishness: 'Which of you shall we say doth love us most?' His ego demands that his daughters flatter him and Goneril and Regan immediately try to out-do each other in their professions of love for their credulous father. Lear's treatment of both Cordelia and Kent is extremely harsh and unjust. Cordelia is disowned and disinherited simply for refusing to pander to Lear's ego ('Here I disclaim all my paternal care, propinquity and property of love'), while Kent is banished for bluntly telling Lear to reverse his 'hideous rashness' and for describing his

treatment of Cordelia as 'evil'. **The Lear that we see in the opening scene is an utterly unappealing, unsympathetic character.**

While Lear is undeniably the architect of his own downfall, our initial disapproval of him ultimately develops into a profound sympathy when we see the intensity of his suffering. While Lear's cruelty is impulsive and unthinking, Goneril and Regan's mistreatment of Lear is coldly pre-meditated. They conspire to strip Lear of his remaining power and dignity: 'Pray you sister, let us sit together.' Lear is profoundly shocked by the disrespect shown to him first by Goneril's servants, and then by Goneril herself ('Are you our daughter?'). He is pained by his sense of powerlessness: 'I am ashamed that thou hast power to shake my manhood thus.' We pity Lear as he senses his growing lack of control over himself ('O let me not be mad, not mad sweet heaven!'), others, and events in general. The stocking of Kent constitutes a deliberate, public show of disrespect towards Lear that shakes him to the very core of his being: 'They could not, would not do it: 'tis worse than murder to do upon respect such violent outrage.' Lear's pitiful running between sisters only sees him stripped of his remaining power and dignity when Goneril and Regan refuse to allow him to keep even a single knight: 'What need one?' We cannot but sympathise with Lear as he pleads with the gods not to let him break down completely in the face of Goneril and Regan's heartless behaviour: '. . . this heart shall break into a hundred thousand flaws, or ere I'll weep.' **The storm scene highlights the**

intensity of Lear's physical and mental suffering. Callously locked out by Regan, the frail old man is exposed to the ferocity of the elements. The pain that drives Lear to insanity is caused by the ingratitude of his 'pelican daughters'. The old king is a particularly pathetic figure in the mock trial scene as he struggles to comprehend his daughters' unnatural behaviour: 'Is there any cause in nature that makes these hard hearts?' Like Edgar, the audience is deeply moved by Lear's anguish: 'My tears begin to take his part so much, they'll mar my counterfeiting.' Finally, it is impossible not to feel profoundly sympathetic towards Lear when he carries Cordelia's lifeless body onto the stage: 'Cordelia, Cordelia, stay a little.' The images of the wheel of fire and the rack effectively suggest the intensity of Lear's suffering. **By the closing scene, we feel that Lear has paid an inordinately high price for his personal failings.**

We also admire Lear for growing through suffering. His pain has a humanising, ennobling effect, and he consequently ends the play a better, wiser, more humble man. Lear gradually learns to see himself more clearly ('I am a very foolish, fond old man'), recognises his wrongdoing ('I did her wrong'), and is filled with guilt and shame at his mistreatment of Cordelia ('If you have poison for me I will drink it'). He ultimately acquires humility, asking for Cordelia's forgiveness ('Pray you now, forgive and forget') and comes to see others in a clear light, recognising that Goneril and Regan flattered him 'like a dog'. He acquires a social conscience, regretting his failure to look after the poor: 'O, I have ta'en too little care of this!' Remarkably, Lear even comes to preach the idea of social justice, arguing that wealth should be distributed more equitably: 'Expose thyself to feel what wretches feel that thou may shake the superflux to them and show the heavens more just.' We admire the manner in which Lear grows in wisdom. He becomes aware of corruption in high places, and of the absence of fairness in the administration of justice in the kingdom: 'Robes and furred gowns hide all. Plate sin with gold and the strong lance of justice hurtless breaks; arm it in rags, a pigmy's straw doth break it.'

The remarkable loyalty of such characters as Kent, the Fool and Gloucester reminds us of an earlier, greater Lear. Kent returns in disguise to serve the king who banished him. His loyalty to Lear is total: 'My life I never held but as a pawn to wage against thine enemies.' Kent's loyalty to Lear is such that he is even prepared to follow him into the next world: 'I have a journey, sir, shortly to go. My master calls me, I must not say no.' The Fool remains with Lear throughout his descent into insanity and endures the worst storm in living memory alongside him. We also see Gloucester risking his life to help Lear. We realise that Lear must essentially be a good and noble character to inspire such unwavering loyalty and respect. We gradually come to see Lear in the same light as those characters who admire him.

In conclusion, Lear displays no redeeming features in the dramatic opening scene. In fact, his foolish and harsh behaviour inevitably alienates the audience. However, Shakespeare ensures that we ultimately sympathise with Lear by powerfully evoking his intense personal suffering. **We realise that Lear is the author of his own demise, but ultimately see him more as victim than villain. We also come to admire Lear for his acquisition of wisdom, self-awareness and humility.**

'Lear grows through a process of intense personal suffering, ending the play a better and wiser man.'

The personal growth of the central character is the dominant theme of the play, *King Lear*. When we meet Lear in the opening scene of the play, he is a deeply flawed and utterly unappealing character. He is arrogant, egocentric (self-centred), spiritually blind. and rash. However, Lear grows through suffering, gradually acquiring humility, self-knowledge and wisdom. **By the close of the play we feel both pity and admiration for the man who appeared to be nothing more than a cruel, foolish tyrant in the dramatic opening scene.**

The opening scene dramatically highlights Lear's weaknesses. Lear is a foolish character – he divides his kingdom on the basis of a ridiculous love-test, believing that he can measure love in terms of words: 'Which of you shall we say doth love us most?' Goneril and Regan do not hesitate to exploit their ageing father's **gullible** nature. Lear is also extremely **rash**, disowning and disinheriting Cordelia because she refuses to flatter him: 'Here I disclaim all my paternal care, propinquity and property of blood . . .' He also banishes Kent for bluntly telling him that he is doing 'evil'. Through Goneril we learn that Lear has always been a **fiery** character ('The best and soundest of his time hath been but rash'). Accustomed to unquestioning obedience, Lear has grown **arrogant**. He is outraged by Kent's intervention: 'Come not between the dragon and his wrath.' The dragon image indicates that **Lear lacks self-knowledge**, suggesting that he sees himself as an all-powerful being, a 'dragon' whose anger must be feared. Regan remarks that Lear 'hath ever but slenderly known himself'. **Lear must acquire self-**

knowledge, before coming to understand others and life in general. He is spiritually blind at the start of the play, but through suffering gains true vision, ultimately coming to see himself and the wider world more clearly.

Lear's personal growth is gradual and uneven. In contrast to Gloucester who gains insight (understanding) in a very sudden manner, Lear's path to self-knowledge and insight is a long, painful one. It must also be pointed out that even as Lear grows in wisdom, he occasionally shows signs of his earlier failings. At different times in the play, Lear displays the foolishness, arrogance, rashness and egocentricity (self-centredness) so dramatically in evidence in the opening scene. **However, Lear's transformation is all the more credible (believable) because it is not a simple process.**

Lear takes his first painful steps on the road to self-knowledge when he is stung by Goneril's 'marble-hearted' ingratitude. Once Goneril has her share of the kingdom, she has no need to flatter or humour Lear any longer. Encouraged by their mistress, Goneril's servants treat Lear with thinly-disguised contempt, while she herself expresses her impatience with his 'insolent retinue' (bad-mannered followers). **Lear is stunned to find himself treated, not as an all-powerful king, but as an irritating old man:** 'Are you our daughter?' Not only does he have difficulty recognising his daughter, he has difficulty recognising himself: 'Does any here know me? This is not Lear. . . . Who is it can tell me who I am?' **Lear's self-image is shaken by Goneril's display of filial ingratitude (which he describes as being**

'sharper than a serpent's tooth') and he painfully acknowledges his own foolishness and lack of judgement: 'O Lear, Lear, Lear! Beat at this gate that let thy folly in and thy dear judgement out!' Lear's anguish (mental/emotional suffering) is heightened by his awareness of his own powerlessness: 'I am ashamed that thou hast power to shake my manhood thus.' However, even though Lear has gained a degree of self-knowledge, he still displays the rashness that caused so much harm in the opening scene. Goneril is cursed in the strongest terms imaginable: 'Into her womb convey sterility . . . .'

The next step on the road to self-knowledge is taken when, speaking of Cordelia, Lear remarks to the Fool, 'I did her wrong'. It is ironic that as Lear begins to gain insight he simultaneously edges closer to insanity. Shocked by Goneril's ingratitude and pained by the knowledge that he gave her the power to humiliate him, Lear struggles to keep his sanity: 'O let me not be mad, not mad sweet heaven!' While the disintegration of his self-image lies at the root of Lear's loss of sanity, the onset (beginning) of madness is accelerated by his towering rages.

Lear is foolish to believe that Regan will treat him better than Goneril, but again learns through painful experience. When he arrives at Regan's castle, he is horrified to find his servant Kent in the stocks: 'They could not, would not do it; 'tis worse than murder to do upon respect such violent outrage.' Stung by this public insult, he senses the madness rising up within him: 'O how this mother (disease) swells up toward my heart!' Lear initially refuses to believe that Regan could be as ungrateful as Goneril: 'Thou shall never have my curse . . . thou better know'st the offices of nature, bond of childhood, effects of courtesy, dues of gratitude.' However, when

Goneril arrives and takes Regan by the hand, it is clear that the two sisters are acting as one against Lear to strip him of his remaining power and dignity. Regan coldly reminds Lear of his powerlessness in a strikingly callous remark: 'I pray you father, being weak, seem so.' We see how much Lear still has to learn when he tries to measure love in terms of the number of knights each sister will allow him to have. He tells Goneril: 'Thy fifty yet doth double five-and-twenty, and thou art twice her love.' When his daughters refuse to allow him to keep even a single knight, Lear rants powerlessly, threatening them with 'the terrors of the earth'. **However, he continues to grow through suffering, showing signs of self-knowledge when he describes himself as 'a poor old man as full of grief as age'.** Sadly, he moves ever closer to insanity: 'O fool, I shall go mad!'

In the storm scene Lear's suffering is so intense that he finally loses his sanity. Kent tells us that 'all the power of his wits have given way to his impatience'. **The positive aspect to Lear's torment is that he paradoxically acquires 'reason in madness'.** He sees himself for what he is: 'A poor, infirm, weak and despised old man.' He shows an admirable concern for others, ushering the Fool into the hovel ahead of him ('I have one part in my heart that's sorry yet for thee'). He also acquires a social conscience, realising that he neglected the poor who do not even have adequate shelter from the storm: 'O, I have taken too little care of this.' Lear even preaches the idea of social justice, suggesting that wealth should be distributed more fairly: 'Expose thyself to feel what wretches feel that thou mayest shake the superflux to them and show the heavens more just.' We see further evidence of Lear's new-found wisdom when he sees Poor Tom as an example of the reality of humankind: 'A poor bare forked animal.'

It must be pointed out that even as Lear gradually grows and learns, he continues to display some of his old failings. This fact makes his personal transformation more realistic – he doesn't change suddenly or completely. On the heath Lear cries out for universal destruction because of his own intense suffering: 'And thou all-shaking thunder, strike flat the thick rotundity of the world.' This is a reminder of **Lear's egocentric (self-centred) nature.** He views everything in terms of his own experience, concluding that Poor Tom could only have been reduced to his miserable state by his ungrateful daughters. When Kent points out that Poor Tom has no daughters, we again see **Lear's rash and fiery nature:** 'Death traitor! Nothing could have subdued nature to such a lowness but his unkind daughters.'

The pain of his daughters' filial ingratitude is so intense that Lear almost welcomes the storm as a distraction, reflecting that it 'will not give me leave to ponder on things would hurt me more'. On the heath, Lear occasionally becomes tranquil, but, when he calms down, he remembers how his daughters have mistreated him and another towering rage follows. **The mock trial highlights Lear's inner torment as he struggles to understand his daughters' 'hard hearts'. Lear continues to grow through his suffering, now acknowledging that Goneril and Regan flattered him 'like a dog'. However, the gradual, uneven nature of his personal development is again apparent when he arrogantly declares, 'I am the king himself . . . When I do stare, see how the subject quakes'.** Here we are reminded of the dragon image from the opening scene.

There are many examples of what Edgar describes as Lear's 'reason in madness'. Lear wisely tells the blind Gloucester that 'a man may see how this world goes with no eyes'. He comes to realise that the world is unjust and corrupt, observing that the rich can avoid justice, while the poor are always punished for any wrongdoing: 'Through tattered clothes small vices do appear: robes and furred gowns hide all.'

We get further evidence of Lear's personal development when his sense of 'burning shame' prevents him from rushing to Cordelia. We are reminded of the intensity of Lear's suffering when he finally meets his beloved daughter: 'I am bound upon a wheel of fire that mine own tears do scald like molten lead.' The dramatic nature of Lear's transformation is apparent when he describes himself as 'a very foolish, fond old man' and begs Cordelia's forgiveness ('. . . pray you now, forgive and forget'). He is so contrite (guilty) that he is even prepared to drink poison.

The closing scene brings unbearable anguish for Lear when he carries Cordelia's lifeless body onto the stage: 'Howl, howl, howl, howl! O, you are men of stones.' This dramatic scene reminds us that in some ways Lear remains unchanged. We again see his rashness in the immediate aftermath of Cordelia's murder: 'A plague upon you, murderers, traitors all.' **However, while Lear's personal transformation may not be total, it is certainly dramatic. We cannot but feel admiration for a man who acquires wisdom and humility through intense personal suffering. In the course of the play Lear is truly stretched 'upon the rack of this tough world', but ends the play a better and wiser man.**

'King Lear – A Tragic Hero?'

King Lear is a true tragic hero. As the play opens he is a king with all the power and prestige that accompany this position. A tragic hero possesses a major flaw which brings about a catastrophe (disaster). Lear's tragic flaw is his rashness. Underlying this rashness are his arrogance, spiritual blindness and lack of judgement. The catastrophe brought about by Lear's flawed character causes immense suffering for Lear and for others. Lear descends from a position of absolute power to one where he owns nothing except the clothes on his back, while his kingdom is plunged into a state of chaos because of his tragic mistakes. As a tragic hero, Lear should retain our sympathy (to some degree, at least) and, as the play unfolds, we feel both pity and admiration for him. He grows through suffering, ultimately becoming a better and wiser man. What really casts Lear in the role of a tragic hero is the fact that wisdom and humility come too late for him to alter the disastrous sequence of events caused by his destructive rashness. The mood at the close of the play is particularly bleak as the audience is overwhelmed by a terrible sense of tragedy.

The play opens with Lear as a figure of immense power and authority. He is 'every inch a king'. He is almost a god-like figure as he leans over the map and proclaims how he will divide up the kingdom. His subjects are loyal and respectful. Kent addresses Lear in reverential tones ('Royal Lear whom I have ever honoured as my king, loved as my father . . .'), before going on to deliver a blunt warning to his master after he has disowned and disinherited Cordelia: 'Reserve thy state, and in thy best consideration, check this hideous rashness.'

The autocratic (tyrannical) Lear sees himself as an all-powerful being as he warns Kent, 'Come not between the dragon and his wrath . . .'

However, for all his power, Lear is a flawed character. It is his human weaknesses that bring about his downfall and cause so much suffering for both himself and others. In this sense, he is the typical tragic hero. Lear is dangerously rash in his decision-making. He is arrogant and lacking in judgement and self-knowledge. Lear's rashness is the main cause of the catastrophe which affects both himself and his entire kingdom. He disowns Cordelia, his one true daughter: 'Here I disclaim all my paternal care, propinquity and property of blood . . .' In this one moment of terrible impetuosity, Lear sets in motion a train of disastrous events which lead to his own downfall and to the deaths of many of the participants in the opening scene. He unleashes evil forces which ultimately assume complete control of his kingdom. In cutting himself off from his one true daughter, Lear puts himself at the mercy of Goneril and Regan – a decision he lives to regret. By the close of the opening scene, the evil sisters are already conspiring (secretly plotting) against Lear: 'Pray you, let us hit together . . .' Lear's destructive rashness is also to be seen in his impulsive decision to banish Kent. Not only does Lear banish his most loyal servant for attempting to make him aware of his foolishness, he also threatens him with capital punishment (i.e. death).

Lear pays a high price for his human weaknesses as he is driven to the point of insanity by Goneril and Regan's ingratitude and callousness (lack of feeling). While we realise that Lear is the architect of his own downfall, we still sympathise with him as he is rejected and belittled by his ungrateful daughters. Stung by Goneril's 'marble-hearted' ingratitude, Lear naively expects Regan to treat him better, only to realise that his two daughters are acting as one against him. Regan coldly reminds Lear of his powerlessness: 'I pray you father, being weak, seem so.' The two sisters strip Lear of his remaining power and dignity when they refuse to allow him to have even a single knight, coldly asking, 'What need one?' Locked out in the worst storm in living memory, Lear struggles in vain to retain his sanity. The pain of his daughters' filial ingratitude is such that he calls out for universal destruction: 'And thou all-shaking thunder, smite flat the thick rotundity of the world! Crack nature's moulds, all germens spill at once that make ingrateful man!' In the mock trial scene, Lear pathetically tries to understand his daughters' 'hard hearts'. **The images of the wheel of fire ('I am bound upon a wheel of fire that mine own tears do scald like molten lead') and the rack (used by Kent in the closing scene) underline the intensity of Lear's suffering.**

As Lear loses his sanity the forces of darkness, unleashed by his initial foolishness, take complete control of his world. Evil is depressingly dominant for much of the play because Lear gives it the opportunity to thrive. Edgar is reduced to the level of a mad beggar by Edmund's scheming, Gloucester is savagely tortured for going to assist Lear, while Goneril and Regan plumb new depths of evil in their rivalry over Edmund.

Like all great tragic heroes, Lear comes to acknowledge his own mistakes. He grows through suffering. He realises that he did Cordelia wrong and, towards the close of the play, begs her forgiveness ('Pray you now, forgive and forget'). He realises that Goneril and Regan flattered him 'like a dog'. He comes to see himself as 'a poor, infirm, weak, despised old man'. He also acquires a social conscience, recognising that he neglected the poor when he was king ('O, I have taken too little care of this'). We see his compassion for others as he ushers the Fool into the hovel ahead of him ('In boy, go first'). He achieves a degree of wisdom, declaring that man is 'a poor bare forked animal'. He also comes to see that the system of justice is corrupt because 'robes and furred gowns hide all' (i.e. the rich avoid justice while the poor are always punished for any wrongdoing).

Lear is a classic tragic hero in that while he becomes a better and wiser man, his acquisition of self-knowledge comes too late for him to undo the harm that he has done. The hope offered by the counter-movement against evil is all-too-brief. The counter-action against the forces of evil begins almost as soon as Cordelia and Kent are unjustly banished by Lear. The two are in regular contact and Kent looks forward to co-operating with Cordelia in setting right the wrongs done to Lear ('seeking to give losses their remedies'). Gloucester also goes to Lear's assistance: '. . . the king, my old master, must be relieved.' Hope is heightened when Lear and Cordelia are reconciled. However, the defeat of Cordelia's forces extinguishes this hope and from this point Lear's suffering reaches new and heartbreaking levels of intensity. Cordelia is hanged after Edmund ordered her execution, and Lear's grief knows no bounds: 'Howl, howl, howl, howl! O, you are men of stones.' **The happiness that Lear had anticipated following his reconciliation with Cordelia is cruelly snatched from him:** 'Why should a dog, a horse, a rat, have life and thou no life at all?' This poignant scene brings the full extent of the tragedy into sharp focus. Lear dies, having truly been stretched 'upon the rack of this tough world'.

The ending of the play is particularly bleak. Lear and Cordelia are both dead. The death of Cordelia is particularly depressing because she is the epitome of virtue and the play's most innocent victim. Lear's kingdom has been profoundly disrupted by the forces of evil, and, in Kent's words, 'all's cheerless, dark and deadly'.

'The sub-plot reflects and reinforces the key themes of the main plot.'

Plot and sub-plot run side by side, at times connecting and becoming interwoven. A cursory reading of the play indicates the striking similarities between plot and sub-plot. The sub-plot reflects and reinforces key ideas in the main plot, underlining the universal nature of such themes as moral blindness and redemption through suffering.

Both Gloucester and Lear are gullible, rash and morally blind. Just as Lear falls victim to the 'glib and oily' flattery of Goneril and Regan, Gloucester's credulous nature is easily exploited by Edmund. Both men are manipulated with consummate ease by children who prove to be callous and unnatural. Gloucester shares Lear's rashness, reacting impulsively to Edmund's revelation of Edgar's 'treachery'. Without ever affording Edgar the opportunity to defend his character and reputation, Gloucester immediately condemns him: 'Abhorred villain! Unnatural, detested, brutish villain! Worse than brutish!' Shortly afterwards, Gloucester reduces his loyal and loving son Edgar to the level of a hunted criminal, just as Lear had forced his one true daughter, Cordelia, into exile. 'Let him fly far: Not in this land shall he remain uncaught; and found – dispatch.' In the same scene, Gloucester disinherits Edgar, promising Edmund that he shall inherit his lands: '. . . of my land, loyal and natural boy, I'll work the means to make thee capable.' Morally blind, neither Gloucester nor Lear is capable of seeing themselves or others clearly in the early stages of the play.

While Gloucester and Lear share similar flaws, they are utterly contrasting personalities. While Lear is arrogant and domineering, Gloucester is passive and weak. His weakness of character is apparent when he makes no attempt to support Kent in highlighting the rash, foolish and unjust nature of Lear's actions in the dramatic opening scene. Initially manipulated by Edmund for his own evil ends, he is later manipulated by Edgar for the noble-minded purpose of ridding him of his suicidal despair. Edmund laughs at Gloucester's superstitious nature, describing as 'the excellent foppery of the world' the tendency to blame our disasters on 'the sun, the moon and the stars', when, in fact, they originate in 'our own behaviour'. Edgar exploits his father's gullible nature for a worthy purpose when he persuades him that he was led to jump from the cliffs at Dover by a demon in the form of a beggar, before convincing him that he is still alive through 'a miracle' and that the gods have 'preserved' his life. Having earlier believed that the gods wantonly killed men for their 'sport', Gloucester now prays to the 'ever-gentle gods' not to allow him to be tempted to die 'before you please'.

Notwithstanding their flaws, both Gloucester and Lear are both essentially noble characters. Gloucester protests against Kent being placed in the stocks, rightly pointing out to Cornwall that Lear will be angered by this act of blatant disrespect towards him: 'Let me beseech your Grace, not to do so . . . the king must take it ill that he is so slightly valued in his messenger.' While this protest has no impact on Cornwall's thinking, it serves to highlight Gloucester's sense of justice and fundamental decency. His finer qualities are again to be seen when he sympathises with the stocked Kent: 'I am sorry for thee, friend.' Gloucester's noble nature is also evident in his determination to go to Lear's assistance even at the risk of his own life: 'Though I die for it, as no less is threatened me, the king, my old master, must be relieved.'

Both Gloucester and Lear are victims of filial ingratitude. Goneril, Regan and Edmund show no respect for the natural bond that should closely bind child and parent (Edmund hypocritically claims to have told Edgar of 'how manifold and strong a bond the child was bound to the father'). However, both Gloucester and Lear are themselves initially guilty of blatantly disregarding these bonds in their unjust and harsh treatment of Edgar and Cordelia.

Both Gloucester and Lear undergo dramatic personal transformations in the course of the play, with both acquiring self-knowledge and moral vision (qualities which are inextricably linked since one cannot see others and the world in general clearly until one sees oneself clearly) **through suffering**. Both are enlightened by their intense torment, ending the play better and wiser men. **Both gain insight in an ironic manner. In Edgar's words, Lear gains 'reason in madness', while Gloucester acquires moral vision at the very moment** that he loses his physical sight: 'Oh my follies! Then Edgar was abused; kind gods forgive me that, and prosper him!' The irony of simultaneously losing his physical sight and acquiring moral vision is not lost on Gloucester: 'I stumbled when I saw . . .' In striking contrast to Lear's gradual acquisition of insight, Gloucester's attainment of understanding is sudden and dramatic.

Both Gloucester and Lear show concern for others, even in their own suffering. Lear ushers the fool into the hovel ahead of him ('Poor fool and knave, I have one part of my heart that's sorry yet for thee'), while Gloucester expresses his concern for the old man who has been guiding him since he was thrown out at the gates of his own castle: 'Thy comforts can do me no good at all; thee they may hurt.'

Both Gloucester and Lear acquire a social conscience in the course of their personal growth, learning to care for the poor and the unfortunate. Observing the 'poor naked wretches' on the moor, Lear concludes that he took 'too little care of this' when he was king. He goes on to preach the gospel of social justice: 'Take physic pomp; expose thyself to feel what wretches feel that thou mayest shake the superflux to them and show the heavens more just.' Gloucester similarly argues for a more equitable distribution of wealth so that 'distribution should undo excess and each man have enough.' Similar to Lear, Gloucester comes to see wealth as an obstacle to moral vision; he speaks of 'the superfluous and lust-dieted man . . . that will not see because he doth not feel.'

Gloucester and Lear are both rescued by the children they had treated so unjustly, with both Edgar and Cordelia ultimately giving consolation and hope to their respective tormented fathers. Edgar is

Cordelia's counterpart in the sub-plot – both are noble-minded, loving and forgiving. Edgar and Cordelia are portrayed as healing agents, tending to and healing the fathers who have wronged them. Edgar sets out to rid Gloucester of his deep despair and suicidal tendencies ('Why I do trifle thus with his despair is done to cure it'), while Cordelia hopes that her love will 'repair those violent harms' done to Lear by Goneril and Regan ('Restoration hang thy medicine on my lips').

Both Lear and Gloucester pay the ultimate price for their own failings, with both experiencing the extremes of joy and grief before they die. Lear experiences the inexpressible joy of being reconciled with Cordelia, before being crushed by grief at her tragic death. Gloucester dies almost as Lear does. Edgar describes how his father reacted when he finally revealed his true identity to him: '. . . his flawed heart . . . twixt two extremes of passion, joy and grief, burst smilingly.'

'Evil is vividly and frighteningly portrayed in the play.

A number of characters in the play display a frightening capacity for evil and for savage cruelty. When we consider that some of the greatest cruelties are inflicted on fathers by their own children and by children on their own fathers, we realise that the natural bonds that ordinarily bind families together can sometimes be broken in ways that are truly shocking.

Goneril is, from the beginning, transparently false. Insincerity drips from her words of flattery when she tells Lear, 'Sir, I love you more than words can wield the matter, dearer man eye-sight, space and liberty'. No sooner has she got her share of the kingdom than she starts to plot against Lear, conspiring with her sister against him: 'Pray you, let us hit together.' She encourages her servants to openly neglect Lear, ensuring that he clearly understands that he is not wanted: 'Put on what weary negligence you please.' Goneril sends a message to Regan, telling her to treat Lear as she has done: 'I'll write straight to my sister to hold my very course.' She insults Lear by telling him that he is old and doting: 'All's not offence that indiscretion finds and

dotage terms so.' Along with Regan, she humiliates Lear by not allowing him to keep a single knight. Goneril wants immediate revenge on Gloucester when she discovers that he has been assisting Lear: 'Pluck out his eyes!' **Her cruelty is boundless as we see when she urges Edmund to kill her husband, Albany and when she herself poisons Regan** because she regards her sister as her rival for Edmund's affections.

Regan is as hypocritical as Goneril and, similar to her sister, has no qualms about using 'the glib and oily art' of flattery to ingratiate herself with (win the favour of) Lear before the kingdom is divided. We see her cruelty when she insists that Kent be kept in the stocks all day and 'all night too'. She is well aware that the stocking of Kent is a direct insult to Lear, with Gloucester reminding her that 'the king must take it ill that he is so slightly valued in his messenger'. Regan belittles Lear by refusing to see him when he first arrives at Gloucester's castle. In a particularly cruel put-down, she coldly reminds Lear of his powerlessness: 'I pray you father, being weak, seem so.' Regan is the epitome (embodiment/personification) of filial ingratitude. When Lear pathetically reminds her that he gave her 'all', she callously replies, 'And in good time you gave it'. Along with Goneril, she strips Lear of what is left of his power and dignity by denying him the right to have even a single knight: 'What need one?' She callously orders the doors of Gloucester's castle to be closed against Lear when he rushes out into the storm: 'O Sir, to wilful men the injuries that they themselves procure must be their schoolmasters.' **Like Goneril, Regan is cruel and vengeful, looking to punish Gloucester when it becomes known that he has helped Lear: 'Hang him instantly!' The depth of Regan's savagery is almost beyond belief.** She demands that Gloucester's second eye be cut from his head: 'One side will mock another, the other too.' This scene is the most vivid and frightening depiction of evil. Not satisfied with physically torturing the unfortunate old man, she also torments him mentally. When Gloucester cries out for his son Edmund, Regan delights in telling him that it was Edmund who betrayed him: 'Thou call'st on him that hates thee: it was he who made the overtures of thy treason to us, who is too good to pity thee.' **Regan heartlessly throws the blind Gloucester out of his own castle, declaring that he can 'smell his way to Dover'.** Appalled by her cruelty, one of Regan's servants remarks, 'If she live long . . . women will all turn out monsters'. Regan later regrets not having killed Gloucester because his pitiable state is turning people against them, and promises to reward Oswald if he kills 'the blind traitor'. **Animal imagery underscores Goneril and Regan's inhuman cruelty** ('pelican daughters', 'tigers, not daughters', 'monsters of the deep' etc.).

Similar to Goneril and Regan, Edmund is capable of frightening evil and cruelty.

What is particularly horrifying about the evil in the play is that its chief victims are elderly parents who suffer at the hands of ungrateful, unfeeling children. **Edmund coldly and ruthlessly exploits Gloucester's gullibility and Edgar's nobility in order to advance himself:** 'A credulous father and a brother noble whose nature is so far from doing wrong that he suspects none.' **Edmund betrays Gloucester to Cornwall** in the full knowledge that his father will be severely punished for assisting Lear. **He deceives both Goneril and Regan into believing that he loves them in order to achieve his own ends**, cynically delighting in his cleverness: 'To both these sisters have I sworn my love, each jealous of the other as the stung are of the adder.' **He plans to use Albany to help him defeat the French, before Goneril arranges her husband's 'speedy taking-off'** after the battle has been won. **Edmund orders the executions of both Lear and Cordelia** because he sees them as potential threats to his ambition to achieve absolute power.

Cornwall is a suitable husband for Regan in that he is equally cruel and vindictive. It is he who orders that Kent be placed in the stocks. **He belittles Lear** by refusing to meet him when he first arrives at Gloucester's castle. Most horrifyingly, **he gouges out Gloucester's eyes in an act of monstrous savagery.**

Oswald is a minor character, but is despicably cruel and evil. He treats Lear with visible disrespect, addressing him as 'my lady's master'. **He is prepared to kill the blind, defenceless Gloucester** in order to advance himself: 'That eyeless head of mine was first framed to raise my fortunes.'

In conclusion, while evil is present in every Shakespearian tragedy, it is depicted in a particularly frightening and vivid manner in *King Lear*.

'The evil characters in the play are far more interesting than the good.'

The central characters in the play tend towards extremes of good or evil and consequently may seem one-dimensional and sometimes lacking in credibility. However, evil of its very nature is more interesting than good. While Cordelia and Edgar are hugely admirable characters who redeem their respective fathers and help to restore the natural order, they are not nearly as interesting as their evil counterparts. **Goneril, Regan and Edmund fascinate us because of the sheer depth of their evil and cruelty.**

Cordelia is a shining example of filial love and loyalty. She bears no grudge against Lear after he has unjustly disowned and disinherited her. Even after she departs for her new home in France, Cordelia continues to be informed (through Kent) of Lear's plight. Her love and concern for her father prompt her to lead a French expedition to rescue him: 'No blown ambition doth our arms incite, but love, dear love and our aged father's right.' Cordelia is utterly forgiving of her father, and in fact asks his blessing. She acts as a healing agent, comforting and consoling Lear in his darkest hour. **As the personification of goodness, Cordelia cannot but be respected and admired. However, she is too perfect to excite our interest, being depicted as an almost saintly figure** ('. . . she shook the holy water from her heavenly eyes'). **Similar to Cordelia, Edgar is admirable, but not particularly interesting because he too is perhaps too good to be believable.** He does not hesitate to forgive the father who wronged him. We see his loving, forgiving

nature in his desire to cure Gloucester of his self-pity. Like Cordelia, Edgar acts as a healing agent, easing his father's suffering. We also see his nobility when he forgives Edmund.

Goneril is the most contemptible of the evil characters. While Regan is no less evil, it is Goneril who is the dominant sister. We see her sickening hypocrisy in the opening scene when she claims to love Lear 'more than words can wield the matter'. It is Goneril who suggests that she and Regan conspire together against Lear after he has handed over his kingdom to them: 'Pray you, let us hit together.' **It is Goneril who initiates most of the evil schemes against Lear**, humiliating him in a calculated, cold-blooded manner. She encourages her servants to openly neglect and disrespect him and strips him of his remaining power and dignity by denying him the right to have even a single knight. Her extraordinary cruelty can be seen in her vicious desire to avenge herself on Gloucester: 'Pluck out his eyes!' **Goneril does not hesitate to undertake any act of evil, no matter how appalling.** We see her complete lack of conscience when she plans the death of her own husband and poisons her sister. At no point does Goneril display even a hint of conscience. **She is a truly hideous human being whose capacity for evil and cruelty both appals and fascinates.** When her villainy has been revealed and all is lost, Goneril does not hesitate to take her own life.

Regan may not be as formidable a character as Goneril, but she is no less evil, perpetrating some of the most shocking acts of cruelty in the play. Her

treatment of Lear is utterly callous. It is hard to believe that any daughter could display such a complete lack of feeling towards her own father. When Lear pathetically points out that he gave his daughters 'all', Regan contemptuously replies, 'And in good time you gave it'. When Lear rushes out into the storm, **Regan orders that the gates of the castle be closed against him**, leaving her aged father to face the unforgiving elements. **Regan seems to have an insatiable appetite for savagery, and takes a perverse delight in physical torture.** It is she who extends Kent's time in the stocks ('Till noon! Till night my lord, and all night too') and demands that Gloucester's second eye be cut from his head ('One side will mock another, the other too'). The blind Gloucester is then left at the castle gates to 'smell his way to Dover'. **It is the almost unbelievable depth of Regan's savagery that fascinates the audience – it is difficult to believe that a woman in particular could be capable of such monstrous cruelty.**

Edmund is one of the most interesting characters in the play. Similar to both Goneril and Regan, Edmund is extraordinarily evil. **It is difficult to grasp the depth of the cruelty that these evil characters display towards their own fathers and siblings.** Edmund does not hesitate to betray Gloucester to Cornwall even though he knows that Gloucester will face torture and, possibly, death for assisting Lear. **While Edmund is an utterly amoral character, he fascinates us on a number of levels.** We almost have a grudging admiration for his determination to defy society and rise above the lowly circumstances of his birth: 'Edmund the base shall top the legitimate -I grow, I prosper, now gods stand up for bastards!' Edmund is a sharp-witted villain who ruthlessly exploits Gloucester's gullibility and Edgar's nobility. He coldly sees people either as aids or obstacles to the achievement of his goals. **Edmund is a more credible character than Goneril or Regan because he is not as one-dimensional, displaying some redeeming features in the closing scene.** He exchanges forgiveness with Edgar and accepts that justice has been done: 'The wheel is come full circle.' **We admire his philosophical attitude and lack of self-pity. He also makes a belated effort to do some good by revealing that Lear and Cordelia are to be executed. The grim satisfaction that he takes in the thought of having been loved by two sisters is another indication of his humanity.** The irony that in death 'all three now marry in an instant' is not lost on Edmund, who remains sharp-witted to the end.

In conclusion, the evil characters are much more interesting than their moral opposites. The good characters are simply too perfect to be entirely believable. Furthermore, the evil characters fascinate us with the almost unbelievable depth of their cruelty.

'The Importance of Kent'

From the opening scene, Kent wins the admiration of the audience – he is loyal, courageous and shrewd. Kent is a very important character in the play, performing a number of key dramatic functions.

Kent is the only character to highlight the gravity of Lear's foolishness in the dramatic opening scene: '. . . be Kent unmannerly when Lear is mad . . . Think'st thou that duty shall have dread to speak when power to flattery bows?' When everyone else is silenced by Lear's fury, Kent considers it his duty to confront the king and attempt to make him aware of the great mistake he is making when he disowns Cordelia. He urges Lear to 'see better', bluntly telling him, 'I tell thee thou dost evil'. Kent clearly perceives that Lear's ill-judged behaviour is more than mere folly, it is 'hideous rashness' and 'evil'.

Kent unwittingly helps to bring the quarrel between Lear and his evil daughters into the open. Kent's undisguised contempt for Oswald and his bluntness when subsequently questioned by Cornwall results in his being placed in the stocks. Kent points out that, since he is the king's messenger, this degrading punishment represents an open insult to Lear. Unsurprisingly, when Lear arrives he is shocked and enraged to find Kent in the stocks: '. . . 'tis worse than murder to do upon respect such violent outrage.' From this point on the battle-lines between good and evil are clearly drawn.

One of Kent's most important dramatic functions is to maintain the link between Lear and Cordelia. Kent has kept Cordelia informed of Lear's plight and shares her determination to set right the wrongs done to the king: '. . . and shall find time from this enormous state seeking to give losses their remedies.' After Cordelia lands in England, Kent sends a messenger to Dover to inform her of Lear's 'unnatural and bemadding sorrow'. Kent keeps Cordelia in the minds of the audience during her absence.

Kent updates the audience on important military and political developments. Through Kent we learn of the growing division between Albany and Cornwall: 'There is division, although as yet the face of it be covered . . . 'twixt Albany and Cornwall.' Through Kent we learn that the forces of good are assembling to rescue Lear: 'From France there comes a power into this scattered kingdom.'

Kent regularly comments on and clarifies Lear's mental state for the audience: 'His wits begin to unsettle', 'All the power of his wits have given way to his impatience', '. . . . his wits are gone', ' . . . sometime in his better tune remembers what we are come about.' Kent also explains why Lear is reluctant to meet Cordelia: '. . . burning shame detains him from Cordelia.'

Kent is important for what he represents. He is the epitome of fidelity (loyalty). His allegiance to Lear is absolute and unwavering. Kent's love for Lear is the guiding force of his life. It is no exaggeration to state that Kent lives for Lear: 'My life I never held but as a pawn to wage against thine enemies.' It is this loyalty which prompts Kent to risk Lear's wrath by intervening when he sees the dramatic nature of the king's rashness. Despite being unjustly banished, Kent's loyalty to Lear never diminishes and he returns in disguise to serve him in any capacity he can: 'Now banished Kent, if thou canst serve where thou dost stand condemned, so may it come, thy master whom thou lovest shall find thee full of labours.' Kent is infuriated by Oswald's blatant disrespect for Lear and defends his master's honour by tripping up the unmannerly servant and pushing him out. Kent watches over Lear as the storm rages on the heath, guiding him to the shelter of a hovel. When Lear asks him, 'Wilt break my heart?' Kent's response reflects his deep affection for and absolute loyalty to his master: 'I had rather break mine own.' Even when Lear loses his sanity, Kent never fails to address him respectfully: 'Good my Lord . . .', 'Sir . . .' When the bewildered Lear seems to recognise him at the close of the play ('Are you not Kent?'), Kent explains that he has followed his master's 'sad steps' from the beginning of his troubles. Kent shows great understanding of and sympathy towards his king in his final agony. While others hope to revive the dying Lear, Kent knows that Lear has suffered enough and that it would not be right to further prolong his agony: 'Vex not his ghost: O let him pass! He hates him that would upon the rack of this tough world stretch him out longer.' Kent's unswerving loyalty to Lear is such that, when the king dies, he is determined, in the noble manner of an ancient Roman, to be at his side in the next world also. It is for this reason that he rejects Albany's offer of joining with himself and Edgar in ruling the kingdom: 'I have a journey, sir, shortly to go. My master calls me, I must not say no.' **Kent's selfless loyalty is inspiring, while his fundamental goodness helps to counterbalance the evil in the play.**

Kent's loyalty to Lear reminds us that Lear was not always the rash and foolish figure we see in the opening scene. His extraordinary fidelity to the king strongly suggests to us that there was an earlier, greater Lear who inspired such loyalty in the wise and noble Kent.

'The transformation of Albany'

Albany's dramatic transformation from ineffectual, dominated husband to strong, assertive leader is one of the most uplifting aspects of the play. His transformation is as total as it is dramatic. Little wonder that, in Act 4 Scene 2, a bewildered Oswald says of Albany: '. . . never man so changed.' By the close of the play, Albany has developed into a figure of real substance and authority and plays an important role in the restoration of peace and order.

When the audience first encounters Albany, he leaves us decidedly unimpressed. He seems to live in the shadow of his forceful, domineering wife, Goneril. He doesn't utter a word of concern about Lear's glaring mistreatment of Cordelia in the opening scene. Albany does make an attempt to take issue with his wife over her harsh treatment of Lear ('I cannot be so partial, Goneril, to the great love I bear you.'), but his feeble protest is contemptuously dismissed by his arrogant wife: 'Pray you, content.' Goneril regards Albany with undisguised disdain, scorning his 'milky gentleness' and 'want of wisdom'. Goneril perceives Lear's one hundred knights to be a potential threat to her power, and demands that the old king reduce his retinue. However, she neither consults nor informs Albany about this matter. Albany appears to be genuinely bewildered by Lear's fury: 'My lord, I am guiltless as I am ignorant of what hath moved you.' He seems to be a well-meaning, but weak character, incapable of acting (or even thinking) independently of his imperious (dictatorial) wife.

While we are unsure how it happened, Albany undergoes a truly dramatic personal transformation. He is presented in a far more positive light in the later stages of the play and gradually wins our respect and admiration. Albany finds himself in a difficult position when the French force lands. While his sympathies lie with Lear and Cordelia (who leads the French force), he has an inescapable duty to repel a French army on English territory. Oswald is clearly taken aback by the extent of Albany's transformation: '. . . never man so changed. I told him of the army that was landed; he smiled at it . . . What most he should dislike seems pleasant to him; what like, offensive.' Goneril completely misinterprets Albany's reluctance to engage the French force when she attributes this hesitancy to 'the cowish terror of his spirit'. Goneril, at this point, appears to be utterly unaware that her once 'mild-mannered' husband has undergone a change of truly dramatic proportions. However, Albany leaves her in no doubt but that she is now dealing with a very changed man when he bluntly tells his evil wife what he thinks of her: 'O Goneril, you are not worth the dust which the rude wind blows in your face.' He is convinced that his wife's unnatural treatment of Lear will ultimately be her undoing: 'She that herself will sliver and disbranch from her material sap perforce must wither and come to deadly use.' Albany now regards Goneril with total revulsion as he tells her that 'filths savour but themselves'.

A firm believer in the notion of divine justice, Albany is convinced that 'the heavens' will 'tame these vile offences'. He regards Cornwall's death as divine justice at work: 'This shows you are above you justicers that these our nether crimes so speedily can venge.' In this scene we see Albany as a man capable of anger and action. His passionate hatred of Goneril is such that he could physically tear her asunder ('tear thy flesh and bones'). Albany's earlier timidity is nowhere evident in this scene; instead we see a newly assertive, forceful leader possessed of and motivated by strong moral principles. At the close of this scene, Albany clearly aligns himself with the forces of good and promises to avenge the outrage of Gloucester's eyes.

In the final Act of the play, Albany emerges as a major force, playing a significant role in the restoration of peace and order to the kingdom. Edmund criticises Albany for being 'self-reproving'(self-critical) and we can see in this criticism Albany's regrets that he has not taken action sooner against the injustice and cruelty visited on both Lear and Gloucester. While reluctant to take up arms against Cordelia, Albany knows that intervention by a foreign force must be opposed. However, we learn from Edmund that Albany intends showing mercy to both Lear and Cordelia ('As for the mercy which he intends to Lear and Cordelia . . .'). Albany acknowledges the justice of the revolt of many of his own people, who have, he says, been 'forced to cry out' by the harshness of the regime ('the rigour of our state') ruling in place of Lear.

The last scene of the play helps us to appreciate more fully the full strength of Albany's character. Pragmatism demanded that he ally himself with Goneril, Regan and Edmund against the French invasion. However, when the external threat has been dealt with, Albany takes charge, impressing us with his dignity and authority. His strength of character is obvious in his refusal to tolerate Edmund's arrogance: 'I hold you as a subject of this war, not as a brother.' He arrests Edmund and Goneril ('this gilded serpent') for 'capital treason'. Albany emerges as a man of action willing, if necessary, to fight Edmund himself in trial by combat (he is the first to throw down his glove to Edmund). When Goneril states that, according to the rules of knighthood, Edmund is not obliged to accept a challenge from a person of lesser rank (the unknown warrior who challenges Edmund is the disguised Edgar), Albany puts her firmly in her place: 'Shut your mouth, dame . . .' Albany is also sufficiently perceptive to realise that Goneril may attempt to commit suicide ('Go after her: she's desperate; govern her.') He also recognises the nobility of the disguised Edgar: '. . . thy very gait did prophesy a royal nobleness.'

Albany displays many of the qualities required of a good and strong leader. He is compassionate and sensitive. He is deeply moved by Edgar's account of Gloucester's suffering and death ('I am almost ready to dissolve hearing of this') and by the intensity of Lear's grief at Cordelia's death ('Fall and cease'). **However, he only shows sympathy towards those deserving of it. He barely reacts to news of his wife's death, seeing Goneril's demise as divine justice:** 'This judgement of the heavens, that makes us tremble, touches us not with pity.' Tragically, while preoccupied with all that is happening around him, Albany seems to forget Cordelia and Lear and the fact that they must now be in a position of great danger. When Edmund confesses to having ordered their executions, Albany makes a belated and ultimately vain attempt to save them, telling Edgar to 'Run, run, O, run!' He subsequently dismisses news of Edmund's death as 'but a trifle here'. **At the close of the play, Albany promises that justice will be done in the kingdom:** 'All friends shall taste the wages of their virtue, and all foes the cup of their deservings.' **Along with Edgar, Albany will play an important role in restoring the health of 'the gored state' and in reinstating the natural order.**

'The theme of madness is central to the play.'

Madness is one of the central themes of the play. Madness, in its various forms, is a theme that relates to Lear, Edgar and the Fool. While we sympathise with Lear when he is pained to the point of insanity by the ingratitude and callousness of his 'pelican daughters', there is a positive aspect to Lear's madness, as there is to Gloucester's blindness. In his madness Lear acquires a peculiar type of wisdom – a wisdom that is encapsulated in Edgar's paradoxical expression: 'reason in madness.' When Lear acquires 'reason in madness', he is able to see himself, others and society in general more clearly than ever before. The Fool was also regarded as mad, but his idiotic antics conceal a sharp wit. While the Fool may or may not be entirely sane, he is certainly wise and commonsensical. The final character to whom this theme relates is of course Edgar, who is forced by his brother's treachery to adopt the disguise of a mad Bedlam beggar in order to avoid arrest. Act 3 Scene 6 brings all three of these 'madmen' together as Lear imagines himself putting his ungrateful daughters on trial. In this memorable scene we observe Lear's genuine insanity, Edgar's feigned madness and the Fool's half-foolish jests.

Lear's madness has its origins in Goneril and Regan's unnatural ingratitude. When

Lear is first rebuked and attacked by Goneril, the shock to his system is immense. His self-image is dramatically undermined: 'This is not Lear . . . Who is it that can tell me who I am?' The realisation of the injustice he did to Cordelia ('I did her wrong') combined with the pain of Goneril's 'monster ingratitude' cause Lear to fear for his sanity: 'O let me not be mad, not mad, sweet heaven!' The sight of Kent in the stocks (''tis worse than murder to do upon respect such violent outrage'), and Cornwall's refusal to meet him are further insults to Lear's royal dignity. Lear now struggles to resist the insanity rising within him: 'O how this mother swells up toward my heart! *Hysterica passio* down, thou climbing sorrow, thy element's below!' Regan's contemptuous ejection of him ('. . . being weak, seem so') is the next great shock to his system. **While Lear is very much the architect of his own downfall, we cannot but feel pity for a powerless old man who can only rave helplessly against his daughters' filial ingratitude.** When he declares 'O Fool, I shall go mad', it is clear that he is losing the battle to retain the balance of his mind. **Lear's towering rages accelerate the onset of madness.**

The storm on the heath reflects the storm in Lear's mind. Yet even as his 'wits begin to turn', Lear shows signs of growing through suffering. He begins to acquire insight and humility, seeing himself now as 'a poor, infirm, weak and despised old man.' The mentally unstable king displays a new concern for others when he ushers the Fool into the hovel in front of him: 'In boy, go first.' Even though he is now on the verge of insanity, he becomes aware of his failings as a king. He realises that he neglected the poor and now preaches the doctrine of social justice: 'O I have taken too little care of this! . . . Expose thyself to feel what wretches feel, that

thou may shake the superflux to them and show the heavens more just.' Lear's belief that Poor Tom's misery is attributable to 'his unkind daughters' prompts the concerned Fool to suggest that 'This cold night will turn us all to fools or madmen.' As Lear tears off his clothes in an attempt to identify with 'unaccommodated man', it is clear that he has lost the balance of his mind. Kent simply says: 'All the power of his wits have given way to his impatience.' The 'trial scene' sees Lear's insanity reach a peak. In this bizarre scene he struggles to understand his daughters' callousness as he wonders, 'is there any cause in nature that makes these hard hearts?'

Like Edgar ('My tears begin to take his part so much, they'll mar my counterfeiting'), the audience is deeply moved by Lear's intense suffering. Yet Lear continues to grow through his mental torment. Further evidence of Lear's personal growth comes when Kent informs us that 'burning shame' prevents Lear from going to Cordelia. Lear gradually acquires moral vision. He now realises that Goneril and Regan flattered him 'like a dog'. He wisely tells the blind Gloucester that 'A man may see how this world goes with no eyes.' He becomes aware of corruption in high places and of social inequalities: 'through tattered clothes small vices do appear. Robes and furred gowns hide all.' Little wonder that Edgar should speak of Lear's 'reason in madness'.

The ennobling, humanising effects of Lear's mental suffering are most strikingly apparent when he meets Cordelia. Now lucid (clear-minded), Lear displays self-knowledge and humility, describing himself as 'a very foolish, fond old man.' His sense of guilt in relation to Cordelia is so overwhelming that he would willingly drink poison if that would somehow prove the depth of his shame and regret. Lear's personal redemption is complete when he is reconciled with Cordelia. When he is arrested, the increasingly philosophical king only wishes for himself and Cordelia to be together so that they can ponder the meaning of life ('the mystery of things'). **While we cannot but sympathise with Lear in his intense suffering, his madness has a positive dimension. Lear's acquisition of 'reason in madness' enables him to see himself, others and the world in general more clearly.**

While the Fool was generally regarded as a madman, he clearly possesses a sharp wit. His primary dramatic function is to make Lear more aware of his foolishness. **The Fool is able to speak his mind to Lear precisely because he is regarded as a madman.** Lear describes him as 'a bitter fool' because he speaks the bitter truth, while Goneril refers to him as Lear's 'all-licensed Fool' because his apparent madness allows him to say whatever he likes. As Kent shrewdly observes, the Fool is no ordinary comic buffoon: 'This is not altogether Fool, my Lord.'

The Fool continually reminds Lear of his foolishness: 'Thou hadst little wit in thy bald crown when thou gavest thy golden one away', '. . . thou madest thy daughters thy mother', 'thou shouldst not have been old till thou hadst been wise'. The Fool disguises many of his philosophical utterances with nonsense songs: 'Fathers that wear rags/Do make their children blind.' He is the voice of Lear's conscience, the nagging inner voice that relentlessly reminds him of his wrongdoing. He is also sufficiently perceptive to realise the consequences of his master's intense suffering on the heath: 'This cold night will turn us all to fools and madmen.' Once the Fool has prompted Lear to reflect on his folly, his dramatic function is fulfilled, and he takes no further part in the action.

Edgar adopts the disguise of a mad Bedlam beggar for purposes of survival. His brother's falseness and his father's rashness have reduced him to the level of a hunted fugitive and, with all of the ports closely guarded, Edgar is forced adopt the persona of a madman: 'I will preserve myself; and am bethought to take the basest and most poorest shape.' Edgar's assumed madness has a definite purpose: self-preservation. While Edgar is able to keep up the pretence of being mad for a long time, he is so deeply moved by his father's suffering that he nearly dispenses with his act: 'My tears begin to take his part so much, they'll mar my counterfeiting.' **Edgar's 'madness' also has a very positive aspect in that it enables him to stay alive, go on to redeem his father and play his part in restoring the natural order. He assumes the role of a madman in order to protect his own life, but dispenses with his disguise as soon as his country needs him.**

Of the trio of 'madmen' who find themselves together on the heath (Lear, the Fool and Poor Tom), only Edgar is entirely sane. His feigned madness is a contrast to Lear's real madness and helps to relieve the dramatic tension. When Lear declares that Poor Tom's misery is attributable to his 'unkind daughters', it is clear that he has finally lost the balance of his mind. Obsessed with the ingratitude of his own daughters, Lear cannot see that Edgar does not have any daughters. **The exchanges between the real madman (Lear), the official madman (the Fool), and the pretended madman (Edgar) make for one of the most memorable scenes in the play.** Now at the height of his madness, Lear finds in Edgar a true image of the basic humanity he wants to share: 'unaccommodated man is no more but such a poor, bare, forked animal as thou art.'

At one level the mock trial scene is **bizarrely comic** as the mad Lear, the blanketed Edgar and the Fool preside over the mock trial of Goneril and Regan. **However, the mock trial serves a significant thematic purpose:** the fact that Lear appoints a fool and an apparent madman to pass judgement on his daughters suggests that he has now grown in wisdom to the point where he perceives that sanity and reason have nothing to do with justice as it is administered in his kingdom.

In conclusion, the play presents us with three very different kinds of 'madness'. While Lear's madness is a human response to the pain of his daughters' filial ingratitude,

Edgar's 'madness' is a matter of choice. **However, in both cases madness, real or feigned, is the result of the natural bonds that should bind families together being broken.** It is the ingratitude and treachery of those closest to them that reduces both Lear and Edgar to the level of madmen. **As an 'official' madman, the Fool fulfils a traditional role in the royal court,** entertaining the king with his witty observations and clever rhymes. **However, the Fool's unofficial role as Lear's conscience is more important** as, under the guise of madness, he points out Lear's mistakes to him, helping him to grow in wisdom and become more self-aware.

'The play explores the meaning of love.'

King Lear **is notable as much for its exploration of love as it is for its portrayal of evil.** From the impressive sincerity of France's love for Cordelia in the opening scene through to the healing, redemptive love of Cordelia and Edgar for Lear and Gloucester respectively in the latter stages of the drama, love is a central theme of the play.

Having witnessed and been repelled by the false love of Goneril and Regan, the audience is greatly impressed with the genuine nature of France's love for Cordelia. After being disowned and disinherited by Lear, Cordelia understandably fears for her reputation, requesting Lear to make it known that she has not lost his favour because of any dishonourable action on her part. However, it is immediately apparent that France is aware of the strangeness of Lear's behaviour towards Cordelia when he asks the king how the daughter 'who even now was your best object, the argument of your praise, balm of your age' could in a moment commit

an act 'so monstrous' to completely fall from favour. He is incredulous when he learns that Cordelia has lost everything simply because of her unwillingness to flatter Lear. In contrast to the romantic Paris who believes that Cordelia 'is herself a dowry', the mercenary-minded Burgundy is unwilling to marry Cordelia without the portion of the kingdom promised him. Paris openly expresses his love for her at this point: 'Fairest Cordelia, thou art most rich, being poor; most choice, forsaken; and most loved, despised!' **Paris' love for Cordelia highlights the fact that true love is never influenced by material considerations: 'Love is not love when it is mingled with regards that stand aloof from the entire point.'**

Kent's love for Lear is one of the most positive and uplifting aspects of the play. It is no overstatement to say that Kent lives for Lear: 'Royal Lear, whom I have ever honoured as my king, loved as my father, as my master followed, as my great patron thought on in my prayers . . .' Kent's love for Lear means that he sees it as his inescapable duty to make the king aware of any mistakes he is making that may ultimately cause him suffering. He describes Lear's decision to disown and disinherit Cordelia as 'hideous rashness'. After Kent is banished and threatened with death, he still returns in disguise to serve Lear as a humble servant: 'Now banished Kent, if thou canst serve where thou dost stand condemned, so may it come, thy master, whom thou lov'st, shall find thee full of labours.' Kent remains with Lear throughout his painful journey to self-awareness and wisdom. He never fails to defend Lear's honour, ending up in the stocks after beating the despicable Oswald for disrespecting Lear. It is Kent who leads Lear to the shelter of a hovel in the dramatic storm scene and who ensures that Cordelia remains informed about Lear's plight. In the closing scene, Kent is deeply pained by Lear's heartbreak at the death of his beloved Cordelia, insisting that no attempt be made to revive him if he loses consciousness: 'O let him pass! He hates him that would upon the rack of this tough world stretch him out longer.' Kent's love for and loyalty to Lear does not end with the latter's death. He refuses the offer to join Albany and Edgar in ruling the kingdom because of his enduring devotion to Lear: 'I have a journey, sir, shortly to go; my master calls me, I must not say no.' **Kent's love for Lear reminds us that unwavering loyalty is a key feature of real love.**

Cordelia's love for Lear is another of the play's most inspiring features. In total contrast to her sisters' hollow declarations of love for Lear, Cordelia's love for her father is genuine and deep. Once she becomes aware of Lear's plight, she leads an expedition to England to rescue him. Cordelia's motivation for this military intervention has nothing to do with political ambition, and everything to do with her loving concern for her father: 'No blown ambition doth our arms incite, but love, dear love and our aged father's right.' The scene where she meets Lear is deeply moving. She struggles to come to terms with the appalling cruelty inflicted on her father, telling Kent that she would have kept her enemy's dog close to her fire on the night that Lear was forced to endure a particularly violent storm on the moor. Cordelia is seen as the very embodiment of love and forgiveness as she tenderly addresses Lear: 'O my dear father! Restoration, hang thy medicine on my lips, and let this kiss repair those violent harms that my sisters have in thy reverence made!' Remarkably, Cordelia even asks Lear's blessing: 'O! Look upon me sir, and hold your hands in benediction o'er me.' **Cordelia's love for Lear indicates that a capacity for forgiveness is an integral aspect of love, while also highlighting the redemptive power of love.**

Edgar's enduring love for Gloucester is another of the play's most heartening (uplifting) features. Notwithstanding the fact that he has been reduced to the level of a hunted criminal by Gloucester's rashness and has been forced to adopt the disguise of a mad Bedlam beggar in order to survive, Edmund, like Cordelia, bears no feelings of resentment towards his father. Seeing his father's dark despair and desire to end his life, Edgar engages in a kindly deception, tricking the credulous (gullible) and disorientated Gloucester into believing that he has fallen from the steep cliffs of Dover and that the gods have saved his life: 'Thy life's a miracle.' Edgar's loving action rids Gloucester of his suicidal tendencies, with the latter now proclaiming: '. . . henceforth I'll bear affliction till it do cry out itself "Enough, enough", and die.' **Edgar's love for Gloucester reinforces the idea that love is always kind**

and forgiving and can be redemptive.

Unsurprisingly, the relationships involving Goneril and Regan tell us a great deal about what love should not involve. Their transparent flattery of Lear immediately suggests the insincerity of their declarations of 'love' for their father. Their attempts to ingratiate themselves with him are far removed from genuine expressions of love since they are motivated solely by the desire for self-advancement.

All of these relationships help us to better understand the nature and meaning of love. We see that love is not influenced by material considerations and that love based on loyalty and a willingness to forgive has the power to redeem characters who, like Lear and Gloucester, have lost their way in life through their spiritual blindness.

'Describe a dramatic scene in the play.'

Act 3 Scene 7 is one of the most dramatic scenes in the play, indeed in any Shakespearian drama. This is the scene in which Gloucester's eyes are gouged out in an act of monstrous cruelty.

Gloucester bravely goes to Lear's assistance when he learns of the plot upon his life. Gloucester does not realise that he has been betrayed by his son Edmund in whom he confided this dramatic news. We know that Cornwall has sworn to Edmund that he will have his revenge on Gloucester for this act of 'treachery' and fear for Gloucester. **The irony whereby the audience knows more than the character adds to the dramatic nature of this scene.**

This scene opens dramatically with Cornwall ordering Gloucester's arrest and Goneril ('Hang him instantly!') **and Regan** ('Pluck out his eyes!') **trying to outdo each other in their vengeful bloodlust.** When Cornwall tells Edmund to leave because 'the revenges we are bound to take upon your treacherous father are not fit for your beholding', our fears for Gloucester intensify. When Gloucester arrives, he is immediately bound. We sympathise with Gloucester who, sensing that these evil characters mean to harm him, pathetically reminds them that he is their host. However, since the evil sisters show scant regard for the natural bond that should link parent and child, they are unlikely to display any respect for the natural bond that should link a host and his guests. Goneril, Regan and Cornwall are intent on revenge and will abuse Gloucester's hospitality in the most dramatic and horrifying way imaginable. Regan starts the cruel process of revenge when she shows her disrespect for Gloucester by plucking his beard.

The tension mounts as Gloucester is bound and interrogated about his involvement in the French landing and his knowledge of Lear's situation. Gloucester shows admirable courage and loyalty to Lear in philosophically accepting his predicament: 'I am tied to the stake, and I must stand the course.' When Regan asks Gloucester why he sent Lear to Dover, his response is charged with irony: 'Because I would not see thy cruel nails pluck out his poor old eyes; nor thy cruel sister in his anointed flesh stick bearish fangs.' Like all of the other noble characters in the play, Gloucester believes in the idea of divine justice, defiantly telling his captors: '. . . but I shall see the winged vengeance overtake such children.' However, the evil characters will first have their revenge on him.

There follows one of the most horrifying moments in any Shakespearian drama as Cornwall, in an act of unimaginable savagery, gouges out one of Gloucester's eyes. However, even this act of barbarity does not satisfy Regan who, clearly feeling that no punishment is adequate for a man who has helped her father, demands that Gloucester's second eye be cut from his head: 'One side will mock another; the other too.'

More drama and physical action follows when, in an instinctive act of humanity, one of Cornwall's servants intervenes on behalf of Gloucester. In the sword fight that ensues, Cornwall is mortally wounded and the noble servant stabbed from behind by Regan. **Cornwall's wound does not prevent him from completing his vicious blinding of Gloucester:** 'Out vile jelly! Where is thy lustre now?'

Gloucester endures further suffering when, in his agony and blindness, he calls out for his son Edmund. Regan, not satisfied with Gloucester's physical torture, delights in tormenting him mentally by revealing that it was Edmund who betrayed him: 'Thou call'st on him that hates thee, it was he who made the overtures of thy treasons to us . . .'

Gloucester now experiences a sudden, dramatic moment of self-awareness: 'O my follies! Then Edgar was abused. Kind gods, forgive me that and prosper him.' While Lear acquires insight in a slow, gradual manner, Gloucester gains understanding in an instant. **The irony in Gloucester gaining spiritual vision at the very moment that he is made physically blind adds to the dramatic qualities of this scene.**

Almost unbelievably, Gloucester has to endure even more misery when Regan orders that he be thrown out of his own castle: 'Go thrust him out at the gates, and let him smell his way to Dover.' This is yet another dramatic example of the evil sisters' seemingly insatiable appetite for cruelty.

This scene dramatically highlights the depths of inhumanity and savagery of which people are capable. The fact that two female characters are involved and delight in physical torture adds to the barbarity of Gloucester's blinding. This scene is also important because it sees the death of the first of the evil characters. Like Gloucester, Albany subscribes to the notion of divine justice. When he learns of Cornwall's death, he sees it as an example of the gods punishing evil-doers: 'This shows you are above you justicers that these our nether crimes so speedily can venge.'

'Imagery and Symbolism in the play.'

Certain images recur throughout *King Lear*. These patterns of imagery convey key themes, portray characters and help to create the distinctive atmosphere of the play.

Animal Imagery
There are numerous references to animals in the course of the play. Animal images suggest the unnatural cruelty of Goneril and Regan and underline their lack of humanity. Lear angrily describes Goneril as a 'detested kite' and speaks of her 'monster ingratitude'. Speaking to Regan of the pain of Goneril's ingratitude, Lear (pointing to his heart) tells

her, 'O Regan, she hath tied sharp-toothed unkindness like a vulture, here'. He later refers to his two 'pelican daughters'. Albany is horrified by Goneril and Regan's bestial cruelty, describing them as 'tigers, not daughters'. He declares that if such unnatural cruelty goes unchecked, the human world may become like that of the wild beasts: '. . . humanity must perforce prey on itself like monsters of the deep.' Kent speaks of Lear's 'dog-hearted daughters'. Serpent imagery suggests Goneril and Regan's falseness: in the closing scene, Albany orders the arrest of 'the gilded serpent' that is Goneril. Kent uses animal imagery to highlight the insidiously destructive evil of 'smiling rogues' like Oswald who undermine the natural bonds that link families: '. . . like rats oft bite the holy cords a-twain which are too intrinse to unloose.' Animal imagery suggests a society based on the law of the jungle where only the strongest and the most ruthless survive and where there is little or no room for humanity or compassion.

Images of Suffering and Violence

King Lear is a play characterised by intense suffering. This suffering is physical, mental and spiritual in nature. The pain of his daughters' ingratitude is such that Lear declares that his heart 'shall break into a hundred thousand flaws'. Two key images underscore the intensity of Lear's anguish. Speaking to Cordelia, Lear imagines himself as a tortured soul: 'I am bound upon a wheel of fire that mine own tears do scald like molten lead.' At the close of the play, Kent insists that his royal master be allowed to die since death will release him from the agonies of life: 'O let him pass! He hates him that would upon the rack of this tough world stretch him out longer.'

The violent behaviour of human beings is often linked with that of animals. Speaking to Goneril, Regan and Cornwall Gloucester explains his loyalty to Lear in the following terms: 'Because I would not see thy cruel nails pluck out his poor old eyes, nor thy fierce sister in his anointed flesh stick bearish fangs.' The blinding of Gloucester is an act of savage cruelty. Bound to a chair and disrespectfully plucked by the beard, Gloucester accepts that he is 'tied to the stake' and 'must stand the course'. He has both eyes gouged out ('One side will mock the other, the other too', says the inhuman Regan), and is thrown out of his own castle to 'smell his way to Dover'. The image of the blinded Gloucester stumbling in his world of darkness is particularly powerful, dramatically underscoring the savage cruelty of the evil characters.

Clothing Imagery: Appearance and Reality

Clothing imagery suggests the contrast between appearance and reality that lies at the heart of this play and indeed all Shakespearian tragedies. Clothing is a symbol of wealth and social status and is associated with the dishonesty of those in positions of power. As Lear grows in wisdom, he declares, 'Through tattered clothes small vices do appear, robes and furred gowns hide all. Plate sin with gold and the strong lance of justice hurtless breaks: arm it in rags, a pigmy's straw doth pierce it.' Lear has learned much by the time he makes this pronouncement. He had initially confused appearance with reality, accepting his daughters' declarations of love at face value.

Edgar's nakedness (Gloucester refers to him as 'this naked soul') contrasts with the 'furred gowns' of the nobility and suggests his honesty. Edgar has nothing to hide behind. Lear tears off his clothes in order to be like Edgar: '. . . unaccommodated man is no more but such a poor, bare, forked animal as thou art. Off, off, you lendings! Come, unbutton here.' Lear is closest to self-knowledge when he dispenses with the clothing symbolic of wealth, high social status and deception. He runs about in the storm 'unbonneted' and 'bareheaded', reducing himself to the level of the poorest of his subjects, and sharing in their deprivation and suffering.

Storm Imagery

The storm on the moor suggests that nature is in sympathy with Lear's suffering. The storm is symbolic both of the storm in Lear's mind and of the disorder and turbulence in society that follows the shattering of the natural bonds that bind families and wider society together: 'Blow winds and crack your cheeks! Rage! Blow! You cataracts and hurricanes spout . . .' In his intense suffering, Lear cries out for universal destruction: 'Strike flat the thick rotundity of the world! Crack nature's moulds. All germens spill at once, that make ingrateful man!' The unnatural intensity of the storm may also symbolise the unnatural cruelty of Goneril and Regan. Kent describes the storm as the worst in living memory: 'Since I was a man, such sheets of fire, such bursts of horrid thunder, such groans of roaring wind and rain, I never remember to have heard.'

'King Lear is a very gloomy play.'

The play is, in many respects, a very dark drama. Evil is dominant for much of the play. Lear and Gloucester suffer intensely and indeed all of the central characters suffer to some degree as a result of the disruption of the natural order. The ending is especially dark with the death of Cordelia and Lear's heartbreak. **However, the play has a number of positive aspects that serve to relieve the gloom.** Both Lear and Gloucester grow through suffering, and both characters are redeemed (rescued) by loving children. Also, good ultimately triumphs over evil.

The ease with which the evil characters deceive others, and the fact that evil seems to thrive for much of the play creates a sense of gloom. Goneril and Regan employ the 'glib and oily art' of flattery to easily fool their doting father into giving them their share of the kingdom: 'I love you more than words can wield the matter . . .' Edmund similarly manipulates the gullible and rash Gloucester with consummate (expert) ease, convincing him that the loyal and loving Edgar is plotting against him. He also takes advantage of his brother's trusting nature: 'A credulous father and a brother noble, whose nature is so far from doing harms that he suspects none: on whose foolish honesty my practices ride easily.' The scheming of the evil characters reduces Lear to a madman, deprives Gloucester of his sight and forces Edgar to play the part of a Bedlam beggar. The defeat of the French force led by Cordelia intensifies (heightens / increases) the sense of gloom.

The extreme suffering of Lear and Gloucester is another gloomy aspect of the play. Both Lear and Gloucester suffer intensely as a result of filial ingratitude. Goneril and Regan's unnatural behaviour causes Lear such extreme spiritual agony that he eventually loses his sanity, while Gloucester suffers intense physical pain as well as mental anguish as a consequence of Edmund's betrayal of him. Lear is stripped of all dignity by his 'pelican daughters'. Goneril's servants treat Lear with visible contempt while Regan places his messenger in the stocks, and refuses to see him. The final humiliation comes when the two evil sisters deny Lear even a single knight. It is impossible not to feel sympathy for 'a poor old man as full of grief as age' who can do no more than rant helplessly when he finally sees Goneril and Regan for the 'unnatural hags' that they are. Lear realises too late his utter folly (foolishness) in handing over his royal authority to ungrateful daughters who now have the power to humiliate him. The image of Lear 'bound upon a wheel of fire' underlines the intensity of his suffering, as does Kent's description of Lear being stretched 'upon the rack of this tough world'. Gloucester's intense suffering also adds to the overall sense of gloom. The brutal gouging out of Gloucester's eyes is one of the most horrifying and repulsive moments in Shakespearian literature. His extreme physical pain is matched by his mental anguish when Regan delights in telling him that it was Edmund who betrayed him,

The ending of the play is very grim. The death of Cordelia is particularly tragic since she is seen as the embodiment of goodness and love. Lear's unspeakable grief as he leans over the dead body of Cordelia is deeply moving: 'Why should a dog, a horse, a rat have life, and thou no breath at all?' Like Kent, we are affected by Lear's pitiful death. The death of Gloucester, who dies ''twixt two extremes of passion, joy and grief', further contributes to the sense of despondency that envelops the close of the play.

However, it would be an overstatement to describe King Lear as 'overwhelmingly gloomy' because the play is not without its positive, uplifting aspects. While Lear and Gloucester both suffer intensely, they grow and learn through suffering, ending the play as better, wiser men. Both men ultimately acquire self-knowledge and moral vision. Lear comes to see himself as 'a very foolish fond old man'. He eventually sees Goneril and Regan for the 'unnatural hags' that they are, and humbly begs Cordelia's forgiveness: 'You must bear with me; pray you now, forget and forgive: I am old and foolish.' Lear also acquires a social conscience, regretting his neglect of the 'poor naked wretches' he sees on the heath and preaching the doctrine of social justice: 'Expose thyself to what wretches feel, that thou mayst shake the superflux to them and show the heavens more just.' He also comes to see the falseness and corruption of political life: 'Robes and furred gowns hide all.' **Gloucester similarly grows through suffering. Ironically he gains moral vision at the moment he loses his physical sight.** He finally realises that he misjudged Edgar: 'O my follies! Then Edgar was abused. Kind Gods forgive me that and prosper him!' Like Lear, he also displays a new concern for the poor: 'So distribution should undo excess, and each man have enough.'

Cordelia and Edgar are shining examples of filial love and forgiveness, redeeming their respective fathers despite the great wrongs done to them. Cordelia's intervention in English affairs is motivated solely by an admirable concern for her father, Lear: 'No blown ambition doth our arms incite, but love, dear love and our aged father's right.' She acts as a healing agent: 'Restoration hang thy medicine on my lips and let this kiss repair those violent harms that my two sisters have in thy reverence made!' Cordelia bears no grudge against her father, insisting that she has 'no cause' to resent him, and even seeks his blessing. Edgar's kindly deception of his father cures Gloucester of his despair. Convinced that he has fallen from the Cliffs of Dover, and that the gods have saved his life ('Thy life's a miracle!'), Gloucester regains the will to live. **Edgar's positive philosophy also helps to**

lift the gloom: 'The worst returns to laughter.'

Kent and the Fool are inspiring examples of loyalty, remaining with and supporting Lear through his darkest hours. Kent even returns in disguise to serve the man who had earlier banished him: 'Now banished Kent, if thou canst serve where thou dost stand condemned, so may it come, thy master, whom thou lovest shall find thee full of labours.' Kent literally lives for Lear: 'My life I never held but as a pawn to wage against thy enemies.' At the close of the play the ever loyal Kent prepares to follow his master into the next world: 'I have a journey, sir, shortly to go: My master calls me, I must not say no.' The Fool never abandons Lear, remaining with him even in the eye of the fiercest storm in living memory: 'But I will tarry, the Fool will stay.'

Albany's emergence as a strong character and force for good is another positive aspect of the play. In the early stages of this drama, Albany appears to be a weak, ineffectual character, living in the shadow of his domineering wife. However, as the play unfolds, Albany develops into a stronger, more assertive character who finally tells Goneril what he really thinks of her: 'O Goneril, you are not worth the dust which the rude wind blows in your face.' He warns her that she will pay the price for her 'vile offences', and is so angry with her that he declares he would like to tear her limb from limb. No longer the 'milk-liver'd' man scorned by his wife, Albany is now capable of anger and action and promises to avenge the outrage of Gloucester's eyes. While he is compelled to do battle with the French force, he plans to be merciful towards both Lear and Cordelia. At the close of the play he plays an important part in bringing peace and order again to the realm. He is personally courageous and is prepared to engage Edmund in trial by combat, until

Edgar emerges to champion his cause. He condemns Goneril and Edmund's treachery, and has no sympathy whatsoever for them when they die. He promises to reward friends and punish enemies: 'All friends shall taste the wages of their virtue, and all foes the cup of their deservings.' **Albany's development into a leader of real substance offers hope for the future.**

The humanity and glimmer of conscience that Edmund reveals in the final scene also helps to lift the gloom that shrouds the close of the play. He is moved by Edgar's account of Gloucester's death, and makes a belated effort to undo some of the evil he had intended by revealing that he has signed Lear and Cordelia's death warrants: 'Some good I mean to do despite mine own nature.' Here we see that even the villainous Edmund is not entirely devoid of humanity.

Most importantly, good ultimately triumphs over evil. All of the evil characters die at the close of the play. While the evil characters initially prosper, evil is ultimately seen to be self-destructive: Goneril poisons Regan so that she can have Edmund for herself and takes her own life when her treachery is revealed, while Edmund's evil earns its own reward when he is killed by the brother he wronged.

In conclusion, by the close of the play all the characters, good and bad, have suffered as a result of the disruption of the natural order. However, suffering brings wisdom to both Lear and Gloucester and the natural order is restored in the closing scene. Albany and Edgar will restore the kingdom to health. **Although evil is defeated at a high price, good ultimately triumphs. The triumph of good over evil leaves us feeling optimistic for a brighter future. While this play is undeniably dark, it is certainly not overwhelmingly gloomy.**

'Why study the play?'

King Lear, like all of Shakespeare's tragedies, remains relevant to a modern-day audience. The play makes for compelling viewing because the plot is full of often surprising twists and turns and is rich in dramatic incident. The play abounds with truly dramatic scenes: the opening scene where the rash and arrogant Lear banishes the two people who love him the most and gives his two evil daughters power and authority over him; Act 3 Scene 7 where the unspeakably cruel blinding of Gloucester takes place; the storm scene where the anguished Lear cries out for universal destruction; and the heartbreakingly sad and deeply moving final scene. Everyone loves a good story, and the tale of King Lear and his daughters is precisely that.

The play presents us with themes that are enduringly relevant. Firstly, it is based on the fascinating and age-old struggle between good and evil. Evil is vividly and frighteningly portrayed in the play. Goneril and Regan display unnatural depths of cruelty, treating Lear with visible contempt after he foolishly hands the kingdom over to them. When Lear protests against the placing of his messenger in the stocks, Regan's response is dripping with contempt for her now powerless father: 'I pray you father, being weak, seem so.' Goneril and Regan heartlessly strip Lear of his remaining power and dignity, refusing to allow him to keep even a single knight ('What need one?'). Edmund is one of Shakespeare's most opportunistic and ruthless villains. Devoid of any sense of morality, Edmund believes in the law of the jungle: 'Thou, Nature, art my goddess . . .' He does not hesitate to betray his own father after he goes to Lear's assistance, even though he knows that Gloucester will face dire punishment when he returns. Evil initially prospers, but is ultimately defeated by the forces of good. In this sense the play is very reassuring: it asserts the inevitable triumph of justice, with the forces of evil ultimately preying upon and destroying each other. The play powerfully demonstrates the self-destructive nature of evil.

King Lear offers us a range of insights into the parent-child relationship, a theme of obvious universal relevance. We see how families and wider society are thrown into turmoil when the natural bonds that link family members are broken. In this play, both Lear and Gloucester are the first to shatter the parent-child bond when their rashness causes them to misjudge and subsequently mistreat Cordelia and Edgar respectively. Both Lear and Gloucester suffer extreme torment when they are in turn mistreated by their ungrateful and unfeeling children – Lear is driven to the point of insanity by the filial ingratitude of Goneril and Regan, while Gloucester suffers both mentally and physically after Edmund betrays him.

The play highlights the human capacity for personal growth. Both Lear and Gloucester grow through intense personal suffering, ending the play as better, wiser men. Both men ultimately come to see themselves, others and society in general more clearly. There is a memorably ironic quality to the manner in which both men attain self-knowledge and wisdom. Lear acquires what Edgar describes as 'reason in madness', while Gloucester gains moral vision at the very moment that he loses his physical vision ('I stumbled when I saw').

We are also provided with inspiring examples of the redeeming power of love.

Lear and Gloucester are saved by Cordelia and Edgar respectively, loyal and loving children who bear no grudge against the fathers who had treated them so unjustly. Cordelia insists that she has 'no cause' to resent Lear in any way. Her only desire is to ease the pain that her evil sisters have caused Lear: 'O my dear father! Restoration, hang thy medicine on my lips, and let this kiss repair those violent harms that my two sisters have in thy reverence made.' Edgar similarly redeems Gloucester when he cures him of his despair by deceiving him into believing that he has fallen from the Cliffs of Dover and that the gods have saved him: 'Thy life's a miracle!'

The play also presents us with uplifting examples of nobility and loyalty in the persons of Kent and the Fool respectively. Kent devotes his entire life to Lear's service. Even though he is a nobleman, Kent returns in disguise to serve Lear in any way he can after he has been banished from the realm by the rash king: 'Now, banished Kent, if thou canst serve where thou dost stand condemned, so may it come, thy master, whom thou lov'st, shall find thee full of labours.' Kent's loyalty to Lear is total and unwavering; even death is not regarded as a barrier to his extraordinary fidelity to his master. Even though Albany asks him to join Edgar and himself in ruling the kingdom, Kent refuses the offer because, in the manner of an ancient Roman, he is determined to follow his master into the next world: 'I have a journey, sir, shortly to go; my master calls me, I must not say no.' The Fool similarly follows Lear through his painful journey towards self-awareness. Like Kent, the Fool does not hesitate to highlight Lear's foolish behaviour; indeed he sees it as his primary duty to relentlessly remind Lear of all that he has done wrong ('. . . thou hadst little wit in thy bald crown when thou gavest thy golden one away', '. . . thou madest thy daughters thy mothers').The Fool's remarkable loyalty to Lear is best seen when he remains with him on the wild moor throughout the worst storm in living memory. It is here that we see the Fool's loving concern for Lear: 'Good nuncle, in and ask thy daughters' blessing. Here's a night pities neither wise man nor fool.'

The fact that the sub-plot reflects and reinforces key themes in the main plot underlines the universality of these themes.

The Characters

LEAR

While Lear initially appears to be nothing more than an arrogant, autocratic tyrant, we gradually realise that he is essentially a noble, but tragically flawed character. We sympathise with Lear in his suffering and admire his acquisition of humility, insight (vision) and self-knowledge, **However, our sympathy for Lear must not blind us to the reality that he is very much the architect of his own downfall.** Lear's description of himself as a man 'more sinn'd against than sinning' is essentially correct. We naturally sympathise with a 'fond, foolish old man' who is deliberately and callously humiliated by his 'pelican daughters' and pained to the point of insanity by their ingratitude. However, it is Lear's tragically-flawed character and his initial disruption of the natural order (brought about by his selfish abdication from power and his unnatural treatment of the loyal and loving Cordelia), that sets an ultimately tragic train of events in motion.

From the opening scene, we are aware of a number of weaknesses in Lear's character. Lear is concerned only for himself; he is selfish and egocentric. His self-centred attitude is strikingly evident in his desire to enjoy the trappings of power, without any of the responsibilities: 'Only we shall retain the name, and all the additions to a king; the sway revenue, execution of the rest, beloved sons be yours.' **Lear is also extremely arrogant**, reacting angrily to Kent's efforts to make him aware of his own wrongdoing in relation to Cordelia. Lear's self-image underscores his arrogance. He sees himself as a fearsome 'dragon' whose 'wrath' is to be avoided. Lear is gullible and susceptible to flattery, as the 'love test' shows. **Lear is fiery and rash** – he disinherits and disowns Cordelia because she refuses to pander to his ego and banishes Kent because he urges him to 'check this hideous rashness'. The rashness, which Lear displays in the opening scene, is no isolated moral lapse - it is again evident in the violent language used to curse Goneril: 'into her womb convey sterility; dry up in her the organs of increase . . .'

Lear lacks self-knowledge and moral vision. In Regan's words, Lear 'hath ever but slenderly known himself'. Lear must acquire self-knowledge before coming to understand others and the world in general. It is only through suffering that Lear acquires humility and insight. **Lear's spiritual or moral growth is gradual and painful.** While he ironically acquires 'reason in madness', his personal development is uneven. Even as he acquires self-understanding, Lear at different times displays the naivety, arrogance, rashness and egocentricity (self-centred nature) so dramatically in evidence in the opening scene.

When Goneril treats her father with open disrespect, the effect on Lear is profound. When Lear was king, he had no conception of himself as a man, rather ridiculously seeing himself as a terrifying dragon-like figure. When he gives away his power and authority, he is treated not as an all-powerful king but as an irritating old man. As a result, his self-image is severely shaken: 'Who is it that can tell me who I am?' Stung by what he sees as Goneril's 'marble-hearted' ingratitude Lear takes his first painful steps on the road to self-knowledge: 'O Lear, Lear, Lear! Beat at the gate that led thy folly in and thy dear judgement out!' The realisation that he is powerless to respond to Goneril adds to his frustration and anguish. Lear's acknowledgement that his treatment of Cordelia was wrong marks another step in his personal growth. He tells the Fool: 'I did her wrong'. It is ironic that as Lear begins to acquire insight, he simultaneously edges closer to insanity: 'O, let me not be mad, not mad, sweet heaven! Keep me in temper: I would not be mad.' It is the disintegration of his self-image that lies at the root of Lear's loss of sanity. The actual onset of madness is accelerated by his towering rages.

Lear is further humiliated when his servant Kent is placed in the stocks. He reacts with disbelief to this deliberate act of blatant disrespect: 'They durst not do it; they could not, would not do't; 'tis worse than murder to do upon respect such violent outrage.' Lear senses how close he is to insanity: 'O, how this mother swells up toward my heart!' We are reminded of Lear's continuing spiritual blindness when he is unable or unwilling to see that Goneril and Regan are fundamentally alike. Naively, he tells Regan: 'Thou shalt never have my curse . . . thou better knows't the offices of nature, bond of childhood, effects of courtesy, dues of gratitude.' Goneril and Regan's treatment of their father is particularly reprehensible because of its deliberate, pre-meditated nature. Lear realises that his daughters are acting as one against him when Regan takes Goneril by the hand. We cannot but sympathise with a powerless old man who pathetically points out, 'I gave you all'.

While Lear grows through suffering, his acquisition of self-knowledge is a gradual process. Lear foolishly continues to believe that he can measure love. In the opening scene, he believed that he could measure love on the basis of words; now he believes that he can measure love in terms of the number of knights he is to be allowed: 'Thy fifty yet doth double five-and-twenty, and thou art twice her love.' Having given up all of his power and authority, his daughters now strip him of his dignity: 'What need one?' Lear's sanity is profoundly shaken: 'O fool, I shall go mad!' Lear's 'heart-struck injuries' result in what Kent aptly describes as 'bemadding sorrow.'

The storm scene represents the climax of the play; it is a scene full of drama and irony. Stripped of his authority, dignity, even his very clothes, Lear acquires 'reason in madness'. He sees himself for what he is: 'A poor, infirm, weak and despised old man.' He shows his humanity in his concern for the Fool and realises that, as king, he neglected the poor. Lear's newly-discovered social conscience prompts him to preach the idea of social justice, as he suggests that wealth should be distributed more fairly: 'Expose thyself to what wretches feel that thou mayest shake the superflux to them and show the heavens more just.'

Lear's towering rages accelerate and finally precipitate (bring about) the onset of madness. On the heath, Lear feels his wits 'begin to turn'. By the end of the storm scene, Kent observes that 'all the power of his wits have given way to his impatience.' While he promises to be 'the pattern of all patience', tranquillity inevitably leads to reflection, recollection, and another 'high rage'. In this sense, Lear's behaviour on the moor assumes a cyclical pattern.

In the storm scene we see many examples of Lear's acquisition of 'reason in madness'. He wisely tells the blind Gloucester that 'A man may see how this world goes with no eyes'. He realises that appearances can be deceptive: 'Robes and furr'd gowns hide all.' The clothing image suggests how clothes (symbolising wealth and material possessions) can blind people to their own and to others' shortcomings. Lear himself is closest to nature and to self-knowledge when he is naked on the moors in the eye of the storm. He becomes aware of the unjust, corrupt nature of the world in which he lives: 'Plate sin with gold and the strong lance of justice hurtless breaks: arm it in rags, a pigmy's straw doth pierce it.' In other words, he realises that wealthy people are never punished for their wrongdoing.

A further indication of Lear's personal growth is the 'burning shame' that he feels in relation to Cordelia. The extent of Lear's anguish and torment is clear in his initial reaction to seeing Cordelia; he imagines himself 'bound upon a wheel of fire that mine own tears do scald like molten lead.' Lear now sees himself for what he is: 'a very foolish, fond old man.' He realises that he is not in his 'perfect mind' but knows that Cordelia has

'cause' not to love him: 'If you have poison for me, I will drink it.' Lear has acquired humility and self-understanding and now seeks forgiveness: 'You must bear with me; pray you now; forget and forgive: I am old and foolish.'

Lear's enduring rashness is evident in the immediate aftermath of Cordelia's death when he curses all of those around him: 'A plague upon you, murderers, traitors all.' Lear's personal growth is uneven in the sense that even as he grows, certain ingrained weaknesses persist. However, we cannot but be deeply moved by Lear's intense grief at Cordelia's death : 'Howl, howl, howl, howl! O, you are men of stones!' While we are fully cognisant (aware) of Lear's responsibility for Cordelia's death (it was he who set the entire train of tragic events in motion in the opening scene), we cannot but sympathise with an old man who ends the play a better and wiser character having been truly stretched on the rack of life.

KEY ADJECTIVES

Initially:
- rash, impetuous, impulsive
- arrogant
- foolish
- gullible, naive, credulous
- unjust, harsh

Ultimately:
- rash (his most ingrained weakness through to the close of the play
- humble
- wise, perceptive (to a degree)
- compassionate, caring

GLOUCESTER

Like Lear, Gloucester is initially gullible, rash and morally blind. In the same way that Lear falls victim to the 'glib and oily' flattery of Goneril and Regan, Gloucester's credulous nature is easily exploited by Edmund. **Gloucester, like Lear, is rash in his reactions,** impulsively condemning Edgar

without any objective evidence of his guilt: 'Abhorred villain! Unnatural, detested brutish villain! The manner in which Gloucester disinherits Edgar is strikingly similar to Lear's treatment of Cordelia, being similarly rash and unjust. Without ever giving Edgar an opportunity to defend his reputation and honour, Gloucester makes a fugitive of his loyal son before going on to impetuously declare that Edmund will be his heir : '. . . of my land loyal and natural boy, I'll work the means to make thee capable.'

Gloucester is a decidedly weak though good-natured man, making no effort to support Kent in challenging Lear's dangerously foolish decision-making in the opening scene. He strikes us as an ineffectual character who is easily manipulated – initially by Edmund for his own evil ends and later by Edgar for the compassionate purpose of ridding him of his despair. Edmund laughs at Gloucester's superstitious nature, describing as 'the excellent foppery of the world' the tendency to blame our disasters on 'the sun, the moon and the stars'. Gloucester's superstitious nature is to be seen in his belief that the gods dictate the course of human life: 'As flies to wanton boys are we to the gods; they kill us for their sport.' Edgar exploits his father's superstitious nature for a noble purpose when he tricks him into believing that he has jumped from the cliff at Dover, before convincing him that the gods have spared his life ('Thy life's a miracle'), thereby renewing Gloucester's desire to live and accept whatever life presents him with.

Gloucester is a flawed but essentially noble and decent character. He protests against Kent being placed in the stocks, pointing out to Cornwall that Lear will be angered by this act of blatant disrespect towards him: 'Let me beseech your grace not to do so . . . the king must take it ill that he is so slightly valued in his messenger.' Gloucester's gentle protest is ignored, but reflects his sense of justice. His noble nature is also evident in his determination to help Lear even at the risk of his own life: 'Though I die for it, as no less is threatened me, the king my old master must be relieved.'

Gloucester displays a stoical (philosophical acceptance of life's varying fortunes) **side to his character when he is tortured by Cornwall:** 'I am tied to the stake, and I must stand the course.'

Similar to Lear, Gloucester acquires self-knowledge and moral vision through intense suffering. Both are enlightened by their sufferings and both gain insight in an ironic fashion. While Lear acquires 'reason in madness', Gloucester acquires inner or spiritual vision at the moment he is made physically blind: 'O my follies! Then Edgar was abused, kind gods, forgive me that, and prosper him!' Gloucester acknowledges the irony of simultaneously losing his physical sight and acquiring moral vision when he remarks, 'I stumbled when I saw . . .' While Lear's personal growth is a protracted (drawn out) process, Gloucester's acquisition of insight is sudden and dramatic.

Gloucester learns to care for others. Lear's concern on the moor for the Fool is reflected in Gloucester's concern for the old man who guides him after he has been blinded: '. . . good friend, be gone; thy comforts can do me no good at all; thee, they may harm.' Both learn to care for the poor and unfortunate and come to subscribe to the idea of social justice. Gloucester declares that 'distribution should undo excess and each man have enough.' He learns that wealth can contribute to spiritual blindness, speaking of 'the superfluous and lust-dieted man . . . that will not see because he doth not feel.'

Gloucester pays the ultimate price for his failings. Like Lear, Gloucester experiences both joy and grief before his death. Edgar describes how his father reacted when he finally revealed his true identity to him: 'his flawed heart . . . 'twixt two extremes of passion, joy and grief, burst smilingly.'

KEY ADJECTIVES

Initially:
- gullible, credulous, naive
- superstitious
- rash, impetuous, impulsive
- unjust, harsh

Ultimately:
- wiser
- philosophical
- caring, compassionate

CORDELIA

While her appearances are rare and her contributions limited, Cordelia's character remains etched indelibly (forever imprinted) on our memories. Cordelia plays a central role in the drama. Had she gone along with Lear's whims and pandered to his ego, the whole tragedy might have been avoided. However, if Cordelia had flattered her father, she would not have been true to herself and to those aspects of her character which earn our admiration. Like Edgar, she is a shining example of filial love and loyalty. Her genuine affection and capacity for forgiveness stand in stark contrast to the false love and vengeful natures of her sisters.

In the dramatic opening scene, Cordelia's courage and integrity are immediately evident. Even though she risks losing her inheritance, she refuses to employ the 'glib and oily art' of flattery so effectively used by her sisters. Cordelia's motto is to 'love and be silent'. Her love for her father is genuine: 'I am sure my love's more richer than my tongue.' She prefaces her declaration of love for her father by stating, 'I cannot leave my heart into my mouth', reflecting her inability to engage in the ingratiating art of flattery. In refusing to flatter her father, Cordelia makes a brave and principled stand against both Lear's foolish pride and her sisters' sickening hypocrisy. While Cordelia's declaration of love for Lear ('I love your majesty according to my bond; nor more nor less') suggests cold indifference rather than genuine affection, her love for her father is real. Her declaration of love is characterised by economy of language and – more importantly – sincerity of feeling. Cordelia believes that actions say a great deal more than words: '. . . what I well intend, I'll do't before I speak.' While we admire her courage and spirit, it is her stubborn refusal to humour a foolish, sentimental old man by participating in his childish 'love test' which brings about the catastrophe.

Cordelia's strong character is again evident when she confronts her father in front of the whole assembly and asks Lear to 'make known' that she has not fallen from favour because of some 'unchaste action or dishonour'd step.' Cordelia displays great composure throughout this opening scene; she remains firmly in control of her emotions and, though treated very unjustly, never expresses anger or resentment.

Cordelia is shrewd and sharp-witted, seeing her sisters for what they are: 'I know you what you are.' She believes that their true natures will become apparent in time: 'Time shall unfold what plaited cunning hides.' **Her loving and forgiving nature** is evident in her concern for her father now that he is dependent on Goneril and Regan: 'I would prefer him to a better place.'

Cordelia's royalty of nature is reflected in the manner in which she responds to the news of Lear's suffering: she is described as being 'a queen over her passion'. She responds to Kent's letter (informing her of her father's plight) with 'patience and sorrow' rather than anger. Cordelia is deeply moved by Lear's suffering but, as in the opening scene, does not allow her emotions to overwhelm her. She is regarded as an almost saintly figure: '. . . she shook the holy water from her heavenly eyes.'

Her generous and forgiving nature is reflected in her desire to restore Lear's 'bereaved sense'. She would willingly give all of her material wealth to anyone who could restore her father to health: 'he that helps him take all my outward worth.' She is perceptive and recognises that Lear's 'ungovern'd rage' not only exacerbates his mental condition but threatens to 'dissolve' his life. The depth of her love for her father is evident when she explains the motivation behind the French intervention: 'No blown ambition doth our arms incite, but love, dear love and our aged father's right.'

Cordelia displays her leadership qualities when she leads the French expedition to rescue Lear. After landing in Dover a messenger arrives to inform her that the British forces are marching towards them. However, Cordelia is already aware of this development and has ensured that her forces are ready: ''Tis known before; our preparation stands in expectation of them.'

Cordelia is seen as a healing agent who comforts and consoles her suffering father: 'Restoration hang thy medicine on my lips; and let this kiss repair those violent harms that my two sisters have in thy reverence made!' Her innate (natural) goodness is such that she finds it difficult to comprehend the depth of her sisters' cruelty: 'Mine enemy's dog, though he had bit me, should have stood that night against my fire.' She bears no ill-will towards her father. Cordelia tells Lear that she has 'no cause' to be angry. Her forgiving, warm nature brings out the good qualities in Lear. He is a much humbler man now and readily admits to his faults. Cordelia's strength of character and concern for her father are evident when she and Lear are taken prisoner by Edmund: 'For thee, oppress'd king, am I cast down, myself could else out-frown false fortune's frown.' Like Edgar, Cordelia, is ever sensitive to the sufferings of others but refuses to indulge in self-pity.

If Goneril and Regan are the embodiments of evil, Cordelia is the personification of goodness. Aside from a stubborn streak, she epitomises all that is best in human nature. Her virtue is a necessary counterweight to the evil represented by her sisters. She is a model of filial love and loyalty and her death is the darkest moment in the play.

KEY ADJECTIVES

- good, virtuous
- honest, sincere, candid
- stubborn, obstinate (slightly)
- brave, courageous
- shrewd, perceptive, astute

- calm, composed
- capable
- loving, tender, affectionate
- forgiving, compassionate

EDGAR

Edgar undergoes significant personal development in the course of the play. While he may initially be regarded as a credulous, malleable (easily influenced) character, he ultimately emerges as an impressively capable figure and a force for good. Like Lear, Gloucester and Albany, Edgar grows as a character, learning from his own painful experience and from witnessing the suffering of others at first hand. In the course of his personal development, Edgar always retains his nobility of mind. Like Cordelia, Edgar is a shining example of goodness and a model of filial love and loyalty. Like her, he too is wronged by his father but bears no resentment towards him. Both Edgar and Cordelia act as healing agents, easing the suffering of their respective fathers.

While Edgar initially strikes us as a gullible, rather lightweight character who is easily manipulated by his more cunning brother, it should be remembered that it is his fundamentally noble nature which prevents him from suspecting that it is Edmund who is the 'villain' who has blackened his reputation.

As the play unfolds, Edgar displays great inner strength and endurance. He is optimistic, stoical and resourceful. He never succumbs to despair or self-pity, even when he is forced 'to take the basest and most poorest shape'. In assuming the guise of a mad beggar, Edgar demonstrates his resourcefulness. He makes light of his own suffering. When he witnesses Lear's anguish, he dismisses his own pain: 'How light and portable my pain seems now when that which makes me bend makes the king bow.'

Edgar is extremely sensitive to the suffering of others. He is deeply moved by the intensity of Lear's pain: 'My tears begin to take his part so much, they'll mar my counterfeiting.' He is so affected by the heartbreaking sight of the blinded Gloucester that he finds it difficult to keep up his pretence (act) as Poor Tom ('I cannot daub it further').

Edgar's noble and forgiving nature is evident in his desire to cure Gloucester of his self-pity: 'Why I do trifle thus with his despair is done to cure it.' The pretence of leading Gloucester to the edge of the cliffs at Dover is an innocent deception, which is designed to restore his father's will to live. While Gloucester is initially angry to find that he is still alive, Edgar convinces him that his life is a 'miracle' and that 'the clearest gods, who make them honours of men's impossibilities' have preserved him. While Edmund had earlier exploited Gloucester's gullibility for his own evil ends, Edgar exploits his father's credulous nature for a noble purpose. Edgar's plan is successful, and from this point Gloucester is determined to accept whatever the gods have in store for him: 'Henceforth I'll bear affliction till it do cry out itself "Enough, enough" and die.' Gloucester, who had earlier compared the gods to 'wanton boys' who kill flies (men) for 'their sport', now prays to the 'ever-gentle gods' that his 'worser spirit' will never again tempt him to end his life.

Edgar is a man of action. When the cowardly Oswald raises his sword against Gloucester's 'eyeless head', Edgar confronts this 'serviceable villain' and kills him. Edgar later accuses Edmund in a direct manner and challenges him to deny the truth of his accusations: '. . . thou art a traitor/False to thy gods, thy brother and thy father./Conspirant 'gainst this high, illustrious prince.' Before his brother dies, Edgar nobly and generously exchanges forgiveness with him.

Throughout the play Edgar never accepts that life will not improve, regardless of

how low an ebb his fortunes may be at: 'The worst returns to laughter', '. . . .the worst is not so long as we can say "This is the worst"'. Edgar's cheerful confidence comes not only from his optimistic temperament, but from his unshakeable faith in the 'clearest gods'. He has a deep and unwavering faith in the ultimate triumph of good over evil. He regards Edmund's death as divine justice as work: 'The gods are just, and of our pleasant vices make instruments to plague us.'

In an age when the natural bonds that should bind families together are often shattered without a thought, Edgar, like Cordelia stands out as a model of filial love and loyalty. His **admirable stoicism**

(acceptance of life's varying fortunes) is reflected in the advice which he offers to Gloucester: 'Men must endure their going hence, even as their coming hither: Ripeness is all.' At his lowest point, when he is forced to play the part of a mad Bedlam beggar ('the lowest and most dejected thing of fortune'), Edgar remains **resilient and optimistic**. He helps not only to ease his father's suffering but to restore the natural order. **After an unpromising beginning, Edgar develops into a character of real substance who, by the close of the drama, is set to play a central role in ensuring the recovery and future welfare of the state.**

KEY ADJECTIVES

- noble, honourable, virtuous
- credulous, gullible (initially)
- resilient, strong, tough, stoical
- resourceful, capable
- optimistic, cheerful, positive

- brave, courageous
- forgiving, compassionate
- loyal, devoted
- loving

KENT

From the opening scene Kent wins the admiration of the audience – he is loyal, courageous, blunt and perceptive. Kent continues to demonstrate these traits throughout the play.

Kent's loyalty to Lear is absolute and unwavering. Kent's love for Lear is the guiding force of his life; it is no exaggeration to say that Kent lives for Lear: 'My life I never held but as a pawn to wage against thine enemies.' Kent's love and respect for Lear are evident in the manner in which he addresses his king: 'Royal Lear, whom I have ever honoured as my king, loved as my father, as my

master followed, as my great patron thought on in my prayers.' However, Kent's love for and devotion to Lear do not blind him to Lear's faults, on the contrary, it is these very qualities that compel him to confront the king and highlight the gravity of his wrongdoing. '. . . be Kent unmannerly when Lear is mad . . . Reverse thy doom and in thy best consideration check this hideous rashness.' When all others are intimidated by Lear's fury and remain silent in the face of his blatantly unjust treatment of Cordelia, Kent counsels him to 'see better', before bluntly telling him: 'I'll tell thee thou dost evil.' Kent is perceptive and sees people for what they are. He expresses his respect and concern for Cordelia

('The gods to their dear shelter, take thee, maid'). He sees through Goneril and Regan's flattery and doubts if their actions will match their words: 'And your large speeches may your deeds approve/That good effects may spring from words of love.'

Despite Lear's harsh mistreatment of him, Kent's loyalty to his master never wavers. Even after being banished and threatened with death, he is determined to return in disguise and serve Lear in some capacity: 'Now, banish'd Kent,/If thou canst serve where thou dost stand condemn'd, so may it come, thy master, whom thou lovest shall find thee full of labours.' Kent is infuriated by Oswald's blatant lack of respect for Lear, and does not let it pass unpunished, immediately tripping Oswald up and pushing him out. There is no element of tact or diplomacy in Kent's make-up; on the contrary, he can be quite a fiery character.

It is Kent's undisguised contempt for Oswald and his subsequent blunt responses to Cornwall that result in him being placed in the stocks. Kent is aware that Oswald has come as Goneril's messenger 'with letters against the king'. He subjects this 'cowardly rascal' to a tongue-lashing before drawing his sword and beating him, accusing him of taking 'the puppet's part' against the royalty of his mistress' (Goneril) father. When questioned by Cornwall, Kent is typically direct: '. . . anger hath a privilege.' He later tells Cornwall, 'I am no flatterer'. Cornwall orders that this 'stubborn ancient knave' be placed in the stocks. Kent points out that since he is the king's messenger, this degrading punishment is in fact an insult to Lear: 'You shall do small respect, show too bold malice against the grace and person of my master, stocking his messenger.' Lear is incensed to find Kent in the stocks ('. . . 'tis worse than murder to do upon respect such violent outrage') and in the dramatic scene which

follows comes to realise the full extent of his foolishness. This episode brings the quarrel between Lear and his daughters into the open, with the battle-lines between good and evil now clear to be seen.

Significantly, Kent's soliloquy at the end of this scene reveals that he has succeeded in getting news of Lear's predicament to Cordelia. Kent resolves to co-operate with Cordelia in her efforts to set right the wrongs done in the kingdom: 'seeking to give losses their remedies.' In helping to re-establish links between Lear and Cordelia, Kent performs one of his most important dramatic functions. In Act 3, Scene 1 Kent asks the gentleman to hurry to Dover to report on Lear's 'unnatural and bemadding sorrow'. While this gentleman does not know Kent, the latter proudly asserts that he is 'a gentleman of blood and breeding' and as such that he speaks the truth. Kent gives the gentleman a ring which Cordelia will recognise. Through Kent's later conversation with the gentleman we learn of Cordelia's response to the news of Lear's suffering. Her reaction to the news contained in Kent's letters is characterised by 'patience and sorrow'. Kent helps to keep Cordelia in the minds of the audience when she is not on stage.

Kent updates the audience on important political and military developments. He informs us of the growing division between Albany and Cornwall: 'There is division, although as yet the face of it be covered with mutual cunning, 'twixt Albany and Cornwall'. Through Kent we learn that the forces of good are now assembling and are on their way to rescue Lear: '. . . from France there comes a power into this scattered Kingdom.'

Kent regularly comments on and clarifies Lear's mental state for the audience: 'His wits begin to unsettle'; 'All the power of his wits have given way to his impatience'; '. . . his wits are gone'; '. . . sometime in his better tune remembers what we are come about.' Kent also explains why Lear is reluctant to meet Cordelia: '. . . burning shame detains him from Cordelia.'

Kent remains with and watches over Lear as the storm rages on the heath, guiding his master towards the shelter of a hovel. Lear asks him, 'Wilt break my heart?' Kent's response reflects his deep affection and absolute fidelity (loyalty) to his master: 'I had rather break mine own.' Again that loyalty does not prevent Kent from speaking the truth to Lear. When Lear, with typical egocentricity, blames Poor Tom's miserable condition on his daughters, Kent tells him: 'He hath no daughters, sir.' Recognising that Lear's angry outbursts exacerbate (worsen) his mental condition, the concerned Kent urges Lear to be patient: 'Sir, where is the patience now that you so oft have boasted to retain?' Even when Lear loses his sanity, Kent never fails to address him respectfully: 'Good my lord . . .'; 'Sir . . .'

Kent is an admirably philosophical character who believes that life is governed by the stars: 'it is the stars, the stars above us, that govern our conditions.' He believes that the wheel of fortune always turns full circle. After he has been placed in the stocks, Kent looks forward to better times ahead: 'Fortune, good night: smile once more, turn thy wheel.'

Kent's affection for and total loyalty to his master are strikingly evident in the closing stages of the play. Cordelia thanks Kent for his loyalty to Lear: 'O thou good Kent, how shall I live and work to match thy goodness?' Kent's own heart is close to breaking point when he witnesses Lear's overwhelming grief at Cordelia's death: 'Break, heart; I prithee, break!' Kent has followed his master's 'sad steps' through all his sorrow and suffering and shows great compassion for his king in his final agony. While others hope to revive the dying Lear, Kent knows that Lear has suffered enough and that it would be cruel to prolong his agony further: 'Vex not his ghost: O, let him pass! He hates him that would upon the rack of this tough world stretch him out longer.' Kent's loyalty to Lear is not limited to the physical world; his devotion to his master is such that he wishes to join him in death: 'I have a journey, sir, shortly to go, my master calls me, I must not say no.' Kent's unwavering loyalty to Lear reminds us that we are witnessing the downfall of a once-great man. Through Kent's eyes we see an earlier, greater Lear – a man whose finer qualities inspired such selfless devotion in the noble Kent.

KEY ADJECTIVES

- loyal, devoted
- loving (towards Lear)
- shrewd, perceptive, astute
- blunt, direct
- courageous, fearless
- philosophical

THE FOOL

The Fool is no ordinary court jester introduced into the play for the sole purpose of providing a little levity and relieving the tension of the drama. It would probably be incorrect to regard him as an entirely sane man pretending to be mad (the evidence of the play suggests that he was well-suited to playing the role of court jester), yet he possesses penetrating insight and sound common sense. **In relentlessly reminding Lear of his foolishness, the Fool helps his old master to achieve self-knowledge.** The Fool displays remarkable loyalty, remaining with Lear throughout his descent into insanity. He also shows a real and sincere concern for Lear's welfare.

Lear describes his jester as 'a bitter fool' because he tells Lear the bitter truth at all times: 'Thou hadst little wit in thy bald crown when thou gavest thy golden one away.' The fool recognises that the truth is not always well-received: 'Truth's a dog must to kennel,' but nonetheless never refrains from giving full rein to his caustic (sarcastic/barbed) wit in reminding Lear of the errors of his ways. When Lear asks him: 'Dost thou call me fool, boy?' The Fool's response is typically sharp: 'All thy other titles thou hast given away; that thou wast born with.' The Fool reminds Lear that he has given Goneril and Regan power and authority over him: '. . . thou madest thy daughters thy mother. Emphasising that Lear has left himself at the mercy of his daughters, the Fool tells him that even a snail has a house and would not 'leave his horns without a case'. Determined to make his master aware of his mistakes and shortcomings, the Fool never spares Lear's feelings: 'Thou shouldst not have been old till thou hadst been wise.' The Fool disguises many of his highly philosophical reflections with nonsense songs: 'Fathers that wear rags do make their children blind.' There is a sharp edge to the Fool's wit and his seemingly meaningless songs often contain an element of truth. Goneril describes the Fool as 'all-licensed' because he seems to be allowed to say whatever he likes. The Fool can speak his mind precisely because he is regarded as an idiot. Kent acknowledges the Fool's sharp wit: 'This is not altogether fool, my Lord.'

The Fool's most striking quality is his loyalty to Lear. In one of his songs, he informs Lear that while his knights have already gone, he will stay: 'But I will tarry; the fool will stay.' As Lear faces the fury of the storm tormented by his daughters' filial ingratitude, the Fool is still with him, doing his best to keep up the spirits of the king in his blackest hour. The Fool has a real and sincere concern for Lear's welfare. He is worried about the destructive effects of the storm on Lear's mind, as well as the obvious physical hardship which it brings: 'Good nuncle, in, and ask thy daughter's blessing: here's a night pities neither wise men nor fools.' Throughout the play, the Fool continually reminds Lear of the foolishness of his abdication. However, he makes no attempt to impart any moral lessons during the storm, fearing the effects of the violent tempest on Lear's mind: 'This cold night will turn us all to fools and madmen.'

The Fool's purpose is to prompt Lear to reflect on those foolish actions which gave rise to the tragedy. He is Lear's conscience, his inner voice that relentlessly reminds him of his foolishness. The Fool helps and supports Lear on his painful spiritual journey to self-knowledge. **Once Lear has acquired self-knowledge, the Fool's dramatic role is fulfilled and we neither see nor hear of him beyond the storm scene.**

KEY ADJECTIVES

- loyal, devoted
- courageous
- insightful, wise
- blunt, direct
- caring (towards Lear)

GONERIL

Goneril is the most abhorrent of the evil characters. Her sister is equally evil, but Goneril is stronger and more repulsive than Regan and dominates this sibling relationship. There are no moral depths that Goneril will not plumb in her utterly ruthless pursuit of her ambitions.

In the opening scene we clearly see her hypocrisy when she claims to love her father, 'more than words can wield the matter'. She is cunning and unscrupulous in the way she uses flattery to achieve her ends. She tells Regan what she really thinks of Lear, criticising his 'poor judgement' and 'unruly waywardness'. Having seen Cordelia suffer because of Lear's rashness, Goneril is determined to ensure that she never suffers because of his fiery nature. She conspires with Regan to further undermine (weaken) Lear's position: 'Pray you, let's hit together.' It is Goneril who insists that they take action against Lear without delay: 'We must do something and in the heat' (without delay).

Goneril's utter contempt for Lear is obvious when she refers to him as an 'idle old man that still would manage those authorities that he hath given away.' When she witnesses Lear's behaviour in her castle, she disdainfully concludes that, 'Old fools are babes again.' Goneril encourages Oswald and her other servants to neglect and openly disrespect Lear: 'Put on what weary negligence you please.' Along with Regan, she is determined to take away all that remains of Lear's kingly dignity. She complains about Lear's 'insolent retinue' (bad-mannered knights) before going on to dismiss half of them in an instant. Lear had naively expected his daughters to treat him like a king, but this blatant insult to his status opens his eyes to his daughter's true nature. Lear curses Goneril in the strongest terms imaginable, but she is unmoved by his vitriolic attack. While both Goneril and Regan deliberately humiliate Lear, it is Goneril who initiates most of the schemes to undermine Lear's status. She writes to Regan, urging her to treat Lear as she has done ('hold my very course'). When the enraged Lear leaves her home to go to Regan's, Goneril follows shortly afterwards to ensure that Regan acts on her instructions. She is the more enterprising and domineering of the two evil sisters.

As the play unfolds, we see the growing gap between Goneril and her husband. She regards Albany with contempt, and is disparaging (insulting) in what she regards as his 'milky gentleness' and 'cowish terror'. Goneril is attracted to Edmund, an ambitious, ruthless man of action, perhaps seeing in him a kindred spirit. This attraction appears to be the only indication of her humanity.

Goneril's extraordinary cruelty is dramatically displayed in her desire to

avenge herself on Gloucester: 'Pluck out his eyes!' She has no reservations about any action, however evil. Most strikingly, she displays no qualms of conscience about planning her husband's death. Edgar is horrified to discover this 'plot upon her virtuous husband's life'. In her letter to Edmund, Goneril writes that he will have 'many opportunities' to 'cut him [Albany] off'. Goneril's ruthlessness is further reflected in her poisoning of Regan. She also adds her name to Edmund's on the death warrant for Lear and Cordelia. Her calculated humiliation of Lear only hints at the depths of evil demonstrated later in the play.

Unsurprisingly, Goneril is a strong, capable leader. While she initially claims that she would sooner lose the battle against the French than lose Edmund to Regan, her more practical side quickly asserts itself as she perceives the necessity of unity in the face of the enemy: 'Combine together 'gainst the enemy; for these domestic and particular broils are not the question here.'

Ruthless, vengeful and utterly devoid of humanity, she is a truly monstrous character. She possesses no redeeming traits and may be regarded as the embodiment of evil. Hesitation is not part of Goneril's make-up and her unhesitating suicide is entirely in keeping with her character.

A series of images suggest that Goneril is devoid (without) of humanity. She is a 'detested kite", a 'sea-monster', 'a devil', 'a fiend', a 'gilded serpent', 'a vulture'. For Lear, the pain of her filial ingratitude is 'sharper than a serpent's tooth'. These images suggest her formidable, but despicable, character.

KEY ADJECTIVES

- evil, malevolent, malicious
- amoral (no morals)
- false, deceptive, hypocritical
- ambitious
- ruthless, inhuman, callous, cruel
- domineering, autocratic
- strong, capable, practical
- despicable, contemptible, vile, detestable

REGAN

Like Goneril, Regan is innately evil and capable of savage cruelty. These evil sisters are fundamentally alike in that their actions are never influenced either by conscience or by normal human feelings. However, as early as the end of the opening scene, we see that Regan tends to be dominated by Goneril, who is the more domineering, more active sister.

Regan's hypocrisy is evident in the opening scene. There is irony in Regan's suggestion that she is made of 'the self metal' as her sister, because both are equally false and evil. Her response to Lear's love test is to claim that Goneril's expression of love 'comes too short' – an early sign of rivalry that destroys their relationship later in the play. Regan's treatment of Lear is callous. She emphasises Lear's advanced age

('O, sir you are old, nature in you stands on the very verge of her confine') and his powerlessness ('I pray you, father, being weak, seem so'). Nowhere is her filial ingratitude more obvious than in her contemptuous response to Lear's pathetic attempt to remind his unnatural daughters of his generosity towards them ('I gave you all . . .'): 'And in good time you gave it.' Her utter lack of feeling for her father is strikingly evident when she shuts the doors of her castle against him: 'O, sir, to wilful men the injuries that they themselves procure must be their schoolmasters.' Lear is left to face what Kent later describes as the worst storm in living memory. Stunned by the depth of this cruelty, Cordelia later remarks that she would have kept her enemy's dog by her fire on the night of that most violent of storms. Regan, in contrast, displays not a trace of filial love or loyalty towards her father, whom she contemptuously refers to as 'the lunatic king'. It is little wonder that in the mock trial scene the insane Lear asks, 'Is there any cause in nature that makes these hard hearts?'

We see Regan's vindictiveness when she countermands her husband's order and lengthens Kent's punishment in the stocks. No sooner has Cornwall ordered that Kent is to remain in the stocks 'till noon', than Regan immediately orders that he is to remain there 'all night too'. That she is no less evil than Goneril is particularly clear from the role she plays in the mutilation of Gloucester. She initially demands that he be hanged 'instantly'. When Gloucester still possesses one eye, she cruelly says: 'One eye will mock another, the other too.' The servant who goes to Gloucester's assistance is stabbed in the back by Regan, and she takes a cruel delight in informing Gloucester that it was Edmund who betrayed him: '. . . it was he that made the overture of thy treasons to us, who is too good to pity thee.' She callously tells Gloucester to 'smell his way to Dover'. Regan's ruthlessness is again evident when she later remarks that 'it was great ignorance Gloucester's eyes being out to let him live.' She promises to reward Oswald if he kills Gloucester: 'Preferment falls on him that cuts him off.'

Regan's rivalry with and jealousy of Goneril is such that she is willing to open a private letter from her sister to Edmund. Regan's passion for Edmund ultimately leads to her handing her title, her soldiers and her prisoners over to him and calling the world to witness that she has made him her 'lord and master'. It is ironic that Goneril and Regan, who were so utterly unfeeling towards their aged father, should be destroyed by the depth of their feeling for a man who cares nothing for either of them: 'Which of them shall I take? Both? One? Or neither?'

While Goneril and Regan are united in evil and display a number of similar characteristics, they are not entirely alike. Regan is weaker in character than Goneril, tending initially to live in her sister's shadow. Goneril and Regan eventually turn out to be each other's greatest enemy as their partnership is destroyed by their intense jealousy of each other over Edmund. Their actions reveal how low human beings can sink when they are utterly insensitive to the feelings of others, while the fate of these malevolent sisters shows us that evil is ultimately self-destructive.

KEY ADJECTIVES

- evil, malevolent, malicious
- ruthless, callous, unfeeling, unscrupulous
- false, deceptive, hypocritical
- amoral
- contemptible, despicable

EDMUND

Like Goneril and Regan, Edmund is extraordinarily evil. He is utterly unprincipled and totally amoral (has no moral principles). He is motivated entirely by self-interest and has no feelings for anybody else, regarding others either as aids or obstacles to the achievement of his ambitions. He betrays his own father and turns his brother's life upside down. He orders the deaths of Lear and Cordelia and deceives two sisters, turning them into mortal enemies. However, while neither Goneril nor Regan possess any redeeming features, Edgar is in some respects an attractive villain.

Edmund's illegitimacy is no excuse for his evilness and villainy but it does, to an extent, influence our feelings towards him. It is understandable that Edmund is bitter. Having the misfortune to be born outside of wedlock, he will not, in the normal course of events, inherit anything from his father. His first soliloquy (Act 1, Scene 3) earns him a degree of sympathy and even admiration because he is so determined to rise above the circumstances of his birth and 'fashion' his own future. Edmund is a proud, clever villain who cannot accept society's view of him as 'base' (low) when he knows that he has a 'mind as generous and shape as true as honest madam's issue'. He shows resolve in his assertion that he will 'top the legitimate' and defiance as he challenges the gods to 'stand up for bastards'.

He displays a single-minded will to succeed and believes that he has the power to shape his own destiny.

Edmund is a sharp-witted villain with the capacity to perceive (the ability to see) the strengths and weaknesses of others and to plan his schemes accordingly. He is also entirely unscrupulous in the pursuit of his ambition to possess his father's lands and ultimately, the crown. He forges a letter to supplant (replace) his brother Edgar as heir to the earldom. He ruthlessly exploits his father's credulous (gullible) nature and his brother's noble-mindedness: 'A credulous father and a brother noble whose nature is so far from doing harms that he suspects none.' Edmund cunningly wounds himself to impress the gullible Gloucester with his apparent loyalty. He is a ruthless opportunist who turns every situation to his own advantage. When Gloucester confides in him regarding the letter which tells of the French landing and informs him of his intention to help Lear, Edmund immediately decides to betray him: 'This courtesy, forbid thee, shall the duke instantly know; and of that letter too.'

Edmund's hypocrisy is evident when, speaking with Gloucester, he describes Goneril and Regan's treatment of Lear as 'savage and unnatural'. He betrays his own father in the certain knowledge that Gloucester will be severely punished for his 'treason'. Edmund's hypocrisy is again evident in his apparent reluctance to inform Cornwall of Gloucester's intentions: 'O heavens! that this treason were not, or not I the detector.' In reality, he is entirely unmoved by his callous (unfeeling) action, believing that 'the younger rises when the old doth fall.' Goneril and Regan are exploited in a similar fashion to advance Edmund's selfish goals. In Act 5 Edmund reflects nonchalantly (casually) on his double-dealing in relation to the two sisters: 'To both these sisters have I sworn my love; each jealous of the other, as the stung are of the adder.' Albany is to be used to help win the battle before 'her who would be rid of him' (Goneril) devises ' his speedy taking'. Lear and Cordelia are to be killed, not for personal reasons, but because they represent a political threat. Edmund believes that both have the power 'to pluck the common bosom on their side', i.e. to win popular support. Intelligent and charming, hypocritical and ruthless, Edmund is utterly insensitive to the human suffering which results from his single-minded desire to defy society and achieve wealth, status and power.

Edmund displays some redeeming features in the final scene. When he is unsuccessful in his ambitious designs, he accepts his failure without showing personal animosity (hatred). **He exchanges forgiveness with Edgar and accepts that divine justice has been done:** 'The wheel is come full circle.' He also displays a touch of humanity and a glimmer of conscience. Edgar's description of Gloucester's suffering and death prompts Edmund to respond: 'This speech of yours hath moved me and shall perchance do good . . .' As he nears death, Edmund attempts to do 'some good . . . despite of mine own nature' by revealing that he has ordered the deaths of Lear and Cordelia. The grim pleasure which he takes in the thought of having been loved by two sisters is another indication of his humanity: 'Yet Edmund was beloved: The one the other poison'd for my sake and after slew herself.' The irony that all three are, in a sense, married in death ('all three now marry in an instant') is not lost on him. While Edmund's attitude towards and treatment of others throughout the play is reprehensible, his final words and actions hint at his humanity and prevent him from being viewed as a complete monster. Edmund is a more believable and more interesting character than Goneril and Regan because he is not wholly evil.

KEY ADJECTIVES

- ambitious, determined
- false, deceptive, hypocritical, two-faced
- clever, resourceful, quick-witted
- ruthless, unscrupulous
- humane (to some extent at the very end of the play)

OSWALD

Oswald is a truly contemptible character. Encouraged by his mistress, Goneril, Oswald treats Lear with blatant disrespect. When Lear asks him: 'Who am I, sir?' Oswald contemptuously replies: 'My lady's father.' Oswald's cowardice is displayed when, confronted by the angry Kent, he shouts for help. He subsequently lies to Cornwall, suggesting that he had 'spared' Kent because of his advanced age. Oswald is to be despised for drawing his sword against the 'eyeless head' of Gloucester in order to advance himself ('to raise my own fortunes'). He runs from Kent, but is willing to kill a blind old man. **He is a servile character** (fawning, excessively respectful), ever anxious to ingratiate himself with (please) his superiors. His only redeeming trait (positive quality) is his absolute loyalty to his mistress Goneril; indeed, with his dying breath he asks Edgar to give the letters which he carries to Edmund. Edgar accurately describes Oswald as 'a serviceable villain as duteous to the vices of thy mistress as badness would desire'.

KEY ADJECTIVES

- disrespectful, discourteous, insolent
- cowardly
- servile, obsequious, fawning

CORNWALL

Cornwall seems to be a suitable husband for Regan in that he is equally cruel and vengeful. He appears to be dominated by his wife. When Regan suggests that 'wilful men' must learn from 'the injuries that they themselves procure' and closes her doors against Lear, Cornwall's response is, 'My Regan counsels well'. After Cornwall orders that Kent is to remain in the stocks 'till noon', Regan insists on a more severe punishment: '. . . and all night too.' Cornwall is rather gullible in that he too is impressed with Edmund's apparent loyalty to his father early in the play: 'For you, Edmund, whose virtue and obedience doth this instant so much commend itself, you shall be ours.' Cornwall's vengeful nature is to be seen in his anticipation of Gloucester's return from his attempt to assist Lear: 'I will have my revenge ere I depart his house.' We see his brutality and cruelty when he gouges out Gloucester's eyes: 'Out, vile jelly! Where is thy lustre now?' Although his character is only sketched (not developed fully), he displays no redeeming features.

KEY ADJECTIVES

- evil, malevolent
- gullible, credulous
- cruel, vengeful

Comparative Study

Texts

- **Lies of Silence** – Brian Moore

- **Dancing at Lughnasa** – Brian Friel

- **Il Postino** – Michael Radford

Modes of Comparison

A. Cultural Context

Lies of Silence

This text is set in Belfast in the 1980s when the Northern 'Troubles' are at their peak. The cultural context is dominated by the deep-rooted political/religious conflict in the North of Ireland. The violence that springs from this age-old quarrel has a very real impact on the lives of the central characters in this text. As a hotel manager, Michael Dillon is acutely aware of the necessity for tight security. The Clarence Hotel had been bombed the previous year. Each car entering the hotel grounds is checked by guards, while its occupants have to undergo a body search. In the opening pages of the text, Michael is depressed by the familiar sight of policemen climbing out of an armoured car, 'wearing combat jackets, their revolvers cowboy-low on their thighs.' Watching them cautiously cross the street, Michael feels strangely dejected: 'Why should he stay, why should anyone in their senses stay here?'

Lies of Silence **highlights the depth of the religious divide and its attendant (accompanying) bitterness in Northern Ireland.** In this text, religion is portrayed in a negative light as a cause of division. Of course, in Northern Ireland religious and political divisions have, historically, coincided, with the Protestant population being loyal to Britain, and the Catholic population being nationalist. When religious divisions lead to narrow-mindedness, hatred, and even violence, this is known as sectarianism. Both Protestants and Catholics are seen to be sectarian, as can be seen in Michael's reference to 'Protestant prejudice and Catholic cant'. He speaks of the narrow-mindedness of the priests who taught him ('priests whose sectarian views perfectly propagated the divisive bitterness' at the heart of the Northern conflict), while describing the Orange Order as 'that fount of Protestant prejudice against the third of Ulster's people who are Catholics.' Significantly, the two religious figures that are specifically mentioned are immersed in sectarian politics: the Reverend Alun Pottinger is a leading member of the Orange Order, while Father Connolly is closely linked with the IRA. It is the desire to assassinate Pottinger that prompts a number of IRA men to take over Dillon's house and order him to drive a car with a bomb into the grounds of the Clarence Hotel on the day that Pottinger is delivering a speech. They threaten to kill Moira, his wife, if he refuses to co-operate with them.

Historically, the Catholic community has been subjected to discrimination, particularly in the areas of political power and employment, since the foundation of the Northern Ireland state. Moira's father, Joe, tells of how 'a Catholic would never get a job if there was a Protestant up for it.' He goes on to describe what happened when Catholics started looking for their civil rights in the late 1960s: 'And then in the sixties the civil rights marches started and it was on the telly an' the whole world saw the Prods beatin' us up and the police helpin' them.' Michael also speaks of discrimination against Catholics in the course of a disagreement with Moira: 'The Protestants here are never going to share jobs and power with Catholics unless they're forced into it.' While Michael himself does not believe in religion or indeed in God, religious difference is a hugely important factor in this story.

While the paramilitary groups on both sides of the religious divide initially grew

out of the ancient political/religious quarrel, they quickly gravitate towards a range of gangster-type activities. When the gunmen start to order her about, Moira vents her anger at them, pointing out that they have no democratic mandate to represent or act on behalf of the Catholic community in Northern Ireland, suggesting that if there were a vote the following day among Catholics, the IRA 'wouldn't get five per cent of it.' Moira goes on to declare bitterly that the IRA men who have taken over her house, and indeed all paramilitaries regardless of whether they are of a green or orange hue, are now simply engaged in common criminal activities: 'You're just a bunch of crooks, IRA or UDA, Protestants or Catholics, you're all in the same business. Racketeers, the bunch of you! There isn't a building site in this city or a pub that you or the UDA don't hold up for protection money.' Moira's father, Joe, is outraged by the IRA's virtual kidnapping of his daughter. He sarcastically dismisses the idea of the Catholic community being 'protected' by the IRA, describing the organisation as 'a bunch of thugs, that has no programme except killin' people.'

In addition to the violent conflict that casts a dark shadow over everyone's life in Northern Ireland, family life is another key element of the cultural context in *Lies of Silence*. Family life in the Dillon household is strained and problematic. Moira's deteriorating relationship with Michael undermines her self-confidence and causes her to feel insecure: 'You're bored with me, you married me because you fancied me and now I've lost my good looks you couldn't care less about me.' Moira correctly perceives that Michael had married her for her good looks and because he liked the idea of other men envying him his tall, beautiful wife. From the beginning of the text it is apparent that

Michael and Moira's marriage has broken down as Michael is having an affair with a Canadian woman named Andrea. Michael had planned to leave Moira on the day that the IRA take himself and his wife hostage in their own home.

Poverty is a striking feature of the cultural context of *Lies of Silence*, although it does not directly affect the lives of the main characters. In this text Northern Ireland is in an economic slump and there is intense competition for jobs. The text refers to 'a continuing plague of poverty' which blight the lives of thousands of working-class people 'whose highest ambition was a job in a shipyard or a mill'. Unemployed for years and mired in poverty, many working-class people are devoid of hope. Poverty inevitably intensifies sectarian tensions. The text suggests that it is the working classes on both sides of the religious divide that are most virulently sectarian, referring to 'graffiti-fouled barricaded slums where the city's Protestant and Catholic poor confronted each other, year in and year out, in a stasis of hatred, fear and mistrust.' Working-class people are portrayed as the victims of their leaders, political and religious, who stoke the fires of sectarianism in their own selfish interests. Dillon expresses his anger at the 'lies told to poor Protestant working people about the Catholics, lies told to poor Catholic working people about the Protestants, lies from parliaments and pulpits, lies at rallies and funeral orations, and, above all, lies of silence from those in Westminster who did not want to face the injustices of Ulster's status quo'. The idea of successive British governments ignoring the injustices perpetrated for generations against Catholics in Northern Ireland is disturbing.

Class division is another significant aspect of the society in which the story is located. Interestingly, and in sharp contrast to the working classes who are bitterly divided along religious lines, middle-class Catholics and Protestants are portrayed, for the most part, as happily co-existing. Michael Dillon lives in 'a quiet, unpublicised, middle-class Belfast where Protestants and Catholics lived side by side, joined by class, by economic ties, even by intermarriage, in a way the poor could never be.' It seems that the majority of the comfortable middle-classes attach greater importance to socio-economic factors than religious difference. Dillon's neighbour, Mr Harbinson (a retired bank manager), 'was no more a religious Protestant than Dillon was a religious Catholic'. Like the vast majority of the Catholic and Protestant people in Ulster, he 'just wanted to get on with his life without any interference from men in woollen masks.' While the gunman Kevin disparagingly addresses Moira as 'You stuck-up wee bourgeois bitch', Moira in fact comes from a strongly working-class background, with her parents living on the Falls Road. If the gunman was confused, it was because education had erased Moira's 'broad Belfast accent'. It is interesting to note that Moira was the first member of her extended family to earn a university degree. We see how her parents are acutely aware of their working-class background whenever Michael (whose background is upper middle-class) comes to visit. Her mother sets out her best china and silver, and ironed linen napkins replace the paper napkins they normally use. Moira's parents are visibly awkward in Dillon's company and are described as feeling 'ill at ease' in his parents' presence.

Lies of Silence is set in a patriarchal (male-dominated) world. While Moira appears to be a stronger character than Dillon, courageously defying the IRA, it is Dillon who makes all the important decisions, moral and practical. The IRA is an organisation dominated by men, while the business world in which Dillon works is clearly male-dominated, with his peers and superiors all male. Father Connolly is another male authority figure, as is the Reverend Alun Pottinger.

It is interesting to note how Dillon's attitude towards his home in Ulster changes as the time for his departure for a new job and a new life in London draws near. The warmth he feels at his send-off party seems to stir new feelings within him towards the world that, up to this point, appeared only to depress and anger him. Surrounded by hotel employees who clearly care for him, Michael feels a deep sense of belonging: 'He wondered if he ever again would feel so close to and inspire such affection from people who worked for him. He had left this place and had come back unwillingly, but now, looking at the people around him, hearing the familiar Northern accents, he knew that this was home . . .'

Ultimately, it is the violent nature of the world in which Dillon lives that claims his life. Having defied the IRA by informing the police of their plan to blow up the Clarence Hotel, Michael (along with Andrea) departs for London some time later. Despite separate warnings from both Moira and Andrea and a very clear warning from Father Connolly, Michael initially refuses to be persuaded or intimidated into not identifying one of the gunmen whose face he had seen when the IRA had taken over their house. However, once he is in London with Andrea, Michael experiences a new sense of happiness, which is conveyed in the memorable image of the two kissing and 'her happiness flow[ing] into him like a current.' Michael now has a new, more positive, perspective on his life: 'She was right. They were here. Everything had changed. Everything.' Following 'the happiest day in his whole life', he changes his mind about testifying against the IRA, but it is too late. The following day, the unsuspecting Dillon leaves a man into his apartment to check the gas meter. After establishing Dillon's identity, the little red-haired man whistles as though he were calling a dog – he is in fact indicating to his two accomplices that they had the right apartment and the right man. Seconds later, two unmasked youths arrive at the door and shoot Michael Dillon dead. Ultimately, he could not escape the violent nature of the world into which he was born and where he worked for most of his life. The republican paramilitaries Dillon had dared to defy are predictably ruthless in dealing with a threat to one of their own members and do not hesitate to order his assassination.

KEY POINTS

- The cultural context is dominated by the bitter, violent and age-old religious/ political quarrel in Northern Ireland.
- Family life is at the point of breakdown at the opening of the text, with Michael Dillon about to leave his wife Moira.
- Poverty is a feature of the world of the text, although it does not impact directly on the lives of the protagonists.
- Class division and class consciousness are features of this world.
- This text is set in a male-dominated society.
- Dillon's feelings towards Belfast change towards the close of the text. His feelings of depression and anger that were caused by living in Ulster in the early part of the text ultimately give way to a sense of belonging, a realisation that Ulster is his home.
- Dillon is ultimately a victim of the violent world in which he had spent most of his life. It is sadly ironic that he is killed the day after 'the happiest day in his whole life'.

Dancing at Lughnasa

Similar to *Lies of Silence*, this text is set in Ireland, but in a different location and era. *Dancing at Lughnasa* is set in Donegal in the 1930s. Here, the Mundy sisters live in a world of poverty and limited opportunity.

In sharp contrast to *Lies of Silence* family life in this text is generally stable (until the close of the text, when it is disrupted by external factors) and loving.

Interestingly, the family unit in this text is not the traditional nuclear family (father, mother, child/children). Instead we have a family of five sisters, one of whom – Chris – has a young son, Michael. Father Jack, the sisters' only brother, once again becomes part of the family after he returns from his missionary work in Uganda. The Mundys are a closely united family. Kate is the mother figure and the head of the house. Inevitably, the sisters have their occasional disagreements; most obviously, they disagree in relation to attending the Harvest Dance. Notwithstanding occasional moments of conflict, family life in the Mundy household is generally more stable and less problematic than family life in *Lies of Silence*. There is a sense of warmth and support within the Mundy home that is not in evidence in the Dillon household. The closeness of the Mundy sisters is vividly evident in the scene where they all dance wildly around the house to the music of Marconi, the radio. Michael, a character in the text as well as the narrator, recalls this very special moment: 'And when I remember the kitchen throbbing with the best of Irish music beamed to us all the way from Dublin, and my mother and her sisters suddenly catching hands and dancing a spontaneous step-dance and laughing – screaming! – like excited schoolgirls . . .' In their wild, joyous, unrestrained dancing, the Mundy sisters seem to briefly escape all that oppresses them such as poverty, social expectations and an overbearing clergy.

While poverty is a feature of the world of *Lies of Silence*, it does not impact directly on the lives of the protagonists, as it does in *Dancing at Lughnasa*. The Mundy sisters have to contend with a range of problems associated with poverty, including unemployment and emigration. Kate is a teacher in the local primary school and is the only wage-earner in the family. Agnes and Rose make a little money knitting gloves at home. Chris and Maggie work around the house and have no income. The house furnishings are described as 'austere', while the clothes of all the sisters 'reflect their lean circumstances'. Maggie remembers how, as children, they never had butter on their soda bread going to school, only home-made jam. As adults the Mundy sisters often struggle to put food on the table. At one point Maggie points out that they have 'three eggs' and soda bread to feed seven people (Gerry, Michael's father, is on one of his rare visits at the time)

for their evening meal. However, the family's circumstances become truly dire after Kate loses her job on the whim of the vindictive parish priest angered by Father Jack's bizarre behaviour, and Agnes and Rose lose the little money they make from their part-time home knitting when a knitting factory opens up in the locality: 'The Industrial Revolution had finally caught up with Ballybeg.' While Gerry appears occasionally, he has no sense of responsibility and does nothing practical to help Michael or his mother, Chris. The family's desperate circumstances ultimately prompt Agnes and Rose to selflessly leave the family home and go to England in the hope of easing the family's plight. Despite their sisters' exhaustive efforts to locate them, they never see either Agnes or Rose again. Reflecting on their possible reasons for leaving, Michael considers the possibility that 'perhaps the two just wanted . . . away.' Many years later Michael discovers that his aunts worked as cleaners in the Underground and in factories in London until Rose could no longer get work. Tragically, their lives had fallen apart shortly afterwards and they ended up on the streets, without shelter, and with only alcohol to comfort them. Almost inevitably, Agnes dies of exposure and Michael finds Rose two days before she dies in a grim hospice, but, sadly and perhaps unsurprisingly, she does not recognise the nephew she had last seen as a young boy.

The world of this text also highlights other forms of poverty, most notably social poverty. The Mundy sisters have no social life, and are totally deprived of opportunities for romance and excitement of any kind. Sadly, they live in a world where women of a certain age are deemed too old for love and romance. Clearly frustrated with their constrained lives, the sisters long for self-fulfilment. While Kate detests Gerry's irresponsibility, she, like all of her sisters, is spellbound by the sight of Chris and Gerry dancing together. Agnes is particularly captivated by Gerry, and may even be in love with him (an idea that is supported by the final tableau where Gerry is sitting next to Agnes on the garden seat). When Kate is loosely linked with Austin Morgan, a shopkeeper in town (and indeed teased by the innocent Rose) she blushes. Maggie fondly remembers Brian McGuinness, who was the great love of her life although she never went out with him; instead he went out with her best friend, Bernie O'Donnell, before emigrating to Australia. 'Simple' Rose is besotted with the married, but separated, Danny Bradley. When Agnes suggests that all the sisters go to the harvest dance together and dance 'like we used to', and Kate appears to give some consideration to the idea, the entire household is briefly charged with an electric excitement. Agnes is overwhelmed by joy as she anticipates going dancing for the first time in many years: 'And I don't care how young they are, how drunk and dirty and sweaty they are. I want to dance, Kate. It's the Festival of Lughnasa. I'm only thirty-five. I want to dance.' However, when Rose begins to dance with wild abandon around the house, Kate panics and declares that they will not be going to the dance: 'Do you want the whole countryside to be laughing at us? – women of our years? – mature women, *dancing*?' Kate's clenching argument is to remind her sisters: 'And this is Father Jack's home – we must never forget that – ever.' Given their largely isolated and dull lives, it is little wonder that Marconi, as the radio is called, assumes such importance in the Mundy sisters' daily lives (Michael speaks of 'the sheer magic of that radio'). It serves primarily as a source of music and also as a link with the world beyond Ballybeg and Donegal.

Similar to *Lies of Silence*, religion is an important factor in this world. This is entirely unsurprising given the unchallengeable power and position of the Catholic Church in Ireland in the 1930s. In both texts, religion is portrayed in a negative light. We see religion at the root of inter-community hatred and bitterness in *Lies of Silence*, with Catholic priests and Protestants ministers often to the forefront in fomenting (encouraging / stirring up discord) such destructive passions. In *Dancing at Lughnasa*, the unseen parish priest is similarly depicted in an unchristian light. In dismissing Kate from her teaching position in the local school, he deprives the Mundy family of their main breadwinner. While he claims that falling numbers are the reason for her dismissal, the reality has much more to do with his disdain for Kate's brother Father Jack, who has returned from his missionary work in Uganda, immersed in the beliefs and rituals of those native people whom he was charged with converting to Catholicism. In everyday parlance, Jack had 'gone native' out in Africa. It seems that Kate was well aware of the parish priest's antipathy towards Jack, as she comments on it early in the play: 'I met the parish priest. I don't know what has happened to that man. But ever since Jack came home, he can hardly look me in the eye.'

Unlike *Lies of Silence*, class division is not a feature of the world of *Dancing at Lughnasa*. This is not to suggest that rural Ireland was some type of classless utopia in that era (or indeed in any era since); it is simply that the focus of the play is fixed so firmly on the Mundy household that we see little of wider society.

One of the most obvious downsides to living in a small community in Ireland in the 1930s (and indeed for decades later) was the preoccupation with 'reputation'. Kate, the mother figure in the Mundy family, is very image conscious, being keenly aware of how she and her sisters may be perceived by the wider community. Michael recalls how, when Father Jack first went to Africa, the local newspaper would often have an article on 'our own leper priest', as they called him because Ballybeg was proud of him, as was all of Donegal. Michael remembers his family enjoying 'a small share of that fame'. Significantly, he goes on to point out 'that little bit of status' that Father Jack's fame conferred on them 'must have helped my aunts to bear the shame Mother brought on the household by having me – as it was called then – out of wedlock.' With Jack's behaviour becoming increasingly bizarre (particularly his distinct lack of interest in saying Mass) Kate is determined that no one beyond the family will know anything about the dramatic change her brother has undergone: 'This must be kept in the family, Maggie! Not a word of this must go outside these walls – d'you hear? – not a syllable!' We see further evidence of Kate's obsession with the family's reputation when she objects to Maggie's suggestion that the police be informed of Rose's disappearance after Rose announcing her determination to meet with Danny Bradley: 'You're going to no police, Maggie. If she's involved with that Bradley creature, I'm not going to have it broadcast all over . . .'

Similar to *Lies of Silence*, this text is also set in a male-dominated environment. The parish priest is the main authority figure in the lives of the Mundy sisters. His treatment of Kate is harsh and unjust – it is the kind of spiteful behaviour that represents the very antithesis of Christianity. Sadly, Kate has no option but to accept his decision to dismiss her for the 'sins' of her brother, Jack, regardless of the patent injustice of this decision. Father Jack had always been looked up to as a hero by his sisters, until they see how he has been strangely transformed when he returns,

espousing pagan, as opposed to Christian beliefs. There are only two other men mentioned in the text: Austen Morgan is a shopkeeper in town and seemingly one of Ballybeg's leading businessmen (it is sadly ironic that Kate ends up tutoring Austen's children). Finally, while Gerry is an utterly irresponsible figure, he is never turned away from the Mundy household on those rare occasions he chooses to pay Chris and Michael a visit. It would be no understatement to say that Gerry dominates Chris's life – she never refuses to dance with him and to embrace him, and she is always heartbroken after he leaves. This is a world where women generally remain at home. At this time employment opportunities for women were very limited. Kate works as a teacher, while Chris later works in the new knitting factory. The Mundy sisters' struggle to survive suggests that women in this era generally needed to marry to ensure their financial security.

What makes the world of *Dancing at Lughnasa* particularly interesting and unique (in terms of this comparative study) is the fact that it has an alternative pagan culture running alongside the community's orthodox Catholic way of life. This pagan culture pays homage to the god Lugh on the Festival of Lughnasa. With heavy drinking and wild, unrestrained dancing, this pagan celebration, which is marked by bonfires in 'the black hills', is quite similar to the celebratory pagan occasions in Africa, for example the Festival of the New Yam, as described by Father Jack ('And then we dance – and dance –and dance . . . That palm wine! They dole it out in horns! You lose all sense of time . . . !'). Having departed for Uganda a fully committed Catholic missionary, Father Jack returns with a very different set of beliefs and values. We see clearly how fundamentally his perspective and values have altered when, instead of reproving Gerry for his lack of responsibility in relation to Chris and Michael (as Kate expected), he befriends him. Jack is also happy to see that Chris has 'a love child', pointing out that in Uganda 'women are eager to have love-children', and that 'the more love-children you have, the more fortunate your household is thought to be.'

It is difficult to avoid the sense that the world of *Dancing at Lughnasa* is on the point of significant change. Most obviously, the radio that 'obsessed' the Mundy family will ultimately expose them to the modernising, liberalising influences of the wider world. More negatively, the fact that Agnes and Rose feel compelled to leave for London suggests that De Valera's vision of Irish society as a nation of self-sufficient people living 'in frugal comfort' on the land and devoted to both their religious and Gaelic traditions would never be anything more than a romantic illusion. This is because Ireland lacked the capacity to provide for its people's most basic needs and, more importantly, the vast majority of people (even then) wanted an element of comfort and variety in their lives. Kate seems to sense that her world is already in a state of flux when she tells Maggie: 'You perform your duties as best you can – because you believe in responsibilities and obligations and good order.

And then suddenly, suddenly you realise that hair cracks are appearing everywhere, that control is slipping away, that the whole thing is so fragile it can't be held together much longer. It's all about to collapse, Maggie.'

Ultimately, the harshness of the world in which the Mundy sisters live seems to overwhelm them. Poverty forces Agnes and Rose to emigrate to London in search of work. Tragically, the sisters eventually find themselves living on the streets – a grim fate that ultimately claims both of their lives. Chris spent the rest of her life working in the knitting factory – 'and hated every day of it.' Father Jack dies within a year of returning home, leaving Kate inconsolable. Kate herself does nothing for a number of years before getting the job of tutoring Austen Morgan's young family. Gerry Evans's visits became increasingly infrequent, until eventually they stopped entirely (Michael later learns that Gerry had been leading a double life, having a family in Wales, with a son Michael's age, while continuing his relationship with Chris). Michael sums up the sense of gloom that engulfed the Mundy household when the time came for him to leave: '. . . much of the spirit and fun had gone out of their lives; and when my time came to go away, in the selfish way of young men, I was happy to escape.'

KEY POINTS OF COMPARISON
Lies of Silence **and** *Dancing at Lughnasa*

- Family life in this text is more stable and more loving than in *Lies of Silence*.
- Similar to *Lies of Silence* poverty is also a feature of the world of this text. However, in contrast to the aforementioned text where poverty does not directly affect the protagonists, poverty impacts in a very real and destructive manner on the lives of the Mundy sisters.
- In addition to their obvious material poverty, the Mundy family also has to contend with a type of social poverty. The sisters seem to rarely leave home, with few references to outside friends or social opportunities/outlets. They are clearly frustrated with their constrained lives and long for romance and excitement.
- As in *Lies of Silence* the protagonists in this text live in a patriarchal society – women's inferior status to men is, naturally, much more pronounced in *Dancing at Lughnasa* because this text is set in an earlier era.
- Religion is a very important factor in the worlds of both texts, and is portrayed in a negative manner in both.
- While rural Ireland was most certainly not a classless society in the 1930s, the fact that the focus of *Dancing at Lughnasa* remains largely fixed on the family home, means that we are afforded very few insights into wider society at that time. In contrast, the class divisions in *Lies of Silence* are explored much more fully.
- Unlike *Lies of Silence*, violence is not a feature of the world of *Dancing at Lughnasa*.
- The world of *Dancing at Lughnasa* is unique in the sense that there is, what might be termed, a counterculture (in the form of the enduring popular attachment to such pre-Christian festivals as the Feast of Lughnasa) existing side-by-side with orthodox Catholic culture.
- There is a strong sense that the world of *Dancing at Lughnasa* is on the point of significant change.
- Ultimately, the world in which the Mundy sisters live seems to overwhelm them, its harshness ultimately breaking up the family and stealing much of the spirit and joy from their lives.

Il Postino

Unlike *Lies of Silence* and *Dancing at Lughnasa*, both of which are set in Ireland (although in different eras), *Il Postino* is set in Capri, an island off the coast of Naples, in the 1950s. Mario's world resembles that of the Mundy family in its remoteness and poverty. It also shares a number of other cultural features with both of the other comparative texts.

Similar to *Dancing at Lughnasa*, poverty is a prominent factor in the world of *Il Postino*. The opening scenes of the film bring the poor standard of living on the island into clear focus. Fishing is the main livelihood on the island, and fishermen have to literally work from dawn to dusk to make a meagre living. Much to his father's frustration, Mario is not suited to the life of a fisherman, regularly complaining of the 'damp boats'. Mario becomes animated only when he reads a postcard from some friends who have emigrated to America, and whose new life he clearly envies. The houses in the town are generally dilapidated. Mario's house is sparsely furnished and, like all of the other houses on the island, without running water. The local café in which Beatrice works for her aunt is dull and functional. There are no cars to be seen on the streets, with bicycles and donkeys the most popular forms of transport. Mario himself travels everywhere on his bicycle.

Illiteracy is very prevalent (widespread) on the island. Mario qualifies for the position of temporary postman because he can just about read and write and has a bicycle. Later we see that Beatrice's aunt cannot read what she assumes to be Mario's pornographic poems to her niece, and brings them to the priest to read them (the poems were in fact written by Pablo Neruda, a middle-class poet and writer from Chile).

The quality of Mario's family life is closer to that of the Mundys in *Dancing at Lughnasa* than that of the Dillons in *Lies of Silence*. While Mario seems to be less than happy living at home with his taciturn (uncommunicative) father, he is happy and contented when he marries Beatrice, the love of his life.

Similar to *Lies of Silence*, the world of *Il Postino* is marked by class divisions, although these social divisions are much deeper in the former text. Social divisions are not very pronounced in *Il Postino* because the majority of the local community consists of simple people struggling to wrest a living from the sea. However, we get an insight into the class divisions in wider society when Di Cosimo, the local politician, arrives on the island with his cigar-smoking entourage to canvas the votes of the local people. Di Cosimo's attitude towards the islanders is, at best, condescending. Of course, another (more important) visitor is Pablo Neruda. The elegant manner in which Neruda's house is furnished as well as his possession of the latest technology (a tape recorder) casts Mario's poverty into sharp relief (highlights his poverty by means of contrast).

As is the case in both *Lies of Silence* and *Dancing at Lughnasa*, *Il Postino* is set in a male-dominated world. While all three texts present us with strong female characters, such as Beatrice's aunt (a formidable woman) in this text, they are ultimately subordinate to men. Real power rests with the men in each world. The chief authority figures in *Il Postino* are the politician and the priest. The politician, Di Cosimo, is a contemptible figure, lacking in integrity and unscrupulous in his deception and manipulation of the local people. He promises the locals that he will personally ensure that a waterworks will be established on the island (up to this point water has been shipped out to the island once a month from the mainland) simply to garner the votes he needs to get elected. While Rosa is naively impressed with Di Cosimo's election pledges and spends money expanding and upgrading her cafe to cope with the expected increase in business when the additional workers would arrive on the island, the water project is again cynically shelved after Di Cosimo is elected. Rosa is powerless to do anything about Di Cosimo's lies, even though they have cost her a lot of money. Beatrice is a beautiful, sensuous young woman, whose chief dramatic purpose is to act as a source of inspiration for Mario's poetry. She is not developed in any meaningful way as a character. This is also the case with Neruda's wife, Mathilde, who is only seen in relation to her famous husband.

Religion plays an important role in the worlds of all three texts, but only in *Il Postino* is religion portrayed in a generally positive light. While religion is a cause of division in *Lies of Silence*, it brings the local people (who are very religious) together in *Il Postino* – they turn out en masse for the blessing of the fishing boats and for a religious pageant. They also accord the priest a position of respect at all important social occasions, such as Mario and Beatrice's wedding celebration. Interestingly, when the local priest objects to Neruda being Mario's witness (because he is a communist), Mario is prepared to defy him (suggesting that the priest, while respected, is not as powerful as his counterpart in *Dancing at Lughnasa*). A potentially serious conflict is circumvented by Neruda arriving in the church to pray.

The most important aspect of the cultural context where Mario's development is concerned is his friendship with Pablo Neruda, the renowned poet and communist writer from Chile, who, exiled from his homeland, spends some time in Capri. When the film opens, we get the impression that Mario is unhappy with his life. He is clearly not suited to being a fisherman and envies those friends of his who have emigrated to America. His innocence and simplicity are to be seen in his childish delight in wearing his postman's hat. The volume of post arriving on the island is very low because the bulk of the islanders are illiterate, but it increases dramatically when Neruda comes to live on Capri. Mario's sole task as a temporary postman is to deliver Neruda's post, and it is through this role that the two men gradually get to know each other. Mario's interest in Neruda is initially unrelated to his literary stature, springing instead from what Mario sees as Neruda's remarkable success with women ('Women go crazy for his poetry', he tells Giorgio). Mario wants Neruda to help him to write a poem that will win the heart of Beatrice, the love of his life. Neruda finally agrees and Mario not only wins Beatrice's heart, but embarks on his poetic education. We see this when he asks Neruda to explain the meaning of a metaphor. The contrast between the polished, middle-class Neruda and the initially awkward, self-conscious Mario is strikingly apparent. However, under Neruda's influence, Mario undergoes a dramatic personal transformation, developing into a more confident, more articulate character. Exposure to Neruda's communist beliefs makes Mario more conscious of class-based injustice and exploitation. He is angered by the sight of Di Cosimo's cronies looking to buy fish on the cheap from the local fishermen, and is unafraid of taking on the unprincipled, dishonest Di Cosimo in the café and exposing his promises as lies. Neruda plays a key role in helping Mario to discover and develop his hidden talent. When Neruda first asks Mario to speak into the tape recorder and describe something on the island that is beautiful, he can think of nothing. However, towards the close of the film, the first poem he composes reflects his appreciation of the island's natural beauty when he records such things as the sound of the waves gently lapping on the shore, the wind in the bushes, 'the sad nets belonging to my father' and the sound of Pablito's heartbeat in Beatrice's womb.

Only in *Il Postino* do we see a sense of camaraderie among the local people. This is vividly evident in the way they laugh loudly together when they see themselves in the newsreel, telling of Pablo Neruda's impending arrival on their island. One of the most appealing aspects of the world of this text is the support extended to Mario by Beatrice, Rosa and, particularly, Giorgio after Neruda is allowed to return home to Chile. Mario had innocently expected that Neruda would maintain some degree of contact with him (he had told Mario that he would write to him), but this does not happen. It is truly uplifting to see those closest to Mario gather round and support him in his unspoken disappointment, as together they follow Neruda's travels and speeches in the newspapers. Giorgio, the postmaster, also helps Mario to record the various sounds of the island in Mario's earliest artistic endeavour.

Mario dedicates this poem to Neruda. When Neruda finally returns to Capri, Beatrice gives him this recording after describing how Mario had met his death, adding to Neruda's sense of guilt by pointing out that Mario had insisted that their son be called Pablito (as another expression of his gratitude to his friend and mentor).

Mario's death is particularly tragic, because he dies in a violent crush after leaving his peaceful island home to deliver a poem dedicated to Pablo Neruda at a communist rally on the mainland. However, by the end of his short life he has already achieved a great deal. In contrast to the protagonists in both *Lies of Silence* and *Dancing at Lughnasa*, Mario rises above the limitations of the world into which he was born to discover and develop his poetic talent, while achieving personal happiness with Beatrice. Most remarkably, Mario grows to the point where he has the confidence to address a large political rally and read his own poem as a further expression of his gratitude to the man who had played such a significant role in his personal development.

KEY POINTS OF COMPARISON
Lies of Silence, Dancing at Lughnasa and *Il Postino*

- Both *Lies of Silence* and *Dancing at Lughnasa* are set in Ireland (although in different eras), while *Il Postino* is located on the island of Capri, off the coast of Naples.
- While family life in both *Dancing at Lughnasa* and *Il Postino* is generally stable and loving, family life in *Lies of Silence* is strained and problematic.
- Poverty is a feature of the worlds of all three texts, having a direct and significant impact on the quality of the protagonists' lives in both *Dancing at Lughnasa* and *Il Postino*.

- All three texts are set in male-dominated societies. Women's inferior status to men is particularly marked in *Dancing at Lughnasa* because it is set in rural Ireland in the 1930s.
- Religion is a key feature of the worlds of all three texts, but only in *Il Postino* is it portrayed in a generally positive light.
- Social divisions are a feature of the worlds of all three texts, particularly *Lies of Silence* where the divisions are both religious/political and class-based. While both of the other texts are set in class-divided worlds, class division is not a major issue in either *Dancing at Lughnasa* or *Il Postino*.
- Only in *Lies of Silence* are conflict and violence significant aspects of everyday life. While Mario dies a victim of random violence on the mainland, life on Capri is peaceful.
- Only in *Il Postino* do we see a genuine sense of camaraderie among the local people. We see this most memorably in Giorgio's unstinting support for Mario after Neruda leaves the island and fails to maintain contact with him.
- Only in *Dancing at Lughnasa* do we encounter a world where an earlier, pre-Christian culture survives alongside the culture of the era in which the text is set.
- It is also only in *Dancing at Lughnasa* that we sense a world on the brink of significant change.
- Unlike the protagonists in both of the other comparative texts, Mario in *Il Postino* rises above the difficulties and limitations of the world into which he was born to realise his potential and achieve personal happiness with Beatrice.

B. General Vision and Viewpoint

Lies of Silence

The general vision or viewpoint relates to the authorial/directorial outlook on life. This viewpoint inevitably influences our perspective on the text and on the world in which it is set. The vision of an author can be conveyed through the manner in which the plot opens, develops and ends, through key characters and relationships, through the type of society in which the text is located and also through language and imagery. Often, the dominant viewpoint of a text can be reflected in a key moment.

Lies of Silence is set in Northern Ireland, in a bitterly divided society dominated by an age-old political/religious conflict. While the text is not without moments of light, the viewpoint it offers is largely dark and grim, with the violence associated with this ancient tribal feud ultimately claiming the life of the central character, Michael Dillon.

The gloomy manner in which this text opens sets the tone for the generally pessimistic novel that follows. In the opening pages of the novel, Michael is depressed by the familiar sight of armed policemen jumping out of an armoured car. The image of their revolvers 'cowboy-low on their thighs' suggests the idea of a lawless 'Wild West' type of society. Michael feels strangely dejected by the sight of the policemen cautiously crossing the street: 'Tonight, this familiar sight depressed him. Why should he stay, why should anyone in their senses stay here?'

The quality and outcome of the key relationships in the text varies (Michael and Andrea are briefly happy), but, overall, adds to the pervasive sense of gloom. When the text opens, it is already apparent that Michael's marriage to Moira is effectively over, with Michael already involved with another woman named Andrea, a young Canadian journalist. While Michael plans to leave Moira, he has not told her at this point: 'He was married and hiding their affair from his wife'. While Andrea pressures him to be truthful with Moira, **Michael, lacking in moral courage, postpones telling his wife that their marriage is over. He had married Moira for the wrong reasons.** He liked the idea of other men envying him his beautiful wife: 'She was tall, beautiful and very flirtatious.' Moira struggled with bulimia ever before she married Dillon, and the problem recurs whenever she feels anxious or depressed. She quickly perceives Michael's loss of interest in her: 'You're bored with me, you married me because you fancied me and now I've lost my looks, you couldn't care less about me.' Shortly after this observation, Michael kisses Moira 'a traitor's kiss'. As the text unfolds, Michael realises that his love for Moira 'had not been love, but a form of self-deceit'. **When he eventually builds himself up to tell Moira that he is leaving her, she is not entirely surprised, having already seen him holding hands with Andrea.**

Shortly afterwards, Moira does a television interview in which she strongly denounces the IRA. While Moira's defiance of the IRA is undoubtedly courageous, it inevitably places her in some danger. More significantly, from Michael's viewpoint, she lets slip to a journalist the fact that Michael had seen one of the gunmen, a revelation that would ultimately lead to his assassination.

The portrayal of society is dominated by the deep-rooted and violent sectarian conflict that envelops the world of the text in a sense of darkness and gloom. Inevitably, this sectarianism is to be found on both sides of the religious divide. Michael speaks of 'priests whose sectarian views perfectly propagated the divisive bitterness' at the heart of the Northern conflict, while describing the Orange Order as 'that fount of Protestant prejudice against the third of Ulster's people who are Catholics.' **What is particularly depressing is that the two religious figures that are specifically mentioned are themselves immersed in sectarian politics:** the Reverend Alun Pottinger is a leading member of the dogmatically anti-Catholic Orange Order and delivers 'sermons of religious hatred', while Father Connolly is directly linked with the IRA and is portrayed as an apologist for their activities.

Poverty is another dispiriting aspect of the society in which the text is located. High levels of unemployment intensify competition for jobs, with the corollary (natural consequence) being a heightening of sectarian tensions. It is the working classes on both sides of the religious divide who are portrayed as being the most vehemently sectarian. The text presents us with the disheartening image of 'graffiti-fouled barricaded slums where the city's Protestant and Catholic poor confronted each other, year in and year out, in a stasis of hatred, fear and mistrust'. Dillon would seem to be expressing the authorial viewpoint when he expresses his anger at the 'lies told to poor Protestant working people about the Catholics, lies told to poor Catholic working people about the Protestants, lies from parliaments and pulpits, lies at rallies and funeral orations, and, above all, lies of silence from those in Westminster who did not want to face the injustices of Ulster's status quo'. **The idea of ordinary working people being the victims of both their political and religious leaders who perpetuate religious enmities in their own selfish interests is both disturbing and depressing.**

At first it seems that the text is going to conclude in a bright, optimistic manner. Once Michael and Andrea have 'escaped' to London, he experiences a new sense of happiness in both his personal and professional lives. At the end of one particularly joyful day with Andrea, Michael 'wanted to say to her that he had never been so happy, that today was the happiest day in his whole life'. Professionally, Michael had been unhappy for some time, but the prospect of managing the Wellington Hotel in London rekindles his enthusiasm for the only business he truly knows: 'Was this the turning point he had so often dreamed of, the end of useless daydreams, of nostalgia for his student days, of that failed hope of writing poetry . . .?' The positive mood continues with Michael and Moira speaking to each other in a caring manner, with each expressing concern for the other's safety. Following an intense internal debate, Michael decides that he will not risk his life by testifying against the IRA man whose face he had seen. Tragically, the happy ending that (however unlikely) seems to be in the offing fails to materialise, with Michael's change of heart coming too late to save him from the assassins dispatched to silence him. **At the close of the text, the world of the novel is enveloped in a sense of darkness, gloom and pessimism.**

KEY POINTS

- *Lies of Silence* presents us with a vision of life that is largely dark and gloomy.
- The manner in which this text opens immediately conveys a sense of despondency.
- The quality and outcome of the key relationships varies, but, overall, heightens the sense of pessimism that pervades the text.
- The vision of society is particularly grim.
- The end of the novel is realistic, but utterly depressing nonetheless.

Dancing at Lughnasa

Similar to _Lies of Silence_, _Dancing at Lughnasa_ presents us with a vision of life that is essentially dark and depressing. However, few texts are entirely pessimistic, and in _Dancing at Lughnasa_ there are moments of light and laughter that briefly lift the general air of despondency.

In contrast to the dark manner in which _Lies of Silence_ opens, this text begins on a nostalgic note as Michael (who is both narrator and character) **recalls the summer of 1936. A number of significant events that held out the prospect of happiness are mentioned.** The Mundy family acquires their first wireless set that summer, calling it Marconi. The wireless provides the family with music and, in Michael's words, 'it obsessed us'. Father Jack, the only brother of the five Mundy sisters, returns from the missions in Uganda where he had worked for twenty-five years in a leper colony. Finally, Michael's father, Gerry, appears twice that summer to visit Michael and his mother, Chris. All of these significant events occur against the backdrop of the annual Festival of Lughnasa, a pre-Christian celebration of the harvest that is associated with excessive drinking and wild, unrestrained dancing in the Black Hills.

The vision of family life combines negative and positive features. The Mundy sisters have to contend with a range of problems associated with poverty. The house furnishings are described as 'austere', while the clothes the sisters wear 'reflect their lean circumstances'. References to 'three eggs' and 'two tomatoes' further highlight their straitened (impoverished) circumstances. They also have to cope with the embarrassment of Father Jack's strange transformation – he appears to

have 'gone native' during his twenty-five years abroad as a missionary, regularly speaking of various pagan rituals, while studiously avoiding the subject of Mass. The 'leper priest' who had once been such a great source of pride for the family becomes a source of embarrassment. It is Father Jack's bizarre behaviour that causes the vindictive parish priest to sack Kate from her position in the local primary school, leaving the already poor Mundy family without its only wage earner. Gerry, Michael's father, occasionally visits Chris, but, utterly irresponsible, contributes nothing to the family budget. **All of these factors convey a sense of gloom, but the manner in which the family responds to adversity helps to counter the gloom to some extent.**

The key relationships in this text are, for the most part, within the family (the notable exception being Chris' relationship with Gerry). Notwithstanding their occasional and inevitable disagreements, the Mundy family is closely united. In sharp contrast to the negativity associated with family life in _Lies of Silence_, the love and togetherness of the Mundy family is one of the most positive aspects of _Dancing at Lughnasa_. Poverty does not break the family's spirit, epitomised by Maggie's wonderful wit. Her response to having to prepare a meal for the family with only three eggs typifies her uplifting sense of humour: 'Not a great larder, but a nice challenge to someone like myself. Right. My suggestion is . . . Eggs Ballybeg . . .' While Michael's arrival would have been a source of embarrassment in small-town Ireland at that time, the young boy is cherished by all of the sisters. Their love for him is such that he has effectively got five mothers rather than one. Rose is described as 'simple', but is never treated in any way differently – on the contrary, she is greatly loved and shares a special bond with Agnes. Father Jack is the unwitting cause of Kate losing her job, but is always treated with great care and respect by his sisters. While the pagan rituals he regularly speaks of are embarrassing to Kate, they suggest a joyful, expressive, life-affirming type of religion: 'And then we dance – and dance – and dance – children, men, women, most of them lepers, many of them with misshapen limbs, with missing limbs – dancing, believe it or not, for days on end! It's the most wonderful sight you have ever seen!' While Kate admits to being frightened by the dramatic change in Jack ('Completely changed. He's not our Jack at all.'), Maggie again brings a smile to our faces with another humorous remark: 'A clatter of lepers trying to do the Military Two-Step.' Earlier she had wittily feigned shock at learning that Okawa (which the confused Jack often called Maggie) was the name of Jack's house boy in Uganda: 'Damnit. I thought it was Swahili for gorgeous.' Notwithstanding his lack of any sense of responsibility towards his son Michael, Gerry's arrival lifts the mood of the Mundy household. Chris is keenly aware of Gerry's failings, but is still delighted to see him. Maggie observes that Chris 'laughs all the time with him', while even Kate, watching Chris dance with Gerry, remarks, 'Her whole face alters when she's happy, doesn't it?' With his walking stick, straw hat, and talk of distant places, Gerry is a colourful presence in a world of dull routine. All of the sisters are transfixed by the sight of Chris and Gerry dancing together.

Perhaps the darkest aspect of this text's vision of society is the repression of women. In contrast to the wealth of social opportunities and the sexual liberation enjoyed by the female characters in *Lies of Silence*, the Mundy sisters have no social outlets and, as Kate always reminds them, are of an age when going to dances **(such as those that take place during the Festival of Lughnasa) would be frowned upon. This is, of course, a realistic portrayal of Irish society in the 1930s, when the Catholic Church, whose authority was beyond challenge, dictated a deeply conservative and restrictive morality, particularly in matters relating to male-female relationships.** The effects of living in a world where, as women on the brink of middle age, they are deemed to be too old for romance, love and marriage, leads to considerable frustration on the part of all the sisters as they crave emotional (and possibly sexual) fulfilment. Chris cannot hide her delight at seeing Gerry, although she knows he has no intention of remaining with her. It seems that Agnes is also attracted to Gerry, and may even be in love with him. Agnes is prepared to spend the five pounds she has saved on bringing her sisters to the festival dance: 'And I don't care how young they are, how drunk and dirty and sweaty they are. I want to dance, Kate. It's the Festival of Lughnasa. I'm only thirty-five. I want to dance.' Rose is infatuated with Danny Bradley, a married man whose wife has left him and gone to England. Maggie speaks of Brian McGuinness, a young man she 'was keen on' when she was a teenager. We can see Maggie's personal frustration through her humour: 'Wonderful Wild Woodbine. Next best thing to a wonderful, wild man.' Even Kate appears to harbour a romantic interest in Austen Morgan, the local shopkeeper who ultimately marries 'a wee young thing from Carrickfad.' Sadly, the sisters do not go to the festival dance in the black hills. After a moment's hesitation, Kate, ever conscious of the family's image, tells them that they cannot go: 'Do you want the whole countryside to be laughing at us? – mature women, *dancing*?'

The Mundy sisters' frustration with and

desire to defy the restrictions of society's strict moral code can be seen in the wonderfully uplifting dance they perform around the house. The dance is spontaneous and joyful. It starts as the sound of Irish dance music ('The Mason's Apron', performed by a céilí band) on the wireless gradually increases in volume. It is Maggie who is the first to dance as, 'animated by a look of defiance, of aggression', she 'emits a raucous *Yaaaah!*' and throws herself into a wild dance with total abandon. She invites her sisters to join her and, within a few seconds, Rose, Agnes and Chris begin to dance and soon they are all 'doing a dance that is almost recognisable'. While Kate initially remonstrates with the others, she soon joins them, leaping to her feet, throwing her head back and emitting a loud 'Yaaaah!' Kate dances alone, as her movement 'simultaneously controlled and frantic' takes her quickly around the kitchen and out into the garden. Kate's dancing is described as being 'out of character and at the same time ominous of some deep and true emotion'. The sisters' dancing suggests 'a sense of order being deliberately subverted'. While the sisters are described as looking 'slightly ashamed' when the dance ends, it is significant that they are also said to look 'slightly defiant'. **This truly joyous scene is the most inspiring moment in the entire play, dramatically highlighting the resilience of the family's spirit in a harsh and oppressive world. There is no scene comparable to this in** *Lies of Silence*.

Similar to *Lies of Silence*, **society in this text is depicted in an essentially negative manner.** Poverty is a feature of the worlds of both texts, but this poverty impacts in a far more dramatic manner on the lives of the protagonists in *Dancing at Lughnasa*. Indeed, just as violence blights the lives of the protagonists in *Lies of Silence*, so does financial hardship afflict the lives of the Mundy family. In both texts the church is portrayed in an unsympathetic light, with the priest in Ballybeg comparable to the Reverend Alun Pottinger and Father Connolly in his unchristian behaviour. In neither text do women enjoy full equality with men, but this inequality is far more pronounced in *Dancing at Lughnasa* because of the era in which it is set.

As in *Lies of Silence*, **the manner in which** *Dancing at Lughnasa* **ends underscores the generally negative outlook of the text.** After a knitting factory is established in Ballybeg, Agnes and Rose lose their part-time jobs as home knitters. Shortly afterwards they leave for England and are never seen again, despite the family's exhaustive efforts to locate them. When Michael finally tracks them down in London twenty-five years later, he learns that the inseparable sisters had worked as cleaners, ultimately ending up on the streets when Rose could no longer find work and Agnes could not support them both. They had ended up sleeping on the streets, sustaining themselves with what alcohol they could afford. Michael informs us that Agnes had died of exposure, while Rose died shortly after he finds her in a grim hospice. Jack dies within a year of returning home, leaving Kate in particular 'inconsolable' for months. Gerry departs for the civil war in Spain and thereafter his visits became increasingly infrequent until they eventually stop entirely. Later, in the mid-fifties, Michael receives a letter from a young man of his own age in Wales who had found his name and address among his father's personal belongings. The revelation that Gerry had been leading a double life for so many years heightens the sense of gloom at the close of the text, underlining the insincerity of his routine proposals of marriage to Chris and further highlighting the shallowness and selfishness of his character.

However, unlike *Lies of Silence*, the ending of *Dancing at Lughnasa* is not entirely bleak and pessimistic. The memory that continues to linger in Michael's memory is of his mother and aunts dancing around the house. The sisters' dancing is suggestive of their enduring joy in life, their resilient spirit, their ability to transcend their many problems and their defiance of the repressive society in which they live: 'Dancing as if the very heart of life and all its hopes might be found in those assuaging notes and those hushed rhythms and in those silent and hypnotic movements. Dancing as if language no longer existed because words were no longer necessary . . .'

KEY POINTS OF COMPARISON
Lies of Silence and *Dancing at Lughnasa*

- Both texts present us with largely dark visions of life, but there is more light and laughter in *Dancing at Lughnasa*.
- In contrast to *Lies of Silence* which opens on a gloomy note, *Dancing at Lughnasa* begins with a sense of nostalgia as Michael recalls the summer of 1936.
- Family life in *Dancing at Lughnasa* is presented in a much more positive light than in *Lies of Silence*.
- Key relationships are portrayed in a more optimistic light in *Dancing at Lughnasa* (where the key relationships are mainly within the family) than in *Lies of Silence*.
- The societies in which both texts are set are presented in a grim light, with the portrayal of religion (or, more particularly, its representatives) being extremely negative.
- In both *Lies of Silence* and *Dancing at Lughnasa* one key factor is at the root of the despondent atmosphere that pervades both texts: just as sectarian violence blights the lives of the protagonists in *Lies of Silence*, so does poverty afflict the lives of the Mundy family.
- Both texts end in a depressing manner, but the ending to *Dancing at Lughnasa* is not entirely pessimistic, as the memory that dominates Michael's memory is that of his mother and aunts dancing around the house in an uplifting act of joy and defiance.

Il Postino

In contrast to both of the other comparative texts, the overall vision of Il Postino is optimistic. While the protagonists in both *Lies of Silence* and *Dancing at Lughnasa* are ultimately overwhelmed by the harsh worlds in which they live, Mario rises above the difficulties and limitations of his world to realise his potential and achieve personal happiness.

Similar to Lies of Silence, this text opens in a rather gloomy manner with Mario struggling to communicate with his taciturn father. The relationship between father and son is obviously strained. When Mario shows his father a postcard from America and speaks at some length about friends of his who have gone there, his visibly frustrated father tells him to get a job, reminding him that he's 'not a child any more'. Mario's father, like most of the men on the island, earns a meagre living as a fisherman. Similar to the home of the Mundy family in *Dancing at Lughnasa*, the sparsely furnished house in which Mario and his father live is a reflection of their impoverished circumstances; to make matters worse, they have just run out of water when his father goes to wash his hands.

Family life in Il Postino resembles that in Dancing at Lughnasa more than Lies of Silence. While family life is strained and problematical when Mario is living with his reticent father, the quality of his family life improves dramatically after he marries Beatrice, the love of his life. When Beatrice becomes pregnant, there is a wonderful sense of joy, with the image of Mario listening to the sound of his baby's heartbeat being particularly uplifting.

In sharp contrast to Lies of Silence, the key relationships in Il Postino are depicted in a very positive light. **The most important relationship in the text is that between Mario and Pablo Neruda, the Chilean poet and communist who, exiled from his homeland, spends some time in Capri.** At first the relationship between Mario and Neruda is detached, but the two gradually grow close after Mario (acutely aware of Neruda's reputation as a ladies' man and of the number of letters he receives from women) asks the renowned poet to help him win the heart of Beatrice, a beautiful young woman, who works for her aunt Rosa in the local café. Reciting lines from Neruda's poems helps Mario to win Beatrice's love. When Neruda asks him about this, Mario's response reveals a sharp understanding of the nature of poetry: '. . . poetry doesn't belong to those who write it, but to those who need it.' More than that, reading Neruda's work sparks Mario's interest in poetry and he discusses the art of poetry with his new mentor in Neruda's home and on the beach, beginning with a discussion of metaphors. He tells Neruda that he can personally relate to one of his lines, 'I am tired of being a man'. When Mario asks Beatrice to marry him, he asks Neruda (as a gesture of his gratitude to him) to be his best man. Mario is also influenced by Neruda's communist philosophy, becoming keenly conscious of social injustices. Most significantly, Mario grows in confidence through his relationship with Neruda, who is both his friend and mentor. We see a new, confident and assertive Mario as he takes issue with members of a local politician's entourage who are trying to buy fish cheaply from local fishermen. While we are impressed with Mario's personal development, the fishermen are clearly angry at his intervention! Mario also challenges Di Cosimo. The cynical politician promised before the elections that waterworks would be constructed on the island, but now announces that the project is to be postponed. Mario is sad when Neruda leaves the island, and is understandably dejected when he fails to maintain contact with him. However, Neruda's impact on Mario's personal growth is considerable as we see Mario write his own poetry. He uses Neruda's tape recorder to record the wondrous and inspiring sounds of the island. He also writes a poem dedicated to Pablo Neruda, and is invited to read this poem at a large communist rally on the mainland. It is a measure of Mario's impressive personal development that he is prepared to address such a large gathering and read his poem.

The other important relationships in Mario's life are similarly portrayed in a very optimistic manner. Mario achieves personal happiness when he marries the beautiful Beatrice. Beatrice clearly loves him and is certainly impressed with his poetic achievements. Both his father and Rosa (Beatrice's aunt who initially had little time for 'a man whose only capital is the fungus between his toes') come to respect Mario. Another uplifting relationship is that between Mario and Giorgio, the postmaster. It is these friends who support Mario following Neruda's failure to stay in contact with his protégé, helping Mario to trace Neruda's travels through newspaper cuttings. Giorgio also helps Mario to record the sounds of the island as part of his first poem. The wonderful support network that Mario enjoys reminds us of the closeness and supportive nature of the Mundy family in *Dancing at Lughnasa*.

Similar to both *Lies of Silence* and *Dancing at Lughnasa*, the society in which this text is set is, in some respects, rather depressing. Once again we see a world of dispiriting poverty and few opportunities, a world where the cynical cigar-smoking politician, Di Cosimo and even the sophisticated Pablo Neruda visibly differ from the local community because of their relative wealth. As in both *Lies of Silence* and *Dancing at Lughnasa* this text is set in a patriarchal society where the authority figures (the politician, Di Cosimo, and the priest) are both male.

While Mario's death may suggest that *Il Postino* ends on a gloomy note, this tragic, but random, event does not significantly detract from the optimism created by all that he has achieved in his life before his tragic death. In contrast to the protagonists in both of the other comparative texts, who (notwithstanding the enduring spirit of the Mundy sisters epitomised by their joyful, defiant dance) are ultimately crushed by the harshness of the worlds in which they live, **Mario rises above the constraints and problems of his world to realise his potential and achieve personal happiness with Beatrice.**

It could be argued that the absence of a 'happy ever after' ending grounds the uplifting tale of Mario's personal development in the often harsh and painful reality of life. Other factors also give this essentially optimistic text a sense of realism, such as Neruda's failure to keep in contact with Mario and the fact that Mario never saw his son Pablito (the name representing another expression of his respect for, and gratitude to, Neruda). Also, we can see Beatrice's understandable, but controlled, anger at these happenings when Neruda and his wife finally return to Capri after a five-year absence. The image of Neruda alone on the beach reminds us of his earlier conversations with Mario on this beach – conversations that set Mario on the road to writing his own poems. Sadly, Mario had only begun to realise his potential when he met his untimely death. However, the manner in which he rose above the limitations of the society in which he lived to achieve all that he did cannot but inspire the audience.

KEY POINTS OF COMPARISON
Lies of Silence, Dancing at Lughnasa and *Il Postino*

- While the overall visions of life in both *Lies of Silence* and *Dancing at Lughnasa* are largely pessimistic, the outlook on life in *Il Postino* is essentially optimistic.
- Both *Lies of Silence* and *Il Postino* open in a gloomy manner, while *Dancing at Lughnasa* begins with a sense of nostalgia.
- In contrast to *Lies of Silence*, family life in both *Dancing at Lughnasa* and *Il Postino* is portrayed in a generally positive manner.
- Similar to *Dancing at Lughnasa* (where the key relationships are generally within the family), but in contrast to *Lies of Silence*, the key relationships in *Il Postino* are portrayed in a very positive light.
- The societies in which all three texts are set share some rather depressing features, with poverty, for example, impacting in a very real way on the lives of the protagonists in both *Dancing at Lughnasa* and *Il Postino*.
- While Mario's random death obviously means that *Il Postino* does not conclude in an entirely optimistic manner, it is a realistic reminder of the harshness of life where 'happy ever after' endings are rare. Yet Mario's untimely death does not significantly detract from the overall sense of optimism conveyed by the text. In contrast, both of the other comparative texts, particularly *Lies of Silence*, conclude in a pessimistic manner.

C. Literary Genre

Lies of Silence

Literary genre focuses on the ways that texts tell their stories. While novelists, playwrights and film directors all employ some narrative techniques distinctive to their own particular art, there are also many similarities between the narrative methods they use. *Lies of Silence*, a novel which belongs to the thriller genre, is set in Northern Ireland in the 1980s when 'The Troubles' were at their peak and paramilitary violence was endemic in Ulster. The author, Brian Moore employs a variety of techniques to tell his story.

The opening lines of the novel indicate that this is a third person narrative: 'At a quarter to nine, just before going off work, Dillon went down to reception to check the staff roster for tomorrow.' Again, we see the third person narration in the closing lines of the novel: 'They raised their revolvers. They were not wearing masks. This time, there would be no witnesses.' A third person narrative implies that the story is told by an omniscient (all-knowing) narrator. **However, it is quickly apparent that we view much of the unfolding action through the eyes of Michael Dillon.** As he observes a police armoured car approach him and soldiers emerge from it, with 'their revolvers cowboy-low on their thighs', he feels depressed by this everyday sight: 'Why should he stay, why should anyone in their senses stay here?' When we are viewing events through Dillon's eyes, Brian Moore writes in the present tense, giving Dillon's thoughts a sense of immediacy. There are occasions when the text reads as if it were Dillon's stream of consciousness. This technique enables the author to bring home to the reader the depth of Dillon's plight after the IRA place him in a moral dilemma – a classic 'Catch 22', no-win situation. For example, as Dillon passes his old Catholic boarding school, driving towards the Clarence Hotel with a bomb in his car while Moira is being held hostage by the IRA, the narrative reads as if it were Dillon thinking aloud: 'Look at me, look at me . . . See this car on its way to kill innocent people, see my wife in a room with a gun at her head, and then ask your Cardinal if he can still say of these killers that he can see their point of view.' Later, after Moira informs him that she has spoken to a solicitor about a divorce and tells him of her intention 'to do something about the IRA', the narrative again reads like Dillon's thoughts: 'It's spite, it's getting back at me, it's an effort to make herself into a heroine, with me, the cowardly husband, slinking off to England with his girlfriend.' **Despite much of the action being described as if we were looking through Dillon's eyes, we do not always sympathise with him.** For example, his continual procrastination over when to tell Moira that he is leaving her does not impress the reader. After Moira pleads with him not to leave her, we are told that Dillon 'kissed her, a traitor's kiss'. Dillon's lack of moral courage and indecision is again to be seen after Moira arrives unexpectedly at the hotel and sees him holding hands with Andrea: 'It was the moment to tell her, but he knew he could not do it.'

Dialogue is a key element in the telling of this story: it advances the plot, builds up tension and contributes to the creation and development of characters. Dialogue brings characters and situations to life. Throughout the text, the dialogue is never less than powerful and convincing. The early conversations between Dillon and Moira point to a strained relationship on the point of breakdown. Moira perceives that Dillon has lost interest in her: 'You're bored with me, you married me because you fancied me, and now I've lost my looks you couldn't care less about me.' Moira's exchanges with her IRA captors reveal a stronger, defiant side to her character. After deliberately provoking one IRA man by insulting him, his response reminds us that social divisions in Northern Ireland are based on class as well as religion: 'Cheeky, aren't ye? You stuck up wee bourgeois bitch.' This conversation heightens the sense of tension, while the expletive adds to the realism of the scene. The use of dialect further increases the sense of realism. One such example is when one IRA man warns Dillon that the volunteers guarding Moira 'will do a nut job on her' if he does not co-operate with them. Interestingly, when Moira is arguing with the IRA man, her accent changes, so that 'she now spoke in the flat Belfast tones of the gunman himself' (of course, Moira herself was born into a working class family on the Falls Road). Moira refuses to be cowed by the intruders: 'You're just a bunch of crooks, IRA or UDA, Protestants or Catholics, you're all in the same business. Racketeers, the bunch of you.' In this scene, dialogue intensifies the tense atmosphere. After Moira has excoriated (vehemently denounced) the IRA, she is threatened in a very direct manner, with one IRA man coldly warning her, 'Shut your mouth, or I'll shut it for you.' Dialogue also plays an important role in developing the plot. Andrea urges Dillon not to identify Kev (one of the IRA men who had taken over his house) who had been picked up by the police: 'If you identify this Kev, it will be like putting out a contract on your own life.' When Father Connolly warns

Dillon that his life will be in danger if he testifies against Kev ('Let's not have any more killing, Mike'), Dillon is outraged: 'But if I don't testify against your nephew and his friends, I'll be letting them go free to do more killing, won't I?' The reader now fears that, with this defiant response, Dillon has indeed signed his own death warrant.

The narrative structure of *Lies of Silence* is linear, with the story being told in a chronological manner. There is a very strong sense of story with the narrative driving on to the dramatic conclusion. The plot is compelling and, charged with tension, grips and holds the attention of the reader from beginning to end. The main source of tension in the novel is the response of the protagonists (Michael and Moira Dillon) to the dramatic disruption of their lives by the IRA. A second source of tension relates to Michael's personal life: he had been having an affair with a young Canadian journalist named Andrea for a number of months and hiding this affair from his wife. When IRA men take over their home, Michael, in addition to fearing for his life, curses his failure to tell Moira about his affair with Andrea and of his intention of leaving her: 'But how could he turn around tomorrow and tell her, after what had happened tonight? When the IRA order Dillon to drive to the Clarence Hotel with a bomb in his car, warning him that his wife will be killed if he fails to co-operate, he finds himself in a nightmarish moral dilemma. When Dillon reaches the hotel car park, he realises that the IRA are not targeting the hotel, but planning to assassinate the Reverend Alun Pottinger. Sharply aware of the number of innocent people that would be killed if the bomb in his car was detonated, Dillon dashes into a shop, hoping that the IRA volunteer following him does not see him, and dials 999. Fortunately, the IRA did not deliver

on their threat to kill Moira (having left the house long before Dillon's dramatic action) but that does not detract from the painful sense of betrayal Moira feels at Dillon's decision to call in the police and endanger her life. With their lives already in danger, Moira exacerbates (worsens) the situation by doing television interviews and by letting it slip to a newspaper journalist that Michael had seen one of the IRA men. Shortly afterwards, Dillon receives an anonymous phone call from an IRA man who threatens to kill both Moira and Michael. From this point on the tension relentlessly mounts until the dramatic conclusion. The tensions in the text are eventually resolved, but in a tragic manner as the IRA ultimately silence Dillon by sending assassins to kill him in London.

After the plot, the most important aspect of a story is the quality of the characterisation. The characters in *Lies of Silence* come across to the reader as entirely credible flesh-and-blood individuals who, in their complexity, are never less than convincing. While we sympathise with Michael Dillon (particularly in the unenviable moral dilemma in which he finds himself), because we see so much of the action through his eyes, we do not always admire him. Certainly his deception of Moira over a number of months and his endless procrastination over when to tell her that he is leaving her leave us feeling very unimpressed with both his lack of integrity and moral cowardice. While Moira initially seems to be a rather weak, needy character, preoccupied with her appearance, her defiance of the IRA shows great courage and strength of character. Even the minor characters are depicted in an entirely believable manner. The IRA men are not portrayed in a uniform, stereotypical manner, but instead come across as distinct individuals – while Kev is portrayed as excitable and aggressive, the unnamed fat guard appears to be more humane and the tall gunman coldly ruthless and menacing.

The use of vivid imagery and detailed description help the reader to visualise and imaginatively engage with the unfolding action. The image of the soldiers with their revolvers 'cowboy-low on their thighs' conjures up a world of 'Wild West'-type violence and lawlessness. The image of 'graffiti-fouled barricaded slums' conveys the siege mentality of communities riven (torn apart) by age-old tribal hatred. Perhaps the most powerful image is that evoked by the title, with 'lies of silence' suggestive of the cold indifference of British governments towards the injustices perpetrated against Ulster's Catholics. The scene where the IRA enter the Dillon home is described in graphic detail to powerfully convey a sense of threat and fear: 'Behind the disguise of his paramilitary pullover and hooded menacing headmask, the high-pitched voice and adolescent body proclaimed that this was a child with a gun, excited as a child is when suddenly the game becomes dangerous.' The description of one gunman staring at Moira in an overtly sexual manner is chilling: 'Blinking his small eyes, he stared her up and down, from her sandalled feet to her long bare legs, her slender body, her pale face, her long, dark, tumbled hair.'

***Lies of Silence* ends in a tragic but realistic manner.** After telling Father Connolly of his determination to identify Kev, the young gunman whose face he had seen, the IRA godfathers do not hesitate to order his assassination. Ironically, Michael Dillon had been happier than he has ever been the day before his killers arrived. Truly contented with both his personal and professional lives, he had changed his mind about testifying against the young IRA man. Tragically, his change of heart came too late to save his life.

KEY POINTS

- In terms of its genre, *Lies of Silence* is a thriller.
- This novel is set in Northern Ireland in the 1980s when violence and the threat of violence hung like a dark shadow over Ulster.
- This story is a third person narrative, although the reader sees much of the action through the eyes of Michael Dillon.
- Dialogue is very important to the telling of this story, helping to advance the plot, create characters and build up tension.
- The story is told in a linear, chronological manner.
- The plot is powerful and compelling, immediately engaging the interest of the reader and holding it until its dramatic conclusion.
- The characters are complex and entirely credible.
- The author makes very effective use of vivid imagery and detailed description to enable the reader to visualise and imaginatively engage with the unfolding action.
- The novel concludes in a tragic, but realistic, manner.

Dancing at Lughnasa

This play by Brian Friel is set in Ballybeg, a fictional village in County Donegal in the 1930s. If we are to categorise this play in terms of genre, it belongs to the genre of social realism as it realistically portrays the lives of the Mundy family and their struggle to survive in a harsh and oppressive world. Like Brian Moore, Brian Friel employs a range of literary techniques to deliver his story. For every playwright, dialogue is clearly central to creating characters, illustrating developing relationships and advancing the plot. A play is essentially a visual experience, and stage instructions help the reader to visualise the action and better understand the characters. In this play Friel also makes effective use of a narrator and flashbacks, as well as employing such non-verbal means of communication as music, dance and tableau (i.e. a pause in a scene when all of the characters briefly freeze in position). While the dramatist and novelist use some similar methods to tell their stories, the art of the dramatist gives Friel some additional options in terms of how he communicates his tale.

As a third person narrative, the authorial voice in *Lies of Silence* is balanced and objective. This sense of balance and objectivity is also to be seen in *Dancing at Lughnasa* where it is achieved by the variety of viewpoints the different characters in the play express. For example, we see how Kate's view of going to the harvest dance differs from that of her sisters. While the others, particularly Agnes, are desperate to participate in the wild, uninhibited dancing at the harvest dance ('. . . I don't care how young they are, how drunk and sweaty and dirty they are. I want to dance. It's the Festival of Lughnasa. I'm only thirty-five. I want to dance.'), Kate remains the

voice of convention ('Do you want the whole countryside to be laughing at us? – women of our years? – mature women, dancing?')

Obviously, *Dancing at Lughnasa* differs from *Lies of Silence* in its use of a narrator. This play begins and ends with a monologue delivered by the narrator, Michael, who is also a character in the play. Michael recalls the summer of 1936, zooming in on a number of events in particular: the Mundy family's acquisition of their first wireless (which was named Marconi), the arrival home from Africa of the sisters' only brother, Father Jack, and the two visits paid to his family home by Gerry Evans, his father. These events form the basis of the play's narrative. Michael's memories are both joyful and sad: he recollects 'the sheer magic of that radio' and his mother and her sisters 'suddenly catching hands and dancing a spontaneous step-dance and laughing – screaming! – like excited schoolgirls'. He also remembers Father Jack 'shuffling from room to room as if he were searching for something but couldn't remember what'. Interestingly, Michael's opening speech conveys the disquiet he felt as a seven-year-old boy in 1936: 'I had a sense of unease . . . of things changing too quickly before my eyes, of becoming what they ought not to be.'

The use of stage directions is obviously a narrative technique unique to plays. Stage instructions are the only occasions when the voice of the playwright is directly heard. Friel's stage directions are very detailed and are central to conveying the play's distinctive atmosphere. Stage instructions suggest the dull, mundane nature of the Mundy sisters' lives as they go about their daily chores: 'Maggie makes a mash for hens. Agnes knits gloves. Rose carries a basket of turf into the kitchen . . . Chris irons at the kitchen table.' Stage directions point up the poverty of the Mundy family: they speak of 'the austerity of its (their home's) furnishings' and of how the sisters' plain clothing reflects 'their lean circumstances'. **Stage directions also tell us a great deal about particular characters and relationships.** While the circumstances of Michael's birth would have been a cause of social disgrace in Irish society at that time, the fact that he was born 'out of wedlock' in no way colours his aunts' attitude towards him; indeed it would be impossible to imagine any child being more cherished than Michael. The sisters' love for Michael is very evident from the stage instructions. We are told that when Kate enters the scene laden with shopping bags and sees Michael working at his kites, 'her face lights up with pleasure' and that she subsequently kisses him twice on the top of his head. Stage directions convey the excitement all of the Mundy sisters feel when Gerry Evans is seen approaching the house: 'Everybody dashes about in confusion – peering into the tiny mirror, bumping into one another, peeping out the window, combing hair.' **Detailed stage instructions are the closest the dramatist comes to the novelist's descriptive narrative.** This is to be seen most clearly in the lengthy instructions regarding the sisters' spontaneous, joyful dance, where Friel vividly describes the way in which each sister responds to the music on the wireless. For example, we are told that Maggie dances with total abandon, 'arms, legs, hair, long bootlaces flying', while Kate 'dances alone, totally concentrated, totally private; a movement that is simultaneously controlled and frantic . . .'

While dialogue is very important in the telling of Brian Moore's tale in _Lies of Silence_, it is central to the way Brian Friel delivers his story in _Dancing at Lughnasa_. Dialogue is the means by which the dramatist advances the plot and portrays characters and relationships. For example, the conversation that follows Agnes' suggestion that they all go to the harvest dance tells us a great deal about the individual sisters and the world in which they live. Excitement surges through the house, with the sisters almost overwhelmed by the prospect of going to their first dance in many years. Chris says: 'God Aggie, I could dance non-stop all night – all week – all month!' Agnes is so desperate to achieve some degree of self-fulfilment that she cares nothing for how their appearance at the dance might be perceived: 'And I don't care how young they are, how drunk and dirty and sweaty they are. I want to dance, Kate.' We see the elation and innocence of Rose: 'I love you Aggie! I love you more than chocolate biscuits!' After initially hesitating, Kate now asserts her authority, asking if they want the whole countryside laughing at the idea of 'women of our years? – mature women, dancing?' Kate drives home her point by reminding them, 'And this is Father Jack's home –we must never forget that – ever. No, no, we're going to no harvest dance.' This conversation reminds us that Kate is the mother figure in the family and her authority is rarely challenged. We see her preoccupation with image and reputation. Most significantly, this dialogue highlights the other sisters' willingness to defy social expectations in their desperate longing for romance and excitement.

In contrast to _Lies of Silence_ which is presented in a chronological manner, _Dancing at Lughnasa_ makes use of flashback. The play is based on Michael's memories of the summer of 1936, in particular his memories of those events to which he refers in his opening monologue: the Mundy family's acquisition of Marconi, the wireless, the return to Ballybeg of Father Jack after many years in Uganda, and the two visits made by Gerry Evans, his father, that summer. Also, while _Lies of Silence_ has a powerful and compelling plot, _Dancing at Lughnasa_ does not have a particularly strong storyline. The focus of the play is more on characters, relationships, the world of rural Ireland in the 1930s and how the characters cope with the harsh and oppressive world in which they live.

The main tensions in this text originate in the impoverished and restrictive circumstances in which the characters find themselves. Sadly, these tensions are not resolved in a happy manner. Poverty eventually overwhelms the family, with Agnes and Rose emigrating to England in search of work. The Mundy sisters yearn for romance and excitement, but they are as far from achieving self-fulfilment at the close of the text as they are at the beginning.

As in *Lies of Silence* the characters in *Dancing at Lughnasa* are realistic and entirely credible. Each of the sisters possesses her own distinctive personality. Kate, as a schoolteacher and the family's only wage-earner, is the mother figure and, as such, feels she has a duty to safeguard the family's reputation ('Do you want the whole countryside to be laughing at us?'). Maggie, with her wonderful wit, personifies the family's resilience ('Wonderful Wild Woodbine. Next best thing to a wonderful, wild man.') Agnes is a caring character, and has a special relationship with Rose. It is interesting to see that it is Agnes who most passionately articulates the sisters' yearning for romance and excitement when she expresses her desire to go to the harvest dance ('And I don't care how young they are, how drunk and dirty and sweaty they are. I want to dance, Kate. It's the Festival of Lughnasa. I'm only thirty-five, I want to dance.'). Rose, with her disability, displays a child-like innocence ('I love you Aggie! I love you more than chocolate biscuits!'). Chris is a very sensitive character, prone to extremes of emotion. She is visibly transformed by Gerry's occasional visits and heartbroken after he leaves (Kate tells Maggie: 'And Mr Evans is off again for another twelve months and next week or the week after

Christina'll collapse into one of her depressions.'). The sisters' distinctive personalities are also vividly reflected in the individual manner in which they dance around the house to the music of Marconi. Father Jack is a particularly interesting character, returning from his many years in Uganda with an entirely different set of beliefs and values to those he possessed when he left Ballybeg.

In both *Lies of Silence* and *Dancing at Lughnasa* imagery is a significant feature of the narrative technique. The most important image in the play is the dance. Dancing is symbolic of romance, freedom and self-expression. It is associated with the pagan rituals described by Father Jack and with the wild, unrestrained celebrations of the Festival of Lughnasa. When the sisters dance around the house, it is an expression of their joy in life and a reflection of their ability to briefly transcend their problems. As they release their pent-up emotions, we sense that they are also expressing their defiance of the restrictive world in which they live. Dancing also plays a key role in Chris and Gerry's relationship. Romantic and sensuous, their dancing transfixes Chris's sisters.

***Dancing at Lughnasa*, like *Lies of Silence*, concludes in a gloomy manner.** However, unlike the total darkness of the novel's ending, there is some light at the end of the play. Kate is dismissed from her teaching position in the local school by the spiteful priest who is unwilling to forgive her brother Jack for having 'gone native' in Africa. Michael tells us that after losing their home knitting jobs, Agnes and Rose leave for England in search of work. Many years later Michael learns of the grim fate that has befallen the inseparable sisters. Father Jack dies within a year of returning home, without ever again saying Mass. Kate is surprisingly understanding of the pagan rituals of which he regularly spoke, ultimately describing his bizarre behaviour as 'his own distinctive spiritual search'. Gerry Evans' visits become increasingly infrequent, before completely stopping. A letter from a young man his own age in Wales informed Michael that Gerry had died. It turned out that Gerry was married with a family throughout his occasional relationship with Chris. **Despite the sadness of the Mundy family being eventually overwhelmed by the hard, repressive world in which they lived, the ending of the text is not entirely** **pessimistic.** The memory that remains forever etched on Michael's memory is of his mother and aunts dancing around the house. Looking back on it, he describes the dance in spiritual terms, suggesting that 'this wordless ceremony' put them 'in touch with some otherness'. He further evokes the significance of the dance when he suggests that it was as if the sisters believed that 'the very heart of life and all its hopes' might be found within it.

KEY POINTS OF COMPARISON
Lies of Silence and *Dancing at Lughnasa*

- These texts belong to different genres of literature – while *Lies of Silence* is a thriller, *Dancing at Lughnasa* belongs to the genre of social realism.
- While *Lies of Silence* is set in Belfast in the 1980s, *Dancing at Lughnasa* is located in Ballybeg (a fictional village) in Donegal in the 1930s.
- There is a sense of balance and objectivity in the manner in which both tales are delivered. *Lies of Silence* is a third person narrative (although much of the action is viewed through the eyes of Michael Dillon), while *Dancing at Lughnasa* presents us with a variety of viewpoints as different characters express their varying opinions.
- As a play, only *Dancing at Lughnasa* uses stage directions, music, dance and tableau (a pause during or at the end of a scene when all the characters briefly freeze in position).
- While dialogue is important in the telling of Brian Moore's story, it is fundamental to the narrating of Brian Friel's tale.
- While *Lies of Silence* is told in a chronological manner, *Dancing at Lughnasa* makes use of flashback.
- In contrast to *Lies of Silence*, which has a powerful and compelling plot, the storyline in *Dancing at Lughnasa* is not that strong – in the play the focus is more on the characters and the way in which they cope with the harsh, restrictive world in which they live.
- In both texts the main tensions in the narratives have their source in the society in which the protagonists live.
- In both texts, the characters are complex, distinctive and convincing.
- Both Moore and Friel make effective use of imagery in the course of communicating their respective stories.
- Both texts conclude in a gloomy manner. However, unlike the total darkness of the novel's ending, there is some light at the end of the play.

Il Postino

While novelists, dramatists and film directors obviously employ their own distinctive narrative techniques, there remains a significant range of similarities in the way that *Lies of Silence*, *Dancing at Lughnasa* and *Il Postino* deliver their respective tales.

Similar to *Dancing at Lughnasa*, this film belongs to the genre of social realism, vividly portraying Mario's life in a small, generally poor, community. Of course, texts are not always easily labelled, and there is also an element of romance in this film as much of it revolves around Mario's pursuit of the beautiful Beatrice. Similar to *Dancing at Lughnasa*, *Il Postino* communicates its story visually. Similar to *Lies of Silence*, this story is delivered in a chronological manner.

This film differs from both of the other comparative texts in that it is located in Capri, an island of great natural beauty off the coast of Italy.

Similar to both of the other comparative texts, there is a sense of balance and objectivity in the way in which *Il Postino* tells its tale. In the film the camera generally acts as an objective third person narrator. The camera stands outside the action, recording everything and allowing us to get the point of view of different characters in the course of the film. As early as the opening scene in the film we see how frustrated Mario's father is with a son who seems to have an allergy to fishing boats, while not having any other gainful employment. We also see how strongly opposed Beatrice's Aunt Rosa is to her niece's relationship with Mario when she storms into Neruda's home and threatens to shoot Mario if he doesn't stop seeing Beatrice.

While we smile at her obsession with protecting Beatrice's virtue (virginity), this concern would have been shared by many parents/guardians at that time where their daughters were concerned. Unsurprisingly, for most of the film we are viewing the action from Mario's perspective in point-of-view shots. We view the map of South America through Mario's eyes as he circles Chile after learning from the newsreel of Pablo Neruda's imminent arrival on Capri. For Mario, Neruda is 'the poet of love'.

Dialogue is essential to the telling of the story in all three comparative texts. It is central to portraying Mario's developing relationships with both Neruda and Beatrice. When Mario first meets Neruda as he delivers his mail, he has little to say for himself. However, soon afterwards, Mario starts a conversation with Neruda by quoting a line of his poetry. Soon the conversation moves on to a discussion of metaphors. When Mario tells Neruda, 'I'd like to be a poet too', he is advised to walk on the shoreline (presumably in the hope that he might be inspired by the beauty of the sea). Initially, Mario does not seem to appreciate the abundant natural beauty that surrounds them. When Neruda remarks, 'This place is beautiful', Mario replies, 'Think so?' Shortly afterwards, a conversation between the two men on the beach suggests that Mario has an innate (instinctive) talent for poetry. After Neruda has recited a poem about the sea (with wonderful aural qualities), Mario described it as 'weird', before going on to explain, 'The words went back and forth . . . I felt seasick in fact . . . like a boat tossing around on your words.' When Mario first sees Beatrice he is so besotted by her beauty that he is virtually speechless. However, we see how much more expressive he becomes as a result of Neruda's influence. The next time Beatrice passes close to him in the café, he tells her, 'Beatrice, your smile spreads like a butterfly.' Shortly afterwards, Mario sees Beatrice walking on the beach and showers her with poetic compliments. Medium and close-up shots show that she has been spellbound by his poetic compliments (quoted from Neruda's work) and has fallen in love with him.

The main tension in the plot derives from Mario's romantic pursuit of Beatrice and this is resolved in the happiest of manners when the two marry, with Neruda as Mario's witness. **While the plot of *Il Postino* is not as compelling or as gripping as that of *Lies of Silence*** (which is to be expected given that the novel is a thriller), **it is certainly fascinating to watch Mario's journey to self-awareness, his romantic conquest of Beatrice and, most of all, his developing relationship with Neruda.** This text belongs to the genre of social realism, vividly depicting the life of a small, impoverished, but united community on a small island off the coast of Italy in the 1950s.

As in both of the other comparative texts, the characters in *Il Postino* are portrayed in a realistic and credible manner. In the early part of the film, Mario is awkward and has little to say for himself. As the film unfolds, he undergoes a very significant personal transformation (largely as a result of Pablo Neruda's influence), becoming more confident and expressive. While Beatrice is not developed in any great depth as a character, she still emerges as a distinctive individual, being depicted as a sensuous and spirited young woman. Rosa and Giorgio are both strong individual characters as is the gullible, foolish priest who believes that communists eat babies and, on that rather dubious basis, speculates about Pablo Neruda and his wife Mathilde having no children after many years

of marriage. Of course, Neruda himself is convincingly portrayed as an inspiring, romantic, passionate and caring individual.

In comparing film with written texts, it must be remembered that a film director like Michael Radford employs a variety of narrative techniques that are unique to film in the course of telling his story. Such cinematic techniques include a range of camera shots, lighting and a musical soundtrack. *Il Postino* opens with a medium shot of Mario looking wistfully at a postcard that has been sent to him by friends who have emigrated to America. We get a close-up of Mario's face, suggesting that he is in a pensive mood. Medium shots of Mario's bedroom and of the kitchen where he and his father eat indicate a very basic (bordering on impoverished) lifestyle. The darkness of their home underscores the sense of gloom, while the plaintive music that accompanies the opening scene reinforces the idea that Mario is unhappy and yearns (longs) for another way of life. The stunning natural beauty of the island (of which Mario is unaware in the early stages of the film) is captured in a number of memorable long and medium shots.

The developing relationship between Mario and Neruda is conveyed by a medium shot of the latter demonstratively reciting a poem about the sea as the two men sit together on the beach. A long shot of Beatrice playing table football in her aunt's café highlights her striking beauty, while a close-up of Mario's face conveys his speechless awe on seeing this alluring young woman. Later a high-angle shot sees Mario looking down on Beatrice walking on the beach. When he goes down to join her, he conquers her heart with a series of poetic compliments. This scene is soaked in sunshine and light, conveying a sense of optimism and joy. When she returns home to her aunt's café, a series of medium and close-up shots leave both her aunt and the viewer in no doubt but that she is in love with Mario, having been spellbound by his 'metaphors'. After Beatrice defies her aunt and goes to visit Mario, a point of view shot captures Beatrice's sensual nature as she slowly rolls a small ball from her breasts up to her chin. The most poignant camera shot of all is the close-up of Mario in the newsreel as he is called to the platform to read a poem at the huge communist rally – this close-up perfectly captures Mario's pride and joy minutes before his tragic death.

In all three comparative texts imagery is an important aspect of how the story is told. In *Il Postino* the most important image is of the sea. On an obvious level the recurring images of the sparkling blue sea suggests the wondrous natural beauty of the island. On a deeper symbolic level the sea may represent the idea of inspiration, so fundamental to the work of the poet. It is when Neruda recites a poem about the sea that Mario displays his first meaningful insight into the art of the poet. Mario later wins Beatrice's heart when he showers her with romantic metaphors as she walks by the shore. It is also significant that when Mario records some of the beautiful sounds of the island, the first two sounds on the tape are of the sea – small waves that lap gently onto the beach followed by bigger waves that crash onto the shore.

While Mario's death naturally casts a dark shadow over the close of the text, this random happening does not significantly detract from the wonderful sense of optimism that we feel when we reflect on his inspiring life. Mario is the only protagonist in the three comparative texts who transcends the limitations and difficulties of his world as he grows in self-awareness, realises his potential and achieves personal happiness.

KEY POINTS OF COMPARISON
Lies of Silence, Dancing at Lughnasa and *Il Postino*

- These texts belong to different literary genres: *Lies of Silence* is a thriller, while both *Dancing at Lughnasa* and *Il Postino* belong to the genre of social realism (although there is also a strong element of romance in the latter text).
- While both *Lies of Silence* and *Dancing at Lughnasa* are set in Ireland in different eras (the 1980s and 1930s respectively) and in different societies, *Il Postino* is located on the island of Capri off the coast of Naples in Italy in the 1950s.
- There is a sense of balance and objectivity in all three texts. *Lies of Silence* is a third person narrative (although much of the action is viewed through the eyes of Michael Dillon), *Dancing at Lughnasa* presents us with a range of viewpoints from different characters and in *Il Postino* the camera generally acts as a third person narrator.
- While dialogue is obviously fundamental to the telling of the story in *Dancing at Lughnasa*, it is also essential to the telling of the story in both of the other comparative texts.
- While both *Lies of Silence* and *Il Postino* deliver their tales in a chronological manner, *Dancing at Lughnasa* makes use of flashbacks.
- The plot in *Lies of Silence* is the most powerful and compelling of the three texts, which is to be expected given that it is a thriller. However the storylines in both of the other texts are very interesting, while both (belonging to the genre of social realism) vividly depict a particular society at a particular point in time.
- In both *Lies of Silence* and *Dancing at Lughnasa*, the main tensions in the narratives have their source in the society in which the protagonists live, but in *Il Postino* the main tension derives from Mario's romantic pursuit of Beatrice.
- In all three texts the characters are portrayed in a realistic and credible manner.
- In all three texts imagery is an important element in the narrative method, in how the story is told.
- Only *Il Postino* concludes in an optimistic manner (notwithstanding the tragic, random death of Mario).

Guidelines for Answering Exam Questions

1   In the examination you are asked to compare the texts under one of three different modes of comparison. These are:

A. Cultural Context – this refers to the world of the text, meaning the structures, values, rituals and way of life of a particular society. It also refers to the impact of a particular world on the main character(s).

B. The General Vision or Viewpoint – this refers to the authorial / directorial vision of life, while also referring to the impact of a text on the reader/viewer.

C. Literary Genre – this refers to the ways in which a story is told.

2   Comparison means both similarities and differences.

3   Texts must be discussed in relation to each other - identify and explore links between them.

4   Avoid summarising the stories of the texts that you have – your response should be analytical/discursive in approach.

5   There are two types of question: the single essay-type question and the two-part question.

6   The two-part question generally makes reference to a key moment/ key moments. After you identify and describe a key moment, you may range through the text to establish the context and significance of this particular moment.

7   Where the essay-type question is concerned, address the question in your opening paragraph and outline your response to it.

8   While the texts you have studied must be given their full titles in your introduction, you may abbreviate these titles in the remainder of your response.

9   Each paragraph in the essay-type answer should be based on one point of comparison between the texts. Aim to bring the different texts together in each paragraph with a view to producing a coherent comparative analysis.

10   The opening sentence in each paragraph should make the point of comparison.

11   Each point of comparison should be illustrated by relevant and accurate reference to (and possibly quotation from) the texts under discussion. When this is done, the examiner codes the illustrated comparison 'C'. You are not expected to have a 'minimum' number of

'Cs' in your response. It is the quality of the comparative analysis that is most important.

12   Refer back to the terms of the question at intervals to ensure that your response remains focused on the key issues.

13   As well as comparing the texts (which is obviously your main task), show that you have engaged with them on a personal level – give your personal reaction to certain aspects of the texts that have come up for discussion in your response and that had an impact on you.

14   Unless the question clearly states at least two texts on your comparative course, you are expected to discuss all three of your comparative texts.

15   Write a brief conclusion.

16   Use the language of comparative analysis, e.g.:

  – *I noticed in both Text A and Text B that . . .*

  – *Text C differs from both Text A and Text B in that . . .*

  – *While both Text A and Text B highlight this issue, they treat it in a different manner.*

  – *In contrast to Text A, Text B . . .*

  – *Only in Text C do we see . . .*

  – *John in Text A reminds me of Peter in Text B because . . .*

  – *The manner in which A is portrayed in this text differs from its portrayal in my two other comparative texts..*

  – *I was struck by the sharp contrast between the responses of the protagonists when confronted by . . .*

  – *The worlds of both Text A and Text B display a number of common features.*

  – *The vision of society in Text A is much more positive than the vision of society in Text B.*

  – *In all three texts we see . . .*

  – *Similarly . . .*

  – *Once again . . .*

Sample Answers

A. THE CULTURAL CONTEXT

'The cultural context can have a significant influence on the behaviour of the central character/characters in a text.'

Compare the way in which the behaviour of the central characters in at least two of your texts is influenced by the cultural context of those texts.

(Leaving Certificate HL 2007)

I certainly agree with the above statement. The texts I have studied for my comparative course are: *Lies of Silence* by Brian Moore, *Dancing at Lughnasa* by Brian Friel and *Il Postino*, directed by Michael Radford. The main characters in these texts are inevitably, and significantly, influenced by the cultural contexts of these texts.

Family life is a key aspect of the cultural context. When *Lies of Silence* opens it is apparent that Michael Dillon's marriage to Moira is on the point of breaking up. Their relationship has become strained and problematic, and Michael is having an affair with a young Canadian journalist named Andrea. Moira's deteriorating relationship with Michael heightens her sense of insecurity: 'You're bored with me, you married me because you fancied me and now I've lost my good looks you couldn't care less about me.' While Dillon plans to tell Moira about his relationship with Andrea, he procrastinates, (defers telling her) until Moira finds out for herself when she sees Michael holding hands with Andrea in the hotel. Moira's sense of betrayal is heightened when, after being placed in an unenviable moral dilemma, Michael chooses to alert the police to the bomb in his car – even at the risk of Moira being killed by the IRA volunteers holding her captive in their home. Moira's sense of betrayal is clearly a factor in her decision to do a television interview about their encounter with the IRA (against the advice of the police) – an act that places both Michael's and her own life in danger. Here we get an early example of a protagonist's actions being influenced by the cultural context.

As in *Lies of Silence* we see how the cultural context of *Dancing at Lughnasa* impacts significantly on the behaviour of the central characters. In contrast to the unstable family situation in *Lies of Silence*, the Mundy family in *Dancing at Lughnasa* is close and loving. While the sisters have their occasional disagreements, there is a sense of warmth within the Mundy home that is not evident in the Dillon household. While a child born 'out of wedlock' would normally have been a cause of embarrassment in rural Ireland at that time, Chris' son, Michael, is cherished by all of the sisters, seeming to have five mothers rather than one. Jack is also greatly loved when he returns from his lengthy stay in Uganda, despite having 'gone native' and talking so enthusiastically about pagan rituals, while indicating no interest whatsoever in saying Mass. It is the sisters' love for and devotion to each other that prompts Agnes and Rose to emigrate to England after Kate loses her job in the local school and they lose their jobs as part-time home knitters. Similar to Dillon in *Lies of Silence*, Mario in *Il Postino* does not have a happy family life when he is living with his largely silent father who is visibly frustrated with his son's lack of a job and complaints about the dampness of the boats. Mario defies his father's and society's expectation that he would be a fisherman when he gets a job as a part-time postman, whose only task is to deliver mail to Pablo Neruda, the Chilean poet and communist who chooses Capri as his place of exile. After gradually building up a relationship with Neruda, the latter quickly becomes the most important influence on Mario's life, helping him to become aware of his poetic talent and win the heart of the beautiful Beatrice.

While the most striking feature of the cultural context in *Lies of Silence* is sectarian violence, the most prominent feature of the world of *Dancing at Lughnasa* is poverty. In contrast to these deeply negative social features, the most important factor in Mario's world is an individual man – Pablo Neruda, who proves to be a wonderfully positive influence on Mario. In each text we can see how the cultural context significantly influences the behaviour of the central characters.

In *Lies of Silence* we see that Michael's behaviour is significantly influenced by the society in which he lives. Raised in a world of bitter sectarian divisions, he speaks of the narrow-mindedness of the priests who taught him ('priests whose sectarian views perfectly propagated the divisive bitterness' at the heart of the Northern conflict), while describing the Orange Order as 'that fount of Protestant prejudice against the third of Ulster's people who are Catholics'. After Moira lets it slip to a print journalist that Michael had seen one of the IRA men who had taken over their house for the purposes of bombing the Clarence Hotel and killing Alun Pottinger, Michael is paid a visit by a priest named Father Connolly, whose nephew is the IRA man he can identify. When the priest attempts to contextualise the entire episode, and minimise his nephew's guilt, Michael is enraged: 'If the police find that boy, Kev – vicious little bastard that he is – I'll make sure he's a lot older before he gets a chance to kill anybody else.' It is Michael's deep resentment of the bitter sectarianism at the heart of the Northern conflict and of the religious figures that often perpetuate it that prompts him to defy the IRA and, in effect, sign his own death warrant. This is a classic example of behaviour being influenced by cultural factors. When Michael changes his mind about testifying, it is too late – assassins have already been dispatched to silence him.

Just as sectarian violence is the most destructive aspect of the world of *Lies of Silence*, poverty is the most damaging aspect of the world of *Dancing at*

Lughnasa. The Mundy sisters have to contend with a range of problems associated with poverty, including unemployment and emigration. While the family live in straitened (impoverished) circumstances in the early part of the text (there are references to 'austere' furnishings, 'lean circumstances' 'three eggs', etc.), their situation becomes truly dire after Kate is sacked by the parish priest as 'punishment' for her brother Jack having 'gone native' during his lengthy stay in Uganda. It is destitution that drives Agnes and Rose to depart for England in search of employment and forces Chris to take a job she truly hates in the knitting factory.

A second form of poverty that is just as destructive of the Mundy sisters' prospects of achieving happiness is a type of social poverty that deprives them of opportunities for romance or excitement. The Mundy sisters have no social life and there is abundance evidence of their emotional and sexual frustration at living in a world that deems them too old to attend the harvest dance at Lughnasa (the sisters range in age from twenty-six to forty). All of the sisters are transfixed by the sight of Chris and Gerry dancing together. Agnes is particularly captivated by Gerry and may even be in love with him. Kate is loosely linked with Austen Morgan, a local shopkeeper (who later marries 'a wee young thing from Carrickfad'). Maggie fondly remembers Brian McGuinness, the great love of her love, although she never went out with him. Even 'simple' Rose is infatuated with Danny Bradley, a married man whose wife has left him and gone to England. When Agnes suggests that all the sisters go to the harvest dance 'like we used to', the household erupts in excitement. Agnes is overwhelmed by joy as she anticipates going dancing for the first time in many years: 'And I don't care how young they are, how drunk and dirty and sweaty they are. I want to dance, Kate'. However, after brief consideration, Kate declares that they will not be going to the dance: 'Do you want the whole countryside to be laughing at us? – women of our years? – mature women, dancing?' Kate's preoccupation with image and reputation is typical of Irish society in the 1930s when Catholic morality dictated repressive sexual attitudes.

Shortly after their hopes of going to the harvest dance have been crushed, the sisters, listening to 'The Mason's Apron' on the wireless, begin a spontaneous, joyful dance around the house. The dance expresses their frustration with and desire to defy the restrictions of society's strict moral code. The stage directions tell us that the sisters' dancing suggests 'a sense of order being deliberately subverted'. While the sisters are described as looking 'slightly ashamed' when the dance ends, it is significant that they are also said to look 'slightly defiant'. This truly joyous scene is the most inspiring moment in the entire play, dramatically highlighting the resilience of the family's spirit in a truly harsh and repressive world. There is no scene comparable to this in either of the other texts. Here again we see how the cultural context influences the behaviour of the protagonists.

In contrast to the negative cultural factors that ultimately result in Michael Dillon being killed and the Mundy family being broken up, Mario in *Il Postino* lives in a society which is poor, but very supportive of him. The greatest influence on Mario is, obviously, Pablo Neruda, who is central to Mario's dramatic personal development. Mario's interest in Neruda initially springs from what he sees as Neruda's remarkable success with women ('Women go crazy for his poetry', he tells Giorgio). Mario asks Neruda to help him write a poem that will win the heart of the beautiful Beatrice. Neruda finally agrees and Mario not only wins Beatrice's heart, but also embarks on his journey towards self-awareness as his conversations with Neruda spark his interest in composing his own poems. Initially shy and awkward, Mario gradually grows into a stronger, more assertive and more expressive character. Exposure to Neruda's communist beliefs makes Mario more conscious of injustice and exploitation. He challenges Di Cosimo's cronies when they look to buy fish on the cheap from the local fishermen and later, in the café, exposes Di Cosimo's promises regarding the building of a water works on the island: 'We all knew that as soon as you got elected, the work would come to a halt.' We can see just how much Mario has grown when he composes his first poem, inspired by the natural beauty of the island.

When Neruda had earlier asked him to speak into the tape recorder and say something about the island that was beautiful, Mario could not think of anything to say. However, by the close of the film, Mario, with the assistance of Giorgio (the postmaster and Mario's good friend), records such sounds as waves lapping gently on the shore, the wind in the bushes, 'the sad nets belonging to my father' and Pablito's heartbeat in Beatrice's womb. Mario's new appreciation of beauty is key to his developing poetic talent. Mario's remarkable personal development is perhaps best seen in his willingness to address a huge communist rally on the mainland and read some of his poems.

In conclusion, there is no doubt but that the behaviour of the protagonists in the comparative texts I have studied is significantly influenced, in both positive and negative ways, by the cultural context of a particular text. Cultural influences prompt Michael Dillon to defy the IRA in *Lies of Silence* – an action that costs him his life. The harsh, restrictive world in which the Mundy sisters live in *Dancing at Lughnasa* drives them to express their defiance of that world and release their pent-up emotions in their wonderful, spontaneous dance. Finally, in *Il Postino* we see how the cultural context inspires Mario to grow in self-awareness, develop his poetic talent and achieve personal happiness.

B. THE GENERAL VISION AND VIEWPOINT

'The general vision and viewpoint of texts can be quite similar or very different.'

In the light of the above statement, compare the general vision and viewpoint in at least two texts on your comparative course.

(Leaving Certificate HL 2003)

I agree that the general vision and viewpoint of texts can be quite similar or very different. The general vision or viewpoint refers to the author/playwright/director's outlook on life. This outlook may be conveyed through the manner in which the plot opens, develops and concludes, through key characters and relationships, through the manner in which a particular society is portrayed and also through language and imagery. The texts I have studied for my comparative course are: *Lies of Silence* by Brian Moore, *Dancing at Lughnasa* by Brian Friel and *Il Postino*, directed by Michael Radford. *Lies of Silence* is set in Belfast in the 1980s, in a bitterly divided society dominated by an ancient religious/political conflict. In this text, the outlook on life is dark and grim. *Dancing at Lughnasa* is set in a small village in County Donegal in the 1930s and, while the vision of life in this text is essentially gloomy and pessimistic like that in *Lies of Silence*, there are moments of light and laughter that occasionally lift the general air of despondency. In sharp contrast to both of these texts, *Il Postino* offers us a vision of life that is largely optimistic.

The gloomy manner in which *Lies of Silence* opens sets the tone for the generally dark novel that follows. Michael Dillon is depressed by the everyday sight of armed policemen jumping out of an armoured car, their revolvers 'cowboy-low on their thighs'. This image is suggestive of a lawless, 'Wild West' type of society. This familiar sight sets Dillon thinking about his life in violent Belfast: 'Why should he stay, why should anyone in their senses stay here?' In contrast to the dark manner in which *Lies of Silence* opens, *Dancing at Lughnasa* begins on a nostalgic note as Michael, who is both narrator and character, recalls the summer of 1936. It was then that a number of significant events seemed to hold out the prospect of happiness, namely: the Mundy family's acquisition of their first wireless set; the sisters' brother, Father Jack, returning home after many years in Africa on the missions; and the two visits of Gerry, Michael's absent father. Similar to *Lies of Silence*, *Il Postino* opens in a rather gloomy manner. The opening shot of the film is of Mario looking closely at a postcard from America. His expression suggests that he envies those friends of his who seem to have achieved prosperity in a new world, indicating that he is unhappy with his own life. Mario's struggle to make conversation with his uncommunicative father adds to the sense of gloom.

The quality and outcome of the key relationships in *Lies of Silence* adds to the sense of gloom that pervades the text. While Michael and Andrea are briefly happy towards the close of the text, Michael's relationship with his wife Moira is strained and problematic. It appears that Michael married Moira for the wrong reasons – her good looks – and, when the text opens, it is already apparent that their marriage is over. While Moira struggled with bulimia before she married Michael, the problem recurs whenever she feels stressed or anxious. What compounds Moira's anguish is Michael's failure to tell her that the marriage is over and that he is leaving her. While Michael endlessly procrastinates, Moira finds out the truth for herself when she sees Michael and Andrea holding hands in the hotel. Michael's decision to alert the police to the IRA bomb in his car, at the risk of Moira being killed by her IRA captors, fills her with a sense of betrayal. It is this sense of betrayal that prompts her to do television interviews (against the advice of the police) in which she denounces the IRA, placing both her own and Michael's life in danger.

In contrast to the pessimistic vision of relationships in *Lies of Silence*, the outlook on relationships in *Dancing at Lughnasa* is largely optimistic (the key relationships in this text are, with the exception of Chris's relationship with Gerry, within the family). Despite their occasional and inevitable disagreements, the Mundy family is closely united; indeed the love and togetherness of the family is one of the most positive aspects of the text. Poverty does not break the family's spirit, epitomised by Maggie's wonderful and uplifting wit. When faced with having to prepare the evening meal for seven people with meagre resources, she is undaunted: 'Not a great larder, but a nice challenge to someone like myself.' While Michael and Father Jack might have been regarded as sources of embarrassment in rural Ireland at that time (Michael, Chris' son, was born 'out of wedlock', while Jack had 'gone native' during the course of his many years in Uganda on the missions), both are loved and cherished. Similar to *Dancing at Lughnasa,* the key relationships in *Il Postino* are presented in a very positive light. As Mario's friendship with Neruda develops, the Chilean poet becomes his mentor, helping Mario to become aware of his poetic talent and to conquer the heart of the beautiful Beatrice. Mario has a loving relationship with Beatrice, and also has a close friendship with Giorgio, the local postmaster.

The societies in which all three texts are set are portrayed in a generally negative light. Society in *Lies of Silence* is depicted in a very pessimistic manner. The bitter and violent sectarian conflict envelops the text in a sense of darkness and gloom. Poverty is another dispiriting aspect of the society in which the text is located. It is the working classes on both sides of the religious divide that are portrayed as being the most vehemently sectarian. The text presents us with the disheartening image of 'graffiti-fouled barricaded slums where the city's Protestant and Catholic poor confronted each other, year in and year out, in a stasis of hatred, fear and mistrust'. Dillon would seem to be expressing the authorial viewpoint when he expresses his anger at the 'lies told to poor Protestant working people about the Catholics, lies told to poor Catholic working people about the Protestants, lies from parliaments and pulpits, lies at rallies and funeral orations, and, above all, lies of silence from those in Westminster who did not want to face the injustices of Ulster's status quo'. The idea of ordinary working people being the victims of both their political and religious leaders who perpetuate religious enmities and allow injustices to fester in their own selfish interests is depressing and disturbing. Society in *Dancing at Lughnasa* is similarly portrayed in a negative light. Poverty impacts in a very destructive manner on the Mundys' family life, with Agnes and Rose feeling compelled to leave for England in search of employment after Kate loses her job in the local school and they lose their jobs as part-time knitters. Perhaps the darkest aspect of this text's vision of society is the repression of women. The effects of living in a world where, as women on the brink of middle-age, they are deemed to be too old for romance, love and marriage leads to considerable frustration on the part of all the sisters as they crave emotional (and possibly sexual) fulfilment. The Mundy sisters' frustration with and desire to defy the restrictions of society's strict moral code (as dictated by the Catholic Church) can be seen in the wonderfully uplifting dance they perform around the house. Similar to both of the other texts, society in *Il Postino* is also portrayed in a rather depressing light. Once again, we see a world of dispiriting poverty and few opportunities, a world where the cynical politician Di Cosimo and Mario's mentor, Pablo Neruda, visibly contrast with the local community because of their relative wealth.

The manner in which a text concludes tells us a great deal about its creator's outlook on life. In *Lies of Silence* it seems as if the text is set to conclude in a bright, optimistic manner. Having gone to London with Andrea, Michael experiences a new sense of happiness in both his personal and professional lives. After one particularly joyful day with Andrea, Michael wants to tell her that he had never been so happy. In terms of his job, Michael's enthusiasm for hotel management is rekindled by the challenging prospect of managing the prestigious Wellington Hotel. Tragically, the happy ending that (however unlikely) seems to be in the offing fails to materialise. While Michael changes his mind about testifying against the IRA man whose face he had seen, his change of heart comes too late to save him from an assassin's bullet. At the close of the text, the world of the novel is enshrouded in a sense of darkness, despondency and hopelessness.

Similar to *Lies of Silence*, the manner in which *Dancing at Lughnasa* concludes underlines the generally gloomy vision of the text. Having left for England, Agnes and Rose are never seen again until, twenty five years later, Michael finally locates them in London – by this time Agnes was dead and Rose was in a grim hospice, close to death. Tragically, the sisters had ended up on the streets where exposure and malnourishment broke their health. Jack died within a year of returning home, leaving Kate, in particular, feeling 'inconsolable'. Michael tells us that Gerry's visits became increasingly irregular, before stopping entirely. A letter from a young man his own age informs Michael that Gerry Evans had a family in Wales all the time he was involved with Chris. The realisation that Gerry had been leading a double life for so many years adds to the sense of gloom at the close of the text. However, unlike *Lies of Silence*, the ending of *Dancing at Lughnasa* is not totally bleak and pessimistic. The memory that continues to linger in Michael's mind is of his mother and aunts dancing around the house. The sisters' dancing is symbolic of their resilient spirit, their enduring joy in life, their ability to transcend their many problems and their defiance of the repressive world in which they live.

While Mario's death obviously casts a shadow over the conclusion of *Il Postino*, this tragic, but random happening does not significantly detract from the sense of optimism created by all he had achieved in his life before his untimely death. In contrast to the protagonists in both of the other texts who (notwithstanding the enduring spirit of the Mundy sisters epitomised by their joyful, defiant dance) are ultimately crushed by the harshness of the worlds in which they live, Mario rises above the constraints and difficulties of his world to grow in self-awareness, realise his potential (to some extent) and achieve personal happiness with Beatrice.

In conclusion, the foregoing discussion has established that it is certainly true that the general vision and viewpoint of texts can be quite similar or very different. In all three texts the outlook on certain aspects of life is quite similar, while the vision of other aspects of life is sharply different. There are few texts where the vision or viewpoint is entirely optimistic or entirely pessimistic. To sum up, the dominant outlook on life in both *Lies of Silence* and *Dancing at Lughnasa* is similarly dark and pessimistic, while, in contrast, the dominant vision of life in *Il Postino* is bright and optimistic.

C. LITERARY GENRE

Write a talk to be given to Leaving Certificate students in which you explain the term Literary Genre and show them how to compare the telling of stories in at least two texts from the comparative course.

(Leaving Certificate HL 2005)

Good afternoon students,

Literary genre refers to the ways texts tell their stories. In comparing texts you will find some similarities in the way they tell their tales, but also some differences. It is important to remember that novelists, playwrights and film directors employ some narrative techniques distinctive to their own particular art. There are some key questions that need to be asked in the course of comparing the way different texts tell their stories: To what literary genre does the text belong? From whose point of view is it narrated? Is the story told chronologically (as events occur) or does the author/playwright/director make use of flashbacks? Is the plot compelling and powerful? Are the characters convincing or stereotypical? Is dialogue used to good effect? Do particular images make a powerful impact on us? The texts I will compare in terms of this mode of comparison (literary genre) are *Lies of Silence* by Brian Moore, *Dancing at Lughnasa* by Brian Friel and *Il Postino*, directed by Michael Radford.

Let's begin by comparing the genres of these three texts. *Lies of Silence* belongs to the thriller genre. It is set in Belfast in the 1980s when sectarian violence is at a peak. *Dancing at Lughnasa* is set in Ballybeg, a fictional village in rural Donegal and belongs to the genre of social realism, depicting the way of life of the Mundy family in the harsh and repressive world that was Ireland in the 1930s. *Il Postino* also belongs to the genre of social realism, portraying the life of a generally poor fishing community on the island of Capri (off the coast of Naples) in the 1950s. There is also a strong element of romance in this text, with Mario's pursuit of Beatrice a key aspect of the plot.

Now, we will compare the narrative voice in these texts. From whose point of view is the story being told? *Lies of Silence* is a third person narrative – which implies that the story is told by an omniscient (all-knowing) narrator. This is evident in the opening lines of the novel ('At a quarter to nine, just before going off to work, Dillon went down to reception to check the staff roster for tomorrow.') and in the closing lines of the text ('They raised their revolvers. They were not wearing masks. This time there would be no witnesses.'). However, we also view much of the action through Dillon's eyes, with the text at times reading as if it were his stream of consciousness: 'Look at me, look at me! . . . . See this car on its way to kill innocent people, see my wife in a room with a gun to her head . . .' As a third person narrative, the authorial voice in *Lies of Silence* is balanced and objective.

This sense of balance and objectivity is also evident in *Dancing at Lughnasa* where it is achieved by the variety of viewpoints expressed by the different characters. A good example of varying viewpoints is when Agnes passionately declares her desire to go to the harvest dance, with its wild, uninhibited dancing ('. . . I don't care how young they are, how drunk and sweaty they are. I want to dance. It's the Festival of Lughnasa. I'm only thirty-five. I want to dance.'). However, Kate remains the voice of convention, worried about how it might appear if the sisters went to the dance and released their pent-up emotions ('Do you want the whole countryside to be laughing at us? – women of our age? – mature women, dancing?'). Similar to both of the other texts, we can also see a sense of balance and objectivity in the way in which *Il Postino* delivers its story. In the film the camera generally acts as a third person narrator, standing outside the action, recording everything and allowing us to get the viewpoints of different characters in the course of the film. For example, we see how strongly opposed Beatrice's Aunt Rosa is to her niece's relationship with Mario when she storms into Neruda's home and threatens to shoot Mario if he doesn't stop seeing Beatrice. While we smile at her obsession with protecting Beatrice's virtue, this concern would have been shared by many parents/guardians at that time where their daughters were concerned.

We also need to consider the importance of dialogue as a narrative technique in our comparative texts. In *Lies of Silence* dialogue advances the plot and contributes to the creation and development of characters. Throughout the text, the dialogue is never less than powerful and convincing. Moira's exchanges with her IRA captors reveal a stronger, defiant side to her character. After deliberately provoking one IRA man by insulting him, his response indicates his working class background: 'Cheeky, aren't ye? You stuck up wee bourgeois bitch.' This response heightens the sense of tension, while the expletive adds to the realism of the scene. The use of dialect further heightens the sense of realism – one such example is when an IRA man warns Dillon that the volunteers guarding Moira 'will do a nut job on her' if he does not co-operate with them.

While dialogue is very important to the way Moore tells his story, it is fundamental to the manner in which Friel delivers his tale in *Dancing at Lughnasa*. In the play, dialogue is the means by which the dramatist advances the plot and portrays characters and relationships. For example, the conversation that follows Agnes' suggestion that they all go to the harvest dance tells us a great deal about the individual sisters and the world in which they live. The sisters, with the exception of Kate, are desperate to do something different and exciting. However, when Kate sees Rose dancing wildly in anticipation of going to the dance, she declares that they cannot go because, as 'mature women', the whole countryside would be 'laughing at us'. This conversation reminds us that Kate is the mother figure in the family and her authority is rarely challenged. We see her preoccupation with image and reputation. Most significantly, this dialogue highlights the other sisters' willingness to defy social expectations in their desperate longing for romance and excitement. Dialogue is central to portraying Mario's developing relationships with both Neruda and Beatrice. While Mario has little to say for himself when he first meets Neruda, a conversation between the two men on the beach suggests that Mario has a natural poetic talent. After Neruda has recited a poem about the sea (with wonderful aural qualities), Mario's response is impressively perceptive: 'The words went back and forth . . . I felt seasick in fact . . . like a boat tossing around on your words.' When Mario first sees Beatrice he is so besotted by her beauty that he is virtually speechless. However, we see how much more expressive he becomes as a result of Neruda's influence – the next time Beatrice passes close to him in the café, he tells her, 'Beatrice, your smile spreads like a butterfly'. Shortly afterwards, Mario sees Beatrice walking on the beach and showers her with poetic compliments. Medium and close-up shots show that she has been entranced by Mario's metaphors (quoted from Neruda's work) and has fallen in love with him.

While both *Lies of Silence* and *Il Postino* are presented in a chronological manner, *Dancing at Lughnasa*, in contrast, makes use of flashback. The play is book-ended by Michael's monologues telling of his memories of the summer of 1936 – in other words, the action unfolds within the framework of Michael's memories of that summer. Also, while *Lies of Silence* has a powerful and compelling plot with the narrative driving on to the dramatic conclusion, *Dancing at Lughnasa* does not have a particularly strong storyline. The focus of the play is more on characters, relationships and the harsh, restrictive world that was rural Ireland in the 1930s. While the plot of *Il Postino* is not as gripping as that of *Lies of Silence* (which is unsurprising given that the novel is a thriller), our interest is certainly engaged by Mario' pursuit of the beautiful Beatrice and, more importantly, by his developing relationship with Neruda. Also, as in *Dancing at Lughnasa*, we get a vivid portrayal of a particular society at a particular point in time – in this instance, the small, generally poor, but united community on a small island off the coast of Italy in the 1950s.

After the plot, we need to compare the quality of characterisation. In all three texts the characters come across to the reader/viewer as entirely credible flesh-and-blood individuals who, in their distinctness and complexity, are never less than convincing. In *Lies of Silence* we sympathise with Michael Dillon because we see so much of the action through his eyes, but we do not always admire him. His deception of Moira over a number of months and his endless indecision about when to tell her leaves us feeling very unimpressed with his lack of integrity and moral cowardice. While Moira initially appears to be a rather weak, dependent character, preoccupied with her appearance, she later displays a stronger side to her character in her defiance of the IRA. In *Dancing at Lughnasa* each sister has her own individual personality. Kate, as a schoolteacher and the mother figure in the family regards it as her duty to safeguard the family's reputation in a world where gossip is rife. Maggie is memorable for her wonderful wit ('Wonderful Wild Woodbine. Next best thing to a wonderful wild man.'). Agnes is a caring character, who enjoys a special relationship with Rose, while Chris is a very sensitive individual, prone to emotional extremes – she is visibly transformed by Gerry's occasional visits and heartbroken after he leaves. In *Il Postino* the characters are similarly portrayed in an entirely realistic manner. Mario undergoes a very significant personal transformation. While he is awkward and self-conscious in the early part of the film, he develops into a more confident, more expressive character as he comes under the influence of Neruda. Both Rosa and Giorgio are depicted as strong characters and, while Beatrice is not developed in any great depth as a character, she too emerges as a distinctive individual, being depicted as a sensuous and spirited young woman.

Finally, we must remember that the novelist, playwright and film director employ narrative methods distinctive to their own particular art. For example, *Lies of Silence* makes effective use of vivid imagery and detailed description to help the reader visualise and imaginatively engage with the unfolding action. The image of the soldiers with their revolvers 'cowboy-low' on their thighs conjures up a world of 'Wild West' type violence and lawlessness. The scene where the IRA enter the Dillon home is described in graphic detail to powerfully convey a sense of threat and fear.

The use of stage directions in *Dancing at Lughnasa* is obviously a narrative technique unique to plays. Stage directions are the only occasions when the voice of the playwright is directly heard. Friel's stage directions are very detailed and are central to conveying the play's distinctive atmosphere. Stage instructions suggest the dull, mundane nature of the Mundy sisters' lives as they go about their daily chores: 'Maggie makes a mash for hens. Agnes knits gloves. Rose carries a basket of turf into the kitchen . . . Chris irons at the kitchen table.' Stage directions point up the poverty of the Mundy family: they speak of 'the austerity of its (their home's) furnishings' and of how the sisters' plain clothing reflects 'their lean circumstances'.

Of course, as a film director, Michael Radford employs a variety of narrative techniques that are unique to film in the telling of his story. Such cinematic techniques include a range of camera shots, lighting and a musical soundtrack. *Il Postino* opens with a medium shot of Mario looking wistfully at a postcard that has been sent to him by friends who have emigrated to America. We get a close-up of Mario's face, suggesting that he is in a pensive mood. Medium shots of Mario's bedroom and of the kitchen where he and his father eat indicate a very basic lifestyle. The darkness of their home underscores the sense of gloom, while the plaintive music that accompanies the opening scene reinforces the idea that Mario is unhappy and yearns for another way of life.

In conclusion, you can now see that while there may be a range of similarities between texts in terms of the narrative methods they employ, no two texts are exactly the same in the manner in which they tell their stories. I hope this talk has helped you to better understand the meaning of the term 'Literary Genre' and that you now feel more confident about comparing your comparative texts where this mode of comparison is concerned. Thank you for your attention.

Poetry

JOHN KEATS

Biographical Note

Keats was born in Finsbury, close to London, England in 1795. He was the eldest of five children. He was educated in a small, private boarding school. In 1804 Keats' father was killed in a riding accident. While Keats' mother, Frances, married again, her second marriage was unhappy and the children were raised by their grandparents. His mother suffered from depression and later contracted tuberculosis, dying in 1810. Keats, who had devotedly nursed her through her illness, was devastated. At just fourteen years of age, he was parentless. In 1811 Keats left school to take up an apprenticeship as a surgeon. However, he never had any real interest in this work, eventually feeling repelled by it. Poetry was becoming increasingly important in his life, and in May 1816 he had his first poem published in the *Examiner*, a sonnet entitled *O Solitude! if I must with thee dwell*. Keats' first volume of poetry, *Poems*, was published in 1817. Later that year, he wrote a four thousand word epic poem, *Endymion: A Poetic Romance*. The opening line of this famous poem remains instantly recognisable: 'A thing of beauty is a joy forever.'

On a personal level, Keats' life involved a great deal of pain and loss. His brother Tom contracted tuberculosis, dying from the illness in 1818. From a young age, Keats was fearful for his own life, as we see in his sonnet *When I have fears that I may cease to be*. Keats' greatest fear was that he would die before he had expressed all of the ideas that were teeming in his fertile imagination.

Keats produced the bulk of his poetic work in a highly productive four-year period between 1817 and 1820. One of his most famous achievements was his development of his theory of Negative Capability. In essence this theory suggests that the poet may harbour doubts and uncertainties, and not feel compelled to reach definite conclusions. Keats himself explained this theory as 'when a man is capable of being in uncertainties, mysteries, doubts, without any irritable reaching after fact and reason'. Keats, of course, belonged to the Romantic Movement, which began in the early nineteenth century and ended some fifty years later. Central to the Romantics' beliefs were the power of the imagination to see truths, the importance of man as an individual rather than as a social being, the need for man to re-establish an intimate relationship with the natural world and the necessity of developing a new poetic language that was as close as possible to everyday speech.

In 1820 Keats started to cough up blood and, with his medical training, immediately understood its grave implications. For a time he was looked after by Frances (Fanny) Brawne, the great love of his life and the woman to whom he was engaged, and her mother in their home in Hampstead. His friends advised a spell in Italy, as it was widely believed at the time that tubercular patients would benefit from being in a warm climate. However, Keats did not improve and he died in Rome in 1821. He was, remarkably, only twenty-six years old. At his own request, the following epitaph was inscribed on his tombstone: 'Here lies one whose name was writ on water.'

To One Who Has Been Long in City Pent

The opening lines of this Petrarchan sonnet convey the contrast between the confinement of the city and the vast expanse of the beautiful sky. The sky is personified, with Keats speaking of 'the fair / And open face of heaven' and 'the smile of the blue firmament'. The restorative powers of nature are conveyed by the image of the poet, fatigued from life in the city, happily relaxing in the pleasantly long grass, reading 'a gentle tale of love and languishment'.

The sestet is dominated by a sense of melancholy as the poet returns home in the evening. As he hears the song of the nightingale ('the notes of Philomel') and watches the clouds sail by, Keats 'mourns' the rapid passing of the day. The closing lines compare the passing of this uplifting day to the falling of an angel's tear from heaven to earth.

References to breathing a prayer (presumably in gratitude for the beauty of the sky), heaven and 'an angel's tear' suggest Keats' awareness of a divine power behind the beautiful countryside.

KEY POINTS

- Key themes are the rejuvenating powers of nature and the transient nature of beauty and happiness ('that day so soon has glided by').
- Effective use of metaphors and personification.

On First Looking into Chapman's Homer

The reference to Homer in the title calls to mind his epic travel poems and, as we read into it, we see that this poem is dominated by images of travel and exploration. The 'realms of gold' in which Keats has travelled suggest the richness and power of the imagination. The 'many goodly states and kingdoms' and 'many western islands' he has seen represent the different poets whose work he has explored. Homer, whose wisdom is suggested by his 'deep brow', rules his own poetic realm, but Keats could never travel there because he did not understand Greek. However, Chapman's translation of Homer's classic opened the door to the latter's kingdom, enabling Keats to 'breathe in' its pure air:

'I heard Chapman speak out loud and bold'.

Keats draws an analogy between the excitement he felt on discovering Chapman's translation of Homer and that of an astronomer ('some watcher of the skies') on discovering a new planet ('When a new planet swims into his ken'). He also compares his feelings of elation to that felt by the Spanish explorer Cortes when he first set eyes on the Pacific Ocean. Like Cortes and his men staring silently and awestruck at this hitherto undiscovered vast expanse of water, Keats is moved beyond words by his own dramatic discovery of a whole new poetic world: 'and all his men / Look'd at each other with a wild surmise – / Silent, upon a peak in Darien'.

KEY POINTS

- Key theme is the excitement of reading poetry – this poem suggests that poetry opens up new worlds to the reader.
- The poem is dominated by metaphorical language of travel and exploration.
- Written in the form of a Petrarchan sonnet.

When I have Fears that I May Cease to Be

In this sonnet Keats reflects on poetry, love and the transience of life. The repetition of the words 'when' and 'before' reflect his keen awareness of the passage of time. The poet's great fear is that he will die before he has achieved poetic fame or experienced perfect love. While the title of the poem underlines the poet's fear of death, this sonnet also expresses Keats' ambition and love of life.

Keats fears that death will prevent him from giving expression to all of the ideas in his fertile mind, and from realising his full potential as a poet. The metaphor of the harvest suggests the richness and fertility of the poet's imagination. He fears that he may not live long enough to harvest or express all of the ideas in his 'teeming brain'.

The second quatrain develops the idea that Keats may die before he has written all that he hopes to write. He appreciates and wishes to capture the beauty and mystery of the world, symbolised by the personified night sky ('the night's starred face') in his verse. He also wishes to write about the 'high romance', symbolised by the stars. The phrase 'the magic hand of chance' suggests the mysterious nature of the creative process. The references to night and shadows evoke the idea of death.

In the third quatrain Keats considers the possibility of time preventing him from experiencing the magical power of perfect love: 'Never have relish in the fairy power of unreflecting love.' However, he is also sharply aware of the transience of human beauty and of life itself: 'Fair creature of an hour.'

The poem concludes in a despondent manner in the rhyming couplet. When Keats considers 'love and fame' in relation to time, he is filled with a sense of gloom which is reflected in the image of the poet standing alone 'on the shore of the wide world'. Love and fame fade into unimportance or 'nothingness' when they are set against the grim, inescapable reality of life's transience.

KEY POINTS

- Key theme is the insignificance of love and poetic fame when set against the grim reality of life's transience.
- Effective use of imagery (e.g. 'on the shore of the wide world I stand alone'), metaphor (e.g. harvest metaphor), personificaton (e.g. 'the night's starred face').

- Uses Shakespearian sonnet form.
- Sound effects: assonance (e.g. 'fears . . . cease . . . gleaned . . . teeming'), alliteration (e.g. 'wide world') and end-rhyme (e.g. 'brain / grain', 'more / shore') give the poem a musical quality.
- Uses a euphemism ('When I have fears that I may cease to be') when speaking of his own death.
- Tone is ultimately one of despair.

Bright Star

In this sonnet Keats is attracted to the permanence ('would I were steadfast as thou art') and 'splendour' of the 'bright star'. However, he is not enamoured of its detached, isolated existence. Keats describes the star as being hermit-like in its solitude: 'Like nature's patient, sleepless eremite'. Here we again see Keats' tendency to give human qualities to the natural world. As the sonnet develops, the words 'not' and 'no' make clear the poet's rejection of the star.

The star is depicted as watching over the 'moving waters' below. The poet's imagination infuses these waters with 'priestlike' powers as they cleanse 'earth's human shores'. The freshness and purity of the natural world is evoked by metaphor of the 'soft-fallen mask / Of snow upon the mountains and the moors'. Here the alliterative and sibilant 's' sound suggests the tranquillity of this winter scene, while the alliterative 'm' sound adds to the poem's musical qualities.

While the star is 'still steadfast, still unchangeable', it is also cold and remote. Keats is instead drawn to the transitory (transient or passing) but warm and vibrant world of human passion. The poet's idea of perfect happiness would be to be forever 'Pillowed upon my fair love's ripening breast, / To feel forever its soft fall and swell'. This sensuous image with its soft alliterative and sibilant 's' sound conveys the warmth of shared human love which contrasts with and highlights the cold isolation of the star. If the poet cannot forever experience this intensely passionate moment, then he would choose to 'swoon to death'.

In much of Keats' verse we see the tension between the poet's yearning for permanence and immortality, and his desire to enjoy the warm pleasures of real love.

While the transient physical world is a place of sorrow and pain, it is also the realm of passionate experience.

This sonnet resembles both *Ode to a Nightingale* and *Ode on a Grecian Urn* in that in all three poems Keats is drawn to the idea of an unchanging ideal world, before accepting the need to return to reality. Ultimately, permanence is not enough for the poet. The enduring splendour of the cold star, like the timeless perfection of the cold Grecian urn, cannot ultimately satisfy Keats who longs to forever savour the 'sweet unrest' of passionate love.

> **KEY POINTS**
>
> - Key theme is the contrasting attractions of the constant but cold star and the transient but warm world of human passion.
> - Contrasting imagery: coldness and isolation of the star ('in lone splendour hung aloft the night') contrasted with the shared experience of warm human love ('pillowed upon my fair love's ripening breast, / To feel forever its soft rise and fall').
> - Personification of nature: the star is 'like nature's patient, sleepless eremite'.
> - Sound effects: Alliterative and sibilant 's' sound evokes the sense of perfect peace and happiness that accompanies the shared experience of human love.

Ode to a Nightingale

In this poem we see Keats' deep desire to escape from the imperfect, transient physical world into the perfect, immortal world of the nightingale's song. For Keats the bird's song is a symbol of eternal beauty, happiness and freedom.

The opening stanza conveys the poet's gloom and lethargy: 'My heart aches and a drowsy numbness pains / My sense, as though of hemlock I had drunk.' Keats explains his feelings of despondency and inertia by means of a paradox: ''Tis not through envy of thy happy lot, / But being too happy in thine happiness'. The paradoxical notion that pain can be the result of excessive happiness startles and challenges the reader. The opening stanza contrasts the poet's melancholy with the joy and ease of the nightingale's song: the bird 'singest of summer in full-throated ease'.

The poet considers various avenues of escape from the grim world of reality. He considers the possibility of reaching the perfect world of the bird's song by means of alcohol: 'O for a draught of vintage!' The repetition of 'O' underscores his sense of longing. Keats describes the wine in the type of sensuous detail that is characteristic of his poetry. We can almost taste the wine, which has been 'cooled a long age in the deep-delved earth', and visualise 'the beaded bubbles winking at the brim'. The use of alliteration underlines the sensuous appeal of the wine by means of which the poet hopes 'to leave the world unseen' and fade away with the nightingale 'into the forest dim'.

The third stanza accentuates (emphasises) the pain and sorrow of the physical world from which Keats longs to escape. The poet thinks of physical life in terms of 'the weariness, the fever, and the fret'. The transience of life is vividly captured in a particularly grim image: 'Where youth grows pale and spectre-thin and dies.' The poet believes that Beauty and Love (their personification underlines their importance to Keats) cannot survive in a world of transience: 'Where Beauty cannot keep her lustrous eyes, / Or new Love pine at them beyond tomorrow.'

In stanza four Keats emphatically dismisses the idea of using wine to reach the perfect world of the nightingale's song, proclaiming that he will instead access it through the power of the imagination: 'Away! away! for I will fly to thee, / Not charioted by Bacchus and his pards, / But on the viewless wings of Poesy.' Through the power of his imagination, Keats finds himself in the world of the nightingale: 'Already with thee!'

Stanza five depicts the ideal world of the nightingale's song. This is a world rich in sensuous appeal, a world of darkness and tranquillity where the poet can smell the 'soft incense' that 'hangs upon the boughs', taste the 'dewy wine' and hear 'the murmurous haunt of flies on summer eves.' While the references to 'embalmed darkness' and to flies are suggestive of death and decay, Keats does not view death as something threatening – indeed at the start of the next stanza he even admits to having been 'half in love with easeful Death'.

The poet has considered the possibility of escaping harsh, painful reality through death. The idea of dying when the nightingale is 'pouring forth' his soul 'in such an ecstasy' appeals to the poet. As in *Bright Star,* he longs to forever capture a moment of perfect joy by dying when he is at his happiest. Here Keats sees death as a means of achieving total happiness. However, he realises that death is not the answer to his problems since it would deprive him of the perfect pleasure of the bird's song: 'To thy high requiem become a sod.'

In the seventh stanza Keats contrasts his own mortality with the immortality of the bird's song: 'Thou wast not born for death, immortal bird!' The beautiful song, which the poet has just enjoyed, has been experienced 'in ancient days by emperor and clown'. Keats suggests that the nightingale's song has had an uplifting and inspiring effect on people from ancient and biblical times through to the present. The song fires our imaginations, allowing us to experience a rare and special beauty: 'Charmed magic casements, opening on the foam of perilous seas, in faery lands forlorn.'

The word 'forlorn' acts as a reminder to the poet of the inescapable reality of loneliness and misery. It is like a tolling funeral bell signalling the end of the poet's imaginative experience. As the bird's 'plaintive anthem' fades, Keats realises that the imagination cannot offer him a lasting means of escape: 'Adieu! The fancy cannot cheat so well as she is famed to do'. The wonderful, magical experience stimulated by the bird's song is over and the poet returns to the world of reality. At the close of the poem Keats is back where he began, wondering if the power of his imagination has enabled him to experience a truly visionary moment or merely provided him with the means of temporarily escaping from reality: 'Was it a vision or a waking dream?'

KEY POINTS

- Key themes are the transience and pain of life and the poet's yearning to escape from reality into a world of lasting happiness and perfection.
- The contrast between the perfection and permanence of the bird's song and the imperfection and transience of real life is sharply drawn.
- Sensuous imagery – note stanzas 2 and 5 in particular.
- Symbolism: the bird's song is a symbol of lasting beauty and perfection.
- Sound effects: alliteration (e.g. 'Deep-delved', 'beaded bubbles'), assonance (e.g. 'blown . . . glooms'), sibilance (e.g. 'Singest of summer in full-throated ease'), etc.

Ode on a Grecian Urn

This poem is similar in theme to *Ode to a Nightingale*. In both poems we see Keats' desire for permanence and immortality in a world of transience. The Grecian urn, like the nightingale's song, is a symbol of lasting perfection. However, in both poems Keats also acknowledges that he cannot remain forever in an ideal world conjured up by the imagination. In both poems he concludes that, having experienced perfect, timeless beauty, he must return to reality.

In the opening stanza Keats addresses the urn, which depicts pastoral (rural) scenes of a pagan festival. The metaphors of the 'still unravished bride of quietness' and 'foster child of silence' evoke the stillness and tranquillity of the urn. This sense of peace is reinforced by the sibilant 's' sound of the opening lines. Paradoxically, the silent urn can tell a tale more eloquently than the poet and his poem. There is a sense of excitement as Keats brings the lifeless urn to life by entering into the world of the story depicted on its sides: 'What men or gods are these? What maidens loth? / What mad pursuit? What struggle to escape?'

The second stanza opens with Keats asserting that art is superior to reality, that the world of the imagination is superior to the real world. He claims that the music that the piper on the urn is playing is more beautiful than real music because it appeals not to the ear but to the spirit or to the imagination: 'Heard melodies are sweet, but those unheard / Are sweeter.' He also suggests that the love depicted on the urn is superior to real love because it is forever beautiful and forever young. The 'bold lover' will never kiss the maiden he pursues (the repetition of 'never, never' is particularly emphatic) but, while he will never actually experience the 'bliss' of love, that love and her beauty will live eternally, untarnished by the harshness and disappointment of reality: 'For ever wilt thou love, and she be fair!'

The repetition of 'happy' (six times) and 'for ever' (five times) seems to underline the poet's belief in the superiority of art. We do however wonder if the poet is as convinced as he claims to be of the superiority of art over real life. As someone painfully aware of life's transience, Keats understandably delights in this vividly imagined world of eternal youth, timeless music and everlasting love. This perfect work of art has forever captured a variety of happy scenes, effectively freezing them in time. However, there is a suggestion that the love depicted on the urn lacks the vibrancy and warmth of real human passion: 'All breathing human passion far above that leaves a heart high-sorrowful and cloyed / A burning forehead, and a parching tongue.' While human love is subject to change and can involve sorrow and pain, Keats realises that art, although perfect and immortal, is also cold and lifeless.

In stanza four, Keats captures the ritual sacrifice of a heifer in a typically sensuous image: 'that heifer lowing at the skies, and all her silken flanks with garlands dressed. The image of the deserted, lifeless town reinforces the impression of the urn as a cold, lifeless object: 'And little town, thy streets for evermore will silent be.'

In the final stanza Keats moves from contemplating the scenes on the urn to reflecting on the urn itself. As he steps back and looks at the urn, he leaves the world of the imagination and returns to the world of reality. For all its timeless beauty, the urn is ultimately a lifeless artifact, as the poet's references to 'marble men and maidens', 'Thou, silent form' and 'Cold Pastoral!' clearly suggest. He admires the beauty of the urn and its capacity to 'tease us out of thought' (which is suggestive of its capacity to provoke an imaginative, as opposed to an intellectual or logical response). The urn remains 'a friend to man', reminding us that 'Beauty is truth, truth beauty'. While this equation of truth and beauty has provoked much controversy and debate, Keats seems to argue that what the imagination perceives as beauty must be truth.

As in *Ode to a Nightingale,* Keats accepts that he must return from a vividly imagined world of perfect, everlasting beauty to the world of imperfect, transient reality.

KEY POINTS

- Themes include Keats' desire to escape from transitory reality into a timeless world of enduring perfection.
- The contrast between art (perfect and everlasting, but cold) and reality (imperfect and transient, but living) lies at the heart of Keats' inner debate.
- Use of paradoxes, e.g. 'Heard melodies are sweet but those unheard are sweeter'.
- Memorable metaphors, e.g. 'unravished bride of silence', 'foster child of silence', etc.
- Sensuous imagery: e.g. Love is described as leaving 'a heart high-sorrowful and cloyed, / A burning forehead and a parching tongue'.
- The use of regular questions suggests the poet's imaginative engagement with the scenes depicted on the urn, e.g. 'What men or gods are these? What maidens loth?'
- Sound effects: alliteration (e.g. 'marble men and maidens', etc.), assonance (e.g. 'Sylvan historian', etc).

La Belle Dame Sans Merci

This poem is written in the form of a medieval ballad. It tells a story that is full of mystery, drama and uncertainty. As in other Keats' poems there is a contrast between the harshness of the real world and an ideal world of beauty and happiness.

This ballad consists of a dialogue between the knight and an unknown speaker. Stanzas 1–3 are addressed to the knight, while stanzas 4–12 express his reply. As in other Keats' poems, the real world is seen as a place of suffering. The knight looks sickly ('With anguish moist and fever dew), despondent ('So haggard and so woe-begone') and bewildered ('Alone and palely loitering'). The autumnal setting underlines the sense of desolation: 'The sedge has withered from the lake and no birds sing.' Long vowel sounds reinforce the bleak mood ('Alone . . . palely . . . woe . . . fading', etc).

The knight's meeting with this supernatural beauty ('a fairy's child' with 'wild eyes') seems to have been accidental. Everything about her is beautiful and the knight seems to be instantly enchanted by her: 'Full beautiful . . . / Her hair was long, her foot was light.' He immediately starts to woo her with garlands and bracelets of flowers: 'I made a garland for her head and bracelets too'. He put her on his 'pacing steed' and watched her 'all day long'. Once again, this poem is rich in sensuous detail: 'She looked at me as she did love / And made sweet moan . . . She found me roots of relish sweet, / And honey wild and manna-dew.' This mysterious woman speaks a strange language, yet the knight seems to understand her: 'she said / I love thee true.' Later, she took the knight to her mysterious fairy cave. The happy mood is dispelled when this enigmatic beauty is inexplicably overcome by sorrow: 'And there she wept, and sigh'd full sore'. After the knight attempts to console her 'with kisses four', she lulls him asleep.

The knight's strange experience has a nightmarish dimension – he has a vision of 'death-pale' kings, princes and warriors who warn him that he, like them, has been enslaved by 'La Belle Dame Sans Merci'. The image of their 'starved lips . . . gaped wide' is particularly grotesque and frightening. The beautiful, bewitching enchantress is closely associated with death, and may even be the embodiment of death.

At the close of the poem, the knight is back in the real world: 'And I awoke and found me here / On the cold hill's side'. He seems to have escaped from the nightmare, yet he can never escape the inevitability of death. The mood at the close of the poem is particularly bleak, with the knight isolated and seemingly without purpose or direction ('Alone and palely loitering'). The absence of birdsong ('And no birds sing') suggests that the happiness associated with birds singing is no longer possible.

Once again we see the contrast between the ideal world of beauty and happiness that the knight briefly experiences and the harsh world of reality to which he returns at the close of the poem. For a brief time the knight (perhaps representative of Keats) is captivated by a vividly imagined experience of an ideal world. However, like Keats, in both *Ode to a Nightingale* and *Ode on a Grecian Urn,* the knight, too, inevitably returns to reality.

This poem is gloomy in outlook since it suggests that love and death are inseparable. It is similar to *Ode to a Nightingale* in that both poems suggest the impermanence of love ('Where Beauty cannot keep her lustrous eyes, / Or new Love pine at them beyond tomorrow'). It resembles *Ode on a Grecian Urn* in that both poems suggest that love inevitably involves pain ('A burning forehead and a parching tongue').

KEY POINTS

- Key theme is the contrast between the ideal beauty and happiness that the knight briefly experiences, and the harshness of the real world.
- A gloomy poem dominated by images and suggestions of death.
- The atmosphere of the poem is one of darkness and mystery.
- Vivid imagery.
- Repetition (e.g. first and last stanzas are largely similar).

To Autumn

While most poems on the subject of autumn tend to be largely gloomy reflections on death and decay, this poem celebrates the natural abundance of the autumn season. While there are suggestions of death and the passage of time, this is not a poem about life's transience; instead we see Keats delighting in the richness and beauty of the season. The sensuousness, which is a constant feature of Keats' verse, is strikingly evident in this poem. Each stanza deals with a different aspect of the autumnal world.

Stanza one opens with a wonderfully atmospheric description of autumn: 'Seasons of mists and mellow fruitfulness'. The alliterative 'm' ('mists . . . mellow . . . maturing') and repeated 'l' sounds ('mellow', 'apples', 'fill', 'shells', 'cells') suggest a sense of ease and harmony. Personified autumn is addressed in all three stanzas. In stanza one autumn is depicted as a co-conspirator with 'the maturing sun' in bringing about the seemingly unending fruitfulness of the season. Their shared work has an almost sacred quality as they 'load and bless / With fruit the vines that round the thatch-eves run'. Together, they are responsible for the weight of apples that bend the trees. The phrase 'budding more and still more' suggests unending abundance. Even the bees are deceived into thinking that this bountiful season will never end, with their hives full of honey ('For summer has o'er-brimmed their clammy cells'). Tactile imagery conveys the rich bounty of the season: autumn and the sun combine 'to swell the gourd, and plump the hazel shells'.

In the second stanza autumn is personified as various people engaged in the diverse activities of harvesting. She is, in turn, a granary worker, a reaper, a gleaner and finally a cider maker. Autumn is largely inactive in this section of the poem. The images in this stanza are mainly visual. We see autumn 'sitting careless on a granary floor' with her hair 'soft-lifted by the winnowing wind'. The gentle, alliterative 'w' and assonant 'i' sounds create the sense of autumn's hair being lightly lifted by the wind. The image of autumn asleep 'on a half-reaped furrow' evokes a sense of ease. She is in no rush to complete the reaping and harvesting. Her lethargy suggests a sense of fulfillment. A sensuous image suggests how she is drowsy 'with the fume of poppies'. As a cider maker, autumn patiently watches over the production of cider from the abundant apples that had caused the trees to bend in stanza one: 'thou watchest the last oozings hours by hours.' The sibilance of this line underlines the sense of ease and tranquillity. Time is moving on: in the first stanza we could almost touch the ripening fruit, while in the second we can visualise the harvesting and processing of these fruits.

In stanza three time has moved on further and the harvest is done; all that now remains of it is 'the stubble-plains with rosy hue'. While this is a tactile-visual image, the imagery in this stanza is mainly aural. The poet listens to the plaintive music of autumn, the various sounds combining to create a veritable symphony: '. . . in a wailful choir the small gnats mourn . . . lambs loud bleat . . . Hedge-crickets sing . . . The red-breast whistles . . . And gathering swallows twitter in the skies.' There is a clear suggestion of death in this stanza with references to 'the soft-dying day', 'a wailful choir', the mourning gnats and the robin – a bird traditionally associated with winter. Keats is not despondent; he seems to be accepting of this natural process. He does not dwell on life's transience, but instead celebrates the distinctive beauty of autumn.

KEY POINTS

- Key theme is the abundance and distinctive beauty of autumn.
- Sensuous imagery present throughout.
- Sound effects: alliteration (e.g. 'mists and mellow fruitfulness', 'winnowing wind'), assonance (e.g. 'mourn', 'bourn'), sibilance (e.g. 'Thou watchest the last oozings hours by hours'), etc.

Sample Answer

Explain why the poetry of Keats did or did not appeal to you.

The poetry of Keats greatly appealed to me for a range of reasons. Purely on a descriptive level, I love the way he uses sensuous imagery to convey the beauty of the natural world. Few poets appreciate and celebrate beauty like Keats. On a deeper level Keats grapples with some issues of universal relevance in his work, reflecting on such matters as mortality, the pain of life, the search for permanence in a world of change and the power of the imagination. At the heart of much of Keats' poetry are the conflicting attractions of art and reality. While art is perfect and timeless, it can also be cold and lifeless. In contrast, while reality is painful and transient, it can also be vibrant and passionate. We can all relate to Keats' inner struggles as the issues that preoccupy him are universal and timeless. In the context of these inner struggles, another quality I greatly admire about Keats strongly emerges – his realism. Finally, I was impressed with the various sound effects Keats so effectively employs in his verse.

A simple poem that I greatly enjoyed is *To One Who Has Been Long in City Pent.* Weary of the confinement of the city, Keats is rejuvenated by the natural world as he lies back in the long grass reading 'a gentle tale of love and languishment'. I like the way Keats regularly gives human qualities to the natural world, in this poem personifying the sky with his reference to 'the smile of the blue firmament'. However, his realism expresses itself before the sonnet ends when he reminds us of the transience of this uplifting day by comparing its passing to the fall of an angel's tear from heaven to earth.

In *Bright Star* Keats is attracted to the permanence and 'splendour' of the 'bright star'. However, he is not attracted to its detached, isolated existence. Keats sees the star as being hermit-like in its solitude: 'Like nature's patient, sleepless eremite.' The beauty of nature in winter is captured in the memorable image of the 'soft-fallen mask / Of snow upon the mountains'. The alliterative and sibilant 's' sound evokes a sense of perfect peace. While the star is 'still steadfast, still unchangeable', Keats is drawn back to the real world. His idea of perfect happiness would be to be forever 'Pillowed upon my fair love's ripening breast, / To feel forever its soft fall and swell'. This beautiful sensuous image with its soft sibilant and alliterative 's' sound conveys the warmth of shared human love that is ultimately more appealing to the poet than the existence of the immortal, but cold, star. The tension between Keats' yearning for immortality and his desire to enjoy the passionate pleasures of real love is apparent in much of his verse.

I regard *Ode to a Nightingale* as one of the truly great poems. In this poem we see Keats' intense desire to escape from the painful, transient physical world into the perfect immortal world of the nightingale's song. Like many people at difficult moments in their lives, Keats considers alcohol as a possible avenue of escape. He describes the wine in sensuous detail – one of the features of his verse that I particularly enjoy. We can almost taste the wine that has been 'cooled a long age in the deep-delved earth' and visualise 'the beaded bubbles winking at the brim'. The alliterative 'd' and 'b' sounds underscore the sensuous appeal of the wine, by means of which Keats hopes to fade away with the nightingale 'into the forest dim'. When he dismisses the idea of using alcohol to reach the perfect world of the nightingale's song, the poet finally accesses it by means of his imagination, flying there on 'the viewless wings of Poesy'. The world of the nightingale's song is rich in sensuous appeal. Here Keats can smell the 'soft incense' that 'hangs upon the boughs', taste 'the dewy wine' and hear 'the murmurous haunt of flies on summer eves'. However, we can sense the poet's realism asserting itself in the suggestions of death and decay to be found in the references to the 'embalmed darkness' and the murmuring flies. Ultimately, Keats realises that the imagination cannot offer him a lasting means of escape: 'Adieu! adieu! The fancy cannot cheat so well / As she is famed to do'. The wonderful, magical journey inspired by the bird's song is over and the poet returns to the world of reality. I can certainly understand Keats' longing to escape life's problems and transience, but I am impressed with the realism that brings him back to the physical world.

In *Ode on a Grecian Urn* we again see Keats' desire for permanence in a world of transience. The Grecian urn, like the nightingale's song, is a symbol of lasting perfection. The metaphors of the 'still unravished bride of quietness' and 'foster child of silence' effectively evoke the stillness and tranquillity of the urn. In the early part of the poem Keats asserts that art (symbolic of the power of the imagination) is superior to reality when he claims that the music played by the piper in one of the pastoral scenes depicted on the urn is more beautiful than real music because it appeals, not to the ear, but to the spirit or the imagination: 'Heard melodies are sweet, but those unheard / Are sweeter . . .'

Keats also suggests that the everlasting love of the figures on the urn is superior to real human passion. However, we get the impression that he 'doth protest too much' with the repetition of 'happy' when describing this love: 'More happy love! more happy, happy love! / For ever happy and still to be enjoyed.' There is a clear suggestion that the love depicted on the urn lacks the vibrancy and warmth of real human passion: 'All breathing human passion far above, / That leaves a heart high sorrowful and cloy'd, / A burning forehead and a parching tongue.' While human love is subject to change and can involve disappointment and pain, Keats realises that art, although perfect and timeless, is also cold and lifeless. Moving on to another scene portrayed on the urn, the poet captures the ritual sacrifice of a heifer in a typically sensuous image: 'that heifer lowing at the skies, / And all her silken flanks with garlands dressed.' In the final stanza, the poet leaves the world of the imagination and returns to the world of reality. For all its perfection, the urn remains a cold artifact, a mere reflection of real life as Keats' references to 'marble men and maidens', 'thou silent form' and 'Cold Pastoral!' clearly suggest. Another aspect of this poem that I enjoyed is the manner in which Keats leaves us grappling with his controversial declaration that 'Beauty is truth, truth beauty'.

The Keats' poem that I most enjoyed was *To Autumn*. While the title leads us to expect a despondent reflection on transience and death, what we actually get is a wonderful description and celebration of the overflowing abundance of the season. The sensuousness that I particularly admire in Keats' verse is again strikingly evident in this poem. The poem opens with a wonderfully atmospheric description of autumn: 'Season of mists and mellow fruitfulness, / Close bosom-friend of the maturing sun.' The alliterative 'm' ('mists . . . mellow . . . maturing') and repeated 'i' sounds evoke a sense of ease and harmony. Tactile imagery conveys the rich bounty of the season as autumn and sun combine 'to swell the gourd, and plump the hazel shells'. Autumn is brought to life as Keats personifies her as a variety of workers involved in the diverse activities of harvesting. The images in the second stanza of the poem are mainly, but not entirely, visual. We see autumn 'sitting carelessly on a granary floor' with her hair 'soft-lifted by the winnowing wind'. The gentle, alliterative 'w' and assonant 'i' sounds create the sense of autumn's hair being lightly lifted by the wind. The image of autumn asleep 'on a half-reaped furrow' evokes a sense of ease. Another sensuous image portrays her as being drowsy 'with the fume of poppies'. In the final stanza, the harvesting has been completed and all that now remains of the harvest is 'the stubble-plains with rosy hue'. While this is a tactile-visual image, the images in this stanza are predominantly aural. Keats listens to the plaintive music of autumn: 'in a wailful choir the small gnats mourn . . . lambs loud bleat . . . Hedge-crickets sing . . . The red-breast whistles . . . And gathering swallows twitter in the skies.' While the references to 'the soft-dying day', mourning gnats and 'a wailful choir' evoke the idea of death, Keats is not despondent. He is accepting of this natural process and does not dwell on the passage of time, choosing instead to celebrate the unique beauty and richness of autumn.

In conclusion, I would only like to restate my great admiration for and genuine enjoyment of the work of John Keats, a truly great poet.

W.B. Yeats

Biographical Note

Yeats was born in Dublin in 1865. He was one of a family of five children. William was not the only member of the Yeats family who would go on to achieve fame – his brother Jack went on to become a renowned artist. Yeats spent his childhood years between his mother's native Sligo and London. He never settled into life in London, but deeply loved Sligo and the West of Ireland in general. He grew up in an age when nationalist sentiment was on the rise (his father John was a nationalist) and became passionate about the cause of Irish freedom after meeting an ex-Fenian named John O'Leary. For Yeats, O'Leary was the epitome of selfless patriotism and the embodiment of an earlier heroic Ireland – the 'Romantic Ireland' of the past. Yeats became fascinated with ancient Ireland, particularly its folk tales and legends. The publication of *The Wanderings of Oisin and Other Stories* in 1896 established him as a significant literary talent.

Yeats had a keen interest in all matters spiritual, attending many seances and investigating various forms of mysticism. Along with George Russell and a small number of like-minded people, he formed the Dublin Hermetic Society, an unusual club dedicated to the study of spiritualism and even magic. He became particularly interested in Buddhism and the Cabbala, a mysterious branch of Judaism.

In 1889 Yeats met the woman who would become the great love of his life, the beautiful and fascinating Maud Gonne. Yeats' unrequited love for Maud Gonne inspired most of his great love poems. When she married John MacBride, Yeats felt deeply betrayed. Another key influence on Yeats' poetic development was the Anglo-Irish noblewoman Augusta Gregory. Her estate,

Coole Park, became a regular summer retreat for the poet. Their close relationship was based on mutual respect and affection, with Lady Gregory becoming his confidante and a great source of encouragement for him. She was already deeply involved in a revival of Irish literature through an era known as the Celtic Twilight when she befriended Yeats. With their shared interest in Irish heritage, Yeats and Lady Gregory founded the Irish Literary Theatre (which would later become known as the Abbey Theatre) in 1899. Yeats wrote many plays for the Abbey, all based on Gaelic tales and myths. However, from 1910 Yeats channelled his creative energies into his poetry.

It was during this period that Yeats came under the influence of the American poet, Ezra Pound. In 1913 Yeats and Pound lived together in London. Yeats admired the realism and energy of Pound's work. We can see a new realism and directness in Yeats' poetry during this period as he expresses his deep anger at the selfish, cynical nature of middle-class Ireland in *September 1913*, before the 1916 rebellion gave him cause to revise the views as expressed in the poem *Easter 1916*.

In 1917 Yeats married George Hyde-Lees, with whom he went on to have two children. Their marriage was a surprisingly happy one. (He had earlier proposed to Maud Gonne and, following her rejection of him, her daughter, Iseult, who also rejected him). In 1923 Yeats was awarded the prestigious Nobel Prize for Literature. He played a significant role in public affairs, becoming a senator in the upper house of the Oireachtas in 1922, while continuing to write prolifically into old age. He died in 1939 in France, where he was initially buried. Some years later, he was brought home to Ireland and buried in Drumcliffe, County Sligo.

September 1913

Yeats cared passionately about his country, and regularly reflected on the state of the nation in his verse. *September 1913* is a public poem, a political ballad in which Yeats expresses his disillusionment with the Irish middle classes. The historical background to the poem is very relevant since Yeats wrote it in response to a particular set of circumstances. He was prompted to express his contempt for the materialism (being totally preoccupied with material wealth) and philistinism (the inability to appreciate art) of the middle classes by two events in particular: the 1913 Lockout and the lack of support for a gallery to house the Hugh Lane art collection. The Lockout demonstrated the selfish, mercenary-minded nature of Dublin's merchants, while the rejection of the renowned art collection reflected their lack of respect for cultural and artistic values. In essence, the middle classes appeared to have no compassion for their fellow Irishman and no appreciation of art or culture. In this poem, Yeats contrasts the selfishness and cynicism of the merchants with the selflessness and idealism of the heroes of Irish history.

In the opening stanza the poet speaks directly to the merchants. His contempt for their grasping miserliness is suggested by the image of Scrooge-like figures fumbling in 'a greasy till' and adding 'the halfpence to the pence'. The reference to 'shivering prayer' suggests their hypocrisy and cowardice. The ruthless merchants have no qualms about exploiting the workers to the point where they have 'dried the marrow from the bone'. Yeats is being ironic when he suggests that men 'were born to pray and save.' The refrain at the end of stanzas 1–3 makes reference to a patriot and rebel named O'Leary: 'Romantic Ireland's dead and gone, / It's with O'Leary in the grave.'

For Yeats, John O'Leary (one of the founders of the Fenian movement) symbolises the selflessness and idealism of generations of Irish heroes – qualities which, in Yeats opinion, are 'dead and gone'.

In stanza two Yeats points out that the heroes of the past 'were of a different kind'. Their attitudes and values were fundamentally different from those of the merchants. Yeats speaks of those heroes whose names 'stilled the childish play' of the middle-class people he now rebukes. As adults, the merchants are no longer in awe of the great patriots of the past. These heroes had 'little time' to pray or save because they selflessly devoted their lives to the pursuit of a noble dream. The rhetorical question 'And what God help us could they save?' suggests the dismissive reaction of the cold-eyed materialists to men who put little value on, not only money, but their own lives. The repeated refrain, 'Romantic Ireland's dead and gone . . .' emphasises the depth of the poet's disillusionment.

Yeats' anger intensifies and reaches a climax in stanza three with the repetition of 'for this'. The 'this' to which he refers is the mean-spirited Ireland of 1913. Yeats sadly concludes that the sacrifices of the heroes were in vain since they certainly did not die for the type of selfish, cynical society of which he is so critical. The litany (list) of Irish patriots reflects the poet's pride in the contribution of his own class to the cause of Irish freedom. Fitzgerald, Emmet and Tone were, like Yeats, Anglo-Irish Protestants. A gulf of understanding separates the heroes from the merchants, who regard patriotism as a form of madness ('all that delirium of the brave'). While the heroes had a vision of a free Ireland, the merchants' vision does not extend beyond the till in front of them. The self-absorbed merchants cannot understand, let alone appreciate, men who gave so much of themselves in pursuit of a noble ideal.

In the closing stanza Yeats suggests that if the heroes of the past could somehow be recalled to the present, they would be dismissed as madmen, bewitched by the beautiful woman that was Ireland (Ireland was commonly symbolised by a woman in eighteenth century Irish poetry): 'Some woman's yellow hair has maddened every mother's son'. Yeats believes that these heroes would be mocked and denigrated (spoken ill of) in the Ireland of 1913. While these patriots instinctively gave

their lives for a dream ('weighed so lightly what they gave'), the merchants coldly act in their own self-interest. Self-seeking men who live only for personal gain dismiss as mere madness a heroic willingness to die for a dream. The poem ends on a particularly gloomy note: 'But let them be, they're dead and gone . . . ' Yeats sadly concludes that it is futile raising the memories of the heroic dead in the cynical and dispiriting climate of early twentieth-century Ireland. The courage and generosity of spirit epitomised by the patriots of the past seem to be entirely absent in the Ireland of 1913.

KEY POINTS

- Key theme is Yeats' profound disillusionment with the materialism and cynicism of middle-class Ireland.
- The contrast between the inspiring heroic past and the dispiriting, mean-spirited present is sharply drawn by Yeats.
- Yeats juxtaposes the materialistic, cynical merchants with the selfless, idealistic heroes of the past.
- Vivid, concrete imagery ('fumble in a greasy till', etc.).
- Yeats uses irony to underscore his contempt for the merchants' values ('For men were born to pray and save').
- Use of repetition ('for this') underlines the depth of the poet's disappointment and anger.
- Use of colloquial language suggests the merchants' uncomprehending response to the patriotism of previous generations ('And what, God help us, could they save?').
- The repeated refrain ('Romantic Ireland's . . . ') gives further emphasis to the poet's profound disillusionment with the values of middle-class Ireland.

Sailing to Byzantium

In this poem we see Yeats searching for something permanent in a world of change. It is the poet's keen awareness of life's transient (passing) nature and of his own advanced age that sets him thinking about the meaning and

purpose of life. While *September 1913* is a very public poem, this poem is intensely personal in that Yeats lays bare his pain at growing old. However, it has an obvious universal appeal in that ageing is part of the human condition. The philosophical questions that Yeats raises in this poem also have a universal relevance. The question of life's meaning or purpose and the conflict between body and soul are matters that concern us all, especially as we grow older.

For Yeats, Byzantium symbolised an ideal world. The title of the poem suggests the idea of a journey to a perfect world of art. This voyage is a spiritual one prompted by the poet's consciousness of advancing age. In his search for perfection and permanence in a world of imperfection and change, Yeats rejects the physical world in favour of spiritual perfection in art.

The opening stanza reflects the poet's disenchantment with old age. He feels out of place in a world dominated by 'the young in one another's arms', and is painfully aware of the inevitability of old age. While the young couples and the 'birds in the trees' are symbols of life and energy, they are also symbols of transience: 'those dying generations . . .' While such images of rich and abundant natural life as 'the salmon-falls' and 'the mackerel-crowded seas' reflect Yeats' love of life, he reminds us that every living thing ultimately dies: 'Whatever is begotten, born and dies.' Yeats reproaches young people for being preoccupied with physical pleasures ('sensual music', and for neglecting the spirit, the intellect and art: 'all neglect monuments of unageing intellect.' Conscious of the transience of all things physical, Yeats is drawn to the enduring perfection of art.

Yeats' images of the ageing body become increasingly cruel as the poem progresses: he is one of the 'old men' in stanza one, 'a tattered coat upon a stick' in stanza two, and a 'dying animal' in stanza three. The scarecrow image powerfully conveys Yeats' sense of worthlessness as an old man. He believes that an old man is 'a paltry thing' unless the soul can rise above the sad condition of its 'mortal dress'. In essence, Yeats suggests that an old man must concentrate on the spiritual side of life if his existence is to have any meaning. He must strive to achieve spiritual happiness (the personified soul must 'clap its hands and sing') and spiritual perfection. Yeats believes that spiritual perfection can only be achieved through the study of art; the soul must study 'monuments of its own magnificence'. The poet undertakes this inner voyage to Byzantium in the hope of achieving spiritual perfection in art, thereby transcending the limitations of the physical world.

In stanza three Yeats beseeches the Byzantine sages (symbols of spiritual wisdom) to rise from their holy fires, and to teach him how to achieve spiritual perfection: '. . . be the singing masters of my soul.' They will heal his human sufferings and end frustrations which are both physical and spiritual. Yeats' ageing body can no longer satisfy frustrating sensual desires, while his soul is 'sick with desire' for the spiritual perfection which it can only achieve in a world of timeless art. For these reasons Yeats longs for his soul to escape from the confines of his decrepit body and enter into 'the artifice of eternity'. In making this journey to Byzantium, Yeats expresses his preference for the richer and lasting pleasures of the spirit and intellect over the physical pleasures associated with youth.

Yeats believed that, after death, his soul would re-enter the world as the spirit of a person, an animal or a work of art. However, having experienced the intense anguish of growing old, he does not want his soul to take the form of 'any natural thing'. Instead he wants his soul to take the shape of a golden bird, a perfect, timeless artifact and the symbol of spiritual perfection in art. For Yeats, the golden bird represents an ideal existence. However, while we can understand Yeats' attraction to the perfection and permanence of art, the golden bird's existence seems less than ideal. The golden bird may not age like the living birds in the trees in stanza one, but it is lifeless. Also the idea of existing only to 'keep a drowsy emperor awake' seems very dull and monotonous. Perfect art has advantages over real life, but compared to the imagery of teeming life in stanza one, the world of art represented by the golden bird seems cold, artificial and uninspiring. Like all of the great writers and philosophers, Yeats regularly wrestled with the greatest philosophical question of all: the meaning of life. However, we may not agree with the solution to life's transience proposed in this poem. Indeed, so vividly does Yeats evoke the richness of nature in stanza one that it is difficult to imagine him being forever happy with an existence as a timeless, but artificial, golden bird.

KEY POINTS

- Key themes are life's transient nature, the search for permanence in a world of change and the conflict between the physical and the spiritual.
- An intensely personal poem in which Yeats expresses his pain at growing old. However, the issues raised in this poem have an obvious universal relevance.
- The contrast between the imperfect, transient physical world and perfect, timeless art is at the heart of this poem.
- Yeats makes effective use of imagery and symbolism to convey his themes – the scarecrow image suggests the worthlessness of old age, while the golden bird symbolises spiritual perfection in art.
- The use of repetition (the soul must 'sing' and 'louder sing' as the body ages) emphasises the need for an old man to concentrate on the soul.
- Yeats expresses his ideas in a clear, direct manner, ('That is no country for old men', 'An aged man is but a paltry thing', etc.).

The Lake Isle of Innisfree

The theme of this poem is Yeats' desire to escape from the grim, drab urban world to the pastoral utopia that is Innisfree. The poem begins in London's Fleet Street where Yeats heard the sound of running water in a toy fountain in a shop window, and started thinking about the lake water on Innisfree. While this is a very personal poem, it has an obvious universal appeal in that everyone at some point shares the poet's desire to escape to a world of beauty and tranquillity.

The archaic (old fashioned) language at the start of the poem ('I will arise and go now . . .') gives Innisfree a sense of timelessness. Yeats pictures his ideal world in vivid and precise detail: 'And a small cabin build there, of clay and wattles made: / And nine bean-rows will I have there . . .' He imagines himself living a simple, solitary life close to nature: 'And live alone in the bee-loud glade.' The alliterative 'h' sound ('a hive for the honey bee') and the repeated broad vowel sounds ('clay . . . made

. . . glade') help to convey the peacefulness of Innisfree, while the repetition of 'there' underlines the poet's desire to escape to this rural paradise.

The repetition of 'peace' emphasises the poet's desire for a less stressful, more fulfilling way of life. The long lines ('And I shall have some peace there, for peace comes dropping slow') give the poem a slow, relaxed rhythm, suggestive of the slow, relaxed pace of life on Innisfree. Yeats suggests the sounds and colours of Innisfree by appealing to our senses: we can hear the cricket singing and picture noon's 'purple glow'. Again, the repeated broad vowel sounds ('noon . . . glow') help to convey a sense of peace. The imagery used to describe Innisfree is memorable for its freshness and simplicity: 'the veils of the morning', 'midnight's all a glimmer'.

The repetition of the opening line at the beginning of stanza three accentuates Yeats' longing to escape to a simpler, more tranquil world. For Yeats, this yearning to go to Innisfree is no whim or passing fancy. This utopia is constantly on his mind ('always night and day'). The movement from past to present tense is significant. So intense is the poet's longing to escape to Innisfree, and so vivid is his image of this oasis of peace and beauty that he can hear the sound of the lake water deep within his 'heart's core'. In other words, Innisfree is part of his very being. Its appeal is heightened by the implicit contrast with the world of grim reality suggested by the image of 'pavements grey'. The poet's use of sound is particularly effective as alliteration and assonance combine to suggest the gentle sound of the lake water: 'I hear lake water lapping with low sounds by the shore.'

This poem is particularly memorable for its relaxed rhythm and musical qualities. The slow rhythm, the use of repetition and the regular use of alliteration, assonance and end rhyme combine to give this poem a dream-like quality.

Thematically, there are some interesting comparisons and contrasts between this poem and *Sailing to Byzantium*. In both poems there is a longing to escape to a more appealing world. In this poem (written in the early, romantic stage of his career) Yeats' search for a happier, more fulfilling life centres on the physical world, the world of nature. However, in *Sailing to Byzantium*, Yeats rejects the physical world, longing instead for spiritual perfection in a perfect world of art.

KEY POINTS

- Key theme is the poet's desire to escape from the world of grim reality to a pastoral utopia.
- Detailed description of his ideal world (stanza 1).
- Yeats evokes the colours and sounds of Innisfree by appealing to our senses (stanza 2).
- Memorable images ('midnight's all a glimmer, and noon a purple glow', etc.).
- Sharp contrast between the pastoral utopia of Innisfree and the dull, drab urban world suggested by the image of 'pavements grey'.

- Archaic (old fashioned) language suggests the idea of a timeless paradise: 'I will arise and go now . . .'
- Long lines give the poem a slow, relaxed rhythm suggestive of the slow pace of life on Innisfree.
- Repetition of key phrases and words underscore Yeats' longing for a quieter, simpler, more beautiful world.
- Regular use of alliteration ('a hive for the honey bee', 'lake water lapping'), assonance ('low sounds by the shore', 'pavements grey') and end rhyme ('made-glade', 'slow-glow', etc.) add to the poem's musical qualities, creating the sense of a dream-like world.

Easter 1916

This is another of Yeats' public or political poems. Interestingly, in this poem Yeats completely revises the views expressed in *September 1913*. In that poem a bitterly disillusioned Yeats denounced the middle-classes for their materialism and cynicism, sadly concluding that 'Romantic Ireland' was 'dead and gone'. In this poem Yeats implicitly acknowledges that he misjudged the middle classes. The Easter Rising proved that the spirit of self-sacrificing patriotism was in fact very much alive in Ireland. It is to Yeats' credit that he is prepared to admit that he was wrong in his assessment of modern Ireland in general, and of the middle classes in particular.

In the first stanza, Yeats passes some of the men who would later fight in the Easter Rising and sacrifice their lives for the cause of Irish freedom. Before the Rising, Yeats did not take these Irish nationalists seriously. As they emerged from 'counter or desk', it seemed to the poet that these were unremarkable men leading routine lives. The 'eighteenth-century houses' from which they emerged may symbolise the British presence in Ireland. The repetition of 'polite meaningless words' suggests the distance between the poet and these middle-class political activists. Yeats did not think it worthwhile to engage these men in meaningful conversation. In fact, he completely misread them.

Yeats describes how he often had a laugh at their expense 'at the club'. He believed that he lived in a world of fools ('Being certain that they and I but lived where motley is worn'), and that these men were simply posing as revolutionaries. The first stanza ends with a powerful and paradoxical image which encapsulates the complexity of the Easter Rising and the poet's conflicting emotions: 'All changed, changed utterly / A terrible beauty is born.' The Rising and the subsequent executions dramatically altered the poet's and the nation's attitude towards the rebels, and forever changed the course of Irish history. As the paradoxical notion of 'a terrible beauty' suggests, Yeats was very much in two minds about the Rising. The 'beauty' of the insurrection lay in the idealism and courage of the rebels, but the loss of human life and the fanatical insistence on the need for a blood sacrifice gave this beauty a 'terrible' quality. Yeats is to be admired for his detached, balanced attitude towards the Rising – his achievement was all the more remarkable given that he wrote this poem within a few weeks of the leaders of the Rising being executed. Unlike many politicians and indeed historians, Yeats pays tribute to the patriotism of the men of 1916, without being blind to the problematic aspects of the Rising. This poem is clearly much more than a literary flag-waving exercise. Yeats portrays the Easter Rising as the hugely important, but seriously complex, historical event that it is.

In stanza two, Yeats describes some of the leaders of the Rising. He portrays Countess Markievicz as a well-intentioned but uninformed revolutionary ('ignorant goodwill'). There is a suggestion of her fanaticism in the idea that her voice grew 'shrill' from endless political arguments. Patrick Pearse is described as educator and a poet: 'This man had kept a school / And rode our winged horse'. Thomas MacDonagh, Pearse's helper and friend, is presented as an emerging literary force who 'might have won fame in the end'. The most interesting inclusion in this catalogue of rebels that Yeats knew personally is John MacBride. MacBride married Maud Gonne, the love of Yeats' life, and apparently mistreated her. Despite his personal dislike of MacBribe ('a drunken, vainglorious lout'), Yeats acknowledges his role in the Rising. Along with the other leaders of the Rising, MacBride 'resigned his part in the casual comedy' of life and became a figure of real substance, a hero.

The third stanza is dominated by the image of the stone in the stream. Yeats uses the image of the stone in the stream to suggest the impact of the Rising on Irish life and history. The stone also symbolises the fanaticism of the Rising. The idea of stone hearts ('hearts with one purpose alone . . . enchanted to a stone') suggests that the men of 1916 were blindly devoted to a dream, to the exclusion of all other considerations. The image of the stone in the stream suggests that the Rising is a permanent presence or unchangeable reality in the stream of life. Various images of movement and change ('birds that range from cloud to tumbling cloud . . . a horse plashes within it, the long-legged moor-hens dive') and the repetition of 'minute by minute' suggests that the stream of life is ever changing. The closing line in stanza three ('The stone's in the midst of all') underlines the idea that, through their deaths and subsequent transformation into heroes, the men of 1916 have transcended time. The stone that is the Rising will remain as a permanent point of reference in the ever-changing stream of life.

The image of hearts of stone continues into the final stanza: 'Too long a sacrifice can make a stone of the heart.' Yeats refuses to judge the heroes: 'that is Heaven's part.' It is our 'part' or duty to remember ('To murmur name upon name') and to offer comfort, as a mother comforts her child 'when sleep at last has come on limbs that had run wild'. The comparison of the men of 1916 to impulsive children is perhaps the only unsatisfactory aspect of this poem because it seems to suggest that the rebels were somehow not responsible for their actions. Yeats raises another problematic aspect of the Rising when he wonders whether it was necessary since England may have granted Irish freedom (in the form of Home Rule) anyway: 'Was it needless death after all? For England may have kept faith for all that is done and said.' Yeats implicitly acknowledges the rebels' idealism and courage when he writes: 'We know their dream; enough to know they dreamed and are dead'. Even allowing for the possibility that they may have been misguided ('But what if excess of love bewildered them till they died?'), Yeats concludes that the rebels are deserving of their place in Irish history. By listing the names of such dead heroes as 'MacDonagh and MacBride, and Connolly and Pearse', Yeats consciously immortalises them in his verse. The closing lines restate the idea that the Rising transformed men he had once regarded as figures of fun into heroic martyrs: 'Now and in time to be / Wherever green is worn / Are changed, changed utterly.' The poem concludes with the memorable, paradoxical image of the Rising as 'a terrible beauty'. Yeats is acutely aware of the problematic aspects of the Rising (one of the most emotive events in Irish history) that more blinkered commentators would prefer to ignore, but concludes by acknowledging the idealism and courage of the rebels.

Yeats' capacity for self-criticism and detached assessment result in an admirably balanced reflection on the nature and impact of the Easter Rising. This poem is particularly memorable for Yeats' use of powerful imagery and symbolism and simple, direct expression.

KEY POINTS

- Key theme is the nature and impact of the Easter Rising.
- Effective use of imagery and symbolism.
- The use of repetition for emphasis: 'polite meaningless words', 'A terrible beauty is born', 'minute by minute'.
- The use of questions to highlight some of the more uncertain, complex aspects of the Rising, e.g.: 'Was it needless death after all?'
- Simple, everyday language, ('I have met them at close of day', 'He, too, has been changed in his turn', etc.)
- Detached, balanced assessment of the Rising.
- Yeats displays an admirable capacity for self-criticism in acknowledging his underestimation of those men who went on to sacrifice their lives in the Rising.

The Wild Swans at Coole

In this very personal poem Yeats reflects on the passage of time, the beauty of nature and his own sense of sadness as he approaches the autumn of his life. The natural imagery of the opening stanza suggests the beauty, tranquillity and sadness of autumn: 'The trees are in their autumn beauty / The woodland paths are dry / Under the October twilight the water mirrors a still sky.' The alliterative 's' sound helps to convey the sense of peace. The poet's sadness is only hinted at in the opening stanza. The dying year (autumn) and the dying day (twilight) are suggestive of Yeats' melancholy, (sadness), while the image of 'nine-and-fifty swans' (one swan is without a mate) may point to his loneliness. The slow rhythm suggests the poet's reflective mood.

The intensely personal nature of this poem is underlined by the repetition of 'I'. Yeats is very aware of the passage of time: nineteen years have passed since he first counted these swans. On that occasion, Yeats was deeply pained by

Maud Gonne's rejection of him, and the pain of that unrequited (unreturned) love still lingers. Strong, active verbs suggest the power and vitality of the swans: 'I saw . . . all suddenly mount and scatter wheeling . . .' A vivid visual image helps us to picture the swans as they wheel 'in great broken rings'. The noise of the swans' 'clamorous wings' contrasts with and highlights the silence of this autumnal scene.

Yeats regards these swans with awe, describing them as 'brilliant', 'mysterious' and 'beautiful'. The poet now directly expresses his sadness: 'And now my heart is sore'. He recalls how, nineteen years earlier, the sound of the swans' beating wings had lifted his heavy heart: 'All's changed since I . . . trod with a lighter tread'. The alliterative 'b' sound in 'bell-beat' suggests the loud beating of the birds' wings.

Yeats implicitly contrasts himself with the swans. While he is alone, the swans keep their mate for life. While he has inevitably grown old since his last visit to Coole Park, the swans appear to be unageing ('their hearts have not grown old'). While Yeats is weak and weary, the swans are strong and energetic.

The image of 'the still water' further conveys the silence and peacefulness of this autumnal scene. At the close of the poem, Yeats highlights the contrast between his own mortality and the continuity of the natural world. Long after he has grown old or died, the swans will continue to 'delight men's eyes'. Despite the poet's personal sadness, the poem ends on a positive note with this reminder of the enduring, uplifting beauty of the natural world.

KEY POINTS

- Key themes are the passage of time, the poet's sense of sadness as he approaches the autumn of his life and the beauty and continuity of nature.
- An intensely personal poem – note repeated use of 'I'.
- The old, weary, lonely poet is contrasted with the seemingly ever-youthful, energetic, passionate swans.
- Memorable images of the beauty and tranquillity of the natural world ('Under the October twilight the water mirrors a still sky', etc.).
- Yeats generally uses ordinary, everyday language, ensuring that we can easily relate to his themes ('And now my heart is sore', etc.).
- A series of adjectives expresses the sense of awe with which the poet regards the swans: 'brilliant . . . mysterious, beautiful'.
- Effective use of sound: alliteration ('still sky', 'bell-beat', 'cold companionable', 'sore-shore', etc).
- The slow rhythm reflects the poet's meditative (reflective) mood.

The Stare's Nest by My Window

The theme of this poem is Yeats' personal response to the Irish Civil War. While this is obviously a political poem, it is dominated by the natural images of bees 'building' and birds nurturing their young. Yeats is clearly saddened by the violence and destructiveness of this bitter conflict, but looks to the natural world to provide hope in this time of despondency and uncertainty. He hopes that nature will act as a positive counterforce to the hatred, bitterness and pessimism of the civil war. Describing his own response to the war, Yeats wrote that he 'felt an overmastering desire not to grow unhappy or embittered, not to lose all sense of the beauty of nature'.

The image of 'loosening masonry' suggests the sense of disintegration associated with the civil war. The world around the poet seems to be falling apart. The repetition of 'loosening' underscores the idea of destruction and decay. The fact that Yeats speaks of his own wall crumbling ('My wall is loosening . . .') suggests that he has been personally affected by this deeply divisive conflict. Yet even as the man-made world breaks down, the natural world is busy building and creating: 'The bees build . . . The mother birds bring grubs and flies.' While the image of the empty bird's nest suggests the idea of silence and loss, Yeats hopes that the bees will build 'in the empty house of the stare'. He longs for the hard-working bees to replace the productive birds in the empty nest.

The poet goes on to describe his feelings of fear, uncertainty and helplessness. The image of people locked within their own uncertainty ('the key is turned on our uncertainty . . .') is particularly effective. Yeats is only a powerless observer of this internecine (mutually destructive) conflict: '. . . somewhere a man is killed, or a house burned'. In the face of such murderous hatred and violence, Yeats can only repeat his plea for natural world to provide a positive, inspiring image of fruitfulness and continuity.

The vivid image of 'that dead young soldier in his blood' being 'trundled down the road' effectively conveys the full horror of the civil war. Yeats expresses no political viewpoint, instead highlighting the human cost of this bitter conflict.

In the closing stanza, Yeats suggests that idealism has sadly been transformed or twisted into a type of ugly fanaticism: 'We had fed the heart on fantasies, the heart's grown brutal from the fare'. A similar idea is expressed in *Easter 1916* where Yeats speaks of 'hearts . . . enchanted to a stone'. He feels that hatred is now a more powerful force than love: 'More substance in our enmities than in our love'. Given the extreme bitterness of the civil war, Yeats' assessment of the state of the nation at this point in time seems a valid one. The expressive 'O' at the close of the poem ('O honey-bees, come build . . .') accentuates the intensity of the poet's longing for the natural world to provide an image of all that is positive, harmonious and inspiring at a time of division and despair.

An Acre of Grass

This poem is set in the poet's home in Rathfarnham, County Dublin, where he lived for the last seven years of his life. The opening lines suggest that Yeats' house has what he needs to keep him mentally stimulated and physically well. He has his art and his literature ('Picture and book remain') and his 'acre of grass / For air and exercise'. Yeats' ageing and diminishing strength are directly stated: 'Now strength and body goes . . .' The references to midnight and 'an old house' suggest that the poet's life is drawing to a close. The sense of silence and stillness in the old house is clear from the line, 'Where nothing stirs but a mouse'. The silence of the house may suggest the artistic silence of the poet in old age.

In his advanced years, the poet no longer has the sensual desires of a younger man: 'My temptation is quiet'. His primary concern in old age is to discover and reveal 'the truth' of life in his poetry. The creative process requires both inspiration and intellectual effort, but Yeats' 'loose imagination' and 'mill of the mind' seem incapable of making 'the truth known'. The implication of these lines is that the poet's creative powers are, sadly, on the wane.

The third stanza brings a dramatic change in tone as Yeats cries out for 'an old man's frenzy'

so that he can 'remake' himself. There is no sign now of the sense of resignation to the harsh realities of old age apparent in the opening stanzas. Yeats wants to resemble Timon and Lear, Shakespearian characters who raged against old age and, in Lear's case, against the loss of his mental powers. More particularly, the poet wishes to be like William Blake, who continued to write poetry through his old age in relentless pursuit of 'the truth'.

Yeats also wishes that he could be similar to Michelangelo, the renowned Renaissance artist and sculptor and a man whose unquestionable genius enabled him to 'pierce the clouds' and see the truth beyond them. The poet again expresses his desire to be 'inspired by frenzy' so that, possessed of 'an old man's eagle mind' (a phrase suggestive of his hopes of soaring to new intellectual heights in old age), he might 'shake the dead in their shrouds' with his insightful work. This image powerfully conveys the depth of the poet's desire to continue to have a significant impact on the world with his work – even at his advanced age.

The poet's attitude towards his work in old age changes dramatically in the course of this poem. In stanzas 1–2 Yeats seems resigned to the fact that, 'at life's end', his creative powers are waning, leaving him incapable of revealing 'the truth' in his poetry. However, in stanzas 3–4, we see a very different attitude from Yeats as he defiantly expresses his desire to be granted 'an old man's frenzy' that will enable him to be as artistically productive in old age as William Blake and Michelangelo.

KEY POINTS

- Key theme is the poet's desire to remain artistically productive and insightful in old age.
- There is a striking contrast between the poet's resigned attitude towards old age and its diminishing effects on his artistic capability in stanzas 1–2 and his defiant determination to 'remake' himself in stanzas 3–4.
- Effective use of imagery ('the mill of the mind', etc.).
- Literary allusions are interesting.

Politics

The title suggests that socially responsible writers should have an interest in political matters. Given Yeats' serious interest in Irish public affairs, we expect a poem on some important public event. However, what follows is a reflection on youth and love. This brief poem takes the form of a conversation between Yeats and two seemingly well-informed men: '. . . here's a travelled man that knows / What he talks about, / And there's a politician / That has read and thought . . .' The subject of their discussion is the international political and military situation. However, the poet struggles to stay focused on such weighty matters because of a beautiful girl who's standing nearby: 'How can I, that girl standing there, / My attention fix / On Roman or on Russian / Or on Spanish politics . . .'

The men are discussing the likelihood of war:

'And maybe what they say is true / Of war and war's alarms'. Despite the obvious importance of the subject under discussion, the poet's attention shifts from this serious conversation to the beautiful girl nearby. Yeats longs for his youth and the experience of young love again: 'But O that I was young again / And held her in my arms.' Yeats' yearning for the sensual pleasures of youth can be seen in much of his poetry – in *Sailing to Byzantium* he clearly envies 'the young in one another's arms'. The conflict between youth and age, the body and the spirit, life and art are at the heart of much of Yeats' poetry. Sadly, while the poet's longing for the romance and excitement of youth is understandable, ultimately he must accept the limitations and frustrations that accompany the inexorable ageing process.

KEY POINTS

- While the title leads us to expect a poem about some public event, what follows is a meditation on youth and love
- Key theme is the poet's longing for his irretrievable youth and the opportunity to experience young love again.
- The importance of individual human passion is juxtaposed with the importance of significant happenings on the international stage.

An Irish Airman Foresees his Death

In this poem, Yeats adopts the persona of Robert Gregory, the only son of Lady Gregory and a close friend of the poet's, who was killed in 1918 while fighting for the British Royal Flying Corps. The poem opens on a grim note with the speaker predicting his own death with a sense of absolute certainty: 'I know that I shall meet my fate / Somewhere among the clouds above . . . ' The long vowel sounds convey the serious tone in which these words are uttered ('. . . know . . . fate . . . among . . . clouds above . . .'). The fact that the speaker seems to be unmoved by the prospect of imminent death raises a number of questions.

The greater part of this poem is given over to clarifying the speaker's reasons for volunteering for the war. He was not motivated to volunteer because he hated the Germans: 'Those that I fight I do not hate . . ." Neither did he volunteer because of his love for the British people: 'Those that I guard I do not love . . .' The speaker's only allegiance is to his home in County Galway and to the poor people who live there: 'My country is Kilcartan Cross, / My countrymen Kilcartan's poor . . .' These lines evoke Robert Gregory's sympathetic character. However, regardless of how the war ends, these people will not be affected: 'No likely end could bring them loss / Or leave them happier than before.' He did not volunteer because he was forced to do so by 'law' or out of some sense of 'duty', nor was he inspired to volunteer by some stirring political speech or by the patriotic passion of 'cheering crowds'. The manner in which the speaker dismisses all of the usual emotional reasons that prompt people to volunteer for a war suggests that Robert Gregory was a very detached character.

The speaker's motivation for volunteering is not to be found in any 'external' forces or influences, but deep within his own psyche. He was driven to volunteer by his passion for adventure, and by a desire to confront his fate: 'A lonely impulse of delight / Drove (him) to this tumult in the clouds . . .'

The reader is struck by the bleak tone of the closing lines. Having taken account of every aspect of his life ('I balanced all . . .'), the speaker views the future as meaningless and futile: 'The years to come seemed a waste of breath . . .' The repetition of the same phrase to dismiss the past heightens the sense of despondency that envelops the close of the poem. The final lines of the poem reflect the grim logic of a man who regards his life as pointless and who is now prepared to meet his fate 'somewhere among the clouds above'.

In Memory of Eva Gore-Booth and Con Markiewicz

In this poem Yeats remembers the Gore-Booth sisters whom he had first met in 1894. When he wrote this poem in 1927, both sisters were already dead. The sisters were members of the Anglo-Irish aristocracy whose home was Lissadell, a beautiful mansion near Sligo. The opening lines convey a sense of nostalgia as the poet remembers his visit, as a young man, to Lissadell in 1894. Both the house and the Gore sisters are seen as the epitome of beauty, style and elegance: 'The light of the evening, Lissadell, / Great windows, open to the south, / Two girls in silk kimonos, both / Beautiful, one a gazelle.' While Yeats admired the beauty of both sisters, he was particularly attracted to Eva (the 'gazelle' image is suggestive of graceful beauty). The sense of quiet reflection in lines 1–4 is abruptly shattered in line five with personified Autumn portrayed as a 'raving' destructive force that 'shears / blossom from the summer's wreath . . .' This image powerfully expresses the idea of time's relentless destruction of youth and beauty.

Constance, the older of the two sisters, was sentenced to death for her significant role in the 1916 Rising, but was ultimately pardoned and released from prison. Constance remained politically and socially active, being appointed Minister for Labour in the first Dáil Eireann cabinet, and subsequently supporting the Republican side in the Civil War. Yeats was very unimpressed with the sisters' political activities and social agitation, arrogantly dismissing Constance's efforts to help the poor as 'conspiring among the ignorant'. On a personal level, the 'lonely years' that followed the breakdown of her marriage and her separation from her children were largely the result of her almost fanatical commitment to advancing her political and social ideals. Yeats was equally dismissive of Eva's involvement in the Labour and women's suffrage movements in London, denigrating her social vision as 'Some vague Utopia'. Also, he believed that the sisters' revolutionary efforts undermined their youth and beauty and aged them prematurely: Eva is described as 'withered old and skeleton-gaunt'.

Lines 14–19 convey the poet's sense of nostalgia for an earlier time when the Gore-Booth sisters were young and beautiful. Yeats speaks of them as if they were still alive, wishing that he could once again 'speak / of that old Georgian mansion, mix / Pictures of the mind, recall / That table and the talk of youth . . .'

Yeats next addresses the sisters' ghosts, pointing out that they now possess the knowledge that comes with death: 'Dear shadows, now you know it all . . .' He speaks of 'the folly' (foolishness) of their efforts to bring about social and political change, declaring that, 'The innocent and the beautiful / Have no enemy but time . . .' Here we again see one of

Yeats' primary thematic preoccupations: the ageing process and the ravages of time which ultimately reduce the most beautiful of women (in this instance, the Gore-Booth sisters) to a state of skeletal gauntness.

The final passage of the poem is quite complex. Yeats requests the ghosts of the Gore-Booth sisters to, 'Arise and bid me strike a match / And strike another till time catch . . .' Obviously, the poet does not believe that he can literally set time alight – the fire is perhaps a metaphor for great works of art which have the power to transcend (rise above) time. The transience of life is often juxtaposed with the permanence of art in Yeats work (this contrast is at the heart of *Sailing to Byzantium*). The poem concludes with Yeats reflecting on 'the great gazebo' that he and the Gore-Booth sisters and indeed all members of the Anglo-Irish ascendancy class created – the gazebo being emblematic of their civilized, orderly way of life. Of course, theirs was also a life of wealth and privilege which had been gradually disappearing through the final decades of the nineteenth and the early decades of the twentieth centuries. The line 'They convicted us of guilt' suggests how the general population resented the privileged lifestyle of the Anglo-Irish class.

KEY POINTS

- Themes include the poet's nostalgia for an earlier world – a world of grace and elegance symbolised both by Lissadell House and the Gore-Booth sisters. A related theme is the destructive power of time.
- The contrast between the transience of life and the permanence of art is a key feature of the poem.
- Impressive use of imagery and symbolism.
- Effective use of sound: the assonant 'i' sound in the opening lines helps to convey a pleasant mood ('The light of evening, Lissadell . . . Two girls in silk kimonos.') Alliteration also adds to the musicality of the poem ('light / Lissadell', 'both / Beautiful.', 'folly / fight') as does end rhyme ('dreams / seems . . . seek / speak . . . fight / right . . . match / catch, etc.)
- Yeats' attitude towards the two sisters is often arrogant and sexist. He views the working classes in a similarly superior manner (referring to them as 'the ignorant').

Under Ben Bulben

In this poem, Yeats, now in old age, addresses his fellow Irish poets in an authoritative manner: 'Irish poets, learn your trade, / Sing whatever is well made . . .' The word 'trade' suggests that writing poetry is a craft that requires skill and dedication if it is to be mastered. Yeats urges Irish poets to reject the modern poetic style that was becoming established at this time: 'Scorn the sort now growing up / All out of shape from toe to top.' It would seem that Yeats is referring here to free verse, a key feature of the modern poetic method. Yeats was a formalist who strongly adhered to long established poetic forms, rhyme and metre – this poem is written in the time-honoured heroic couplet form, which is well-suited to the poet's authoritative tone. The poet dismisses those who have no appreciation of their history and who break with traditional forms and techniques: 'Their unremembering hearts and heads / Base-born products of base beds . . .' The repetition of 'base' underscores the poet's low regard for the themes and style of modern poetry. Yeats urges his fellow Irish poets to write of Ireland's rich and vibrant past and to acknowledge the contribution of the various classes in Irish society to that past: 'Sing the peasantry, and then / Hard-riding country gentlemen, / The holiness of monks, and after / Porter-drinkers' randy laughter.' However, Yeats does not want the more troubled aspects of Irish history, a history of heroic defiance of conquest and colonisation, to be neglected by contemporary poets: 'Sing the lords and ladies gay / That were beaten into the clay / Through seven heroic centuries . . .' The poet exhorts (encourages) Irish poets to look to the past for inspiration ('Cast your mind on other days') and to in turn inspire the Irish people to remain 'the indomitable Irishry'.

Within six months of completing Section VI of *Under Ben Bulben*, Yeats was dead. Seemingly anticipating his death, the poet gives clear instructions as to where he is to be buried. Looking ahead, Yeats imagines himself buried 'in Drumcliff churchyard'. He writes about his own demise in a totally detached manner: 'Under bare Ben Bulben's head / In Drumcliff churchyard Yeats is laid.' Ben Bulben is a mountain that the poet always loved. The reason for his choice of this particular cemetery is made clear: 'An ancestor was rector there / Long years ago . . .' (The ancestor to whom he refers was his great-grandfather.) While the 'ancient cross' is a conventional symbol of Christianity, Yeats does not want a conventional burial. He does not want a marble headstone, but one made of limestone quarried near the church. He issues clear instructions as to what is to cut into his headstone: 'By his command these words are cut: Cast a cold eye / On life, on death. / Horseman, pass by!' The word 'command' conveys the authoritative tone in which this instruction is delivered. The epitaph seems to suggest that we should view both life and death in a balanced, detached manner. While the words are starkly simple, there may be other levels of meaning to this epitaph. The horseman is a mysterious figure, but is probably a ghostly character that has its origins in ancient Irish mythology. More important is the instruction that he is to 'pass by!' It seems that Yeats does not want anyone to dwell for long on the fact of his death, but to get on with the business of living.

KEY POINTS

- Key theme is the creative / artistic process.
- This poem also reflects Yeats' passionate concern for Ireland and its people.
- Written in a traditional poetic form – the heroic couplet.
- Tone throughout is authoritative.
- Musical qualities include alliteration ('Base-born . . . base', 'lords and ladies', 'bare Ben Bulben's head', etc.), assonance ('toe-to-top', 'hearts and heads', etc.), end rhyme ('trade-made', 'heads-beds', 'gay-clay', etc.).

The Second Coming

Yeats wrote this poem in 1919, a time of global upheaval and chaos. World War I had raged from 1914 to 1918, causing loss of life on a truly obscene scale, while the Russian Revolution had ushered in a new type of totalitarian regime which did not acknowledge the existence of God. In Ireland the IRA were engaged in a bloody conflict with British forces in yet another attempt to win Irish independence. To compound the sense of devastation, a virulent strain of flu cut a swathe through the European continent, leaving millions dead in its wake. Yeats believed that history moved in cycles of 2000 years, and reckoned that the Christian era was drawing to a close at this time of widespread violence and disorder.

The opening lines convey a sense of things spinning out of control as the falcon, moving in ever wider circles, loses contact with the falconer. If we take the falconer to be representative of Christ, then Yeats is suggesting that in this era of violent turmoil, people are moving increasingly further away from God. The language of the first section of this poem evokes a sense of disorder, disintegration and pervasive violence: 'Things fall apart . . . anarchy is loosed upon the world . . . The blood-dimmed tide is loosed . . .' The idea of 'the ceremony of innocence' being 'drowned' in a blood-red sea suggests the end of a world of order and harmony. Confronted by this 'tide' of violence and destruction, good men are weakened by self-doubt and lacking in commitment, while the evil-doers are, in contrast, driven and fanatical: 'The best lack all conviction', while 'the worst / Are full of passionate intensity'.

The second section of this poem opens in a dramatic manner, with Yeats presenting us with his apocalyptical vision of the future: 'Surely some revelation is at hand: / Surely the Second Coming is at hand.' Some biblical knowledge is required to fully understand the poet's thinking in this poem. In the Book of Revelation the Second Coming is associated with the end of the world. While the Second Coming suggests Christ's second coming to judge mankind, it is also associated with the coming of the Antichrist – and it is this monstrous creature that dominates the poet's vision of the future. Yeats goes on to describe a disturbing visionary experience in which he sees a creature with the body of a lion and the head of a man. This creature lives 'somewhere in the sands of the desert'. This unnatural creature would seem to symbolise the Antichrist. This creature's cruel and callous nature is conveyed by a striking simile: 'A gaze blank and pitiless as the sun.' References to 'shadows' and the coming darkness ('The darkness drops again . . .') suggest the evil, sinister atmosphere that surrounds the coming of the 'rough beast' that has been asleep for two thousand years ('twenty centuries of stony sleep'). Even the predatory desert birds are 'indignant' at the coming of this sphinx-like creature which, with 'its hour come round at last, / Slouches towards Bethlehem to be born?' The idea of this nightmarish creature being born in Bethlehem is shocking in its almost sacrilegious distortion of the story of Christ's birth.

The dark, despairing vision of the future that Yeats describes in this poem proved prophetic as the twentieth century unfolded in all its violence and devastation.

KEY POINTS

- A prophetic poem that presents us with an utterly dark vision of the future.
- The title of the poem has obvious biblical connotations.
- This poem juxtaposes two very different ways of life.
- The conflict between these contrasting ways of life is portrayed in a dramatic manner.
- Imagery is powerful and disturbing.

Swift's Epitaph

This poem is based on a loose translation of the Latin epitaph inscribed on Jonathan Swift's monument in St Patrick's Cathedral. Yeats greatly admired Swift, which was unsurprising given their shared Anglo-Irish literary heritage and their common aristocratic elitism. The image in the opening line suggests the dignified nature of Swift's journey to the next stage of his life: 'Swift has sailed into his rest . . .' In the next world he will be free of the 'savage indignation' that drove him to condemn the many and various ills of society. In this world, he will no longer suffer the intense heartache of the moralist frustrated and angry at the vices of the world he lived in – immoral acts can no longer 'lacerate his breast'. Yeats challenges the reader to 'imitate' Swift, if we 'dare'. In addressing the reader as 'World-besotted traveller', the poet suggests that we are obsessed by the pleasures of the world (an implied contrast with the detached, independent-minded Swift). The suggestion that Swift 'served human liberty' is open to question since neither Swift nor Yeats were over-enamoured with democracy. It is more likely that Yeats was speaking of Swift's belief in the freedom of the artist rather than the freedom of the masses.

KEY POINTS

- This poem is Yeats' tribute to Jonathan Swift, whom he regarded as one of his literary predecessors.
- Opening image of Swift 'sailing' to his rest suggests the dignified manner of Swift's voyage to the next stage of his life.
- The precise meaning of the closing line in the poem is open to question.

Sample Answer

W.B. Yeats – A personal response

Yeats' poetry is very appealing because of the rich variety of his themes. His poems are political and personal, public and private. He reflects on such issues as the state of the nation, the beauty and continuity of the natural world, growing old and the desire to find meaning in life. All of these themes have a universal appeal. Yeats' effective use of imagery and symbolism, and the simple, direct manner in which he expresses the essence of his ideas allow us to easily relate to his verse. Another feature of his poetry that I like is his use of contrast to highlight particular ideas.

In *September 1913* Yeats reflects on the materialism and cynicism of the Irish middle classes. Since we currently live in a very materialistic age, the relevance of this poem is very apparent. The vivid image of the Scrooge-like merchants fumbling in 'a greasy till' suggests their greed, while the image of these 'shivering' hypocrites reciting prayer after selfish prayer suggests their lack of concern for others. Yeats expresses his disillusionment with middle-class Ireland in a clear, direct manner in the refrain, 'Romantic Ireland's dead and gone'. Perhaps the most striking feature of this poem is Yeats' contrasting of the selfish, cynical merchants with the selfless, idealistic heroes of the past ('Yet they were of a different kind'). Yeats suggests that the sacrifices of such patriots as Emmet and Tone were entirely in vain since, in the Ireland of 1913, they would be dismissed as madmen, bewitched by the beautiful woman that was Ireland: 'You'd cry: Some woman's yellow hair has maddened every mother's son'. Another memorable aspect of this poem is the biting irony in Yeats' assertion that 'men were born to pray and save' (Yeats has the selfish prayers of the middle classes in mind here). In this poem the poet reminds us that we were born for far greater things, and sets us thinking about our own value systems.

Easter 1916 is well worth reading in that it shows that Yeats was honest enough to admit that he misread the state of the nation in *September 1913*. He acknowledges that before the Easter Rising he underestimated such revolutionaries as Pearse and MacDonagh. When he met them on the street, he only exchanged 'polite, meaningless words' with them. He recalls how he often had a laugh at their expense 'at the club', believing that he lived in a world of fools: 'Being certain that they and I but lived where motley is worn'. He admits that, with the rising, everything 'changed utterly'. As with so many of Yeats' poems, the imagery is particularly memorable, deftly encapsulating key ideas. The powerful, paradoxical image of 'A terrible beauty' conveys the complexity of this key historical event. The beauty of the Rising lay in the courage and idealism of the rebels, but the loss of human life gave it a 'terrible' quality. Another memorable image suggests the impact of the Rising (symbolised by the stone) on 'the stream' of Irish life: 'Hearts with one purpose alone through summer and winter seem enchanted to a stone to trouble the living stream.' The image of the stone also suggests the fanaticism of the rebels: 'Too long a sacrifice can make a stone of the heart.' Again we see how Yeats expresses his ideas in a direct manner when he bluntly describes John MacBride as 'a drunken, vainglorious lout', before acknowledging that 'he, too, has been changed in his turn'. In highlighting MacBride's role in the Rising, Yeats displays an admirable generosity of spirit since MacBride had married the love of his life, Maud Gonne. The poet's contrasting views of the rebels (before and after the Rising) highlight the way in which the Rising dramatically transformed the popular perception of Pearse and his fellow rebels. In this poem he acknowledges that, by sacrificing themselves in the Rising, they resigned their parts 'in the casual comedy' of life, becoming genuine heroes and forever changing the course of Irish history. This poem is remarkable for its very balanced assessment of a very emotive event. Yeats is aware of the problematical aspects of the Rising, but acknowledges the idealism of the rebels and the profound impact of the Rising on Irish life.

In *The Stare's Nest by My Window* Yeats reflects on the Irish Civil War. Since bitter divisions and violence are permanent features of life, this poem has an obvious universal relevance. Its chief appeal lies in Yeats' refusal to be overwhelmed by the gloom that enshrouded the entire country at this time. In this poem the contrast between the world of man and the world of nature is sharply drawn. While man is associated with death and destructiveness, nature is associated with life and continuity. While the image of 'loosening masonry' suggests how the country is falling apart and the grim image of 'that young soldier in his blood' conveys the horror of the war, the contrasting images of bees building and birds nurturing their young reflect the poet's enduring hope. Yeats longs for the natural world to act as a positive counter-force to the negative forces of death and destruction unleashed by the war. He believes that hate is now a stronger force than love: 'More substance in our enmities than in our love.' In a world still dominated by violence and hate, we share Yeats' longing for an image of hope: 'O honey-bees, come build in the empty house of the stare.'

While *The Wild Swans at Coole* is a very personal poem, its universal relevance is clear as Yeats reflects on his own advanced age, the passage of time, and the beauty and continuity of nature as he visits Coole Park for the first time in many years. Vivid imagery conveys the tranquillity and beauty of this autumnal scene: 'Under the October twilight the water mirrors a still sky.' Yeats expresses his personal sadness in a typically direct manner: 'And now my heart is sore.' The source of his melancholy is the lingering memory of his unrequited love for Maud Gonne. This sense of sadness is highlighted when he contrasts himself with the swans. While the swans appear ever-youthful (an illusion), energetic and loving ('Passion and conquest attend upon them still'), Yeats is old, weary and alone. However, the poem ends on a positive note, with an uplifting image of the swans continuing to 'delight men's eyes' long after he has grown old or died. The reader has much to learn from Yeats' appreciation of the beauty and continuity of the natural world.

Nowhere is Yeats' love of nature more apparent than in *The Lake Isle of Innisfree*. In this poem Yeats expresses his desire to escape from the grim, drab urban world to the pastoral utopia that is Innisfree. While this is a very personal poem, it has an obvious universal appeal in that we have all at some point shared the poet's desire to escape to a world of beauty and tranquillity. This desire is expressed clearly and directly in the opening line: 'I will arise and go now, and go to Innisfree.' Sensuous imagery enables us to picture the beauty of Innisfree, and sense its silence: 'lake water lapping with low sounds by the shore.' The repeated 'l' and 'o' sounds are particularly effective in conveying the peacefulness of this idyllic world. We can hear the cricket singing and visualise noon's 'purple glow'. The powerful attraction of Innisfree is underscored by the sharp contrast between 'the pavements grey' of the urban world and the sensuous appeal of this rural paradise.

Thematically, there are some interesting points of comparison and contrast between *Innisfree* and *Sailing to Byzantium*. In both poems there is a desire to escape to a more appealing world. In Innisfree Yeats' search for a happier, more fulfilling life centres on the world of nature. However, in *Byzantium* he longs to escape to a perfect world of art. This is another poem with an obvious universal appeal in that the pain of growing old and the desire for perfect and lasting happiness are part of the human condition (part of being human). The philosophical questions that Yeats raises in this poem are relevant to us all, especially as we grow older.

Yeats' disenchantment with old age is clearly conveyed in the opening lines of *Sailing to Byzantium*: 'That is no country for old men . . . An aged man is but a paltry thing'. The images of the scarecrow ('a tattered coat upon a stick') and the 'dying animal' powerfully underline the poet's sense of the worthlessness of old age. Vivid images suggest the richness and abundance of nature: 'the salmon-falls . . . mackerel-crowded seas.' However, the transience of the physical world is concisely expressed: 'Whatever is begotten, born and dies.' Painfully aware of the impermanence of life, Yeats is drawn to the perfection and immortality of art. He embarks on an imaginary journey to Byzantium where he hopes to transcend (rise above) the limitations of the physical world by achieving spiritual perfection in a world of timeless art. Yeats' desire to forever leave the physical world is stated with typical directness: 'Once out of nature, I shall never take my bodily form from any natural thing.' He longs for his soul to take the shape of a golden bird. For Yeats the golden bird is a symbol of spiritual perfection in art. His rejection of the physical world in favour of spiritual perfection in art raises some interesting philosophical questions. We can understand why he is attracted to the perfect, immortal golden bird, but many readers would find its artificiality and the monotonous nature of its existence (keeping 'a drowsy emperor awake') unappealing. This poem is interesting because, whether or not you agree with his conclusions, Yeats sets us thinking about the meaning and purpose of life by presenting us with contrasting images of youth ('the young in one another's arms') and age (the scarecrow), and art (the golden bird) and reality ('the birds in the trees').

Yeats is unquestionably one of the all-time great literary figures. I found his poetry to be consistently interesting and thought-provoking, with his use of imagery and contrast being particularly effective in conveying his themes.

T.S. Eliot

Biographical Note

T.S. Eliot remains one of the most celebrated and influential poets of the twentieth century. He was a leading member of the Modernist movement that revolutionised English literature in the early decades of the last century. Eliot was born into a prosperous family in St Louis, Missouri in 1888. As a child, Eliot attended a local school. He entered Harvard University in 1906 and, after taking both his BA and MA degrees, seemed set for an academic career. However, he had been writing poems during his early years in Harvard and decided to spend a year in Paris after college in pursuit of his poetic vocation. After spending some years in France and Germany, he moved to England shortly before the outbreak of the First World War in 1914. In 1915, one of Eliot's most famous poems, *The Love Song of J. Alfred Prufrock*, was published. In London he met Ezra Pound, a fellow American poet who was greatly impressed with *Prufrock*, telling Eliot, 'This is as good as anything I have ever seen'. Also in 1915, Eliot married Vivienne Haigh-Wood after a brief courtship. His impulsive marriage led to a major rift in his family. Vivienne's refusal to cross the Atlantic meant that Eliot remained in England, taking his place in literary London.

Marriage forced Eliot into taking a regular job and in 1917 he took up a post in the foreign department of Llyods Bank in London, where he worked for eight years. The job gave him the financial security he needed to return to his poetry, and in 1917 he received a huge boost from the publication of his first book, *Prufrock and Other Observations*. Eliot's best-known work, *The Waste Land*, was first published in 1922 in a literary journal entitled *The Criterion*. Suffused with Eliot's horror of life, this poem reflects the deep disillusionment of the post-war generation. It would become one of the most important and most influential poems of the twentieth century. Publishing house Faber and Gwyer (later Faber and Faber) offered Eliot a job as literary editor, allowing him to escape from the demands of his job in the bank.

Many people were surprised that a man who had penned *The Waste Land*, a poem of philosophical despair depicting the spiritual barrenness of the modern era, was baptised into the Anglican Church in 1927. From this point on, Eliot's poetry addressed explicitly religious issues.

Eliot's reputation as a great poet saw him receive numerous literary awards. In 1926 he delivered the prestigious Clark lectures at Cambridge University, followed in 1932-1933 by the Norton Lectures at Harvard. He received every award the literary world had to offer, culminating in his receiving the Nobel Prize for Literature in 1948.

The Love Song of J. Alfred Prufrock

[handwritten: Marriage proposal ↓]

The epigraph with which the poem opens comes from Dante's *Inferno* (Canto 27, lines 61–66). The speaker is trapped in hell and filled with a sense of hopelessness. Prufrock is similarly trapped in his own private hell, a hell of endless indecision, low self-esteem and fear of rejection. The key themes of this poem are Prufrock's isolation and the difficulty he has in reconciling the needs of his romantic soul with the fears of his conventional and reserved outer self.

[handwritten: → romantic inner vs. reserved outer]

This poem is written in the form of a dramatic monologue that reflects Prufrock's stream of consciousness. It begins with Prufrock setting out on an imaginary journey in the course of which he struggles to resolve his inner conflict regarding asking an unnamed woman a significant, but unspecified, question: 'Let us go then, you and I . . .' The 'you' and 'I' refer to the two sides of Prufrock's character: the outer respectable and timid man and the inner suppressed and frustrated romantic. Eliot portrays the evening in a strikingly original manner, comparing it to a patient 'etherised upon a table'. This image suggests the speaker's feelings of vulnerability, while also evoking a lethargic atmosphere. From the beginning, there is a sense that Prufrock is not facing into this journey with any great energy or enthusiasm. The urban world is portrayed in a very unattractive manner, with Prufrock choosing to travel through the sleazy part of the city. There is a restless, sordid quality to the city ('muttering retreats . . . one-night cheap hotels'). The shabby streets will ultimately bring Prufrock to a room where he hopes to ask 'an overwhelming question'. This adjective suggests both the enormity of the question in the speaker's mind and its capacity to destroy his present lonely, frustrated existence. We do not know the nature of the question ('Oh, do not ask, "What is it?"'), but can assume it involves revealing some aspect of

his hitherto hidden inner self. The room in which the question is to be asked seems to be located in a refined and sophisticated (or possibly shallow and pretentious) middle-class world: 'In the room the women come and go / Talking of Michelangelo.' The fact that the women 'come and go' suggests that this is a world of transient (passing, short-lived) relationships.

An extended metaphor compares the drifting of the fog and smoke through the city to the movements of a cat. The imagery in this section of the poem has a striking sensuous quality: 'The yellow fog that rubs its back upon the window-panes, / . . . Licked its tongue into the corners of the evening, / Lingered upon the pools that stand in drains . . .' It seems that the cat (fog) is going to make a decisive move ('Slipped by the terrace, made a sudden leap . . .'), but ends up falling asleep ('Curled once about the house, and fell asleep'). A seemingly decisive action that ultimately leads to nothing may suggest how Prufrock's journey will ultimately end.

*[handwritten: ← * Symbolism]*

The repetition of 'There will be time' reflects Prufrock's growing anxiety at the thought of asking his 'overwhelming question'. He tries to reassure himself that he has plenty of time to change his mind about asking a question that could profoundly disturb his personal universe. The world in which Prufrock moves is shallow and artificial – it is a world where he is almost certainly not alone in hiding his true, inner self behind a polite, refined exterior: ' . . .there will be time / To prepare a face to meet the faces that you meet . . .' While Prufrock's assertion that, 'There will be time to murder and create' would seem to be ironic and self-deprecating in that he will never possess the creative powers of a genius like Michelangelo, it also suggests that if Prufrock asks this question, he may well 'murder' his

metaphor

cautious and reserved outer self and 'create' a new, confident and expressive man. The tension mounts as Prufrock anticipates the disturbing impact of the question he plans to ask; he imagines it having the resounding effect of a piece of cutlery dropped on a plate ('Time for all the works and days of hands / That lift and drop a question on your plate . . .'). He comforts himself with the thought that his roundabout route through the seedy side of the city allows him time 'for a hundred indecisions, / And for a hundred visions and revisions . . .' The repetition of 'time' (it is mentioned eight times in the Fog Passage) reflects Prufrock's increasing anxiety. Prufrock is clearly afflicted by chronic indecision as he procrastinates endlessly about asking the question. The trivial, mundane nature of his world is conveyed by the reference to 'the taking of a toast and tea'.

The next section of the poem highlights Prufrock's timidity and extreme self-consciousness. His growing tension is evident as he wonders if he will have the courage to enter the room that is his destination: 'And indeed there will be time / To wonder, "Do I dare"? And, "Do I dare?"' He is painfully aware of how others view him as the repetition of 'They will say' indicates: 'They will say: "How his hair is growing thin!" . . . They will say: "But how his arms and legs are thin!"' Prufrock's preoccupation with his appearance is further evident in his desire to dress in a sedate manner: 'My necktie rich and modest, but asserted by a simple pin.' He wonders if he will have the courage to ask a question that would 'disturb the universe'.

Prufrock's life is one of unvarying, monotonous routine: 'For I have known them all already, known them all – / Have known the evenings, mornings, afternoons . . .' The trivial, measured nature of his existence is captured in the evocative image of his life being 'measured out . . .with coffee spoons . . .'

metaphor

Prufrock is a prisoner of other peoples' perception of him – he has been fixed 'in a formulated phrase'. Society has labelled him and he is keenly conscious of people's expectations of him. His feelings of inadequacy and low self-esteem are very apparent when he pictures himself as a trapped insect 'pinned and wriggling on the wall . . .' At this point he wonders how he might approach the asking of this momentous question: 'Then how should I begin / To spit out the butt-ends of my days and ways?' This image suggests the distaste with which Prufrock views his life, while also suggesting that asking the critical question could mark the beginning of a new, fresh and meaningful life.

The sensuous image of the 'white and bare' arms that 'lie along a table, or wrap about a shawl' is a reminder of Prufrock's sensitive and romantic inner self – the hidden side to him that craves expression. He wonders if it is 'perfume from a dress' that caused him to 'digress' from his primary concern, before again asking himself how he should begin to ask this question: 'And should I then presume? / And how should I begin?' He asks himself if he should begin by describing his journey to this room during which he observed 'lonely men in shirt-sleeves, leaning out of windows'. Perhaps this evocation of the isolation and loneliness of modern urban life might serve as a means of approaching the matter of his personal loneliness and hidden passions?

Ultimately, Prufrock's torturous inner debate concludes with the question going unasked and his romantic inner self remaining suppressed. Prufrock is filled with fierce self-disgust at his timidity, seeing himself as 'a pair of ragged claws / Scuttling across the floors of silent seas.' This image of one of the lowest life forms 'scuttling' away from any possible danger powerfully conveys Prufrock's self-contempt. He remains locked by his fears into a 'silent' world where his true self will remain forever repressed.

After the critical moment has passed the tension slackens, and Prufrock succumbs to the lethargic atmosphere that envelops the personified day: 'And the afternoon, the evening, sleeps so peacefully! / Smoothed by long fingers, / Asleep . . .tired . . .or it malingers . . .' He sees himself in the room where 'tea and cake and ices' (another reminder of the triviality of the lives his class lead) are served and where he wondered if he would 'have the strength to force the moment to its crisis'. In the course of his anguished preparation ('wept and fasted, wept and prayed') for his ordeal, he had conjured up images of his social humiliation, imagining his balding head, in a figurative sense, 'brought in upon a platter' for all to scrutinise and ridicule. He had even imagined the footman 'snickering' at his degradation. Ultimately, Prufrock's dread of being a martyr to mockery is expressed simply: 'And in short, I was afraid.'

In attempting to justify his failure to himself, the emotionally inarticulate Prufrock wonders if revealing his inner romantic self 'would . . . have been worth it' if it had resulted in the embarrassment of being told: 'That is not what I meant at all, / That is not it, at all.' His intense anguish at not being able to express and share his deepest feelings is powerfully conveyed in his exclamation: 'It is impossible to say just what I mean!'

Prufrock mocks himself by comparing himself to a number of heroic figures from the Bible, history and literature. He is painfully aware of the sharp contrast between himself and a heroic figure such as John the Baptist: 'I am no prophet.' He similarly contrasts himself with Lazarus, but his inner self will never emerge Lazarus-like 'from the dead . . .'

We observe the steady collapse of Prufrock's self-esteem as he compares himself first to Hamlet, then to Polonius and finally to the Fool, a character from King Lear. Prufrock resembles Hamlet in his indecision, but not in his ability to act decisively ultimately. He compares himself to the 'deferential' and 'cautious' Polonius who was always anxious to please, before finally likening himself to the Fool. However, while the Fool may have been regarded as a 'ridiculous' figure, he was, at heart, sensitive, caring and not without wisdom. Similarly, there is much more to Prufrock than his conventional outer self would suggest.

By the close of the poem, Prufrock accepts that he will never achieve the heroic status of Michelangelo, John the Baptist or Hamlet: 'I grow old . . . I grow old . . .' Having failed to ask the 'overwhelming question', Prufrock's life continues to revolve around trivialities: 'I shall wear the bottoms of my trousers rolled. Shall I part my hair behind? Do I dare to eat a peach?' He imagines himself walking on a beach and hearing 'the mermaids singing, each to each'. The line that follows stands alone for emphasis: 'I do not think they will sing to me.' This line poignantly evokes Prufrock's feelings of isolation and loneliness. The mermaids are associated with the sea which, for Prufrock, represents a world of beauty, romance, happiness and fulfilment. In this ideal world Prufrock's inner and outer selves are integrated: 'We have lingered in the chambers of the sea / By sea-girls wreathed with seaweed red and brown . . .' Sadly, Prufrock has 'lingered in the chambers of the sea' only in his dreams. Ultimately, reality, in the form of 'human voices' intrudes to awaken him from his dream world. The poem ends on a despairing note as Prufrock 'drowns' in a sea of loneliness and isolation, his inner self forever silenced by his extreme self-consciousness and fear of rejection.

KEY POINTS

- This poem is classically modern in terms of its theme (the isolation and loneliness of modern urban man) and method (Eliot shows us the workings of Prufrock's mind – his stream of consciousness – through image and symbol).
- Prufrock's thought processes (which are often disjointed) are presented in the form of an internal monologue.
- This poem has strong dramatic qualities. Eliot presents us with a specific setting, characters, dialogue (internal), conflict and tension.
- The poem explores Prufrock's inner conflict between his romantic inner self's longing to find expression and his deeply conventional outer self's fear of rejection and humiliation.
- Many allusions to historical, literary and biblical figures.
- Contrast is regularly employed (Prufrock compares himself to a number of heroic figures) to highlight Prufrock's feelings of inadequacy.
- Repetition of key words and phrases gives emphasis to important ideas and evokes specific moods.
- While written in free verse form (closer to conversational speech patterns), Eliot makes regular use of rhyme.
- This poem is very pessimistic in outlook.

Preludes

This poem presents the reader with various aspects of the modern urban world. The first Prelude portrays the city in a grim light, using such negative adjectives as 'grimy', 'withered', 'vacant', 'broken' and 'lonely' to directly express a truly dark vision. Similar to *The Love Song of J. Alfred Prufock*, this poem is dramatic in style. We find ourselves in an urban backstreet on a winter evening without any visible human presence. However the 'smell of steaks' and the 'cab-horse' suggest human activity. The image of 'The burnt-out ends of smoky days' compares the end of the day to the butt-ends of cigarettes, suggesting the unpleasant and unhealthy nature of urban

life. There is no escaping the pervasive gloom of the city as 'a gusty shower wraps / The grimy scraps / Of withered leaves about your feet'. The general sense of neglect ('broken blinds and chimney pots') adds to the despondent mood. Even the 'cab-horse' is described as 'lonely'. However, the lighting of the lamp holds out the possibility of hope – hope that the working people (perhaps symbolised by the horse) living in these backstreets may somehow transcend the grime and gloom of the city.

Just as the evening is personified in the first Prelude ('The winter evening settles down'), so is the morning personified in the second ('The morning comes to consciousness'). The second Prelude begins in the morning, a time often associated with freshness, hope and new beginnings. However, any sense of optimism we might feel is quickly dispelled as the personified morning wakes up to 'the faint stale smells of beer'. The negative portrayal of the city continues with the depressing image of 'the sawdust-trampled street / With all its muddy feet . . .' Perhaps the most dispiriting aspect of this section of the poem is the suggestion that urban life is essentially a series of 'masquerades' – in other words, a world of false appearances and deception where people are not always what they appear to be. Almost as disheartening is the reduction of city workers to the level of utilitarian 'hands' (a reminder of the Charles Dickens' novel *Hard Times* where workers are similarly dehumanised and similarly described). Eliot presents the reader with the image of 'all the hands / That are raising dingy shades / In a thousand furnished rooms'. This image also evokes the drab uniformity of urban life where there seems to be no place for individuality.

The third Prelude focuses on an individual woman – a welcome contrast to the mass portrayal of a thousand 'hands' in the second 'Prelude'. This woman appears to be restless and agitated as she 'tossed a blanket from the bed'. Lying on her back, she sees 'The thousand sordid images' that had contributed to the creation of her personality ('. . . of which your soul was constituted'). These images are 'flickering against the ceiling' as if on a cinema screen. As day dawns, the woman hears sparrows, but in this grim world even nature cannot inspire or elevate – we are told that the sparrows are 'in the gutters'. When morning arrives, it is apparent that this woman is not concerned about personal cleanliness: '. . .

clasped the yellow soles of your feet / In the palms of both soiled hands.' These images of neglect highlight the woman's seedy existence, while also evoking the squalid nature of urban life in general. In this Prelude, as in the previous two, the mood is utterly bleak.

The fourth and final Prelude opens with the surreal image of a man's soul 'stretched tight across the skies / That fade behind a city block . . .' This is an image of spiritual suffering, as is the image of his soul 'trampled by insistent feet' – the latter image also being suggestive of the harshness of urban life. Just as the woman's soul will be forever marked by the many 'sordid images' she has absorbed, so is the male speaker's conscience 'blackened' by life in the city.

At this point, a speaker (perhaps the poet) interjects: 'I am moved by fancies that are curled / Around these images, and cling / The notion of some infinitely gentle / Infinitely suffering thing.' These lines would seem to suggest that the speaker is 'moved' to sympathise with the inhabitants of a world devoid of beauty and hope. What this 'infinitely gentle / Infinitely suffering thing' may be is unclear, but it evokes a sense of tenderness and concern against the background of an extremely bleak and depressing urban landscape.

The positive feeling prompted by these lines is very brief, with the final three lines presenting us with a deeply negative response to the misery and suffering of the urban world: 'Wipe your hand across your mouth, and laugh'. The gesture and laugh amount to a cynical dismissal of the grim lives depicted in the poem. Preludes concludes with a depressing, universal image of poverty and hardship: ' . . . ancient women / Gathering fuel in vacant lots.'

KEY POINTS

- Key theme is the dark, depressing nature of modern urban life.
- Objective description in the first two parts of the poem is followed by personal responses to life in the city in the third and fourth sections.
- This poem abounds with negative adjectives describing life in the city: 'burnt-out', 'withered', 'broken', 'lonely', 'stale', 'dingy', 'sordid', 'soiled', etc.
- Different periods of the day are personified in the first two parts of the poem.
- Images generally suggest the drab, dispiriting nature of urban life.
- The outlook in this poem is deeply pessimistic.

Aunt Helen

This poem opens in a coldly factual manner: 'Miss Helen Slingsby was my maiden aunt, / And lived in a small house near a fashionable square / Cared for by servants to the number of four.' There is not a hint of sentiment in lines that are purely informative. We learn that the poet's aunt had a privileged life with four servants tending to her every need. Her life is defined in terms of her unmarried status and her possessions. As a 'maiden aunt', it was likely that her life was devoid of romance and passion. There is no mention of friends or of any kind of meaningful relationship. Her death was greeted by 'silence in heaven / And silence at the end of the street.' It seems that her death does not register with anyone in an emotional sense. No tears are shed at her passing. The poet says nothing of his own feelings towards his aunt – we can assume that he was as detached and unemotional as the tone of the poem suggests. Following her death, the usual rituals were observed: 'The shutters were drawn and the undertaker wiped his feet – / He was aware that this sort of thing had occurred before.' This touch of humour lifts a lifeless poem. The fact that 'The dogs were handsomely provided for' further

suggests Aunt Helen's lack of emotional ties with her relatives (including the poet presumably).

It is difficult to see the significance of the reference to the parrot's death. It sometimes happens that a husband or wife dies shortly after the passing of their lifelong partner – perhaps the parrot was the closest thing Aunt Helen had to a life partner! Here we are again reminded of the emptiness of her life. The fact that 'the Dresden clock continued ticking' suggests that life goes on.

The most memorable aspect of this poem is the description of the servants' behaviour after their employer's death: 'And the footman sat upon the dining table / Holding the second housemaid on his knees – / Who had always been so careful when her mistress lived.' The servants' bawdy behaviour, with its obvious sexual associations, sharply contrasts with the coldness and restraint of Aunt Helen's life. Of course, the upper class society of which she was a part attached great importance to 'civilized' and 'refined' behaviour, while disdaining the unrestrained expression of emotions which was commonly associated with their social 'inferiors'. With their mistress's passing, the servants are no longer slaves to Aunt Helen's standards of order and decorum and, delighting in their new-found freedom, engage in the type of behaviour they know she would have seen as base and despicable.

KEY POINTS

- This poem satirises (mocks) the poet's aunt and her way of life.
- The lifeless nature of the poem is suggestive of his aunt's lifeless existence.

- The poem contrasts the values of the upper and working classes.

- This poem has an unusual structure, being one line short of a sonnet – it would seem that Eliot did not think his aunt worthy of a poem written in this classic poetic form.

- Some touches of humour lift the mood of the poem.

A Game of Chess

A Game of Chess is the second part of The Wasteland, one of Eliot's most celebrated and influential works. This poem is also located in an urban landscape and, similar to Prufrock, portrays personal relationships in a very dark light. Written in 1922, it is commonly believed that this poem reflects the desolation of the post-World War era. This is a complex poem, replete with literary allusions. Even the title of the poem is taken from a play by Thomas Middleton entitled Women beware Women in which each move in a game of chess is closely associated with each step in the seduction of a young woman. This poem juxtaposes two very different worlds: one a world of wealth and privilege, and the other an everyday working-class world.

The opening scene in this poem takes place in the bedroom of a wealthy woman. The lady's ornate chair is compared to a highly polished throne. The phrase 'a burnished throne' is taken from Shakespeare's Antony and Cleopatra – a play whose themes of love, betrayal and tragedy are also apparent in this poem. Lines 1–20 portray this lady's luxurious bedroom in vivid detail: the marble floor, the ornamented mirror, the 'sevenbranched candlelabra' and her 'rich profusion' of jewels that spill out from her satin jewellery cases.

However, the atmosphere in this opulent room is not entirely pleasant. The verb 'lurked' suggests some hidden threatening presence ('In vials of ivory and coloured glass / Unstoppered, lurked her strange, synthetic perfumes'). The odour they release is almost suffocating in its intensity ('And drowned the sense in odours') and causes the senses to become 'troubled' and 'confused'. The air from the window enlivens the candle flame which sends smoke up to the panelled ceiling ('laquearia'). The flame of the fire is a strange 'green and orange' colour, creating a 'sad light'. Ordinarily, one would expect that the flame from the fireplace would be cheery and inviting. Above the antique mantelpiece hangs a painting depicting The change of Philomel. The mythical tale of Philomel's brutal rape at the hands of her brother-in –law, King Tereus,

177

creates a disturbing change of tone. After the cruel rape, Tereus cut her tongue out so she could tell no one of his barbarous crime. Taking pity on Philomel, the gods turned her into a nightingale. While Philomel was violated in her human existence, her nightingale's song will be 'inviolable'. Sadly, she still feels pursued by the world: 'And still she cried, and still the world pursues'. When the poem states that various figures in paintings on the walls 'Leaned out, leaning, hushing the room enclosed', the atmosphere in the room becomes claustrophobic.

At this point, 'footsteps shuffled on the stair', and a man enters the ornate room where the woman has been sitting at her dressing table, brushing her hair. The 'dialogue' that follows reveals much about this woman's state of mind. But to what extent is it a dialogue, since the man's (probably her husband) responses are not placed in inverted commas? Are his responses simply unspoken thoughts? The woman is agitated: 'My nerves are bad tonight. Yes, bad.' Her mental distress is reflected in her desperate pleas not to be left on her own: 'Stay with me. Speak to me.' There is a serious communication problem between the two: 'Why do you never speak to me? . . . I never know what you are thinking.' The woman's disjointed speech ('Speak', 'What?' 'Think') further suggests that she is on the brink of a mental and emotional breakdown. The man's grim and disturbing response (seemingly kept within his head) would seem to indicate that he too is mentally distressed: 'I think we are in rats' alley / Where the dead men lost their bones.' His internal responses are completely unrelated to the woman's questions. Their disconnection seems total, their relationship non-existent.

As is commonly the case with people who are mentally disturbed, the woman finds harsh sounds difficult to bear: 'What is that noise? . . . What is that noise now?' Even the sound of the wind under the door unsettles her. The man's silence further agitates her: 'You know nothing? Do you see nothing? Do you remember / Nothing?' It seems that theirs has been a mutually destructive relationship, with the capitalisation of 'Nothing' suggesting what now connects them. The man appears to be unmoved by the woman's mental torment, attempting to drown out the sound of her increasingly anxious questions with a popular ragtime song, 'that Shakespeherian Rag'. The woman's anguish has now intensified to the point where a nervous breakdown seems imminent: 'I shall rush out as I am, and walk the street / With my hair down.' Her questions continue as she asks, 'What shall we do tomorrow? / What shall we ever do?' The man's response underscores his bleak view of life: 'The hot water at ten. / And if it rains, a closed car at four. / And we shall play a game of chess, / Pressing lidless eyes and waiting for a knock upon the door.' These lines suggest his boredom with life's unvarying nature, with the reference to 'a closed car' evoking a sense of claustrophobic confinement. What is most disturbing is the horrific image of 'pressing lidless eyes' (presumably against the windows of the car). The literary allusion to 'a game of chess' (the title of a play by Thomas Middleton) suggests the idea of betrayal, manipulation and deceit.

The second section of the poem presents us with a very different setting, as the poem moves from the ornate bedroom of a wealthy woman to a working-class pub in the East End of London. A woman is gossiping with her friends about a couple named Lil and Albert, a soldier who has recently been 'demobbed' at the end of World War I. Her narrative is regularly interrupted by a barman shouting, 'Hurry up please its time'. The relationship between Lil and Albert seems to be strained, with the woman telling of how she advised Lil to make herself 'a bit smart'. It seems that Albert is no longer attracted to his wife, having told her to get 'a nice set' of teeth, before adding, 'I swear, I can't bear to look at you.' The woman reminds Lil that after four years of army service, Albert 'wants a good time', warning that if she doesn't 'give it to him, there's others will'. The fact that Lil resents the advice does not in any way discourage the woman from her withering criticism of her appearance: 'You ought to be ashamed, I said, to look so antique (And her only thirty-one.)' Lil's explanation shocks the reader as she explains that it was the pills she took to induce an abortion that aged her so dramatically: 'It's them pills I took, to bring it off, she said.' The harsh, depressing nature of Lil's life becomes clear when the gossiping woman refers to her five children ('and nearly died of young George.)' It is apparent that Albert attaches greater importance to his sexual pleasure than his wife's physical health, but there is little sympathy for Lil's plight: 'Well if Albert won't leave you alone, there it is, I said'. The barman's repeated announcement ('Hurry up please its time') may have another level of meaning beyond his anxiety to close the premises. It may suggest the inexorable passage of time and life's unending pressures.

Given its bleak tone throughout, this poem concludes in a predictably depressing manner, with the Cockney 'Goonight' recalling the final words of Ophelia (in Shakespeare's *Hamlet*) before she commits suicide: 'Good night , ladies, good night, sweet ladies, good night, good night.' The reference to Ophelia underscores the harshness of the world in which this poem is set. Ophelia was the epitome of beauty and innocence, but was ultimately crushed by the cruel nature of a male-dominated world.

KEY POINTS

- The key theme is the breakdown of relationships across all social classes.
- This poem is dramatic in form – specific settings, characters, dialogue, tension, etc.
- The poem is set in contrasting social settings: the ornate bedroom of a wealthy woman, and a working-class pub in the East End of London.
- A highly allusive poem – the numerous literary allusions challenge the reader.
- The modern urban world is portrayed in a very negative light.
- A relentlessly gloomy poem.

~~A Game of Chess~~ → Journey of the Magi

In this poem Eliot imaginatively recreates the well-known story of the Magi or Three Wise Kings. The Magi's journey to Bethlehem was a lengthy and, as described in this poem, difficult one from their kingdoms in the exotic East. Similar to many of Eliot's poems, Journey of the Magi is presented in the form of a dramatic monologue, with one of the Three Wise Kings (we don't know which one) speaking directly to the reader.

This poem may also be read on a metaphorical level, with the Magi's journey to Bethlehem symbolising Eliot's spiritual voyage to the Anglican faith.

The poem begins with a quotation from a sermon delivered by Bishop Lancelot Andrews, a seventeenth century clergyman, on Christmas Day, 1622: 'A cold coming we had of it, / Just the worst time of year / For a journey, and such a long journey: / The ways deep and the weather sharp, / The very dead of winter.' These lines convey the arduous, demanding nature of the journey undertaken by the Magi, a journey that took its toll on man and animal alike. The disgruntled camel men were 'cursing and grumbling / And running away'. Such was the discomfort of the 'sore-footed' camels that they became unmanageable ('refractory'), stubbornly lying down in the snow rather than continuing on with their journey. The contrast between the world of warmth, ease and comfort the Magi had left behind ('The summer palaces on slopes, the terraces, / And the silken girls bringing sherbet.') and the cold, harsh, unwelcoming world they now travel through ('And the cities hostile and the towns unfriendly / And the villages dirty and charging high prices') is strikingly evident. Little wonder the speaker admits that they sometimes 'regretted' leaving their homeland. The repetition of 'and' creates a sense of memories tumbling through the speaker's mind. At this point, the difficulties of the Magi's journey are succinctly summed up: 'A hard time we had of it' (echoing the earlier, 'A cold coming we had of it'). Ultimately, they 'preferred to travel all night', snatching whatever sleep they could, all the time haunted by an inner voice telling them that their challenging journey 'was all folly' (foolishness).

There is a noticeable change of mood in stanza two as the Magi arrive in Bethlehem (although the town is never named). After travelling through harsh and arid terrain for so long, the Magi now find themselves in a very different world. Images of life and fertility ('a temperate valley' that is 'smelling of vegetation', 'a running stream and a water-mill') suggest how the birth of Jesus will impact on the world. However, the imagery that follows is more suggestive of Jesus' death on the cross than of his birth in a stable. The image of 'three trees on the low sky' is clearly symbolic of the three crosses on the hill of Calvary where Jesus endured horrific suffering before he finally died. In a similarly dark vein, the image of hands 'dicing for pieces of silver' evokes both the idea of the soldiers dicing for Jesus' clothing at the foot of the cross, and Judas' betrayal of Jesus for thirty pieces of silver. It seems that the old magus has premonitions of Jesus' suffering and death as he approaches the place of his birth. The Magi arrive 'not a moment too soon' to witness the birth of Jesus. The speaker's response to this momentous occasion is strangely subdued: ' . . . it was (you may say) satisfactory.' How do we account for his muted reaction? Perhaps his sense of awe at witnessing this momentous occasion prevented him from being more expressive, or perhaps his vision of the intense suffering involved in Jesus' destiny negated any sense of joy he may have felt.

The third stanza sees the old man in a reflective mood as he recalls the Magi's journey to Bethlehem ('All this was a long time ago'). He insists he would 'do it again', but struggles with a key question: ' . . .were we led all the way for / Birth or Death?' He acknowledges that he unquestionably witnessed a birth: 'There was a Birth, certainly.' However, the power of Christianity derives from the death and subsequent resurrection of Jesus (Easter being the most important event in the Christian calendar). Before his life changing experience at Bethlehem, the speaker had thought that life and death 'were different'. However, this experience taught him that they are inextricably (inseparably) linked. He describes how the birth of Jesus was 'Hard and bitter agony for us, like Death, our death.' The birth of Jesus marked the birth of the Christian religion and a new era in the history of mankind. It also marked the painful spiritual re-birth of the Magi, the corollary (natural consequence of) being the death of their previous beliefs.

After returning to their kingdoms, the Magi find that they are 'no longer at ease' there, 'in the old dispensation' (religion). Their new religious beliefs meant that they now feel alienated from their own people. The poem concludes with the old magus expressing his desire for 'another death'. Having experienced the death of his old beliefs, he now looks forward to his actual death with a sense of acceptance, after witnessing the birth of Jesus and having had a revelation of Christianity. While he could no longer subscribe to his old pagan beliefs after his experience at Bethlehem, he cannot call himself a Christian because Christianity had not yet been founded, with Jesus yet to begin his teachings.

This poem is open to a metaphorical reading, with the arduous physical and spiritual journey of the Magi being a metaphor for Eliot's difficult spiritual voyage from Agnosticism to Christianity, or, more specifically, Anglicanism. Just as the Magi felt alienated in their own world after their spiritual rebirth, so did Eliot meet with an unsympathetic response from those close to him after his own spiritual voyage brought him to Christ.

KEY POINTS

- Key theme is the difficult, painful nature of spiritual rebirth.
- Similar to other Eliot poems such as *Prufrock*, this poem is written in the form of a dramatic monologue.

- This poem is open to a metaphorical reading, with the Magi's arduous journey to Bethlehem a metaphor for the poet's spiritual voyage to Christ.

- The poem is clearly structured, with its three sections describing the Magi's journey, their arrival in Bethlehem and the impact of witnessing the Nativity on their spiritual beliefs.

- The contrast between the luxurious lives the Magi have left behind and the arduous nature of their journey to Bethlehem is sharply drawn.

- This poem is rich in symbolism, e.g.: The 'three trees on the low sky' evoke the image of the crucifixion, with Christ's cross flanked by two others.

- While the Nativity is generally portrayed as a joyful event, this is a joyless poem, with images of suffering and death predominant.

- Once again, this is a highly allusive poem, with many biblical and some literary references.

from Landscapes 111 Usk

This is one of a series of short lyric poems entitled *Landscapes*. This poem was inspired by his visit to Usk, a small town in South Wales. The two most significant features of Usk are its association with the legendary King Arthur, and its popularity in medieval times as a place of pilgrimage.

This poem consists of several pieces of advice regarding how to approach this area of the Welsh countryside. The first piece of advice is delivered in a commanding tone, instructing the reader not to 'suddenly break the branch' (presumably because this would be a destructive intrusion into the world of nature). With their references to 'lance' and 'Old enchantments', lines 1–5 evoke Usk's associations with the Arthurian legends. Eliot tells the reader not to expect to find 'the white hart behind the white well'. Harts (stags) are no longer to be found in the Welsh countryside and neither, obviously, are knights with lances. While Eliot sees nothing wrong with getting a sense of the wonderful, mysterious Arthurian tales, he urges the reader not to delve too deeply into their magical, mystical aspects ('old enchantments'): 'Let them sleep./ "Gently dip, but not too deep."'

(The words in double quotes are taken from a poem by the Elizabethan writer, George Peel).

Lines 7–11 offer advice that is more positive in nature: 'Lift your eyes / Where the roads dip and where the roads rise.' Eliot advises the reader to focus more on Usk's Christian tradition than on its mythological past if we 'seek' meaning or spiritual fulfilment in life: 'Seek only there / Where the grey light meets the green air / The hermit's chapel, the pilgrim's prayer.' If we focus on 'The hermit's chapel, the pilgrim's prayer', symbols of our Christian faith, we will be better able to 'lift' our eyes and see the presence of God in the undulating hills (suggested by the reference to roads that 'dip' and 'rise') of the Usk countryside ('Where the grey light meets the green air').

One of the most striking features of this poem is its musicality. This musical quality is created through the use of end rhyme ('well-spell', 'sleep-deep', etc.), repetition ('Where the roads dip and where the roads rise', etc.) and alliteration ('break the branch', 'dip . . . deep', etc.).

KEY POINTS

- Key theme is religion – Eliot's later poetry is clearly influenced by his conversion to Anglicanism.
- While many of Eliot's poems reflect his bleak perception of Christianity, lines 7–11 of this poem present us with a more positive attitude towards religion.
- This poem evokes the unique spirit of this area of the Welsh countryside through images associated with Arthurian legend and Christian tradition.
- A poem rich in musical qualities.

Landscapes IV Rannoch, by Glencoe

Similar to *Usk*, this poem is one of a series of poems entitled *Landscapes*. Some knowledge of the historical background to this poem is necessary if the reader is to fully appreciate its meaning. Glencoe was the location of a particularly barbaric and bloody massacre in 1692. Thirty-seven members of the MacDonald clan were surprised and butchered in their beds by forces loyal to the new king, William of Orange (whom the Catholic MacDonalds refused to recognise). Many women and children also died from exposure after their homes were razed to the ground.

The opening lines of this poem convey an image of a grim, forbidding world of death. The mood is dark and despondent: 'Here the crow starves, here the patient stag / Breeds for the rifle.' There is also a sense of claustrophobic confinement – there is 'scarcely room' for the stag to 'leap' or for the crow to 'soar'. The landscape appears to fall away before our very eyes: 'Substance crumbles'.

The terms 'listlessness' and 'languor' refer to a lack of energy ('Listlessness of ancient war, / Languor of broken steel'). It is almost as if the bloodbath that occurred centuries earlier has drained all life and energy from the landscape, leaving it appropriately silent ('apt / In silence'). In the next line, the poet points out that folk memory is strong, continuing to live on long after the bones of the dead have crumbled: 'Memory is strong / Beyond the bone.'

The closing lines suggest that the spirits of the defeated MacDonalds still haunt this area, anxious for revenge and intent on restoring their family's shattered pride. It is as if the spirits of the dead are still battling 'in the long pass', driven on by the long 'Shadow of pride'. Fighting to the death in life, the MacDonald are unlikely to agree with their enemies in the after-life: 'No concurrence of bone.'

A series of negative words ('crumbles', 'broken', 'confused', 'snapped' etc.) reflect the poem's grim mood, while sound effects reinforce this dark atmosphere. The assonant long 'o' sound contributes to the poem's sombre tone ('crow', 'moor', 'cold', 'bone', etc.), while the repeated hard 'c' sound ('Clamour of confused wrong . . .') suggests the harshness of the slaughter that occurred so long ago.

KEY POINTS

- The key theme of this poem is the way in which important events of the past live on in the landscape where they took place.
- Imagery is striking and memorable, effectively suggesting the idea of violence and death.
- Sound effects reinforce the poem's dark atmosphere.

from Four Quartets East Coker IV

In this poem Eliot portrays man's position in the world in allegorical terms (An allegory is a work that can be read both on a literal and symbolic level. The purpose of an allegory is often to highlight a moral or truth). This poem is based on the analogy (comparison between one thing and another) of the world as a hospital. The patients represent mankind and the surgeon is Christ.

The first stanza opens in a dramatic manner as we find ourselves in an operating theatre in the middle of a surgical procedure. 'The wounded surgeon' is Christ, his wounds evoking his suffering as he was nailed to the cross. His scalpel is used to investigate (or possibly remove) the diseased ('distempered') part of the patient. The patient is feverish (in a state of sin), but the surgeon is 'sharp' and compassionate. Employing 'the healer's art', he resolves the mystery ('enigma') of the patient's fever.

The second stanza begins with a paradox: 'Our only health is the disease / If we obey the dying nurse'. For Eliot, health and disease are inextricably bound up together. True spiritual health can only be achieved by the healing of the 'disease' that is original sin ('Adam's curse'). Eliot tells us that we must 'obey the dying nurse' (the Church) whose purpose 'is not to please', but to remind us 'that, to be restored, our sickness must grow worse.' Put simply, we must be prepared to endure suffering and death if we are to achieve healing and spiritual rebirth.

The third stanza opens with a startling metaphor: 'The whole world is our hospital.' This metaphor implies that every human being is spiritually sick from original sin. The idea of the hospital being 'endowed by the ruined millionaire' is paradoxical on two levels. A 'ruined millionaire' would not have the financial resources to endow a hospital. Secondly, such an act would be seen as an act

of charitable goodness. However, 'the ruined millionaire' is Adam and his moral failings meant that he 'endowed' mankind with the stain of original skin. To 'do well' in this hospital is to die of 'the absolute paternal care' that we receive from God the Father. If man accepts this constant divine care he will be redeemed (saved).

Stanza four vividly describes the process of dying and the subsequent cleansing of the soul that takes place in purgatory. The sensuous imagery in this stanza contrasts with the more generalised expression of ideas in the earlier part of the poem. We can almost feel the coldness of death as it 'ascends from feet to knees'. There follows another paradoxical notion with the poet declaring that if he is to be warmed, he 'must freeze / And quake in frigid purgatorial fires'. The final line in this stanza is rather cryptic (mysterious): 'Of which the flame is roses, and the smoke is briars.' Roses are a symbol of love, so perhaps this line suggests that the flames of purgatory burn with divine love, while the reference to 'briars' evokes the image of the crucified Christ with his crown of thorns. The final line then reminds us of the depth of God's love for us (that he would undergo the agony of crucifixion that our souls might be saved). It also suggests the idea of God (on the cross) and man (in the flames of purgatory) united in suffering.

The final stanza again evokes the image of the crucified Christ, but this time in a more vivid, more powerful manner: 'The dripping blood our only drink, / The bloody flesh our only food.' These references to the flesh and blood of Christ clearly suggest how the Sacrament of Communion provides us with spiritual nourishment. The poem closes with the poet wondering how, in the light of Jesus' agonising death on the cross, we still refer to the day of his crucifixion as Good Friday: 'And, in spite of that, we call this Friday good.'

KEY POINTS

- Key theme is Eliot's grim view of Christianity – throughout this poem there is a strong emphasis on the idea of suffering and death (Christ on the cross and man in his everyday life) as the only path to salvation.
- As an allegory, this poem can obviously be read on a metaphorical level.
- This poem contains some interesting paradoxes.
- Imagery is, once again, striking and unusual.
- Tone is didactic (instructive, moralising), with Eliot tending to sermonise the reader.

Sample Answer

T.S. Eliot – A personal response

Support your point of view by reference and quotation.

I found Eliot's poetry challenging, but interesting and rewarding. Although his poems were written in the early part of the last century, his themes remain relevant to the modern day reader. He writes about the isolation of modern urban man, the shallowness of much social interaction, human relationships and his quest for meaning and spiritual fulfilment in life. I admire many aspects of Eliot's poetic style, particularly his use of the 'stream of consciousness' technique (which enables us to see the workings of a person's mind). I also admire the dramatic nature of many of his poems and his unusual and memorable imagery. While the range of his allusions is impressive, it can be difficult to see the meaning and significance of some of his more obscure references. Another aspect of his poetry I do not like is his consistently pessimistic outlook on life.

Notwithstanding the obscurity of the epigraph with which it opens and its pessimistic tone, *The Love Song of J.Alfred Prufrock* is my favourite Eliot poem because of the manner in which it depicts the doubts and uncertainties that afflict us all at different times in our lives, especially when it comes to revealing our innermost selves. This poem is written in the form of a dramatic monologue that reflects Prufrock's stream of consciousness. The opening line in the poem suggests the two sides to his personality: 'Let us go then, you and I . . .' as he sets off on his journey to a room where he hopes to ask an unnamed woman an unspecified question. The 'you' and 'I' represent the two different sides to Prufrock's personality. The dramatic tension in the poem is caused by the conflict between outer respectable and reserved man ('you') and the inner repressed and frustrated romantic ('I'). A strikingly original image ('Like a patient etherised upon a table') suggests Prufrock's feelings of vulnerability at the thought of revealing something of his inner self in asking this question. The artificiality of social interaction in Prufrock's middle-class world is suggested by his need 'To prepare a face to meet the faces that you meet', and by the pretentious conversation of the women who 'come and go / Talking of Michelangelo.' Prufrock's increasing anxiety as he nears his destination is evident in his stream of consciousness: 'Time for you and time for me, / And time yet for a hundred indecisions / And for a hundred visions and revisions.' Another memorable image conveys the trivial, measured nature of his existence: 'I have measured out my life with coffee spoons.' His feeling of self-disgust at failing to ask the question that might have changed his life is powerfully conveyed by the image of the fearful crab: 'I should have been a pair of ragged claws / Scuttling across the floors of silent seas.' A series of literary allusions underline the total collapse of Prufrock's self-esteem as he compares himself to

Hamlet (the classic procrastinator), then to Polonius ('an attendant lord', always 'deferential'), before finally comparing himself to the Fool in *King Lear*. Prufrock's expression of frustration at being unable to ask his 'overwhelming question' is one that most of us can relate to, having also felt emotionally inarticulate at some point in our lives: 'It is impossible to say just what I mean!'

A Game of Chess is a poignant poem that powerfully conveys the despair wrought by the breakdown of (presumably) once loving relationships. This theme has an obvious relevance in today's world where marital breakdown continues to become ever more common. In this poem Eliot depicts the breakdown of relationships in two very different worlds, one a world of wealth and privilege and the other an everyday working class world. The dramatic nature of this poem appealed to me, with its interesting, distinctive characters and effective use of dialogue vividly highlighting the desolation that inevitably follows the fracturing of a relationship. The opening scene in this poem takes place in the bedroom of a wealthy woman. This lady's luxurious bedroom is described in vivid detail: the marble floor, the ornamented mirror and her 'rich profusion' of jewels that spill out from her satin jewellery cases. Clearly, this woman is very materialistic. However, her wealth (as is so often the case in the modern world) brings her no happiness. In fact she seems to be close to a complete mental and emotional collapse. When a man (probably her husband) enters the room where the woman has been sitting at her dressing table, brushing her hair, the 'dialogue' that follows reveals much about this woman's state of mind and a great deal about the quality of their relationship. There is serious doubt as to whether a dialogue actually takes place since the man's responses are not placed in inverted commas. The woman's mental distress is reflected in her desperate pleas not to be left on her own: 'Stay with me. Speak to me.' There is a serious communication problem between the two: 'Why do you never speak to me?' The man's grim and disturbing response (seemingly kept within his head) would seem to indicate that he too is mentally distressed: 'I think we are in rats' alley / Where the dead men lost their bones.' His responses are completely unrelated to the woman's questions. Their disconnection seems total, their relationship non-existent. This poem opened my eyes to the destructive effect of a disintegrating relationship on the mental and emotional balance of the people involved.

The second section of the poem presents us with a very different setting, as the poem moves from the ornate bedroom of a wealthy woman to a working-class pub in the East End of London. Sharing the dramatic quality of the first part of the poem, the urgent dialogue graphically portrays both the breakdown of a marriage and the harshness of a society devoid of compassion for the emotionally wounded. A woman is gossiping with her friends about a couple named Lil and Albert, a soldier who has recently been 'demobbed' at the end of the World War I. The conversation, while dispiriting, is entirely realistic. The relationship between Lil and Albert seems to be strained, with the woman telling of how she advised Lil to make herself 'a bit smart'. It seems that Albert is no longer attracted to his wife, having told her to get 'a nice set' of teeth, before adding, 'I swear, I can't bear to look at you'. The woman reminds Lil that after four years of army service, Albert 'wants a good time', warning that if she doesn't 'give it to him, there's others will'. Lil's explanation for no longer being physically attractive shocked me as she explains that it was the pills she took to induce an abortion that aged her so dramatically: 'It's them pills I took, to bring it off.' The harsh, depressing nature of Lil's life becomes clear when the gossiping woman refers to her five children ('and nearly died of young George.'). I was struck by the harshness of a relationship where a husband attaches greater importance to his sexual pleasure than his wife's physical health, and by the harshness of a society where there is little sympathy for Lil's plight: 'Well if Albert won't leave you alone, there it is, I said.' The barman's repeated announcement ('Hurry up please it's time') may have another level of meaning beyond his anxiety to close the premises, perhaps suggesting the inexorable passage of time and life's unending pressures. While this poem is utterly pessimistic, it is commonly believed that, as part of *The Waste Land,* it reflects the despondency that followed the horrific devastation of World War I.

Once again, this poem provides us with further evidence of the difficulty that Eliot's wide-ranging allusions can present for the reader. There are, for example, references to Shakespeare's *Antony and Cleopatra* and to a play by Thomas Middleton entitled *Women beware Women.* Yet, in another way, this poem has all of the accessibility and appeal of a television soap, such as (appropriately enough) *Eastenders* – we have a returning husband, a wife whom he no longer finds attractive, mention of an abortion and the possibility of an affair (perhaps with the female narrator, who seems to have every sympathy for him!) if the wife fails to 'smarten up'.

The only poem by Eliot that I found to be less than entirely pessimistic is *Journey of the Magi.* The aspect of this poem that I particularly like is its dramatic quality. Similar to *Prufrock* this poem is written in the form of a dramatic monologue. Also, the theme of searching for something meaningful in life cannot but appeal to modern day readers, so many of whom find their own lives devoid of meaning. One of Eliot's great achievements in this poem is transforming remote biblical figures into engaging human beings. He achieves this by highlighting the regrets ('There were times we regretted . . .'), doubts and uncertainties (inner voices 'saying / That this was all folly') that the Magi feel after leaving a world of luxury and ease ('summer palaces', 'silken girls') and facing into 'hostile' cities, 'unfriendly' towns and 'dirty' villages as they journey to witness the birth of the saviour. I think anyone who has ever attempted to follow his/her personal star could relate to the feelings of doubt experienced by the Magi. After travelling through harsh and arid terrain for so long, they find themselves in a very different world, a world of abundance. Images of life and fertility ('a temperate valley' that is 'smelling of vegetation', 'a running stream and a water-mill') suggest how the birth of Jesus will impact on the world. However, this sense of optimism is short-lived, with the imagery that follows more suggestive of Jesus' death on the cross than of his birth in a stable.

In conclusion, while Eliot's poetry can be challenging, it is always interesting and thought-provoking, offering a range of insights into various aspects of modern-day life such as human uncertainty, problematic relationships, the artificiality of a great deal of everyday social discourse, and the sordidness of the urban world.

Patrick Kavanagh

Kavanagh was born in 1904 in Inniskeen in County Monaghan. He was reared on a small farm. His formal education ended at the age of fourteen, after which he became an apprentice shoemaker and helped on the family farm. He was an avid reader and, while he read various types of literature, was particularly interested in poetry. However, he could not admit to his love of poetry for fear of being ridiculed. In 1929 Patrick's father, James, died and Patrick took over the family shoemaking business, while continuing to work on the family farm under his mother's direction. Kavanagh's poems were first published in the *Irish Weekly Independent* in 1928. His work was also published in *The Irish Statesman*, a literary journal edited by AE Russell.

Kavanagh combined the life of a small farmer with that of a poet for a number of years up to 1936. Following the publication of his first collection of poetry in 1936, he departed for London. It was here that he was commissioned to write his autobiography, which was entitled *The Green Fool*. Kavanagh's stay in London was relatively short and he returned to Inniskeen. Unsurprisingly, he found it difficult to settle back into life as a small farmer, since writing was now his main priority. In 1939 he left the 'stony grey soil' of Monaghan and moved to Dublin. Kavanagh was initially accepted by the Dublin literary establishment and spent much of his time conversing with other writers in the Palace Bar. However, he soon tired of the literary set, with the Palace Bar being sarcastically dismissed as 'The Malice Bar'. Kavanagh stayed on in Dublin, eking out a meagre living from his poetry and occasional newspaper and magazine articles. In 1941 he wrote his most famous poem, *The Great Hunger*. During these years he also published *Tarry Flynn*, an autobiographical novel. This novel offers the reader a range of insights into Kavanagh's ambivalent attitude towards life in Monaghan.

In 1955, Kavanagh developed stomach cancer. While the treatment he received involved the removal of a lung, his recovery from this serious illness inspired his spiritual rebirth. Kavanagh's spiritual renewal enabled him to see the beauty, wonder and spiritual richness of the ordinary, everyday world. His spiritual rejuvenation is strikingly evident in the canal bank poems.

Kavanagh died from pneumonia in 1968. His great friend, Anthony Cronin, described how he was made aware of Kavanagh's passing in his memoirs, *Dead as Doornails*: '. . . a friend sent me a cable, saying: "O commemorate me where there is water . . ."'

Inniskeen Road: July Evening

The theme of this poem is the loneliness and isolation of the poet. While many modern poets have addressed this theme, Kavanagh's sense of isolation was particularly acute because the rural society into which he was born was not very understanding of, or sympathetic towards, his poetic vocation. Kavanagh was conscious of being a man apart, regarded by many as a peculiar figure.

In terms of structure, this poem combines the features of a Petrarchan (octave and sestet) and Shakespearian (three quatrains and a rhyming couplet) sonnet. The scene described in the octave (first eight lines) prompts the reflections engaged in by the poet in the sestet.

The opening four lines capture the atmosphere of a country dance in a subtle way. A barn dance was one of the highlights of the local people's rather dull social lives and generated great excitement. The reference to the young people going by 'in twos and threes' highlights the poet's isolation. Kavanagh is an outsider, an onlooker, an observer. The alliterative 'b' sound in 'Billy Brennan's barn' suggests the noisy atmosphere of the barn dance. Local details such as this root the poem in the world of the poet. The young people's sense of excitement and anticipation is suggested by the reference to their unique method of communication: 'And there's the half-talk code of mysteries / And the wink and elbow language of delight.' The word 'code' suggests Kavanagh's exclusion from the carefree group making its way to the dance – he does not understand the young dancers' form of communication. Secrets are shared through gestures which are incomprehensible to the poet.

There is a striking contrast between the first and second quatrains. While lines 1–4 describe the noise and movement of the people making their way to the dance, lines 5–8 convey the silence and stillness of the countryside. The second quatrain depicts the poet as a solitary figure on a deserted road. The assonant long 'o' sound ('no shadow thrown') contributes to the lonely mood. After the crowd passes by, there is neither a shadow to be seen nor a footstep to be heard. When Kavanagh speaks of 'a footfall tapping secrecies of stone', he suggests both the sound of footsteps and of feet beating out the rhythm of the music at the dance. While 'secrecies' suggests the romantic secrets of the dance, this term may also suggest the secrets of the countryside which the poet hopes to unlock while he wanders alone through the world of nature. One of the interesting aspects of this poem is the variety of meanings associated with certain terms.

The sestet reveals that Kavanagh is keenly, indeed painfully, aware of the high price that he must pay for pursuing his poetic vocation: 'I have what every poet hates in spite / Of all the solemen talk of contemplation.' What Kavanagh 'hates' is the loneliness that is an unavoidable aspect of the life of a poet. However, he realises that inspiration requires contemplation, which in turn requires isolation. Solitary reflection is necessary if a poet is to pursue his poetic vocation. However, people are essentially social creatures and while, as a poet, Kavanagh understands and accepts the need for solitude, on a human level he detests the isolation. He compares his 'plight' to that of Alexander Selkirk (a real-life Scottish sailor who chose to go ashore onto a desert island after a disagreement with the captain of his ship) because both men knew the pain of isolation and, in both cases, their isolation was self-imposed. No one forced Selkirk onto a desert island just as no one prevented Kavanagh from going to the barn dance.

Kavanagh sees himself as monarch of this rural kingdom of 'banks and stones and every blooming thing'. The final phrase is ambiguous (has more than one meaning) since 'blooming' could mean either 'blossoming' or 'cursed'. It is likely that Kavanagh is being deliberately ambiguous in order to express his mixed feelings in relation to his isolation. As a poet, Kavanagh accepts that isolation is an undeniable aspect of his poetic vocation. Kavanagh the poet is happy to wander alone through the countryside because he finds inspiration in his solitude. He sees himself as king of nature and regards his kingdom as beautiful and rewarding. However, on a personal level, Kavanagh is frustrated by the loneliness and curses his isolation. This poem offers us some interesting insights into the reality of life for a poet.

KEY POINTS

- Key theme is the loneliness and isolation of the poet.

- Local details (Inniskeen Road, Billy Brennan's barn) root the poem in the world of the poet.

- There is a striking contrast between the noise and movement of the young people going to the dance (lines 1–4) and the silence and stillness of the countryside (lines 5–8).

- Alexander Selkirk is an apt (suitable) symbol of the poet's self-imposed isolation.

- Effective use of sound, e.g: the alliterative 'b' sound suggests the noise of the barn dance, while the assonant long 'o' sound helps to convey the lonely mood ('no shadow thrown').

- This poem is written in sonnet form, combining the features of the Shakespearian and Petrarchan sonnet forms.

- Simple everyday language *(Colloquial)* ensures that the poem is readily accessible.

- The poem ends on an interestingly ambiguous note.

A Christmas Childhood

This poem presents us with a child's vision of the world. It celebrates a child's innocence and sense of wonder, highlighting the young Kavanagh's appreciation of, and excitement at, commonplace sights and sounds. This poem has an obvious universal relevance, reminding the world-weary and the cynical adult world of the beauty and wonder of everyday life and of the special magic of Christmas. In this poem Kavanagh encourages us to believe that if we could somehow regain a child's perspective on life, then we too might once again be able to see the extraordinary in the ordinary.

The opening section of this poem is full of images of everyday life: frost-covered potato pits, cattle tracks, 'a green stone lying sideways in a ditch'. As a child, Kavanagh marvelled at ordinary, everyday sights and sounds, seeing them as special and wondrous: 'How wonderful that was, how wonderful!' The repetition of 'wonderful' and the use of an exclamation mark convey a sense of childlike excitement, suggesting how, for the child, the world around him was literally filled with wonder. The 'music' from 'the paling post' is described as 'magical'. Playing in the hay shed was like heaven itself: 'The light between the ricks of hay and straw / Was a hole in Heaven's gable.'

Childhood is seen as a time of perfect innocence and happiness and is compared to Paradise: 'the gay Garden that was childhood's.' However, like Adam and Eve, Kavanagh lost his innocence and consequently lost Paradise when he gained knowledge: 'O you, Eve, were the world that tempted me to eat the knowledge that grew in clay . . .' While childhood is associated with innocence and closeness to Heaven, adulthood is associated with knowledge and sinfulness.

One of Kavanagh's abiding memories of Christmas is of his father playing the melodeon. The personified stars highlight the power of the child's imagination: 'There were stars in the morning east and they danced to his music.' The sound of his music drifted across the bogs 'to Lennons and Callans'. Once again we see the importance of local details in Kavanagh's poetry. Such details root his poems in the world of Monaghan, his home-place, and reflect his deep affection for that world. The child senses the special magic of Christmas: 'I knew some strange thing had happened.' Both of his parents made music;

while his father played the melodeon, his mother 'made the music of milking'. The alliterative 'm' sound is musical and helps to suggest the musical quality of cows being milked - an everyday sound that would go unnoticed by most. The repeated references to music accentuate the positive, celebratory tone – this poem is a heartwarming celebration of the wonder and magic of childhood.

The child's lively imagination enables him to visualise the story of Christmas unfolding in his own farmyard and in the surrounding countryside. His mother's lamp becomes a star: 'The light of her stable-lamp was a star / And the frost of Bethlehem made it twinkle.' Later in the poem, 'three whin bushes' are magically transformed into 'the Three Wise Kings' riding across the horizon. Everyday objects become aspects of the Christmas story in the young child's fertile imagination.

Sound is again used to good effect when Kavanagh's use of onomatopoeia helps us to hear the sounds of the countryside in winter: 'A water-hen screeched in the bog, / Mass-going feet crunched the wafer-ice on the pot-holes . . .' For the young child, such commonplace sounds are special and wondrous. Even as a young child, Kavanagh possessed the observant eye of the poet: 'My child poet picked out the letters / On the grey stone,/ In silver the wonder of a Christmas townland . . .' The beauty of the frosty countryside in the early morning is captured in a lovely visual image: 'The winking glitter of a frosty dawn.' This is a particularly engaging poem which describes a world of beauty, magic and wonder.

The young Kavanagh was proud of his father's musical ability, remembering how an old man claimed that he could make the melodeon 'talk'. The reference to his own 'box-pleated coat' is an example of the attention to detail that helps the reader to picture this scene from an earlier era. The poet recalls how his penknife (presumably a Christmas present) had a little blade 'for cutting tobacco'. Christmas was of such central importance in the life of the child that he even measured his age in terms of Christmases: 'And I was six Christmases of age'.

The final stanza refers to father, mother and child – this is appropriate because the idea of family (the Holy Family and the poet's own family) is at the very heart of this poem. The closing lines are memorable for the beautiful simile that compares the child's prayer to 'a white rose pinned on the Virgin Mary's blouse'. This simile underscores the child's innocence – an innocence that enabled the young Patrick Kavanagh to see the ordinary as special and astonishing. It is that innocence and sense of wonder that make this poem so charming and heartwarming. The world of happiness and excitement so beautifully evoked in this poem is all the more appealing when set in contrast with the materialistic and cynical age in which the modern reader finds him/herself. While this is a deeply personal poem that describes the wonders of rural Ireland almost a century ago, we can all relate to it because as children we shared Kavanagh's capacity to delight in and be excited by the ordinary, everyday world around us.

KEY POINTS

- Key theme is a child's innocence and sense of wonder.

- This poem presents us with a child's vision of the world.

- Memorable visual images, e.g: 'The winking glitter of a frosty dawn.'

- The use of personification underlines the power of the child's imagination, e.g: 'There were stars in the morning east and they danced to his music.'

- *Imagination* Metaphors suggest how everyday things are magically transformed into aspects of the Christmas story – his mother's stable-lamp is a 'star' and three whin bushes become 'the Three Wise Kings'.

- The simile that compares the child's innocent prayer to 'a white rose pinned on the Virgin Mary's blouse' is particularly memorable.

- Local details ('Lennons and Callans . . . Cassidy's hanging hill') root the wonderful, magical world, so beautifully evoked in this poem, in everyday reality. *(personal)*

- The use of repetition ('How wonderful that was, how wonderful!') underscores the child's sense of excitement.

- Sound is used very effectively: The alliterative, musical 'm' sound suggests the 'music of milking'. The use of onomatopoeia enables us to hear the sounds of the countryside in winter: 'A water-hen screeched . . . mass-going feet crunched the wafer-ice . . .'

- Simple, everyday language. *colloquial*

Advent

The central theme of this poem is spiritual renewal. Kavanagh longs to regain his lost childhood innocence and sense of wonder because these qualities hold the key to his spiritual rejuvenation. The 'lover' to whom this poem is addressed is the poet's inner self. The poet lost his precious childhood innocence because he 'tested and tasted too much'. In other words, he has gained too much knowledge of the world and has overindulged in sensual pleasures. Having grown world-weary and cynical, life no longer holds any mystery or wonder for him. This idea is effectively conveyed by the image of the overly-wide chink (a gap in a door?) which allows everything to be seen and leaves nothing to the imagination or sense of wonder. Since overindulgence in life's pleasures is perceived to be the primary cause of his loss of innocence, the poet believes that the very opposite process – self-denial – can help him to regain this precious quality. The 'dry black bread' and 'sugarless tea' symbolise the self-denial which, ironically, will achieve for Kavanagh a special kind of 'luxury' – childhood innocence. The term 'charm' is richly suggestive of the magical imagination of children. The biblical image in the final two lines of stanza one suggests how Kavanagh, like Adam and Eve, gained knowledge at the expense of his innocence: '. . . we'll return to Doom the knowledge we stole but could not use.' The knowledge that he has acquired has proved to be useless, while his lost childhood innocence was truly precious.

The second stanza draws a clear contrast between the perspectives (points of view) of children and adults. These contrasting perspectives are suggested by a clever paradox: 'And the newness that was in every stale thing when we looked at it as children'. Here Kavanagh suggests the capacity of the innocent child to see beauty, wonder and mystery in those things that the worldly, cynical adult takes for granted. He reminds us that adults and children view the world through very different eyes – what is fresh and new to a child is 'stale' to a world-weary adult. 'Spirit-shocking wonder' is an evocative phrase which suggests how ordinary, commonplace sights such as 'a black slanting Ulster hill' move and excite the child. Stories that adults dismiss as 'the tedious talking of an old fool' are greeted with 'prophetic astonishment' by the child. As in *A Christmas Childhood*, commonplace sights such as 'bog holes' and 'cart tracks' are special to the child. The child's innocence and sense of wonder are suggested by the reference to the remarkable Christmas story: 'old stables where Time begins'. A lively imagination enables the young Kavanagh to see the Christmas story unfolding in his own farmyard.

In the third stanza, the poet anticipates the benefits of his regained innocence. His renewed sense of wonder will help to bring about his spiritual rebirth. The 'O' underlines this sense of anticipation: 'O after Christmas . . .' Commonplace sights and sounds will once again excite the poet, reminding him of the presence of God in the world around him. 'Old phrases' will 'burn' with new meaning and even the sound of butter being churned will be seen to possess its own mysterious quality: 'the whispered argument of a churning.' Kavanagh will savour the spiritual richness of such everyday sights as a man barrowing dung – an image which is suggestive of growth and new life. His renewed innocence will enable him to once again see the extraordinary in the ordinary. He will be filled with wonder 'wherever life pours ordinary plenty'. The poet's regained innocence will be the source of new spiritual riches: 'Won't we be rich, my love and I'. Kavanagh prays that he will be able to resist the temptation to subject everything to cold logic and rational analysis. He does not want to analyse the beauty and wonder out of everyday life. He hopes to marvel at the 'heart-breaking strangeness in dreeping hedges' and delight in 'God's breath in common statement'. After Christmas he will look at everything in an entirely new light. Pleasure and knowledge are associated with the cynical, sinful world of adulthood and are 'thrown into the dustbin'. Kavanagh's new spiritual vision enables him, like Wordsworth, to see God in the natural world: 'And Christ comes with a January flower'. The snowdrop symbolises his regained innocence and a new spiritual beginning.

KEY POINTS

- Key theme is spiritual renewal – which Kavanagh hopes to achieve by regaining a child's innocence and sense of wonder.

- Many images of everyday life.

- Religious imagery suggests the poet's ability to see God in everyday life, e.g.: '. . . old stables where Time begins . . . And Christ comes with a January flower.'

- Poem contrasts the perspectives of children and adults.

- The paradox 'And the newness that was in every stale thing when we looked at it as children' suggests how children and adults view the world through very different eyes.

- Effective use of sound, e.g. the phrase 'the whispered argument of a churning' suggests the sound of butter being churned.

Lines Written on a Seat on the Grand Canal, Dublin

This poem, along with its companion poem *Canal Bank Walk* was written following Kavanagh's recovery from serious illness. These poems reflect his gratitude at being alive and celebrate the beauty, wonder and spiritual richness of everyday life. *Advent* has much in common with the canal bank poems. In *Advent* Kavanagh hopes to regain his childhood innocence and sense of wonder through a process of penance and self-denial, and in the Grand Canal poems, he has clearly regained that precious childlike delight in the simple things of life. The sights and sounds of the canal bank fill the poet with joy and a deep sense of contentment. The mood of the canal bank poems is one of perfect serenity (peace).

The opening lines of this poem suggest the tranquillity of the canal bank. Broad vowel sound ('canal water . . . thus beautifully') contribute to the slow, leisurely pace of the poem. Kavanagh uses childlike language ('stilly, greeny') to suggest his child-like wonder at the beauty and mystery of commonplace things. His sense of awe is conveyed by the adverb 'beautifully' and by the adjectives 'tremendous' and 'fantastic'. Kavanagh truly loved the canal bank and the repetition of 'commemorate' underscores his deep desire to be forever associated with this oasis of tranquillity and beauty. The opening words 'O commemorate . . .' have a biblical tone that reminds us of the final section of *Advent* ('O after Christmas . . .'). The 'Brother' addressed by the poet is the reader, his fellow man.

Water is associated with life and the poet associates the canal waters with new spiritual life. His spiritual renewal is linked to his sense of wonder. Kavanagh's sense of excitement at the commonplace sights of the canal bank prompt him to coin the word 'niagarously'. This word suggests that for the poet the water cascading from the lock is as awesome or (to take a phrase from *Advent*) as 'spirit-shocking' as the Niagara Falls. In the Niagara metaphor Kavanagh uses deliberate exaggeration (known as hyperbole) to underline the wondrous beauty of this commonplace sight. A clever paradox suggests how the roaring waters blot out the harsh sounds of the city, creating a sense of perfect peace. The sibilant 's' sound helps to convey this sense of quietness: 'niagarously roars the falls for those who sit in the tremendous silence of mid-July'. Kavanagh goes on to compare the canal bank to another distant exotic location, suggesting that it is as inspiring as Parnassus (in Greek mythology Parnassus is associated with inspiration). The poet confidently claims that no one who visits the canal bank will fail to be inspired. He believes that the canal waters pour inspiration: 'No one will speak in prose who finds his way to these Parnassian islands'. Kavanagh writes about the beauty and wonder of the canal bank with great zeal. He firmly believes that this beautiful, peaceful sanctuary in the middle of the city is as inspiring as any place on earth. Kavanagh reminds the reader that beauty and wonder are all around us.

A memorable image perfectly captures the beauty and tranquillity of the scene: 'A swan goes by head low with many apologies'. The personification of the bridges suggests how the entire scene comes to life in the mind of the poet: 'Fantastic light looks through the eyes of bridges.' An exclamation of delight ('And look!') further underlines this sense of wonder. His childlike imagination transforms the humble barge from Athy into a source of romance and mystery. Athy is perceived to be as wondrous and as exciting as any exotic 'far-flung' town. The barge brings stories ('mythologies') to excite the imagination of a poet whose regained innocence enables him to see ordinary things in an entirely fresh way. To the poet, the everyday world is truly special.

Kavanagh does not wish to be commemorated by an ostentatious (showy) memorial, but by a humble canal bank seat which may help others to discover, as he did, a sense of deep inner peace and a fresh appreciation of the beauty and wonder of the ordinary, everyday world.

KEY POINTS

- Key theme is the beauty, wonder and spiritual richness of the ordinary, everyday world.

- While this is a deeply personal poem, it has an obvious universal relevance.

- Written in sonnet form.

- Repetition of 'commemorate' accentuates the poet's deep desire to be forever associated with the canal bank.

- Childlike language ('stilly greeny') suggests the poet's sense of childlike wonder.

- Hyperbole (exaggeration) underlines Kavanagh's sense of awe at the beauty of the canal bank: the canal waters roar 'niagarously'.

- A paradox suggests how the roaring waters create a sense of perfect peace: 'Where by a lock niagarously roars / The falls for those who sit in the tremendous silence . . .'

- The sibilant 's' sound helps to convey the tranquillity of the scene.

- Adjectives ('tremendous', 'fantastic') and an adverb ('beautifully') directly express the poet's sense of excitement.

- Memorable images, e.g.: 'A swan goes by head low with many apologies'.

- Personification of the bridges suggests how the entire scene comes to life in the imagination of the poet: 'Fantastic light looks through the eyes of bridges.'

Canal Bank Walk

This poem is similar in theme and tone to *Lines Written on a Seat on the Grand Canal, Dublin*. Here again Kavanagh celebrates those ordinary, everyday things that tend to go unnoticed and unappreciated. This poem expresses the poet's sense of delight and wonder at the beauty and spiritual richness of the sights and sounds of the canal bank. The power of the natural world to heal and rejuvenate (renew) the poet's spirit is the main theme of this poem.

The opening phrase ('Leafy-with-love banks') suggests the richness and fertility of nature. The alliterative 'l' sound is soft and lyrical. The love to which the poet refers may be the romantic love shared by the young couples walking on the canal bank, or it may be divine love – God's love for man as it is expressed through the beauty of the natural world. The waters of the canal are compared to the waters of baptism, 'pouring redemption' for the poet. The canal waters cleanse and renew the poet's spirit. There is a sense of a new spiritual beginning. The use of religious language and imagery is a marked feature of this poem, suggesting Kavanagh's awareness of a divine presence in the natural world. The repeated use of 'I' and 'me' serves as a reminder of the deeply personal nature of this poem.

For the poet, the natural world reflects the glory of God's creation. He will 'do the will of God' by appreciating and enjoying commonplace things. 'Wallow' is a word associated with pleasure, and for Kavanagh 'the habitual, the banal' (ordinary, everyday things) are indeed pleasures to be savoured. The poet's renewed sense of wonder and his fresh appreciation of the everyday world enable him to once more grow spiritually: 'Grow with nature as before I grew.'

Kavanagh notices every detail of this everyday scene, including 'the bright stick trapped' in the reeds. This image may suggest the spiritually-cleansing effects of the canal waters. The image of the breeze joining the couple on the old seat suggests the naturalness of romantic love. The images of the kissing couple and the bird building its nest symbolise the wondrous process of love and new life. For Kavanagh, these everyday sights bear eloquent testimony to the presence of God. The Word of God has a new meaning and relevance for the poet because he can see and hear God in the sights and sounds of the canal bank. The Word of God has a 'delirious beat' which can be detected in the joyous pulse or rhythm of the natural world.

The sestet (final six lines) takes the form of a prayer in which Kavanagh addresses the 'unworn world'. To the poet, the world is again fresh and new, filled with wonder and mystery. The 'O' at the start of the sestet helps to create the prayer-like tone, while the run-on lines suggest a sense of longing. Kavanagh wants to

be 'encaptured' by nature just as 'the bright stick' is 'trapped' in the reeds of the canal. He longs to be absorbed into the natural world so that his soul may be cleansed and renewed. The use of positive adjectives such as 'fabulous' (used to describe the grass), 'bright' and 'new' underlines the poet's sense of wonder and delight (*Lines Written on a Seat* contains similarly positive adjectives: 'tremendous . . . fantastic . . .'). A series of verbs accentuate the sense of longing: 'enrapture . . . encapture . . . feed . . .' Kavanagh is 'delirious', indeed almost overwhelmed by joy at the beautiful natural sights that he beholds. He can hear the voice of God in the rustling of a beech tree ('eternal voices by a beech'). He wants the 'unworn world' to 'feed the gaping need' of his senses, to provide him with the spiritual nourishment he needs to grow. The poet wants to be inspired ('give me ad lib . . .') to express his gratitude to God for the beauty and richness of life in spontaneous prayer. He wants to 'pray unselfconsciously' like an innocent child. Here we are reminded of *Advent* where Kavanagh is dismissive of 'pleasure, knowledge and the conscious hour'.

Kavanagh's assertion that his soul 'needs to be honoured with a new dress' directly expresses his desire for spiritual renewal. His spiritual rejuvenation is achieved through a fresh appreciation of the beauty, wonder and divine aspect of the natural world ('green and blue things') and through a renewed faith which enables him to accept 'arguments that cannot be proven'. Here we are reminded of the poet's prayer in *Advent* to resist the temptation to explain every aspect of life (' . . . and please God we shall not ask for reason's payment').

The poet's religious view of nature is reflected in his use of specifically religious terms: 'pouring redemption . . . the will of God . . . the Word . . . pray . . . for this soul . . . ' In terms of structure, this poem is written in the form of a standard Petrarchan sonnet: the octave celebrates the beauty and wonder of the canal bank, while the sestet expresses Kavanagh's hope that he may be absorbed into the wondrous, spiritually-rejuvenating natural world.

In both of the canal bank poems we find the poet in a joyful, upbeat mood. Kavanagh's unconfined delight in the beauty and wonder of the everyday world enthuses and inspires the reader.

KEY POINTS

- Key themes are (a) the beauty, wonder and spiritual richness of the everyday world, and (b) the spiritually rejuvenating effects of nature.

- This is a deeply personal, but also universally relevant, poem.

- Written in sonnet form.

- Poem opens with a memorable adjective: 'Leafy-with-love banks.'

- Images are drawn from everyday life, e.g: pouring water, a bird building its nest, etc.

- Religious language and imagery suggests Kavanagh's awareness of a divine presence in the everyday world.

- Positive adjectives directly express poet's appreciation of the world around him: 'new', 'delirious', 'fresh', 'fabulous'.

- Kavanagh's observant eye is very apparent, e.g.: he notices 'the bright stick trapped' in the reeds.

- The sestet has a prayer-like tone ('O unworn world . . .') which further suggests the poet's religious view of nature.

- A series of verbs underline the poet's sense of longing: 'enrapture . . . encapture . . . feed . . .'

- Run-on lines further suggest this sense of longing.

Epic

This is a poem about poetry itself. More specifically, it is a poem in which Kavanagh reflects on the poet's ability to create great poetry from local events. In this interesting sonnet, the poet reminds both himself and the reader that great art (in this case, poetry that is timeless and universal) is inspired by the local or parochial.

The reader is surprised both by the shape and content of this poem. The term 'epic' suggests a lengthy poem describing great events and featuring great heroes. However, what we have here is a sonnet dealing with a quarrel over a small area of rocky land in Monaghan. In the context of epic poetry, this local squabble hardly seems to bear comparison with the subject matter of such epic poems as the *Iliad* (which describes the famous siege of Troy).

This poem opens in the manner of a typical epic poem: 'I have lived in important places, times when great events were decided.' However, there is a sense of anti-climax when we learn that this so-called 'great event' was a local squabble over 'half a rood of rock'. Notwithstanding this sense of anti-climax, we are quickly drawn into a poem that is dramatic in form. We have a specific setting (rural Monaghan), characters (the Duffys and McCabes), direct speech, conflict and tension. The details of this local feud (i.e. the actual names of the families involved and the names of local townlands) root this poem in reality. The use of direct speech ('Damn your soul') gives the poem a sense of immediacy, while the use of war imagery heightens the sense of drama ('. . . a no-man's land . . . pitchfork-armed claims . . . blue cast steel').

The observation that 'That was the year of the Munich bother' seems to put this conflict in rural Monaghan in context. Compared to the great events that were unfolding on the international stage in the build-up to World War II, the dispute between the Duffys and the McCabes seems to be petty and insignificant. When Kavanagh asks himself, 'Which was most important?' he is initially – and unsurprisingly - dismissive of the significance of the local quarrel: 'I inclined to lose my faith in Ballyrush and Gortin'. Indeed the use of a rhetorical question suggests that the answer to this question is self-evident.

However, just as poet and reader are thinking of the big political picture and concluding that such local feuds are unimportant in the greater scheme of things, another voice is heard. The poet hears the voice of Homer, the great epic poet, telling him that he 'made the *Iliad* from such a local row'. This suggests that the raw material from which the *Iliad* was fashioned was similar to the seemingly mundane and unimportant conflict between two farming families in County Monaghan. Kavanagh is reminded that great, epic literature can be rooted in parochial happenings. The closing line ('Gods make their own importance') highlights the importance of the poet – it is the poet who makes a personal experience or a local event important. The poem ends on this confident note, with Kavanagh affirming his belief in the importance of the local world of Ballyrush and Gortin, and in the power of the poet to elevate the local to the level of the universal.

KEY POINTS

- The nature of poetry and the work of the poet.

- Poem opens in a rather grand, epic-like manner, suggesting that the poet is about to discuss something of great importance: 'I have lived in important places . . .'

- A dramatic poem with a specific setting, characters, direct speech, conflict and tension.

- War imagery underlines the intensity of the local dispute: 'a no-man's land . . . pitchfork-armed claims . . . blue cast steel . . .'

- The naming of local surnames and Monaghan townlands suggests how this poem grew out of a local happening. Such details also highlight Kavanagh's attachment to his home-place. Much of his poetry is inspired by specific places.

- A rhetorical question sets the reader thinking about the relative importance of the local dispute: 'Which was most important?'

Shancoduff

In this poem we again see Kavanagh's deep affection for the Monaghan countryside in which he grew up. The repetition of 'my black hills' in the first stanza indicates the close personal connection the poet feels with the hills of Shancoduff - this was the name of a local townland where the Kavanagh family had a small farm. This farm consisted of a number of high grassy hills. The personification of the hills suggests that the poet sees them as living entities: 'Lot's wife would not be salt if she had been / Incurious as my black hills . . .' In contrast to Lot's wife, who disobeyed God by looking back at the towns of Sodom and Gomorrah after God had destroyed them for their extreme immorality, Kavanagh's 'black hills' are not tempted to look behind them, appearing admirably steadfast as they 'eternally . . . look north towards Armagh.' The poet suggests that his hills are 'happy' when the light of dawn 'whitens Glassdrummond chapel.'

In the second stanza, we see how Kavanagh also admires his hills for their thrifty hoarding of 'the bright shillings of March' – a reference to the patches of snow that remain sheltered from the sun in the shadow of the hills. The personification of the sun (it 'searches in every pocket' of the hills) suggests how the entire natural world comes to life in the poet's imagination. Hyperbole (deliberate exaggeration) brings the poet's respect for his hills into sharp focus. In describing them as 'my Alps', Kavanagh again displays his capacity to see beauty and wonder in the everyday world. However, we see that he is not blind to the harshness of 'his' hills when he speaks of bringing 'a sheaf of hay' to 'three perishing calves' on Shancoduff. The arduous nature of this task is evoked by comparing it to climbing 'the Materhorn', one of the most challenging of the Alps. References to specific place-names reflect Kavanagh's affection for his home-place – the freezing calves are 'in the field under the Big Forth of Rocksavage.' In the next stanza, he refers to the drovers 'sheltering in the Featherna Bush'.

In the third stanza the poet's love of his hills is again very evident as he imagines 'the sleety winds' fondling 'the rushy beards of Shancoduff'. Even the harsh winds of winter appear to be kind to the poet's beloved hills. Kavanagh gives us an alternative perspective on the hilly fields of Shancoduff with the remarks of the intensely practical cattle-drovers. Unsurprisingly, they are utterly unimpressed with the boggy fields, concluding that the person who owns them must be poor: 'Who owns them hungry hills / that the water-hen and snipe must have forsaken? / A poet? Then by heavens he must be poor.' While Kavanagh views Shancoduff with the sensibility of a poet, the cattle-drovers view it in a completely unsentimental manner, aware only of the fields' very poor agricultural value. The poem ends on an ambiguous note with the poet, having heard the dismissive comments of the drovers, questioning the impact of their remarks on him: 'I hear and is my heart not badly shaken?' This ambiguous attitude towards the inspirational (as opposed to agricultural) value of the largely barren fields of Shancoduff reminds us of his similarly ambiguous outlook on the local countryside in *Inniskeen Road: July Evening*.

KEY POINTS

- Theme is Kavanagh's deep attachment to and affection for Shancoduff.

- Repetition of 'my black hills' underscores his deep personal connection with the hilly fields of Shancoduff.

- The personification of the hills suggests that the poet regards them almost as friends.

- References to specific places indicate the poet's love of the local countryside.

- Poem ends on an ambiguous note.

On Raglan Road

This ballad tells the story of a failed love affair between the poet and a dark-haired woman. The opening stanza describes Kavanagh's first meeting with this woman on Raglan Road. The autumnal setting evokes a sense of darkness and gloom. From the beginning the poet appeared to be filled with a sense of pessimism: '. . . and knew / That her dark hair would weave a snare that I might one day rue.' The word 'snare' suggests the idea of the poet being trapped by this beautiful woman (a rather hackneyed notion guaranteed to raise the hackles of modern-day women). Despite anticipating problems, Kavanagh followed his heart: 'I saw the danger, yet I walked along the enchanted way . . .' The idea of being enchanted by this woman may suggest the magical quality of love, but this idea is open to a negative reading if we take it to mean that the poet was bewitched by a beautiful temptress. The closing line in this stanza reflects Kavanagh's sense of foreboding as he anticipates the relationship ending in sorrow: 'And I said, let grief be a fallen leaf at the dawning of the day.'

In stanza two the poet's essentially bleak view of love is again evident. While the poet and his lover contentedly stroll along Grafton Street, he is keenly conscious of the perils that attend (accompany) a love affair. Love is portrayed as a dangerous balancing act as the lovers walk 'along the ledge of the deep ravine'. It seems that Kavanagh regards a lover's promise ('passion's pledge') as worthless, with many relationships metaphorically ending up at the bottom of this 'deep ravine'. This love affair did not develop as he would have liked: '. . . and I not making hay'. The poet now believes that the relationship ended unhappily because he loved excessively: 'O I loved too much and by such by such is happiness thrown away.'

In the third stanza Kavanagh describes the gifts he gave his beloved. He gave her 'gifts of the mind', gifts of poetry which spoke of her by name and which celebrated her beauty: '. . . I gave her poems to say / With her own name there and her own dark hair like clouds over / fields of May.' He shared the secrets of the artist's creative mind with her, secrets known by 'the true gods of sound and stone / And word and tint.' This line refers to musicians, sculptors, writers and artists. There is a sense here of the poet seeing himself as a member of some superior artistic club. The simile that compares his lover's 'dark hair' to 'clouds' adds to the sense of gloom.

The closing stanza portrays the end of the couple's relationship: 'On a quiet street where old ghosts meet I see her walking now / Away from me so hurriedly . . .' The 'old ghosts' may refer to the couple in an earlier, happier time in their relationship. However, it is difficult to sympathise with the poet when he arrogantly concludes that, as an 'angel', he was wrong to woo 'a creature made of clay'. The concluding line in the poem suggests that his beloved was unworthy of his romantic attention: 'When the angel woos the clay he'd lose his wings at the dawn of day.'

The repetition of 'I' throughout the poem indicates that this is an entirely one-sided portrayal of this love relationship and may suggest that the poet was rather self-absorbed in his attitude towards this relationship.

Since this poem is better known as a song, it is unsurprising that it is replete with (full of) musical qualities. It has an AABB rhyming scheme ('knew – rue', 'way – clay', etc.), while also having many internal rhymes ('grief – leaf', 'much – such', 'tint – stint', 'clay – day', etc). Alliteration ('Raglan Road', 'passion's pledge', 'secret sign', 'dawn of day', etc.) and assonance ('tripped lightly', 'making hay', 'old ghosts', etc.) add to the musicality of this poem.

KEY POINTS

- Theme is a failed love relationship.
- Effective use of simile (e.g: 'dark hair like clouds over fields of May') and metaphor (e.g: 'the enchanted way' suggests the magical nature of falling in love).
- This poem is full of musical qualities: end rhyme, internal rhyme, alliteration and assonance.
- The mood of the poem is bleak.
- The repeated use of 'I' points up the one-sided portrayal of this failed love relationship.

The Hospital

While the title would seem to suggest a poem about suffering, anguish and human mortality, the theme of this poem is, rather surprisingly, love – love for the most functional and (from the reader's perspective) uninspiring aspects of everyday life. The key to Kavanagh's love of the world around him is his fresh appreciation of life following a brush with death. As he recovered from an operation for stomach cancer, the poet experienced a spiritual rebirth which enabled him to see the world around him in a new, inspiring light. This poem is written in the form of a Petrarchan sonnet, consisting of an octet and a sestet.

The poem opens in a rather startling manner: 'A year ago I fell in love with the functional ward / Of a chest hospital . . .' The details that follow evoke a practical, utilitarian and, many would say, un-poetic world: 'square cubicles in a row / Plain concrete, wash basins . . .' This is a world which appears to be devoid of any aesthetically pleasing qualities – 'an art lover's woe', as Kavanagh puts it. The next line emphasises the apparently mundane reality of his stay in hospital: 'Not counting how the fellow in the next bed snored.' However, things that in the past that might have gone unnoticed by the poet are now cherished and loved. In Kavanagh's new vision of life, everything is capable of being loved: 'But nothing whatever is by love debarred, / The common and banal her heat can know.' What was once dull and unremarkable is now charged with excitement: 'The corridor led to a stairway and below / Was the inexhaustible adventure of a gravelled yard.' That 'a gravelled yard' can be seen in terms of endless adventure speaks volume for the transforming power of the poet's imagination, which is sparked by his new love for the commonplace.

Kavanagh's new perspective on life (as described in the octet) is reflected upon and explained in the sestet. Everyday objects such as 'the Rialto Bridge, / The main gate that was bent by a heavy lorry, / The seat at the back of the shed that was a suntrap' are viewed as giving the hospital a special quality. The poet expresses his love for the familiar and the banal by the act of naming them: 'Naming these things is the love-act and its pledge . . .' The final lines of the poem remind us of the power of the poet who, by writing about a subject that he feels passionate about (in this instance the beauty and mystery of the everyday world of the hospital), confers upon it a form of immortality: 'For we must record love's mystery without claptrap, / snatch out of time the passionate transitory.'

KEY POINTS

- Main theme is the poet's love of the ordinary, everyday world.
- Written in the form of a Petrarchan sonnet (octet followed by sestet).
- The octet is descriptive, while the sestet is reflective and explanatory.
- Images are drawn entirely from the everyday world.
- While the poet uses everyday language for the greater part of the poem, the final lines of the sestet are more formal and rhetorical.

{ • Octect – Love for everyday things.
{ • Sestet – Reflects / Explains this love.

The Great Hunger

The title of the poem refers to the Great Famine (1845–48). However, the hunger referred to in the title is a hunger for emotional and sexual fulfillment that characterised life in rural Ireland from the early to the mid-twentieth century. The Great Famine had a profound impact on subsequent patterns of both land ownership and marriage (the two were intimately related). While endless sub-division of the family farm had been a feature of pre-Famine Ireland, rural society thereafter dictated that the family farm would remain intact and would be inherited by the eldest son. However, the son was then effectively forced to remain living with his parents until they died (by which time he may well have been virtually an old man himself) before he could go looking for a suitable wife. The deeply conservative attitude of the Catholic Church towards all matters sexual exacerbated an already difficult situation for bachelor farmers. In essence, sex was regarded as shameful, even sinful and people were forced to repress their sexual instincts. Of course such sexual repression was profoundly unhealthy and deeply frustrating.

The opening line of the poem has obvious biblical connotations: 'Clay is the word and clay is the flesh . . .' (echoing the opening of St John's Gospel: 'And the Word was made flesh and dwelt among us'). But the 'religion' of Maguire and his men is centred on the land they farm. The simile that compares the potato-gatherers to 'mechanised scarecrows' suggests that lives of hardship and loneliness have left them spiritually lifeless. While the Bible is often described as the Book of Life, the reference to the Book of Death evokes the idea of a life-defeating 'religion' that offers no hope of happiness or salvation. Even the natural world is portrayed in a grim manner: 'Here crows gabble over worms and frogs . . .' For Kavanagh, there

is no 'light of imagination' to be found 'in these wet clods'. The image of the men standing in the field 'shivering' reinforces the cold, dark atmosphere that pervades this poem. These men loved the Virgin Mary, while remaining virgins themselves for 'too long'. The speed with which time passes and youth becomes old age is suggested in the line, 'Yesterday was summer'. The summer of these men's lives has long since passed, without them ever having loved a real woman. Each year they had promised themselves they would marry ('Who was it promised marriage to himself / Before apples were hung from the ceilings for Hallowe'en?'), but now they are in the autumn of their lives – lives as barren as the clay they battle to eke a living from. The narrator addresses the reader when he tells us that 'We will stay and watch the tragedy to the last curtain . . .' Tragically, all that awaits Maguire and his fellow bachelor farmers is the inevitability of death. The despair that engulfs their lives is further reflected in the bleak image of the soul rolling down the hillside 'like a bag of wet clay'.

The second stanza opens with images of lethargy and decay: 'A dog lying on a torn jacket under a heeled-up cart, / A horse nosing along the posied headland, trailing a rusty plough.' The passing of time is evoked by the image of 'October playing a symphony on a slack wire paling.' The mood becomes more despairing with the image of the 'flameless' candle suggestive of the death of hope. The metaphor that compares Maguire to a horse constrained by a halter conveys the idea of a life constrained by social expectations. What follows is particularly depressing as the narrator describes how Maguire engaged in self-delusion (probably in an attempt to ease the pain of his loneliness) when, as a younger man, he 'thought himself wiser than any man in the townland' for avoiding 'every net spread' to trap him into marriage. He even 'pretended to his soul' that children were a nuisance around a busy farm ('That children are tedious in hurrying fields of April . . .'). His obsession with farming is described as 'the passion that never needs a wife'.

The third section of the poem sees Maguire groping in the clay as if he is looking for something: 'What is he looking for there?' While he thinks he is searching for a potato, the narrator asserts that 'we know better'. Maguire's groping and probing in the mud has sexual connotations. The imagery in this section of the poem suggests that he is subconsciously searching for something that he has lost – perhaps the opportunity for love and self-fulfilment.

In section four we hear Maguire speaking with and issuing instructions to Joe (presumably a farm labourer) in relation to the many and varying tasks that needed to be done around the farm: 'Move forward the basket and balance it steady / In this hollow. Pull down the shafts of that cart, Joe, / And straddle the horse . . .' Maguire expresses his anger at a neighbour's donkey eating his clover, giving us the impression that he is a cantankerous old man. However, while he seems to be totally focused on the day-to-day practicalities of managing his farm, the narrator indicates that Maguire has doubts about the quality of the life he leads as he belatedly questions the wisdom of the mother who dominated his life: 'And he is not sure now if his mother was right / When she praised the man who made a field his bride.'

The dramatic interjection of the narrator in section five draws the reader's attention to the emptiness and futility of Maguire's life: 'Watch him, watch him, that man on a hill whose spirit / Is a wet sack flapping about the knees of time'. The reader is struck by the spiritual poverty of a man who dedicated his life to ensuring that 'his little fields' remained fertile even as his own body decayed in the earth. The fertility of Maguire's land is juxtaposed with the barrenness of his life.

The sixth section of the poem brings us back to Maguire's youth, the time of his sexual awakening. A farmyard image is employed to convey the young Maguire's suspicions of women: 'He was suspicious in his youth as a rat near strange bread / When girls laughed . . .' This sense of unease was the result of the Catholic Church's puritanical (narrow-minded, disapproving) attitude towards sexuality. The dawning of Maguire's sexuality is evoked by the reference to 'The cry of fillies in season'. The narrator suggests that expressing that sexuality (which would, in the normal course of events, culminate in marriage and children) was his 'destiny'. However, Maguire 'could not walk the easy road to his destiny'. Instead, he was forced to walk the hard road of emotional poverty and repressed sexuality. The line, 'He dreamt / the innocence of young brambles to hooked treachery' evokes the idea of innocence being betrayed by the twisted values of a harsh society. The difficulty of escaping this grim, repressive life is suggested by the image of 'irregular fields' holding those who work in them in a tight grip. The repetition of 'grip' underscores the difficulty of achieving such an escape: 'O the grip. O the grip of irregular fields! No man escapes.' The brutalising effects of rural Ireland in that era are powerfully conveyed by the image of 'a monster hand' taking children and returning them as 'apes'. Here the narrator suggests that lives of physical hardship, sexual repression and spiritual poverty created people who were less than fully human. Maguire now seems to express his regret at the life choices he has made: 'O God if I had been wiser!' The repetition of this expression of regret and the fact that it is accompanied by a sigh underlines the depth of Maguire's sorrow. Long vowel sounds heighten the sense of gloom: 'He looks towards his house and haggard . . .' Painful experience forces Maguire to admit to himself that his mother was 'a liar' when 'she praised the man who made a field his bride'. It seems that he has also come to realise that the narrow-minded, anti-life brand of religion which stifled the expression of his sexuality is far removed from the essence of God's message: 'God's truth is life – even the grotesque shapes of its foulest fire.'

The seventh section of the poem presents us with the image of a horse so hungry for the sweet clover in the neighbouring field that he 'crashes through the whins and stones' separating him from the object of his longing. The horse cannot simply go through the gap into the field of clover because 'in the gap there's a bush weighed with boulders like morality'. The horse is similar to Maguire who is also prevented from reaching that which he desires (sexual fulfillment) because of the 'boulders' of morality. Living in a deeply conservative society where sexuality was virtually equated with sin, Maguire knows that he dare not provoke the ire (anger) of the local priest by challenging Catholic dictums regarding sexual behaviour.

The next stanza conveys a sense of autumnal decay with its references to 'coltsfoot leaves' that are 'holed with rust', falling rain and 'a yellow sun' that reflects 'the poignant light in puddles shaped by hooves'. These lines may suggest that Maguire is in the autumn of his life, with the despondent tone the result of his never having achieved emotional or sexual fulfilment.

In the closing lines of the poem, the narrator calls on the personified Imagination to join him in evaluating Maguire's life: 'And we will watch from the doorway the years run back . . .' Such a process would be best conducted in a calm, quiet atmosphere, undisturbed by the sounds of the farm: 'Be easy, October. No cackle hen, horse neigh, tree sough, duck quack.'

St. 7 Metaphor

KEY POINTS

- Key theme is the dark, grim reality of life in rural Ireland in the first half of the twentieth century.
- This poem is a biting social satire that highlights the socio-economic, religious and cultural forces responsible for the spiritual / emotional poverty and sexual repression that blighted the lives of so many people in rural Ireland in that era.
- The tone of the poem is entirely and relentlessly despairing.
- The imagery of the poem, most of which is drawn from the natural world, is particularly dark.

Sample Answer

Patrick Kavanagh – A personal response

It is little surprise that Kavanagh is one of Ireland's most popular poets. While his poems chart his personal journey through life, they have a timeless, universal appeal. In an age of rampant materialism, Kavanagh reminds us of the beauty, wonder and spiritual richness of everyday things. In an age when distant, exotic locations are presented as the stuff of holiday dreams, Kavanagh highlights the unique mystery and special importance of our own local world. In an age when so many view the world through complacent, often world-weary eyes, Kavanagh allows us to once again look at life through the innocent eyes of a child. In short, this is a poet who, by celebrating that which generally goes unnoticed, helps us to develop a healthier, more rewarding perspective on life. Kavanagh also helps us to better understand the life and work of the poet through his reflections on the isolation associated with his poetic vocation and on the power of the poet to elevate the local to the level of the universal. Among the appealing aspects of Kavanagh's style are his fresh and striking images, the simplicity of his language and his use of local details.

A Christmas Childhood is one of my favourite poems because Kavanagh vividly describes the world as it is seen through the innocent, excited eyes of a young child. It is not only a beautiful celebration of Christmas and childhood; it is also a celebration of family love and home life. Well-chosen adjectives directly express the child's unconfined excitement and delight as he takes in the sights and sounds of his own farmyard: the frost-covered potato-pits are 'wonderful', while the 'music' from the paling posts is 'magical'. Repeated references to light ('The light between the ricks of hay and straw . . . The light of her stable-lamp was a star') and music ('My father played the melodeon . . . my mother made the music of milking') suggest the idea of an enchanted, idyllic world. Childhood is remembered as a type of Paradise, with the metaphor of 'the gay garden that was childhood's' effectively conveying the idea of innocence and perfect happiness. Sadly, like Adam and Eve, Kavanagh lost his innocence and Paradise itself when he gained knowledge. This biblical comparison is very effective, lending universal relevance to a personal experience.

Kavanagh highlights the power of a child's imagination when commonplace sights are magically transformed into aspects of the Christmas story – his mother's stable-lamp is 'a star', while three whin bushes become 'the Three Wise Kings'. The child can see a divine dimension to everyday sights that would go unnoticed by most adults. The use of personification (the stars 'danced' to his father's music) further suggests the transforming power of the child's imagination. This poem is full of wonderful visual and aural images: 'A water-hen screeched in the bog / Mass-going feet crunched the wafer-ice . . .' Local details ('Lennons and Callans . . . Cassidy's hanging Hill') root this special, mystical world in reality. The language throughout this poem is a model of clarity and simplicity: 'My father played the melodeon, my mother milked the cows . . .' It is appropriate that the final stanza refers to father, mother and child because this is very much a poem about family life. The closing simile captures the innocence of the child in a memorable manner: 'And I had a prayer like a white rose pinned on the Virgin Mary's blouse.' Few readers could fail to be moved by this wonderfully heartwarming evocation of the magic of childhood.

In *Advent* we again see that the poet's personal experience has a universal relevance. Again, the language is simple and direct: 'We have tested and tasted too much . . .' In the course of growing up we, like Kavanagh, have gained knowledge and experienced pleasure. The poet reminds us that the price of this knowledge and pleasure was the loss of our childhood innocence and wonder. The image of 'a chink too wide' that leaves nothing to the imagination effectively suggests how adulthood is devoid of wonder. As in A *Christmas Childhood*, Kavanagh refers to the biblical story of Adam and Eve to suggest how knowledge is paid for with lost innocence, again elevating the personal to the level of the universal: '. . . we'll return to Doom the knowledge we stole but could not use'. While the poet's references to 'the dry black bread and sugarless tea of penance' mean little to a modern reader, he certainly makes us aware of the importance of achieving spiritual renewal through regaining our lost childhood innocence: 'charm back the luxury of a child's soul'. In modern-day Ireland, there is a growing awareness that, for all our knowledge and material wealth, we are somehow deficient in a spiritual sense.

Kavanagh effectively highlights the contrasting perspectives of adults and children by means of a paradox: 'And the newness that was in every stale thing when we looked at it as children.' He underlines the need for spiritual renewal when he points out that that which is 'spirit-shocking' and astonishing to a child is 'tedious' to an adult. The innocent child appreciates that which goes unnoticed by the cynical and world-weary adult: 'the bog-holes, cart-tracks, old stables where Time begins'. Kavanagh goes on to anticipate the benefits of his regained innocence. In essence, he will view the world afresh through the appreciative eyes of a child. His new-found spiritual wealth will be based on a fresh appreciation of everyday things – he will be at his happiest 'wherever life pours ordinary plenty'. Instead of continually subjecting everything to rational analysis (we 'analyse God's breath in common statement'), we should simply appreciate and delight in such everyday wonders as the 'heart-breaking strangeness in dreeping hedges'. As in A *Christmas Childhood*, this poem ends with a flower image: 'And Christ comes with a January flower'. The snowdrop is an apt symbol of regained innocence.

Reading Kavanagh's poetry, the reader is struck by the fact that the poet is recording his personal journey through life. In *A Christmas Childhood* he brilliantly evokes the innocence and wonder of childhood. In *Advent* he realises that he has grown worldly and cynical and longs to regain 'the luxury of a child's soul'. In the canal bank poems we see that Kavanagh has achieved spiritual renewal, and once again views the world through the innocent, excited eyes of a child.

Of all of the poems that I have studied, the canal bank poems are the most uplifting and inspiring. These poems are similar in theme, tone and mood. They celebrate the beauty, wonder and spiritual richness of the everyday world. The sense of joy, serenity and gratitude that pervades both poems is so powerfully expressed as to be almost infectious. Having recovered from a serious illness, Kavanagh again views the world around him with a child's sense of wonder and delight. In these poems we see that the poet has truly regained his childhood innocence.

Canal Bank Walk celebrates those commonplace sights and sounds that generally either go unnoticed or are taken for granted. While deeply personal (there are repeated references to 'I' and 'me'), this poem has an undoubted universal relevance in its highlighting of nature's power to heal and rejuvenate the spirit. It certainly appeals to the modern reader whose world-weariness leaves him/her in serious need of spiritual renewal. The richness and fertility of the canal bank is beautifully evoked in the image of 'Leafy-with-love banks'. The alliterative 'l' sound is soft and lyrical, heightening the sense of tranquillity. The image that compares the waters of the canal to the waters of Baptism ('pouring redemption for me') effectively captures the healing power of the natural world. The use of religious language and imagery suggests Kavanagh's awareness of a divine presence in the natural world, and the reader is encouraged to view the everyday world in a spiritual light. Kavanagh declares that he 'will do the will of God' simply by delighting 'in the habitual, the banal'. We are reminded of Wordsworth's deep spiritual response to nature when Kavanagh declares that he will 'grow with nature'. The images of the couple kissing and the bird building its nest evoke the wondrous process of love and new life. The image of 'The bright stick trapped' suggests the cleansing power of the canal waters. For Kavanagh, the Word of God is 'eloquently new' because he can see and hear God in the sights and sounds ('eternal voices by a beech') of the canal bank. Adjectives such as 'fabulous', 'bright' and 'new' underline the poet's deep appreciation of the world around him. He longs to be absorbed into the natural world of 'green and blue' because spiritual renewal is achieved through becoming one with nature. Kavanagh highlights the beauty, wonder and spiritual richness of the everyday world in such a fresh, passionate manner that the reader cannot but be inspired to look at that world in a new light.

The chief appeal of *Lines Written on a Seat on the Grand Canal Dublin* lies in the fact that it is similarly upbeat and celebratory. Again, we see how the everyday world delights the poet, filling him with a deep sense of joy and contentment. Kavanagh longs to be commemorated by a canal bank seat because he wants to be forever associated with the uniquely peaceful and beautiful world of the canal bank. The use of childlike language effectively suggests a sense of childlike wonder: 'so stilly greeny at the heart of summer'. As in *Canal Bank Walk*, positive adjectives directly express the poet's sense of awe at the world around him: 'tremendous . . . fantastic . . .' While Kavanagh uses hyperbole (exaggeration) when he describes the water pouring from the lock as roaring 'niagarously', he genuinely believes that this 'mini-waterfall' is as wondrous as the Niagara Falls. Once again the poet opens our eyes to the extraordinary nature of ordinary things. A clever paradox suggests how the roaring waters pouring from the lock blot out the harsh sounds of the city, creating a sense of perfect peace: 'niagarously roars the falls for those who sit in the tremendous silence of mid-July.' The sibilant 's' sound helps to convey this sense of peace. Kavanagh goes on to suggest that the canal bank is as inspiring as Parnassus (in Greek mythology Parnassus is associated with inspiration). He confidently claims that no one who visits the canal bank will fail to be inspired: 'No one will speak in prose who finds his way to these Parnassian islands.' The poet writes about the beauty, wonder and inspirational aspect of the canal with admirable conviction – he firmly believes that this little piece of the country in the middle of the city is as magnificent and as inspiring as any place on earth. A memorable image perfectly captures the beauty and tranquillity of the scene: 'A swan goes by head low with many apologies.' A childlike exclamation of delight ('And look!') underscores the poet's sense of wonder. The barge from Athy brings the type of exotic tales ('mythologies') that we normally associate with 'far-flung' locations. It is Kavanagh's regained innocence that enables him to see ordinary things as truly special.

I enjoyed reading *Inniskeen Road* because it helped me to better understand the life of the poet. Like other writers, Kavanagh had to make a lot of personal sacrifices for the sake of his art. The price of pursuing his poetic vocation was a degree of isolation from the local community. As he observes the bicycles going by 'in twos and threes', we realise that the poet is often an outsider. The phrase 'the half-talk code of mysteries' suggests the poet's exclusion – he does not understand the young people's mode of communication. A memorable image captures the sense of excitement and anticipation as people make their way to the barn dance: 'the wink and elbow language of delight.' Kavanagh makes effective use of sound in this poem. The alliterative, loud 'b' sound suggests the noise of the barn dance ('Billy Brennan's barn'), while the repeated long 'o' sound ('no shadow thrown') helps to convey the sense of loneliness that envelops the countryside after everyone has passed by. While Kavanagh admits that he 'hates' the isolation involved in being a poet, he accepts that inspiration requires 'contemplation', which in turn requires isolation. The comparison that juxtaposes the poet with Alexander Selkirk is very apt because both men knew the pain of isolation and in both cases their isolation was self-imposed. I was struck by the cleverness of this poem's ambiguous ending ('I am king / of banks and stones and every blooming thing') because it conveys the attitudes of both Kavanagh the everyday man who is frustrated by the loneliness that is part of being a poet, and Kavanagh the poet who finds inspiration in his natural kingdom.

While *Inniskeen Road* offers us insights into the life of the poet, *Epic* helps us to better understand the nature of poetry itself. This memorably dramatic poem reminds us that great literature can be shaped from local happenings. In this poem Kavanagh reflects on the importance of a local land dispute when set alongside the growing international tensions that were propelling Europe towards World War II. The intensity of the conflict between the Duffys and McCabes is suggested by the use of war imagery: 'no man's land . . . pitchfork-armed claims.' The use of direct speech gives the poem a sense of immediacy; the poet hears the Duffys shouting: 'Damn your soul.' We are taken aback by the description of the Munich crisis as 'the Munich bother' – but to the feuding Monaghan families, the problems in Europe were remote and unimportant. In response to the question, 'Which was most important?', Kavanagh, like the reader, is initially dismissive of the importance of the local quarrel, but Homer's ghost makes a dramatic appearance at the close of the poem to remind him that he made the *Iliad* 'from such a local row'. The declaration that 'Gods make their own importance' suggests that the poet confers importance on an event by writing about it. Kavanagh's reflections on the sources of 'great' poetry are expressed in language that is wonderfully simple and clear. This poem confirms Kavanagh's attachment to the local world of 'Ballyrush and Gortin'. The reader is reminded that great literature is both personal/local and universal.

Kavanagh's poetry has a timeless appeal because, more than anything else, he appreciates and loves the ordinary, everyday world. He writes about the beauty and wonder of commonplace things with such passion and conviction that he inspires the reader to look afresh at that which often goes unnoticed. He also writes with great honesty and insight about the life and power of the poet. His fresh images (most of which are drawn from the everyday and natural worlds) and the simplicity of his language add to the appeal of his poetry.

Please Note – As stated in Note to Students, Sample Answers *are significantly longer than the responses expected of candidates in the examination itself. This lengthy response is intended to suggest a wide range of areas for possible discussion.*

Adrienne Rich

Biographical Note

Adrienne Rich was born into a white, middle-class family in Baltimore, USA in 1929, the elder of two daughters. Her father, Arnold, was a doctor and a professor of pathology at John Hopkins University. Her mother, Helen, was a gifted pianist and composer but gave up her career to raise her two daughters. Rich's home environment was intellectually stimulating, with her father continually encouraging her to write poetry and making demands of her intellectually. Rich worked hard to win her father's approval, but later felt stifled by his overbearing intellectual presence.

In 1951 Rich graduated first in her class from Radcliffe College, part of Harvard University, also winning the prestigious Yale Younger Poets Prize for her first book, *A Change of World*. In 1953, Rich married Alfred Conrad, a Harvard economist, and moved to Cambridge, Massachusetts where she bore three sons in the following five years. In 1955 Rich published her second collection, *The Diamond Cutters and Other Poems*. As a wife, mother and prize-winning poet, Rich seemed to have everything – however, she was finding it increasingly difficult to reconcile the demands of her domestic and artistic roles. Rich's growing awareness of her lesbian inclinations inevitably influenced the quality of her married life. In 1963 *Snapshots of a Daughter-in-Law* was published. This volume addresses some of the concerns of modern women and reflects on issues relating to the female poet / artist.

Rich and her husband moved to New York in 1966. During this time she was greatly impressed with the work of Simone de Beauvoir, the French philosopher and feminist and author of *The Second Sex*. Like many other intellectuals, Rich and her husband became actively involved in the Civil Rights movement and, with America becoming involved in Vietnam, in the Anti-War movement. A radical feminist, she channelled most of her energy into the women's movement. Rich saw poetry not just as a means of expression for its own sake, but as a way of bringing about social change – she once said in an interview, 'I happen to think it (poetry) makes a huge difference'. Consequently, her work combines the personal and the political. Her poetry explores and develops theories on the relationship between language, sexuality, oppression and power. Rich left her husband in 1970 after seventeen years of marriage. A prolific writer (she has published sixteen volumes of poetry and four books of non-fiction prose over the past forty years), Rich has received numerous literary awards.

Storm Warnings

The speaker has been closely monitoring the barometer, and it tells of an impending storm, 'The glass has been falling all the afternoon'. The falling pressure of the barometer only confirms what her senses are telling her. She can hear the strengthening wind above the house and see the sky becoming increasingly darker. The wind is personified as a sinister presence 'walking overhead'. The description of the cloud as a 'zone of grey unrest' underscores the sense of threat. The speaker is sufficiently disturbed to set down her book and 'Walk from window to closed window, watching / Boughs strain against the sky'. Alliteration and assonance combine to convey the effect of the gusting wind. The strength of the wind is suggested by the image of the bending branches.

The opening lines of stanza two suggest the idea of the speaker waiting helplessly for the storm to strike, 'when the air / Moves inward toward a silent core of waiting'. There follows the strange idea that time has somehow travelled with the storm, 'How with a single purpose time has travelled / . . . into this polar realm'. As humans we have no power over weather or time. The poet now goes on to connect the weather with human emotions. Storms and human emotions cannot be predicted or controlled, 'Weather abroad / And weather in the heart alike come on / Regardless of prediction'. Just as we cannot prevent a storm, neither do we have any real control over such emotions as love or sadness.

If we could predict what lies ahead and then avoid it, we would achieve 'mastery of elements'. However, our mechanical instruments can only measure, 'clocks and weatherglasses cannot alter'. Holding a clock or a watch 'is not control of time'. Breaking a barometer will not prevent the wind from strengthening, 'the wind will rise, / We can only close the shutters'.

Stanza four brings us back into the house. As night falls ('as the sky goes black'), the speaker does what she can to shut out the storm – she draws the curtains, and lights some candles. The fragility of the flame (protected by glass against 'the keyhole draught') evokes the vulnerability of the speaker in her fragile home. The menacing storm surrounds the house with its 'insistent whine'. The curtains and the candles are the speaker's 'sole defence against the season' that brings storms. The speaker does what experience has taught her to do, 'These are the things that we have learned to do / Who live in troubled regions'. The phrase 'troubled regions' may refer to geographical regions prone to storms, or it could be a metaphorical reference to troubled hearts and minds. In the closing lines of the poem, the 'I' of the speaker becomes 'we', underlining the universality of the poet's observations.

KEY POINTS

- Key theme is the vulnerability of human life – this idea is explored through the poet's vivid description of the approaching storm.
- The poem can be read on a metaphorical level – just as the speaker is vulnerable to the destructive power of the approaching storm, so are we all vulnerable to our uncontrollable emotions ('weather of the heart').

- Use of 'our' and 'we' in the closing lines underscores the universal nature of the poet's reflections.
- Effective use of imagery ('watching / Boughs strain against the sky', etc.).
- Personification of wind gives it a menacing aspect ('winds are walking overhead').
- Formal structure – poem consists of four self-contained stanzas, each made up of seven lines.
- Effective use of sound: alliteration ('walk from window to closed window', etc.) and onomatopoeia ('the insistent whine / Of weather').

Aunt Jennifer's Tigers

The poem opens with the speaker's aunt embroidering on a decorative screen. The image on the screen is full of life, colour and energy, depicting tigers moving through a jungle, 'Aunt Jennifer's tigers prance across a screen, / Bright topaz denizens of a world of green'. With their gleaming ('sleek'), golden ('Bright topaz') coats, they are masters of their jungle domain, and have no fear of the men also depicted on this scene. The tigers move through their 'world of green' with the supreme confidence of medieval knights, 'They pace in sleek chivalric certainty'. This image powerfully reinforces the idea of the tigers as emblems of male power.

Stanza two focuses on the tigers' creator, Aunt Jennifer. In sharp contrast to the strong, dominant, confident tigers, Aunt Jennifer is weak and anxious. Her nervousness is suggested by the image of her 'fingers fluttering through her wool'. A frail, delicate figure, she finds her ivory needle 'hard to pull'. The reference to ivory reminds us of how man dominates his world, hunting and killing elephants for their tusks. The poet's aunt is 'weighed down by 'The massive weight of Uncle's wedding band'. The ring seems to impede her movements, sitting 'heavily' on her

hand. Significantly, the ring she wears is 'Uncle's wedding band'. Marriage is portrayed in a dark, negative light in this poem. Years of marriage have left Aunt Jennifer weak, weary and nervous. The wedding band symbolises her husband's power and control over her. Her frailty ('fluttering fingers') is contrasted with her husband's strength ('massive weight'). The poem implies that the speaker's aunt is oppressed by marriage.

Stanza three imagines Aunt Jennifer after she has died. The speaker pictures her as she was in life – timid and repressed, 'When aunt is dead, her terrified hands will lie / Still ringed by ordeals she was mastered by'. The verbs 'ringed' and 'mastered' suggest that her marriage involved confinement and domination, while the noun 'ordeals' evokes the idea of harsh, painful experiences. In essence, marriage is seen as a limiting, unhappy experience that stifles a woman's personal development. The closing lines contrast the transience of life with the enduring power of art. After Aunt Jennifer has died, 'The tigers in the panel that she made / Will go on prancing, proud and unafraid'. The timeless creatures that she has created will live on, testament to her talent and creativity.

KEY POINTS

- Key theme is marriage and the oppression of women that this institution brings about.
- Sharp contrast between the power and confidence of the tigers and the weakness and timidity of their creator.
- Effective use of imagery and symbolism.
- Formal style – the poem is written in rhyming couplets.
- Regular rhyming scheme (AABB) and alliteration ('chivalric certainty', etc) give the poem a musical quality.

The Uncle Speaks in the Drawing Room

In this poem 'the uncle' addresses an unknown group of people, possibly members of his own family. The use of the definite article ('the') suggests that 'the uncle' is a distant and aloof figure, while the reference to 'the drawing room' evokes the idea of wealth and privilege. References to 'balcony and gate' and 'crystal vase and chandelier' underline the idea of an upper class world removed from everyday reality. The speaker's reference to 'the mob' suggests the idea of a disorderly, threatening crowd. It is a term that is also suggestive of a sense of upper class detachment and superiority, 'I have seen the mob of late / Standing sullen in the square, / Gazing with a sullen stare / At window, balcony and gate'. The repetition of 'sullen' underscores the crowd's simmering resentment. It seems that the focus of their resentment is the speaker's upper class dwelling. The references to 'bitter tones' and 'fingered stones' evoke a menacing mood.

The speaker is unperturbed (undisturbed) by the crowd, dismissing their actions and concerns as 'follies that subside'. He is confident that the scene before him is nothing more than foolishness that will soon go away. However, he clearly feels an element of doubt when he expresses some concern for the safety of his fragile vases and chandelier, 'Let us consider, none the less, / Certain frailties of glass'. The phrase 'in times like these' implies that the poem is set at a time of wide social unrest.

However, having raised the prospect of violence, the speaker acts quickly to allay the fears of those present, 'Not that missiles will be cast; / None as yet dare lift an arm'. However, the phrase 'as yet' means that he is not completely reassuring. The speaker now recalls how his grandfather experienced a situation similar to the one in which they now find themselves. Interestingly, he too was primarily concerned for his glass, 'But the scene recalls a storm / When our grandshire stood aghast / To see his antique ruby bowl / Shivered in a thunder-roll'. The image of a thunderstorm of unrest suggests how threatened his grandfather felt at the time. The ornamental glass objects that so concern the uncle and his grandfather before him are symbols of a distinctive way of life based on wealth, privilege, power and status.

In the closing stanza the speaker reminds those present of their responsibility to protect 'these treasures handed down / From a calmer age'. His deep-rooted class consciousness is evident when he reminds them that these treasures 'are in the keeping of our kind'. He sees the privileged class to which he belongs as guardians of a civilised way of life, protecting these beautiful, delicate creations from the unruly, uncivilised mob, 'We stand between the dead glass-blowers / And murmurings of missile-throwers'. The glass-blowers are mentioned because they produced the 'treasures' symbolic of the life of privilege that the uncle is so anxious to preserve.

KEY POINTS

- Key theme is social unrest – the established social order is threatened by revolutionary forces intent on changing the status quo.
- The speaker is a symbol of the patriarchal (male-dominated) society in which the poem is set, etc.
- The poem raises questions about the nature of power, which is seen to be class and gender based.
- Effective use of imagery and symbolism.
- The language is pompous, the tone arrogant.
- Formal style – the poem is divided into four stanzas of six lines each. Each stanza is self-contained, ending with a full stop.
- Musical qualities: end rhyme ('tones' / 'stones'), alliteration ('Standing sullen'), onomatopoeia ('thunder-roll') and assonance ('Gazing' / 'stare').

Living in Sin

The phrase 'living in sin' belongs to an ealier age when it was used to describe an unmarried couple living together. The 'she' in this poem is a woman who has just moved in with her partner, who seems to be some type of artist or musician. They are living in a studio apartment – a term with connotations of a carefree artistic lifestyle. The poem highlights the contrast between this woman's idealistic vision of how she imagined things would be and the disappointing reality of 'living in sin'.

In her naivety, the woman had given no thought to the actual realities of day-to-day living with her partner. Such mundane, but unavoidable, activities as housework never seem to have crossed her mind, 'She had thought the studio would keep itself; / no dust upon the furniture of love'. She had innocently envisioned a perfect scenario, 'A plate of pears, / A piano with a Persian shawl, a cat / stalking the picturesque amusing mouse'. Inevitably, experience quickly disabused her of such romantic notions. The reality of her new life involves noisy dripping taps, grimy windows, stairs creaking 'under the milkman's tramp', scraps of leftover food and empty bottles. The use of the adjective 'sepulchral' ('three sepulchral bottles') to describe the empty bottles underscores the sense of gloom. Worst of all, the woman has to cope with an infestation of beetles, 'on the kitchen shelf among the saucers / a pair of beetle eyes would fix her own'. There is a humorous quality to the metaphorical language used to describe this infestation – the beetle staring at her is an 'Envoy from a village in the moldings' (skirting boards). Despite her disenchantment with life in the apartment, the woman feels that to utter a word of complaint would be tantamount to an act of betrayal, 'Half heresy'.

Her partner is unperturbed by the untidiness and grime of the apartment. Perhaps he assumes that cleaning and tidying the apartment is his partner's responsibility. In fact, he seems to be oblivious of both the apartment and the woman. He appears to be a lethargic individual, utterly indifferent to everything. He lacks the motivation and discipline to practise his music, 'sounded a dozen notes upon the keyboard, / declared it out of tune, shrugged at the mirror, / rubbed at his beard, went out for cigarettes'. His self-absorbed, uncaring behaviour indicates a relationship that is far removed from the ideal of selfless romantic love. It is easy to see why 'living in sin' has not lived up to the woman's expectations.

Meanwhile, the woman, 'jeered by the minor demons' (perhaps the nagging voice of social conditioning telling her to act like a housewife), sets about tidying and cleaning the apartment, 'pulled back the sheets and made the bed and found / a towel to dust the table-top'. As she works to create a more appealing domestic environment, the coffee pot on the stove boils over – a minor detail reminding us of those everyday frustrations that can wear away at relationships. Despite her unhappiness, the woman is not prepared to leave the awful apartment and her apathetic boyfriend because she is in love, 'By evening she was back in love again'. However, the next phrase indicates how mundane domestic reality has started to undermine her feelings of love, 'though not as wholly'. During the night the woman occasionally wakes to the realisation that another day of unhappiness awaits her, 'she woke sometimes to feel the daylight coming / like a relentless milkman up the stairs'. For the woman there is no lasting escape from her feelings of disillusionment.

KEY POINTS

- Main theme is the contrast between the ideal of romantic love and the actual reality of day-to-day domestic life. Another theme is sexual stereotyping / inequality – it is the woman who is expected to clean the apartment.
- In this poem Rich dispenses with the formal structures and regular rhyming schemes that are a feature of her early work. The poem consists of twenty-six lines of varying lengths. This approach (known as free verse) gives the poem a sense of immediacy and freshness.
- The tone is one of disenchantment.
- Language combines the ordinary / everyday ('She had thought the studio would keep itself', etc.) and the metaphorical ('the daylight coming / like a relentless milkman up the stairs', etc.).

The Roofwalker

At the heart of this poem lies a comparison between the roofwalkers (builders) and the poet. At the time that this poem was written the poet's relationship with her husband was unravelling. The roofwalkers become a metaphor for the poet's personal situation. Lines 1–12 vividly describe these roofwalkers. As night falls, the builders are silhouetted against the dying light. There is a sense of stillness and silence at the end of a day's work, 'It is / quiet after the hammers, / the pulleys hang slack.' The roofwalkers are seen as heroic, larger-than-life figures (Giants). A memorable metaphor compares the builders' poise on the rooftops to the practised balance of sailors 'on a listing deck'. There is a sense of threat in the image of 'the wave / of darkness about to break / on their heads'. The images of the sky as 'a torn sail' and of the builders as sailors 'on a burning deck' accentuate the sense of danger. While the builders may be oblivious of or indifferent to this danger, the threat remains.

Line 13 sees a shift in focus as the poem moves from a description of the external physical world to the inner world of the poet's thoughts and feelings. Rich draws a comparison between herself and the builders: 'I feel like them up there: / exposed, larger than life, / and due to break my neck'. While the builders are exposed to the elements, the poet is emotionally vulnerable following the collapse of her marriage. Just as the builders risk physical injury in a fall from a building, the risks the poet is taking in her personal life are not without danger and she fears that, metaphorically speaking, she may be in for a fall.

The builder metaphor is further developed in the third section of the poem as the poet reflects on the energy invested in carefully constructing a life she is now leaving behind. Imagery suggests the thought, planning and effort that went into creating that life, 'All those blueprints, / closing of gaps, / measurings, calculations'. Now she wonders if it was 'worth while' making such an effort ('infinite exertion') to 'lay / . . . a roof I can't live under'. The roof symbolises the constraints and oppression of marriage from which Rich has now escaped. The poet finally realises that she never wanted that life, 'A life I didn't choose / chose me'. Her marriage had more to do with social conditioning and family expectation than with her own deepest feelings.

The poet feels that she does not have the personal resources (the relevant knowledge, experience, personal skills, etc.) to construct a new life for herself, 'my tools are the wrong ones for what I have to do'. She feels exposed and isolated, 'I'm naked, ignorant'. Her sense of vulnerability is conveyed by the image of 'a naked man fleeing across the roofs'. The closing lines express the poet's feelings of regret at having made the wrong choices in her life up to this point. If she had made different decisions, she could have had a very different life, one she would have felt no need to flee. Instead of being the 'naked man fleeing across the roofs', she could be contentedly 'sitting in the lamplight / against the cream wallpaper / reading – not with indifference – / about a naked man fleeing across the roofs'. Put simply, if things had been slightly different ('with a shade of difference'), she would only ever have read about other people experiencing the feelings of isolation and anguish that she is now experiencing first hand. Personal choices meant the difference between a life of unhappiness and one of contentment.

KEY POINTS

- Key theme is the poet's sense of isolation and vulnerability. Another theme is the consequences of personal choice.
- A deeply personal poem – repeated use of 'I'.
- Builder metaphor is sustained and developed.
- Questions suggest poet's confusion.

Our Whole Life

This poem expresses the poet's frustration with the limitations of language. Since language is a reflection of a particular culture and since Rich is living in a male-dominated world, the language she is forced to use is incapable of fully and honestly expressing the female experience, and indeed serves only to reinforce male values and beliefs. Perceiving the close connection between language and power, the poet understands that a language that essentially reflects the male perspective has the effect of disempowering women. However, as her political activism indicates, Rich did not see women as the only oppressed group – in a society dominated by white, middle-class male values, many sections of society found themselves politically excluded.

The opening lines suggest the inability of language to express truth. The female experience cannot be truthfully expressed because it must be translated into the language of a patriarchal society. The result is the distortion of the female reality, with truth being twisted into 'permissible fibs' that develop into 'a knot of lies'. The image of 'a knot of lies / eating at itself to get undone' suggests how women are entrapped in a male culture whose language denies the expression

of female values and aspirations, effectively disempowering them. The phrase 'Words bitten thru words' suggests a language that is not whole – in other words, a language that is incapable of expressing a range of experiences, perspectives and realities. A vivid image evokes the idea of a language that lacks the power to communicate meaning, 'meanings burnt-off like paint / under the blowtorch'. When it is translated 'into the oppressor's language' (the language of a patriarchal society), the essence of the female experience is lost in translation. The idea of the original meaning not being communicated is expressed in the phrase 'dead letters'. The difficulty that women face in giving voice to their suffering, grievances, dreams and aspirations is compared to the experience of 'Trying to tell the doctor where it hurts'.

The poet reinforces her point with a dramatic, vivid, disturbing image. This image is set in a wartime situation. The poet describes an Algerian walking from his village, burning, 'his whole body a cloud of pain'. Rich points out that 'There are no words for this / except himself'. Language is incapable of expressing his suffering – only the image of the man himself can communicate his pain.

KEY POINTS

- Key theme is the poet's frustration at the inability of language to comprehensively and truthfully express the female experience.
- The tone is one of frustration and anger.
- Effective use of imagery / symbolism – much of the imagery is violent ('a knot of lies eating at itself', 'meanings burnt off', etc), evoking a sense of oppression.

Trying to Talk with a Man

The title suggests the idea of a communication problem, yet what follows sounds much more dramatic, 'Out in this desert we are testing bombs'. (The US government have a nuclear test site in the remote desert of New Mexico.) From the outset it is clear that this poem combines the political and the personal. The following lines literally refer to the destructive power of the bomb ('deformed cliffs'), while on a metaphorical level suggesting an emerging sense of awareness in the female speaker, 'Sometimes I feel an underground river / forcing its way between deformed cliffs / an acute angle of understanding'. The reference to 'this condemned scenery' reminds us of the destruction that will soon be wrought by an exploding bomb.

The poet gives us a snapshot of the life the couple have left behind, listing objects filled with personal meaning and mentioning shared experiences, 'whole LP collections, films we starred in / . . . chocolate-filled Jewish cookies, / the language of love-letters, of suicide notes, / afternoons on the river bank'. While the reader is taken aback by the reference to suicide notes, both the poet and her husband had suicidal tendencies, and consequently were united in their suffering – sadly, as their marriage fell apart, they were united more in their suffering than in their joy.

The speaker now describes the journey to the desert test site, the face of which will soon be altered by the detonation of a nuclear bomb. They drive 'among dull green succulents' (fleshy desert plants) and stop to walk in a desert ghost town. The barren desert and the lifeless, abandoned town evoke a bleak, desolate atmosphere. The couple's lifeless surroundings are symbolic of the death of their relationship. While the speaker and her partner are 'surrounded by a silence' that sounds like the silence of the deserted town, the woman realises that the silence came with them. It is a 'familiar' silence indicative of the couple's strained relationship. Despite their best efforts to 'blot it out', there is no avoiding it in their present situation, 'coming out here we are up against it'. They are compelled to confront the emotional silence that expresses a sad reality – they simply have nothing left to say to each other.

The speaker's honest admission that she feels 'more helpless / with you than without you' indicates that her relationship with her partner has completely collapsed. Basically, she feels that she is better off without him. When they finally engage in conversation, it is without personal content and no meaningful communication takes place. The man talks only of external events relating to the dangers of nuclear testing. While they talk of 'people caring for each other / in emergencies', it is clear that they no longer care for each other. In fact the speaker feels that this relationship may be harmful to her, 'Your dry heat feels like power'. Her partner anxiously paces the floor, the exit signs reflected in his eyes expressing his desire to escape from this failed relationship, 'they reflect lights that spell out EXIT'.

The speaker reflects that while her partner is talking of the danger of nuclear testing, he makes no attempt to address the danger surrounding their relationship, 'talking of the danger / as if it were not ourselves'. In reality, driving out to the desert was not so much about nuclear testing as testing the strength of their relationship, 'as if we were testing anything else'.

KEY POINTS

- Key theme is the breakdown in communication that leads to a breakdown in a relationship.
- The poem combines the personal (the demise of a relationship) and the political (nuclear testing).
- Effective use of imagery and symbolism.
- Language combines the conversational and the metaphorical.
- The mood is pessimistic, the tone is one of frustration.

Diving into the Wreck

The title evokes a sense of adventure and danger. The narrative poem that follows is not simply an account of an exploratory dive into the sea. In its later stages, it becomes apparent that this poem has layers of meaning and is open to a metaphorical reading. The opening stanza describes the diver's preparations for the dive. Concrete, realistic detail paints a vivid picture of the diver's thorough preparations. She has researched the myths relating to the wreck and loaded her camera to record the experience. The fact that she checks the sharpness of her knife blade and the description of the wet suit as 'body armour' suggests an element of danger. The diver is depicted as a brave medieval knight preparing

to go into battle. Clearly inexperienced, the diver finds her diving equipment cumbersome, 'the absurd flippers / . . . the awkward mask'. Unlike Jacques Cousteau, the renowned underwater explorer, who had the support of 'his / assiduous team', she 'is having to do this / . . . alone'.

The diver describes the ladder 'hanging innocently / close to the side of the schooner' in a matter-of-fact manner. While most would regard it simply as a regular piece of maritime equipment, she knows 'what it is for'. The diver knows that this ladder is the gateway to a mysterious undersea world at the bottom of which lies the wreck.

The repetition of 'I go down' and the phrase 'rung after rung' suggest the diver's gradual descent towards the sea. The line 'the oxygen immerses me' is strange, possibly suggesting that she feels trapped in her oxygen mask. She moves down the ladder slowly and with some difficulty, 'My flippers cripple me, / I crawl like an insect down the ladder'. The insect image suggests not only the slowness of the diver's movements, but also her sense of insignificance as she is about to enter the vastness of the sea. The fact that she is undertaking this dive alone heightens the sense of danger. She is without support, without guidance. Inching down the ladder, she knows she will shortly leave her own environment and enter the alien undersea world, 'and there is no one / to tell me when the ocean / will begin'.

The diver senses her immersion in the sea through the changing colours around her. As she descends gradually and moves further away from the light, the undersea world 'is blue and then / it is bluer and then green and then / black'. The absence of punctuation in this section of the poem helps to convey the fluid nature of the world the diver has chosen to enter. While she briefly fears that she might black out, she is reassured by her powerful oxygen mask, 'it pumps my blood with power'. However, she perceives that the concept of power is irrelevant in this undersea world, 'the sea is not a question of power'. This alien environment presents her with a new reality and new challenges, 'I have to learn alone / to turn my body without force / in the deep element'.

The diver is so enthralled by the beauty and wonder of this undersea world, that she almost forgets the purpose of the dive. Everything is different in this undersea world, 'you breathe differently down here'. The image of fish 'swaying their crenellated fans' suggests the protective shape of the shoals as they weave their way between the reefs.

The diver reminds herself why she is here, 'I came to explore the wreck'. The next lines are challenging, 'The words are purposes. / The words are maps'. Perhaps she is referring here to the words of the myths or old stories surrounding the wreck – these words give her a sense of purpose and also guide her. However, it is reality rather than myth that concerns her now, 'I came to see the damage that was done / and the treasures that prevail'. She uses her flashlight to illuminate the wreck, 'I stroke the beam of my lamp / slowly along the flank / of something more permanent / than fish or weed'. This is what she came for – the truth of the wreck, 'the wreck and not the story of the wreck / the thing itself and not the myth'. The image of 'stroking' a beam of light along the wreck indicates the diver's respectful attitude towards the remains of the old vessel.

The speaker personifies the wreck, 'the drowned face always staring / toward the sun' – an image suggestive of the lives lost following the sinking of the ship. Evidence of the initial damage has been worn away by the movements of the sea ('salt and sway'), and what remains is 'this threadbare beauty'. The curved ribs of the ship confidently assert themselves 'among the tentative haunters' (possibly a reference to cautious divers). While the diver perceives a superficial beauty and a certain pride in the old ship, she also describes it as a 'disaster'.

The speaker now identifies herself with mythical sea creatures, 'the mermaid whose dark hair / streams black, the merman in his armoured body / . . . I am she: I am he'. It seems that, following her initial feelings of apprehension, she is now fully confident in this world of water. The idea of being both mermaid and merman suggests a new capacity to view the world from both female and male perspectives. Perhaps Rich is expressing a desire for a sexless world view – a vision of life, a set of beliefs and values to which both men and women contribute equally.

The speaker now identifies with the 'drowned face' of the wreck, 'I am he / whose drowned face sleeps with open eyes'. At this point the wreck seems to be a metaphor for long established social structures and gender roles. Having assumed a new, androgynous (sexless) identity, the poet feels better equipped to explore this wreck. All men and women are intimately connected with the wreck because it has influenced their formation and, in accepting the existing social order, they have played a role in its perpetuation. In so doing, the poet suggests that everybody has

contributed to society losing its way, resulting in this metaphorical 'wreck', 'we are the half-destroyed instruments / that once held to a course / the water-eaten log / the fouled compass'. The reference to treasure in the wreck suggests that exploring it may be a rewarding experience, possibly offering the opportunity to re-define traditional social structures and gender roles.

The closing lines of the poem suggest that people will continue to find their way 'back to this scene' to further explore the wreck. The poet offers no alternative to the existing social framework, instead stressing the need for ongoing exploration of the 'wreck' in the hope of discovering the basis for a more equitable (just) social order where men and women will be equally empowered and equally valued.

KEY POINTS

- On the surface, this poem describes an exploratory dive into a wreck, but on a deeper level it is concerned with exploring social structures and gender roles.
- Effective use of imagery and symbolism.
- Language combines the conversational and the metaphorical.
- Musical qualities: alliteration ('salt and sway', 'circle silently', etc.) and assonance ('checked the edge', 'sun-flooded schooner', etc.).

From a Survivor

In 1953 Rich married Alfred Conrad, an economist and Civil Rights activist. They had three sons together, but their marriage was a difficult one. After seventeen years of marriage, Rich separated from her husband. Some months later, Alfred Conrad committed suicide. In this deeply personal poem Rich reflects on their marriage and on her feelings for her deceased husband.

The poem opens with a reference to their marriage vows, 'The pact that we made was the ordinary pact / of men and women in those days'. Using the term 'pact' to describe their marriage ceremony is unusual since it has connotations of a political or military agreement (battle of the sexes?).

The conversational language employed by Rich gives the poem a wonderful sense of immediacy, 'I don't know who we thought we were / that our personalities / could resist the failures of the race'. She now believes that they were naïve to believe that they could make a success of their marriage in view of the fact that marital breakdown was so prevalent in American society. In their innocence they never anticipated sharing in 'the failures of the race', thinking of themselves 'as special'. However, like most marriages, theirs had its problems and tensions. Despite these problems, her affection for her late husband endures. Her memory of him is clear and distinct, 'Your body is as vivid to me / as it ever was'.

Changes in thinking and attitudes brought about largely by the active feminist movement mean that the poet now has a clearer perspective on her marriage. When she married, marriage was an inherently unequal institution, with the woman expected to be subordinate to her husband. Now she no longer sees her husband as 'a god / . . . with power over my life'.

The poet's love for her husband is again apparent when she wistfully reflects on how, if things had been different, they would be celebrating their twentieth wedding anniversary the following year, 'Next year it would have been twenty years'. Well aware of his great talents, she describes him as being 'wastefully dead'. When the poet speaks of 'the leap / we talked, too late, of making', it seems that she is referring to some mooted change in the nature of their relationship (possibly divorce).

The poem ends on a positive note, with the poet expressing her happiness with her present life, which she describes as 'a succession of brief amazing moments'. The absence of a full stop at the end of the final line suggests that these wonderful moments are ongoing. Tragically, while the poet is a happy 'survivor' of a broken marriage, her husband never had the opportunity to lead a joyful and fulfilling independent existence.

KEY POINTS

- Key theme is the poet's failed marriage and her feelings for her dead husband. Another theme is the changes in male-female relationships.
- A deeply personal poem.
- Conversational language.
- The poem ends on an optimistic note.

Power

In this poem Rich reflects on the life of Nobel Prize winning physicist, Marie Curie who discovered the radioactive elements plutonium and radium. Unfortunately, constant exposure to high levels of radiation resulted in her developing leukaemia, which ultimately claimed her life.

The opening line is rather cryptic (mysterious), 'Living in the earth-deposits of our history'. In view of the poem's title, perhaps the poet is suggesting that the power structures of modern day society are rooted deep in our history.

There follows an image of a mechanical digger throwing up a long buried, amber coloured bottle. The bottle used to contain an old 'cure for fever or melancholy a tonic / for living in this earth in the winters of this climate'. This clearly was one of those 'cure all' potions concocted by some 'quack doctor' or con-man intent on exploiting the weak and gullible. It is commonly said that knowledge is power, and such people used their limited knowledge in an utterly unscrupulous manner to gain a degree of power over desperate people.

The poem now shifts focus, with the poet explaining that she was reading about Marie Curie. Rich claims that Curie 'must have known she suffered from radiation sickness'. It was ironic that the radium she had worked so hard to purify gradually destroyed her health. We are presented with vivid images of her suffering, 'the cataracts on her eyes / the cracked and suppurating (oozing pus) skin of her finger-ends'. Curie suffered intensely for her selfless dedication to her work, eventually being unable to 'hold a test-tube or a pencil'.

The closing lines tell of how Curie died, 'denying / her wounds came from the same source as her power'. It was her work with radium that gave this great scientist her status and power in society, yet this was also what killed her. What most fascinates the poet is that right to the end Curie denied that her illness was caused by continual exposure to radiation.

The poem highlights the contrasting ways that people use power. The phoney doctor from an earlier age used his power to deceive and exploit the weak and the vulnerable. His cynicism is juxtaposed with Curie's idealism. While the 'quack' was interested only in personal gain, Curie gave her life for research that would benefit all mankind.

KEY POINTS

- Key theme is the contrasting ways that men and women use power.
- Vivid description of Curie's suffering.
- Musical qualities: alliteration ('body bombarded', etc.) and assonance ('living on this earth in the winters of this climate', etc.).
- Optimistic ending.

Sample Answer

'Adrienne Rich's poetry is interesting both for its themes and its language'. Discuss.

I am in complete agreement with this statement. Rich is one of the most important and provocative voices in modern day literature. Her themes are always relevant and she often challenges us with her ideas on a range of inter-related issues: male-female relationships, the nature of power, and the role of women in society. While her feminist perspective means that her work has an obvious attraction for a female audience, her appeal is not confined to one gender. Her language is generally clear and direct and her images striking and memorable.

Aunt Jennifer's Tigers set me thinking about how marriage can oppress women. The poem opens with a woman engaged in a traditionally female task – the speaker's aunt is embroidering on a decorative screen. The image on the screen is dominated by powerful, confident tigers moving through their jungle domain with the swagger of medieval knights, 'They pace in sleek chivalric certainty'. This image powerfully reinforces the idea that the tigers are emblems of male power. The tigers' strength and confidence is contrasted with Aunt Jennifer's weakness and nervousness. Her anxiety is captured in the image of her 'fingers fluttering through her wool'. The most striking image in the poem is of 'The massive weight of Uncle's wedding band' sitting 'heavily' on Aunt Jennifer's hand. The ring (significantly it is '*Uncle's* wedding band') seems to restrict and impede her. The weighty wedding band is an apt symbol of her husband's power and control over her. The oppressive nature of marriage is underscored by the contrast between Aunt Jennifer's frailty ('fluttering fingers') and her husband's strength ('massive weight').

An idea that Rich often explores in her verse is the complex, often disappointing reality of male-female relationships. *Living in Sin* is interesting primarily because of its realistic depiction of male–female relationships. Most people could relate to the experience of the woman who finds that the reality of living with her partner in a small studio apartment falls short of the romantic dream. In her naivety, the woman had given no thought to the mundane realities of day-to-day life with her partner. This idea is expressed in everyday language, 'She had thought the studio would keep itself'. The woman had idealistically envisioned a perfect scenario, 'A plate of pears, / A piano with a Persian shawl'. Inevitably, experience reveals the unglamorous truth: noisy dripping taps, grimy windows, scraps of leftover food and empty bottles. Worst of all, she encounters a beetle among the saucers – the beetle is described in a memorably humorous image as an 'Envoy from a village in the moldings'. Aside from the grim physical environment, the woman has to cope with her partner's lethargy and general indifference. He seems to be a musician or composer, but lacks the motivation to practise his music, 'sounded a dozen notes upon the keyboard, / declared it out of tune, shrugged at the mirror, / rubbed at his beard, went out for cigarettes'. The shrugging image perfectly captures her partner's apathetic attitude. This poem provides us with an insight into sexual stereotyping – the man makes no attempt to tackle any domestic tasks and it is the woman who cleans the apartment. Despite her disillusionment, the woman does not leave her indifferent boyfriend and the depressing apartment, 'By evening she was back in love again'. However, the next phrase ('though not as wholly') qualifies this statement, reminding us of how loving feelings and romantic notions are undermined by the humdrum nature of daily domestic life and by the perpetuation of traditional gender roles.

Anyone who has found him/herself in a relationship which is inexorably disintegrating will easily relate to *Trying to Talk with a Man*. In this poem the speaker and her partner have gone into the desert ostensibly to witness the detonation of a nuclear bomb – however, we get the impression that the underlying purpose of this journey is to take stock of their relationship. An excellent visual image suggests how the woman is growing in insight, 'Sometimes I feel an underground river / forcing its way between deformed cliffs / an acute angle of understanding'. This poem highlights Rich's effective use of imagery to convey her themes. The images of a ghost town and the desert effectively suggest the silent, barren nature of the couple's relationship. While the speaker and her partner are 'surrounded by a silence' that sounds like the silence of the deserted town, the speaker realises that the silence has come with them. It is a 'familiar' silence indicative of the couple's problematical relationship. The speaker acknowledges the extent of their problems in language that is admirably simple and direct, 'Out here I feel more helpless / with you than without you'. What I found interesting about this poem was the man's unwillingness to discuss the problems at the heart of the relationship. He talks only of external events such as the danger of nuclear testing, making no attempt to address the danger surrounding the relationship, 'Talking of the danger / as if it were not ourselves'. This poem stands out in my mind because it underlines an almost universal truth – women are more emotionally aware and more emotionally honest than men.

From a Survivor is a deeply personal poem describing the poet's failed marriage. What I found interesting – and indeed uplifting – about this poem was the affectionate nature of the poet's reflections on her late husband and the fact that her brave 'leap' away from her marriage enabled her to find true joy. The conversational language employed by Rich gives this poem a wonderful sense of immediacy, 'I don't know who we thought we were / that our personalities / could resist the failures of our race'. The poet reminds us of the optimism that attends the early stages of romantic relationships, 'Like everybody else, we thought of ourselves as special'. She never anticipated that their marriage, like so many others, would not stand the test of time. Despite the tensions of their marriage, the poet's affection for her late husband endures, 'Your body is as vivid to me / as it ever was'. It was also encouraging to learn that, having come through a difficult period, the poet retains the capacity to find joy in life – she speaks of having experienced 'a succession of brief amazing moments'. Another aspect of this poem that I found interesting was the insight it provided into the changing nature of male-female relationships. Social and cultural changes brought about largely by the active feminist movement mean that the poet now has a clearer perspective on her marriage. When she married, marriage was an intrinsically unequal institution, with the woman expected to be obedient to her husband. In the past the poet had seen her husband as 'a god / . . . with power over my life'. As Rich grew as a person and as a poet, she 'no longer' viewed her husband as godlike.

One of the most interesting and most challenging of Rich's poems is *Our Whole Life*. This poem expresses the poet's frustrations with the limitations of language. Since language is a reflection of a particular culture and since Rich is living in a male-dominated world, the language she is forced to use is incapable of fully and honestly expressing the female experience. Perceiving the close connection between language and power, the poet understands that a language that essentially reflects the male perspective has the effect of disempowering women. The female consciousness cannot be truthfully expressed because it must be translated 'into the oppressor's language'. The result is the distortion of the female reality, with truth being twisted into 'permissible lies' that develop into 'a knot of lies'. The image of 'a knot of lies / eating at itself to get undone' suggests how women are entrapped in a male culture whose language denies the expression of their values and beliefs. Another image evokes the idea of a language that has lost the power to communicate meaning, 'meanings burnt-off like paint / under the blowtorch'. The poem concludes with a dramatic, disturbing image underlining the limitations of language. A badly burnt Algerian villager, a casualty of war, cannot communicate his suffering to the doctor, 'There are no words for this / except himself'.

In conclusion Rich's poetry is interesting both for its ideas and the way in which these ideas are expressed. She explores issues that are relevant to the modern reader in language that is generally clear and accessible, making very effective use of imagery to express her themes.

Derek Walcott

Biographical Note

Derek Walcott was born, one of twins, in 1930 in Saint Lucia in the West Indies. The history of this small island was very troubled because of the devastating impact of colonisation. France and England squabbled over St Lucia (primarily because of its superb natural harbour), with the island eventually becoming part of the British Empire in the nineteenth century. However, French cultural influences on the island remained strong. After the indigenous population had been wiped out by European settlers, many Africans were brought in to work as slaves on the island's sugar plantations. Asian Indians were also brought in to work on the plantations, which were owned by the Europeans. Walcott comes from a mixed-race background, with both of his grandmothers being descended from African slaves and both of his grandfathers being estate owners.

Walcott's father, Warwick, worked as a civil servant and was also a very talented painter and poet. His mother worked as a teacher in the local Methodist school (The majority of the island's population was Catholic). Walcott's father died when he was only one year old, leaving his mother, Alix, to raise the family. While they were poor in material terms, their family life was very rich, with Alix instilling in her children the value and importance of work, as well as respect for the Bible and the arts. She continually encouraged Derek to develop his God-given literary talent. Derek shared these beliefs and was renowned for, among other things, his remarkable work ethic. He displayed an early talent for writing, having his first poem published in a local newspaper when he was just fourteen. After attending the Methodist Primary School, Derek won a scholarship to the prestigious St Mary's College in the town of Castries. His literary talent continued to blossom through secondary school, and he had five plays written and his first collection of poetry published by the time he was sixteen. It was Alix, his ever-supportive mother, who found the money to fund the private publication of Derek's early poems.

From an early stage in his literary career, Walcott realised that no one had written about his own island, St Lucia, and the wider West Indies. He happily took on the role of expressing the Caribbean experience. Much of his work explores the racial complexities of the West Indies and the impact of these complexities on his own life. Interestingly, Walcott also developed a growing interest in Irish literature, particularly Yeats. He was offered a scholarship to study English in the University College of the West Indies in Jamaica, from which he graduated in 1953 with a BA degree. In 1954 Walcott published *The Sea at Dauphin*, which earned him a Rockefeller scholarship to study play-writing and directing in New York. He returned to the West Indies in 1959 and founded the Trinidad Theatre Workshop. Walcott continued to publish many poetry collections and plays over the following thirty years, all the while adding to his considerable international reputation. He published what is widely regarded as his masterpiece, the epic poem *Omeros*, in 1990. In 1992 Walcott's considerable achievements were recognised when he was awarded the Nobel Prize for literature. Since then he has continued to work relentlessly, publishing several acclaimed volumes of poetry as well as a significant collection of essays.

Derek Walcott has been married three times and has three children. He now divides his time between The United States and his home in the West Indies.

A Letter from Brooklyn

This poem opens with a vivid description of the handwriting of an old lady who has written to the poet about her memories of his dead father. The old lady's script is described as 'spidery'. The web image is developed with references to 'a skein', 'thread' and 'filament'. The personification of the letters ('Each character trembling') suggests how the old lady's hand shook as she was writing the letter. Walcott has difficulty following the lady's disjointed train of thought. Her words are described as 'travelling on a skein / Of such frail thoughts its thread is often broken'. The poet visualises the 'veined hand / Pellucid as paper' expressing the thoughts of this elderly lady. While Walcott at times struggles to understand these thoughts, elsewhere her meaning is crystal clear: 'the filament from which a phrase is hung / Dims to my sense, but caught, it shines like steel'. The poet cannot remember this woman's face: 'I forget her face / More easily than my father's yearly dying'. From this we see that Walcott's father's death when he was only a year old is a continuing source of pain for him. Certain details about the old woman such as her 'small, buttoned boots and the place / She kept in our wooden church on those Sundays / Whenever her strength allowed' remain clear in his mind.

In the second stanza, we learn that the aged woman's name is Mable Rawlins. She writes of the poet's parents in the present tense, as if they were still alive: 'and know both your parents'. Her respect for Walcott's father is apparent in how she remembers him: 'Your father was a dutiful, honest, / Faithful, and useful person'. These simple words of sincere admiration prompt the poet to ponder the value of his own fame when set against his father's qualities: 'For such plain praise what fame is recompense?' The images the old lady paints of his father are highly valued by Walcott because he has no such memories himself. She describes how Walcott's father, like the poet himself, was a painter: 'A horn-painter, he painted delicately on horn, / He used to sit around the table and paint pictures'. The simplicity and beauty of this memory suggests a man at peace within himself and, in the poet's view, evokes the presence of God: 'The peace of God needs nothing to adorn / It.' The old lady's absolute belief in a life beyond death reflects the depth of her religious convictions: 'He is twenty-eight years buried . . . , he was called home, /And is, I am sure, doing greater work'.

The third stanza of the poem describes the impact of Mable Rawlins' unshakeable faith on the poet. The paradoxical phrase 'The strength of one frail hand' suggests how this frail old lady's strong religious convictions had a powerful effect on Walcott, restoring his faith in God: 'Restores my duty to the Word'. The image of the 'dim room' in which Miss Rawlins writes suggests her closeness to death. Even though she has 'such short time to live', she still 'spins the blessings of her years'. This metaphor relates back to the opening image of the old lady's 'spidery writing'. Indeed the web is the dominant image in the poem. The latter image suggests that she continues to 'weave' the wisdom acquired over many years. Despite her advanced age, her beauty has not faded since she possesses a spiritual beauty that deeply moves the poet: 'Not withered of beauty if she can bring such tears'. This inner beauty is derived from a lifetime of experience. Walcott is hugely reassured by Mable Rawlins' absolute belief in a life beyond death: 'Heaven is to her the place where painters go, / All who

bring beauty on frail shell or horn'. Such creative people are steadily 'drawn' to Heaven by a 'thread' of 'resilient steel' that may not be apparent in dark periods of a person's life.

The closing lines underscore the impact of Mable Rawlins' letter on the poet, with the repetition of 'I believe' indicating that his religious faith has been dramatically restored. His renewed belief in Heaven means that he no longer mourns the death of his father or indeed the death of any man: 'So this old lady writes and again I believe, / I believe it all, and for no man's death I grieve'.

KEY POINTS

- A deeply personal poem.
- Key theme is the restoration of the poet's religious faith following a letter from an elderly lady who knew his parents, particularly his dead father, well.
- In terms of style, this poem is dominated by the metaphor of a spider's web – like the web, the old lady appears frail, but, in reality, is very resilient.
- Repetition underlines the key theme ('I believe').

Endings

This poem deals with the nature of change, particularly the manner in which things end. It opens with a strong, unequivocal assertion: 'Things do not explode, / they fail, they fade'. Walcott believes that things do not end in a dramatic, explosive manner, but rather draw to a close gradually. The assonant long 'a' sound suggests that change is a drawn-out process.

Two similes reinforce the idea that change occurs by degrees: 'as sunlight fades from the flesh, / as the foam drains quick in the sand'. The fading of a tan and the draining away of foam into the sand indicate that change is a

slow process. Even love, which often begins dramatically (as the metaphor of 'love's lightning flash' suggests) ends quietly ('has no thunderous end'). Love dies as imperceptibly as 'the sound / of flowers fading like the flesh', decaying as gradually as the skin removed from feet by a pumice stone.

The fading of love is depicted as leaving a sense of soundless emptiness. Its demise is seen as a tragedy as heartbreaking as Beethoven's loss of hearing when he was only thirty years old: 'we are left / with the silence that surrounds Beethoven's head'. The gentle nature of change is underscored by the repetition of 'fade' ('fade . . . fades . . . fading').

This poem is full of musical qualities, with the alliterative 'f' ('fail . . . fade . . . fades . . . flash flowers . . . fading . . . flesh'), 'l' ('love's lightning') and 's' ('sound . . . sweating . . . stone . . . shapes . . . silence . . . surrounds') sounds. In overall terms the soft 's' sound, created by a combination of alliteration and sibilance ('Things . . . sunlight . . . fades . . . flesh, etc, etc.) evokes the gentle nature of change.

There is a sensuous quality to much of the poem's imagery; we can visualise the fading of a tan, feel the gently abrasive pumice stone and hear the sound of silence that follows the death of love.

Walcott obviously does not suggest that everything in life ends gradually, highlighting in particular the slow, inevitable demise of love and the transience of natural beauty, symbolised by the flowers.

KEY POINTS

- Key theme is the gradual nature of change.
- Effective use of simile.
- Musical qualities.
- Repetition reinforces the key theme.

Summer Elegies

The title suggests the idea of both joy and loss – summer is generally regarded as a time of pleasure, relaxation and warm contentment, while an elegy is a poem of lamentation (mourning).

This poem is addressed to a woman called Cynthia, with whom the poet enjoyed a passionate relationship. The language is natural and conversational: 'Cynthia, the things we did . . .' The first three stanzas are full of sensuous, erotic images as Walcott describes their lovemaking on a sun-drenched beach. The opening stanza depicts the lovers, driven by desire, becoming bolder as 'the unhooked halter slithered / from sunburnt shoulders'. The sense of growing excitement is evident in the image of the poet 'tremblingly' unfixing the bikini top to reveal 'two white

quarter-moons / unpeeled there like a frisket'. The frisket simile suggests how part of the woman's breasts were screened from the sun. It seems that lovemaking on the beach was a regular feature of this intense relationship when Walcott states how the woman's uncovered breasts 'burnt for afternoons'. The total intimacy of the lovers is evoked by the image of them making 'one shape in the water'. There is a nice humorous touch in the image of an astonished dove gurgling 'Ooos at / the changing shapes of love'.

The fourth stanza opens with the suggestion that the idyllic time shared by the lovers would never end: 'Time lent us the whole island'. However, we are immediately reminded that time inevitably brings change as 'heat and image fade'. This suggests that the warmth of summer and the blissful experience of the lovers on the beach inevitably pass and fade into memory. This natural, inexorable process is effectively conveyed by apt similes that compare the fading of 'heat and image' to the sand soaking up 'foam lace' and to the paling of the tan 'on a striped shoulder blade'.

In the fifth stanza, sensuous imagery conveys the effect of spending endless hours in the sea and soaking up the sun: 'Salt dried in every fissure'. This tactile image is immediately followed by another depicting the peeling of sunburnt skin: 'I peeled the papery tissue / of my dead flesh away'. The sensuous imagery continues in stanza six with Walcott describing how the dead skin 'feathered as I blew it / from reanointed skin'. The term 'reanoint' has obvious religious connotations, but may only be a light-hearted reference to sun oil and to how we, in a sense, worship the summer sun. The reference to 'reanointed skin' is suggestive of new skin appearing under the dead skin. This leads to the poet wondering if 'love could renew itself' like his skin, 'and a new life begin'. These lines indicate that the poet feels a sense of loss following the demise of a once-loving relationship, and may again be looking for love.

Stanza seven sees Walcott reflecting on the perfection and total tranquillity of an idyllic day, where the sea is not disturbed by even a single yacht: 'A halcyon day. No sail'. The smoothness of the sea is compared to cigarette paper, while 'a red thumbnail' may suggest the setting sun. Stanza eight brings us back to the present. The simile 'The bay shines like tinfoil' depicts the sun sparkling on the sea, while the waves are compared to curved wood shavings ('crimps like excelsior') in a rather unappealing simile. The paradox 'All the deck chairs are full. / but the beach is emptier' suggests how a person can feel lonely even in a crowd, again pointing up the poet's sense of loss.

The final stanza evokes the idea of the Garden of Eden with its references to 'the snake' and 'apple tree'. The lovers' passionate hours on the beach were like Paradise itself but, like Adam and Eve, their perfect happiness ('I had her breast to rest on') did not last, as the closing words clearly indicate: 'the rest is history'.

KEY POINTS

- Key themes are the passion of a new relationship and the transience of love.
- Sensuous imagery.
- Many apt similes and metaphors (although those in stanza seven challenge the reader).
- Biblical imagery in closing stanza.
- Conversational language.
- Sound effects: alliteration (e.g. 'sunburnt shoulders', 'sea like cigarette paper smoothed . . . ') assonance (e.g. 'dried in every fissure').

To Norline

This poem is addressed to the poet's third wife and was written some time after their relationship ended. We picture Walcott, having emerged from a house in which everyone else is still asleep, standing on the beach with a cup of coffee in his hand, looking out at the sea. The image of the 'empty' beach and the grey ('slate-coloured') sky conveys a sense of loneliness and sadness, while the image of the personified surf erasing all markings on the sand 'with its sponge' suggests both the transience of human life and the continuity of nature.

Looking into the future, the poet imagines another man doing exactly what he is now doing: 'and someone else will come / from the still-sleeping house, / a coffee mug warming his palm'. This sensuous image prompts a deeply personal, sensuous simile as Walcott recalls a tender moment shared with Norline: ' . . . as my body once cupped yours'. There is a sense of nostalgia and perhaps even yearning in this image of shared love.

Walcott's deep appreciation and love of the natural beauty of the Caribbean is to be seen in his desire to capture in memory the precise movements of 'a salt-sipping tern'. A memorable simile compares his love for such beautiful natural scenes to his deep love for a particular piece of literature: 'like when some line on a page / is loved, and it's hard to turn'. The poet finds it difficult to take his eyes off the tern in the same way that he struggles to leave behind an especially favoured part of some literary text.

While there is certainly a sense of pervasive loneliness and melancholy in this poem, this is counter-balanced by the clear implication that life goes on. The natural world will continue to witness 'slate-coloured dawns', incoming tides erasing all markings on a beach and the eye-catching tern flying just above the water. In the human world, generation after generation will follow the poet in witnessing and appreciating the beauty of this natural scene. Life will go on just as the page will be turned.

KEY POINTS

- Key themes include the beauty of nature, lost love and the transience of life.
- Sensuous imagery.
- Simple, everyday language.

from Omeros

In this poem Walcott takes a traditional poetic form, the epic, and imbues it with his own distinctive West Indian culture, history and, most strikingly of all, language (English Creole). As the title suggests, there are some links between Walcott's epic and Homer's classics, the *Iliad* and the *Odyssey*. This is a dramatic poem, with a specific setting, characters and dialogue. The poem is located on a fishing boat out at sea in the early morning. It is based on a conversation between Achile, the captain, and his mate.

The poem opens with the yawning mate requesting some assistance from Achile. He knows that Achile is not fond of talking, but needs a hand 'Mackerel running'. There is a humorous quality to the opening exchanges. When the mate asks where Achile's mind was the entire night, he is met with the response, 'Africa', prompting him to enquire, 'Oh? You walk?' The fishermen's poverty is suggested by the image of the mate's worn T-shirt, which is now little more than 'a red hole'. The sarcasm continues with the mate suggesting that Achile 'got sunstroke', and should put 'that damn captain-cap' back on his head. The mate is very diligent, working the rods all night, without any sleep. All the while Achile is asleep, 'cradle(d) in the bow'. The mate comes across as an able seafarer who is able to navigate by the stars: 'he had read / The stars and known how far out they were'. While Achile does not seem to be pulling his weight, the mate is not resentful, feeling that he owes Achile a debt of gratitude because he 'took him on / When he was stale-drunk'.

The mate points to a huge albacore, the size of a shark ('mako-size') that he caught during the night. We get a vivid image of the albacore, known in the region by a variety of names such as 'kingfish' and 'ton'; he is 'steel-blue and silver . . . its eyes like a globed window'. The 'globed window' is a memorable metaphor, suggesting the albacore's bulging eyes. This magnificent fish met a brutal end, 'gaffed and clubbed' by the mate. In death it lies on the bottom of the boat, 'gaping, / its blue flakes yielding the oceanic colour'. However, it put up a colossal fight before the mate finally landed it. When the albacore emerged from the freezing depths, it had 'shot, leaping, / Stronger than a stallion's neck tugging its stake, / Sounding, then bursting its trough' in an attempt to break the line that held it fast. This graphic image conveys the impressive power and admirable determination of the fish.

Throughout the mate's titanic struggle with the courageous albacore, Achile had slept like a baby: 'Cradled at the bow / Like a foetus'. When the mate sees land, Achile skilfully steers the boat through the high waves: 'altered the rudder / To keep sideways in the deep troughs without riding / The crests'. When he looks up, Achile sees an 'old man-o-war', also known as a frigate bird, following the herring-gulls. Its effortless gliding and dominance over other birds made this huge bird 'the sea-king'. Basically a pirate bird, the man-o-war steals the gulls' catch, never catching its own. The gulls are described as 'white slaves for a black king'. This perception of the relationship between the gulls and the frigate-bird turns the historical relationship between white and black men on its head, delighting the Caribbean fishermen still paying the price for their ancestors' conquest and enslavement by the white man. Achile is hugely impressed with the frigate-bird: 'Look at that son- / Of-a-bitch stealing his fish for the whole focking week!' As a gull climbs skywards with its catch in its beak (depicted by a striking metaphor: 'with silver bent in its beak'), the pirate seizes his opportunity. We can visualise 'the black magnificent frigate' intercepting the gull ('met the gull / Halfway with the tribute'), causing the gull to drop its mackerel, which the frigate-bird catches before it hits the water. The idea of the gull paying 'tribute' to the man-o-war reinforces the image of this huge bird as the king of its world.

Both fishermen are in awe of 'the sea-king'. Achile cannot contain his feelings of delight and admiration: 'The black bugger beautiful, / Though!' The alliterative 'b' sound underscores the sense of conviction with which this belief is expressed. Achile feels elated as he watches the man-o-war climb ever higher: 'Achile felt the phrase lift / His heart as high as the bird'. He imagines the movement of the bird spelling the name of his great African ancestor and tribal king, Afolabe, in the sky. It is appropriate that the closing lines again return to the perceived royal nature of this magnificent bird. 'The king going home', says

Achile, as he and the mate 'watched the frigate steer into that immensity / Of seraphic space whose cumuli were a gate'. We are reminded of Achile dreaming of Africa the previous night as the frigate navigates its course through the vastness of the sky towards the heavens ('seraphic space') and home through the gates (symbolised by the clouds) of his kingdom.

KEY POINTS

- Key themes include poverty (these fishermen risk their lives in heavy seas to earn a meagre living), the beauty of nature and its impact on man.
- Poem also touches on the impact of colonisation on these Caribbean fishermen.
- Vivid imagery throughout.
- Written in a traditional poetic form – the epic.
- Written in English Creole.

The Young Wife

This poem is concerned with a husband struggling to cope with the death of his young wife. The poem opens in a conversational manner as the speaker addresses the man, urging him to keep busy and to organise himself: 'Make all your sorrow neat'. The image of making the bed symbolises the various household tasks that need to be attended to: 'Plump pillows, soothe the corners / of her favourite coverlet'. The latter phrase is the only personal note sounded in the opening stanza. The grim reality of death is evoked by the advice to 'Write to her mourners'.

The second stanza highlights the depth of the husband's grief. The fact that he returns 'at dusk' in itself conveys a sense of gloom. The previously welcoming living room is now devoid of comfort and warmth and has

acquired a sinister quality, filling the grieving husband with foreboding. The armchair is no longer inviting: 'travel an armchair's ridge', while the space between the arms of the sofa is described in dark, almost biblical, terms as 'the valley of the shadow of the sofas'. The geographical terms 'ridge' and 'valley' evoke the sense of a vast natural landscape, pointing up the huge sense of emptiness that now fills the bereaved husband. What was once a comforting homely landscape has become a grim place associated with death. This idea is reinforced by the reference to the flowers imprinted on the curtains which, in the husband's imagination, have now withered: 'the drapes' dead foliage'.

The third stanza is dominated by the husband's feeling of being a traitor: 'the mirror / which you believe has seen / the traitor you feel you are' But who has he betrayed? In his tormented mind does he feel that he somehow betrayed his wife by being unable to prevent her dying? Does he feel that continuing on represents some kind of betrayal of her? Certainly the mirror image suggests the idea of self-examination and reflection – which naturally follow on the death of a loved one. The clouded mirror may indicate that the husband now struggles to see who he truly is in the absence of his wife.

The husband's grief is expressed in 'the muffled sobbing / the children must not hear' and is reflected in his fear of approaching the drawers that contain his wife's possessions.

In stanza five death is personified as 'that visitor / that sat beside her'. Death is also compared to the wind 'clicking shut the bedroom door'. The bedroom, which was once the realm of love and intimacy, warmth and passion, is now, by implication, filled with coldness. The husband imagines his beloved wife walking off 'arm in arm' with the visitor that is death, 'leaving her wedding photograph in / its lace frame'. There is a sense of betrayal in these lines, as if his wife has left him for another man. Everything he sees is a reminder that she is no longer with him: the drawers that store her belongings, their wedding photograph and 'the telephone / without a voice'.

The heavy burden of grief is conveyed in the lines: 'The weight / we bear on this heavier side / of the grave brings no comfort.' The marriage vows taken by husband and wife saw them

pledge their love to each other until separated by death, and the husband has been brought 'to the very edge / of that promise' through his wife's illness and death. Outside the grief-enshrouded household, nature continues on, with the hawthorn hedge breaking 'happily into blossom'. Sadly, while nature renews itself, the heartbroken husband may never get over his loss and must go on with only grief 'blossoming' in his heart.

The final eleven lines depict life in the house without the presence of the mother. The anguished husband 'keep(s) setting a fork and knife / at her place for supper', finding it difficult to reconcile himself to the fact that his wife is no longer part of their lives. The children are depicted as a positive presence in the house, easing the sense of emptiness: 'The children close in the space / made by a chair removed'. The speaker now expresses some unalterable realities: 'and nothing takes her place, / loved and now deeper loved'.

In the final stanza, the speaker again addresses the husband: 'The children accept your answer' (presumably about where their mother is now). The husband is startled when he hears his children laugh, but this is an indication that life goes on even amidst death, loss and heartbreak. The poem ends on an uplifting note with an image of the smiling mother sitting in her chair, telling them that 'cancer kills everything but love'. The family's shared love will ensure that she always remains with them in spirit. This poem ends with the reassuring idea that love endures beyond death.

KEY POINTS

- Key themes are death, loss and grief.
- Many poignant images.
- Contrast between continuity of nature and man's inexorable movement towards death.
- Mood is one of sadness and loneliness.
- Ending is positive and uplifting.

For Adrian

This poem concerns the death of an eight-year-old boy who speaks to his family through the poet. It is written in a traditional poetic form, the elegy, consisting of a series of unrhymed couplets. Traditionally an elegy was written in memory of some famous or important person, but this poem is written in memory of a young boy who was hugely important to those who loved him. This poem differs from traditional elegies in another way in that it is written in the voice of the dead child, who speaks through the poet. The list of those to whom the poem is dedicated represents the different members of the boy's grieving family.

The boy who speaks to those grieving his death possesses a wisdom that only the dead possess. In the opening couplet the boy invites these people to look at the world through his eyes: 'Look, and you will see that . . . ' He points out that even a seemingly substantial object such as a wardrobe 'is fading', and is, in fact, 'as insubstantial as a sunset'. The boy claims that he can see through people: 'I can see through you, the tissue of your leaves, / the light behind your veins'. Obviously as flesh and blood beings we face the inevitability of death and decay. Adrian wonders why his loved ones are crying: 'Why do you keep sobbing?' Clearly, he believes there is no need to mourn the dead.

Adrian is now keenly aware of the speed with which life passes: 'The days run through the light's fingers like dust / or a child's in a sandpit'. In referring to the timeless stars and sea, Adrian highlights our mortality. He also prompts us to reflect on our relative insignificance in the universe, asking his loved ones: 'Do you think your shadow / can be as long as the desert?'

In dying, Adrian has achieved knowledge 'beyond my eight years'. He claims to 'have more vestal (pure) authority' and to have 'entered a wisdom'. He cannot comprehend why his loved ones still mourn him: 'Why do you miss me? I am not missing you, sisters'. While these words are cold-sounding, Adrian has achieved unimagined happiness and wisdom in his new state of being and now knows that mourning his death is futile. However, he obviously has fond memories of his family, speaking warmly of 'Judith, whose hair will banner like the leopard's', 'Gem sitting in a corner of her pain' and his aunt 'with the soft eyes that have soothed the one who writes this'. Here we are reminded that Adrian is speaking through the poet; it is almost as if they are one.

The boy desperately wants his family to know that he does not want them to endure any more heartbreak and suffering: 'I would not break your heart, and you should know it; /

I would not make you suffer, and you should know it'. Repetition underlines his desire to fill that gap in their knowledge that causes them to grieve his death. He points out that he is 'not suffering', before telling them that he now possesses the wisdom that only comes with death: 'I am wiser, I share the secret that is only a silence'. It is 'a silence' because the dead cannot communicate their wisdom to the living. Adrian explains that he shares this knowledge with tyrant and tramp alike.

In his altered state age is irrelevant, having no place in the world he is part of now: 'I am not young now, nor old, not a child, not a bud / snipped before it flowered'. The latter image is commonly employed to suggest the idea of a person dying before he/she had the opportunity to fulfil his/her potential. This is how Adrian's family perceive his death. However, Adrian is now at one with the natural world: 'I am part of the muscle / of a galloping lion, or a bird keeping low over / dark canes'. These images evoke a sense of power, beauty and harmony. The boy persists in his efforts to make them see death in a new light – not as 'a goodbye', but as 'a different welcome' to a new world. He tells them that they too will see that what he is saying 'is true', but we feel that his mourning family will not comprehend the wisdom of the dead until they themselves share in it.

The poem closes with the poet explaining how he, in a sense, has acted as a medium or bridge between the worlds of the living and the dead: 'All this the child spoke inside me, so I wrote it down'. The final image of Adrian's closing grave as 'the smile of the earth' reinforces the optimistic, uplifting message at the heart of this poem.

KEY POINTS

- Key themes are the passage of time, life after death and the beauty of nature.
- A philosophical poem.
- Mood is generally positive, uplifting.
- Notwithstanding (despite) the occasional high-brow phrase (e.g. 'vestal authority'), the tone is largely childlike.
- Effective use of natural imagery.
- Sound effects: alliteration (e.g. 'furniture is fading'), onomatopoeia (e.g. 'creaking').
- Repetition underlines sense of urgency (' . . . and you should know it').
- Closing simile is particularly memorable.

Saint Lucia's First Communion

This poem opens with a vivid description of young children making their First Communion on Saint Lucia, an island in the West Indies that is the poet's home. The opening line contains a striking metaphor: 'At dusk, on the edge of the asphalt's worn-out ribbon'. On this road the poet (who is in his car) sees a black child 'in white cotton frock', before noticing a 'small field' of similarly attired young girls. This metaphor compares the innocent children to flowers in a field. Not being a Catholic himself, Walcott takes a couple of seconds to realise what event is taking place: 'Ah, it's the First Communion!' The strong sense of colour in the opening stanza is reinforced by the image of 'the pink ribboned missals in their hands'.

The girls' 'stiff plaits' are 'pinned' in place by 'white satin moths' – a metaphor for the moth-shaped hair clips. The words 'stiff' and 'pinned' may be suggestive of the repressive, restrictive nature of religion. The alliterative 'plaits pinned' underscores this sense of restraint. The moth image is developed with the reference to 'the caterpillar's accordion', perhaps suggesting the movement of the children in the procession. The idea of these children 'still pumping out the myth' clearly indicates the poet's religious doubts and uncertainties, as does his reference to unquestioning faith ('belief without an *if*').

The third stanza depicts a typical First Communion scene, with the poet imagining 'thousands of innocents' across Saint Lucia being 'arranged' on church steps by their proud parents, awaiting the taking of photographs. The verb 'arranged' may also evoke a sense of control. Facing into the bright sun for the photograph (suggested by the inventive metaphor, 'the sun's lens'), the parents inevitably squint as they stand alongside their children who are 'erect as candles' (again, possibly suggestive of a sense of control). There is a sinister aspect to this stanza with the reference to darkness coming on 'like their blinded saint's'. Here we are reminded of Saint Lucia, who was blinded by pagans in the course of her horrendous martyrdom.

Stanza four sees the poet overwhelmed by the desire to protect these young innocents from the evil of the world. Imagining the young children to be moths, he longs to 'house each child' in his hands, to 'delicately urge / the last moth delicately in'. The repetition of 'delicately' underlines the depth of the poet's sensitivity towards and concern for these innocent children. The poet pictures innumerable moths creating a 'blizzard' within his car. He would then release them 'on some black hill', and watch them fly 'heavenward before it came on: the prejudice, the evil!' The concluding lines reiterate the poet's desperate desire to insulate the children from the harshness, disappointment and pain (suggested by the image of their innocent eyes being 'lanced' by the headlights) of the world they will grow up in.

KEY POINTS

- Key themes include the poet's fear of innocence being destroyed by prejudice and evil, and his doubts and uncertainties in relation to religion.

- Many striking metaphors.
- Vivid description.
- Effective use of colour: the contrasting black and white of the opening stanza evokes Saint Lucia's history of conquest, colonisation and enslavement (also suggested by references to cotton).
- Compassionate tone, especially in stanzas 4–5.
- Sound effects: alliteration (e.g. 'plaits pinned').
- Repetition in stanzas 4–5 accentuates the poet's sensitivity.

Pentecost

Pentecost refers to the time following Jesus' ascension into heaven. The apostles were together in one room when the Holy Spirit, sounding like a strong wind, appeared to them in the form of tongues of fire, inspiring them to go forth and spread the word of God in the language of the people to whom they were speaking.

This poem presents us with two very different environments, describing their contrasting influences on the poet. Walcott divided his time between Saint Lucia in the West Indies and the United States. The opening stanza clearly expresses the poet's preference for 'a jungle in the head' (suggestive of Walcott's home, Saint Lucia) over 'rootless concrete' (suggestive of a city like New York). A 'jungle in the head' evokes a sense of entangled, confused thoughts, while 'concrete' conveys a feeling of rigidity, an inability to grow and change. The adjective 'rootless' evokes the idea of a shallow world devoid of culture, history and tradition. The poet declares, 'Better to stand bewildered / by the fireflies crooked streets'. Here Walcott reiterates his preference for the confusion and imperfection of his native world. The fireflies are evocative

of the Holy Spirit appearing to the apostles in the form of tongues of fire, having a similarly inspiring effect.

Stanzas 2–3 focus on the world of the city. The image of dim winter lamps suggests the inability of the urban world to enlighten the poet. The city cannot inspire him: 'nor can these tongues of snow (suggestive of New York in winter) / speak for the Holy Ghost'. The paradox of 'the self-increasing silence / of words' suggests that the city does not stimulate him, while the image of 'iron railings' conveys a feeling of entrapment.

Stanza four leaves the reader in no doubt as to which world the poet favours. What was 'better' in the opening stanza is now 'best'. The opening line of this stanza indicates that Walcott is at home in Saint Lucia: 'But best is this night surf / with slow scriptures of sand'. This is where the poet finds the Holy Spirit and his inspiration, and while the cormorant is 'not quite a seraph' (angel), its 'fading cry' has the power to 'propel(s) / through phosphorescent shoal' and to move what, in the poet's childhood gospels, 'used to be called the soul'.

The Sailor Sings back to the Casuarinas

This is an extract from a much longer poem entitled '*The Schooner Flight*' that is narrated by a sailor named Shabine. Coming from a mixed-race Caribbean culture, Shabine inevitably struggles with his identity. In this poem Shabine famously declares: 'I have Dutch, nigger, and English in me, / and either I'm nobody, or I'm a nation'. The poem is written in the form of a monologue.

While this poem is ostensibly about casuarina trees, it explores the deeper issue of colonisation and its impact on the West Indian natives. Sailing past Barbados, Shabine, observing its landscape, speaks to the reader: 'You see them on the low hills of Barbados'. 'Them' refers to casuarina trees or, what the white colonist called, cypresses. The simile 'like windbreaks' suggest that the trees offer protection from strong winds, although to all-powerful hurricanes they are little more than 'needles'. When cloud-like sails ('the cirrus of torn sails') are caught up in these trees, they resemble masts.

Shabine recalls how, when he was a young child ('when I was green like them') he did not believe these trees were 'real cypresses, but casuarinas'. To further confuse matters, the captain calls them Canadian cedars. The speaker shows great tolerance in his willingness to accept these various names, recognising that people from different cultural backgrounds have 'good cause' for giving the trees a particular name. Regardless of what they are called, these trees are a familiar sight to the Caribbean people. As their bodies bend in the wind, these trees seem to 'wail like women / after a storm' when some returning schooner brings news of 'one more sailor drowned again'. But, while men call the trees different names, the trees themselves naturally have little interest in what they are called. Personifying the trees, the speaker suggests that they have 'nothing else in mind / but heavenly leaping or to guard a grave'. While these contrasting images suggest that natives associate the trees with both joyful and mournful moments in their lives, the trees are most associated with feelings of sadness and loss: 'Those casuarinas bend / like cypresses, their hair hangs down in train / like sailors' wives'.

However, the real significance of particular names is addressed from line nineteen on. Shabine claims that 'we live like our names and you would have / to be colonial to know the difference / to know the pain of history words contain'. Language is obviously a reflection of culture and when the colonised begins to use the language of the coloniser, this is a sign of their successful oppression by that coloniser. Names reflect how we perceive ourselves and our place in the world. This idea is strongly evident in the closing lines which are spoken with obvious sarcasm and a hint of anger: ' . . .

if we live like the names our masters please, / by careful mimicry might become men'. These lines evoke the West Indies' historical experience of conquest and colonisation, one of the results of which was the natives' sense of inferiority in relation to their colonial 'masters'.

KEY POINTS

- Key theme is colonisation and its effect on the people of the Caribbean.
- Effective use of simile and metaphor.
- Much of the imagery is strongly visual
- Some use of native dialect, English Creole ('e.g. 'Now captain just call them Canadian cedars').

Sample Answer

Write the text of a talk that you would deliver to your classmates, outlining your response to the poetry of Derek Walcott.

Good afternoon classmates,

I found the poetry of Derek Walcott to be extremely interesting and thought-provoking. He explores themes that are relevant to all of us, for example love and loss, death and the afterlife and the beauty of nature. Among the most interesting aspects of Walcott's work are his reflections on the impact of colonisation on the people of the West Indies. Since our ancestors were also victims of conquest and colonisation, this aspect of his poetry has a particular relevance for us. Where Walcott's style is concerned, I particularly liked the vividness and sensuousness of his imagery.

As teenagers, the subject of love and romance is never far from our thoughts. In *Summer Elegies* Walcott describes his passionate relationship with a woman called Cynthia. I was struck by the sensuous, erotic images employed by the poet to describe their lovemaking on a sun-soaked beach. I could imagine how 'the unhooked halter slithered from sunburnt shoulders'. The total intimacy of the lovers is captured in the image of them making 'one shape in the water'. I must say I really enjoyed the humorous touch in the image of a startled dove gurgling 'Ooos at the changing shapes of love'. Sensuous imagery conveys the effect of spending endless hours in the sea and soaking up the sun: 'Salt dried in every fissure'. This tactile image is followed by another, depicting the peeling of sunburnt skin: 'I peeled the papery tissue of my dead flesh away'. The sensuous imagery continues with Walcott describing how the dead skin 'feathered as I blew it from reanointed skin'. This poem also explores the sense of loss that inevitably follows the end of a deep, loving relationship. The paradox 'All the deck chairs are full, but the beach is emptier' suggests how a person can feel lonely even in a crowd, effectively evoking the sense of loss that everyone at some point in their lives experiences. I like the way the concluding stanza evokes the idea of the Garden of Eden with its references to 'the snake' and 'apple tree'. The lovers' passionate hours were like Paradise itself, but their perfect happiness ('I had her breast to rest on') did not last, as the closing words clearly indicate: 'the rest is history'.

Walcott also reflects on the transience of love in *Endings*. What most impressed me about this poem was the sensuous imagery the poet employs to express the idea of love gradually and inevitably fading away. Walcott uses the visual images of a tan fading and foam soaking into the sand ('as sunlight fades from the flesh, / as the foam drains quick in the sand'), the tactile image of the gently abrasive pumice stone ('fading like the flesh from sweating pumice stone') as well as the aural image of the sound of silence that follows the death of love ('we are left with the silence that surrounds Beethoven's head') to convey his theme. I also enjoyed this poem's many musical qualities such as its alliterative 'f' ('fade . . . fades . . . fading') 'l' ('love's lightning') and 's' ('sound . . . sweating . . . stone . . . shapes . . . shapes . . . silence . . . surrounds') sounds.

The theme of death and the afterlife is one that certainly engages everyone's interest. While Walcott, like most of us, was not without doubts and uncertainties where religion is concerned (as we see in *Saint Lucia's First Communion*) most of his poems on this subject are wonderfully reassuring and uplifting. Reading *A Letter from Brooklyn*, I was struck by the old lady's absolute belief in life beyond death. In her letter to the poet, she speaks of his father in the present tense as if he were still alive: 'He is twenty-eight years buried . . . he was called home, / And is, I am sure, doing greater work'. The paradoxical phrase 'the strength of one frail hand' suggests how this frail old lady's unshakeable faith has a powerful impact on Walcott, restoring his faith in God: 'Restores my duty to the Word'. The repetition of 'I believe' in the closing lines of the poem ('So this old lady writes and again I believe, / I believe it all, and for no man's death I grieve') underlines how his faith has been dramatically renewed.

While the idea of a young child dying inevitably evokes great sadness, the poem *For Adrian* encourages us to look on death in a very different, more positive way. Again, I found this poem to be very reassuring. Speaking through the poet, Adrian explains that in death he has 'entered a wisdom'. Having achieved unimagined happiness and knowledge in his new state of being, Adrian desperately wants his family to know that mourning his death is futile: 'I would not break your heart, and you should know it, / I would not make you suffer, and you should know it'. I love the image of Adrian, in his altered state, at one with nature: 'I am part of the muscle of a galloping lion / or a bird keeping low over dark canes'. These images evoke a sense of energy, beauty and harmony, all positive feelings not normally associated with death. In portraying death in a new light – not as 'a goodbye, but as 'a different welcome' to a new world, Adrian eases our apprehensions of what awaits us beyond death.

One of the most interesting themes in Walcott's work, in my view, is his exploration of the impact of colonisation on the people of the Caribbean. This theme is addressed in *The Sailor Sings back to the Casuarinas*. This poem is narrated by a sailor named Shabine. The impact of colonisation is to be seen on the language of the native people. What were once called casuarina trees are now known as cypresses or red cedars. Shabine understands the significance and power of language: 'we live like our names / and you would have to be colonial to know the difference / to know the pain of history words contain'. Language is obviously a reflection of culture and when the colonised begins to use the language of the coloniser, that is a sign of their successful oppression by that coloniser. Shabine clearly perceives that names reflect how we see ourselves and our place in the world. The closing lines are spoken with obvious sarcasm and more than a hint of anger: 'if we live like the names our masters please, / by careful mimicry might become men'. As an Irish person, whose own nation was subject to conquest and colonisation, these lines have a special relevance for me. Our ancestors shared the historical experience of the people of the West Indies, one of the results of which was a sense of inferiority to their colonial 'masters'.

This theme is also touched on in *from Omeros*. We see the effect of colonisation in the intense poverty of the fishermen who risk their lives in dangerously turbulent seas to make a meagre living. Looking skywards, Achile is delighted to see the man-o-war pilfer the catch of the herring gull. These gulls are described as 'white slaves for a black king'.

This perception of the relationship between the white gulls and the black man-o-war turns the historical relationship between the white and black man on its head, delighting the Caribbean fishermen who are still paying the price for their forefathers' conquest and enslavement by the white men. The idea of the gull paying 'tribute' to the man-o-war reinforces the perception of this huge bird as the king of its world. Both fishermen are in awe of the 'sea king'. Achile cannot contain his feelings of total elation: 'That black bugger, beautiful, / Though!' In conclusion classmates, I found Walcott's poetry to be relevant and engaging. I particularly enjoyed his vivid and sensuous imagery and agree with the widely held view that he is one of the world's greatest living poets. I hope that you found reading his poetry to be as rewarding and enriching as I did.

Michael Longley

Biographical Note

Michael Longley was born in Belfast of English parents in 1939. One of twin boys, his childhood and adolescence were unremarkable and generally happy. His second level education in the Royal Belfast Academical Institution did not stimulate any interest in writing poetry. In 1958 Longley left Belfast for Dublin where he studied Classics at Trinity College. Evidence of his interest in the Classics is to be found in such poems as *Ceasefire* and *Laertes*. In Trinity a close friendship developed between Longley and Derek Mahon, another Northern Irish poet. It was during his time in Trinity that Longley's interest in poetry blossomed and, while he worked briefly as a teacher in Dublin and London, he soon resolved to become a full-time poet.

Longley's verse reflects his affinity for the Irish countryside, which developed over the course of annual family holidays in Donegal and, later, as a married man with his own family, in Mayo.

Much of his poetry reflects his preoccupation with the Northern conflict and its terrible cost in terms of human suffering. With no political axe to grind, Longley's hard-hitting poems on this subject are deeply disturbing, and indeed moving, in their graphic descriptions of violence and its devastating physical and psychological effects. While never directly commenting on any act of sectarian violence, his compassion for its victims (and even for its perpetrators, as we see in *Wounds*) is always strikingly apparent.

Longley's writing is strongly influenced by his relationship with his father, whose life was dominated by his wartime experiences. Longley writes about his father with great tenderness and affection, without shying away from some problematical aspects to their relationship. His father served in the British Army in both the First and Second World Wars, winning the Military Cross in the former conflict. Throughout his life, Longley's father was haunted by nightmarish memories of war. In both *Wounds* and *Wreaths* Longley juxtaposes the violence of the First World War with contemporary sectarian violence in Northern Ireland.

Longley has said that he views himself primarily as a love poet. He writes about his marriage and his love for his wife in a memorable manner, as we see in *An Amish Rug*. Of course, another great love of his life is the Irish countryside, whether it is the countryside of South Belfast where he grew up, or that of County Mayo where he holidays annually. Longley has a deep affection for the Irish landscape and its plants and creatures.

Carrigskeewaun

This poem was inspired by Longley's love of the Mayo landscape. However, he does not idealise the rugged natural world of Carrigskeewaun. His verse is never sentimental or romantic; he consistently presents us with the reality of the natural world, portraying it in all its harshness as well as its beauty. In colloquial terms, 'he tells it as it is'. This poem celebrates the beauty of nature while also acknowledging its harsh aspects and destructive power. While the poet sometimes experiences a sense of harmony with the world of nature, the predominant feeling in this poem is one of exclusion and isolation. He often portrays man as an intruder in the world of nature. There is a strong sense of nature's supremacy (supreme power) over man in this poem. Nature is master here: the ravens 'supervise' the mountain, the swans regard the poet with 'disdain', while the sea pounds the shells into sand. We see the poet alone in this wild landscape, communing (in close touch with) nature. The poet's family is very much peripheral to the action in this poem. He calls out to them in his loneliness on the mountain ('. . . my voice filling the district as I call their names') and is reminded of them by their footprints in the sand, and by the 'smoke from our turf fire'. In his solitude the poet becomes aware not only of the beauty, harshness and power of nature, but also of his own relative insignificance compared to the vast natural world.

This poem presents us with a series of vivid images of the natural world, images so vivid and precise that they resemble snapshots. *The Mountain* immediately conveys a sense of the poet's isolation: 'This is ravens' territory'. Longley is in the ravens' domain – they 'supervise' the landscape from above, and only they have knowledge of the secrets of the mountain ('the marrow of these boulders'). The poet's loneliness is clearly stated ('I stand alone here') and is underscored by the assonant long 'o' sound ('bones . . . boulders'). His sense of solitude is further reflected in his desire 'to gather children about me', to look for company in this forbidding world of death and desolation. He effectively conveys the sense of his voice echoing around the countryside: 'My voice filling the district as I call their names'.

In *The Path* the poet sees himself as an outsider who disturbs the world of nature; he 'dislodges' the mallards, and 'nudges' the swans. His sense of loneliness remains: 'I am left with only one swan'. The poet's eye for natural detail is evident in the precise manner in which he captures the movements of the birds: 'the mallards whose necks strain over the bog to where kittiwakes scrape the waves'. He also deftly captures the swan's haughty elegance as he describes how it regards him with 'gradual disdain'. Longley sees himself as a barely tolerated visitor in the world of nature. However, his knowledgeable listing of the birds' names reflects his love of nature: 'lapwings, curlews, snipe'.

The opening words of *The Strand* ('I discover . . .') suggest a moment of personal awareness. The footprints in the sand point to the past; in time they will inevitably be erased by the sea. The poet seems to become aware of life's transience and of his own mortality. Just as the shells are ultimately reduced to sand, so also is man subject to the destructive power of nature and time. Nature, in the intimidating shape of the pounding sea, seems to make the poet aware of his own relative insignificance. The metaphor used to describe the dry shells gives the sea human qualities: 'the toe and fingernail clippings of the sea'.

The mood in *The Wall* contrasts with the mood in the earlier stanzas. The man-made wall provokes no feelings of unease within the poet. His sense of isolation now gives way to a sense of belonging as he feels a connection with 'all the men who have squatted here'. The mood is peaceful and meditative, and the homely images ('turf smoke . . . steam from a kettle') are comforting. The poet seems to be in harmony with himself and his surroundings. His partner is mentioned but not named ('A table she might have already set'), underlining the idea that human relationships are very much in the background in a poem primarily concerned with the poet's relationship with the natural world.

Significantly, there is no human presence in *The Lake*. However, the poet's imagery is suggestive of his admiration and respect for the beauty and tranquillity of nature. He depicts a scene of idyllic natural beauty as the lake perfectly mirrors the visiting animals: 'Its surface seems tilted to receive the sun perfectly'. The sibilant 's' sound in this line helps to convey the sense of perfect peace and stillness. The image of 'the mare and her foal', set alongside that of the elegant heron, evokes the continuity and harmony of the natural world, while the poet's description of the visiting animals as 'all such special visitors' reflects his reverential attitude towards nature.

KEY POINTS

- Key theme is poet's relationship with the natural world.
- The natural world is portrayed in an unsentimental manner.
- Precise imagery points to the poet's keenly observant eye.
- Effective use of sound (alliteration, assonance, sibilance) helps to evoke particular moods.
- List of birds' names reflects the poet's knowledge and love of nature.

Badger

In this poem the poet again presents us with a precise, unsentimental portrayal of the natural world. While he celebrates the badger's strength and directness, he also highlights man's disruptive effect on the world of nature. Man's intrusion into the world of nature, as portrayed in this poem, is far more dramatic and violent than that described in *Carrigskeewaun*.

In the first section of this poem the poet's respect and admiration for the badger's strength and determination is evident in: 'Pushing the wedge of his body'. The references to 'cromlech and stone circle' and 'the depths of the hill' suggest that there is something ancient and mysterious about the badger. The poet contrasts the movements of the badger with those of the fox and the hare. While the fox's 'zig-zags' suggest its slyness and cunning, the badger's 'straight and narrow' path evokes an image of its direct, cautious nature. The badger is at one with the natural environment: 'Night's silence around his shoulders / His face lit by the moon'. The use of sibilance helps to convey the tranquillity of this nocturnal scene. This is the badger's domain. Just as the raven 'supervises' the mountain, so does the badger 'manage' the earth. In this way the poet suggests that the world of nature belongs to nature's creatures – man's intrusions into this world are, to a greater or lesser degree, disruptive.

In the second section of this poem, we again see the poet's love of precise detail: 'An intestine taking in patches of dog's mercury, brambles'. This listing of plants' names reflects the poet's knowledge and love of nature. It is ironic that while the badger is hunted ('a head with a price on it'), he is also a respected creature: 'a name that parishes borrow'.

In the final section of the poem, the digging out and death of the badger is described. It is ironic and paradoxical that the poet should use the language and imagery of birth to describe the badger's demise: 'It is a difficult delivery once the tongs take hold'. The sett, which is implicitly compared to a womb in the ground that sustained the badger, now becomes his place of death. The alliterative 'd' sound ('digger . . . dog . . . difficult delivery') combined with the long 'o' sound ('Once the tongs take hold') helps to convey the grim mood. Again we see the poet's love of precise detail when he describes how the badger 'lifted cow-pats for beetles'. For all his strength, the badger is 'vulnerable' – particularly to ruthless hunters. The poet's description of the badger's death is devoid of sentimentality. The hunter becomes the hunted. A series of verbs ('dragging . . . turned . . . tilted') suggest the badger's desperate struggle to survive. While Longley's impersonal tone implies a lack of emotional involvement on his part, his feelings for the badger are implicit in his vivid images. He uses coldly precise descriptions rather than explicit comments to evoke an emotional response in the reader. (We find a similarly cold tone and apparent lack of feeling in his descriptions of sectarian violence.) Just as the poet does not explicitly express his admiration or sympathy for the badger, neither does he directly condemn his hunters. However, the contrast between the naturalness of the badger digging into the earth and the unnaturalness of an inoffensive animal being dug from his sett is striking. While there is no overt didactic (morally instructive) quality to this poem, the poet's exact descriptions and graphic images speak for themselves.

KEY POINTS

- Key themes are the poet's admiration for the badger and nature's vulnerability to man's violent intrusions.
- The badger is portrayed in an unsentimental manner.
- Respect for the badger and contempt for the hunters is implicit rather than explicit.
- Precise, detailed descriptions.
- Unusual imagery – imagery of birth used to describe the badger's death.
- Use of sound effects (alliteration, assonance, sibilance) helps to create mood.
- Listing technique (plants' names) suggests the poet's knowledge and love of nature.

Last Requests

Intimate relationship with father

This poem is an elegy (poem of remembrance) for the poet's father who died of an illness related to an old war wound. The central theme of the poem is the father–son relationship. The first part of this poem deals with his father's apparent death in the trenches in the First World War, while the second part deals with his father's actual death in hospital many years later. Both parts of the poem revolve around the contrast between appearance and reality. In the first stanza the poet's father seemed to be buried alive, but in reality was not dead. In the second stanza the poet initially thought that his dying father was blowing him a kiss, when in reality he was gesturing for a cigarette.

Longley presents us with the harsh reality of war when he describes how his father was abandoned by his 'batman' (personal servant), who stole his 'pocket watch and cigarette case'. There is no sign here of the comradeship that we usually associate with soldiers in times of war. However, the poet (who does not express moral judgements in his poetry) makes no comment on the batman's behaviour. There is a humorous quality to the poet's description of his father's determination to stay alive: 'But your lungs surfaced to take a long remembered drag.' The poet may be suggesting here that his father's love of cigarettes heightened his desire to survive! He was not ready to have his epitaph written just yet: 'Heart contradicting as an epitaph / The two initials you had scratched on gold.'

As his father lay on his death-bed, the poet momentarily believed that his father blew him a kiss. However, he is a consistently honest poet who never draws back from the harsh or disappointing realities of life. We again see his lack of sentimentality when he quickly corrects himself: 'But the bony fingers that waved to and fro were asking for a Woodbine'. The image of 'the bony fingers' is suggestive of the frailty of his aged father. Longley's reference to a specific brand of cigarette links his father's final hours with the battlefields of the First World War where many soldiers requested a Woodbine with their dying breaths. For forty years his father had smoked each Woodbine 'like a sacrament', in respectful memory of fallen comrades. The poet could not relate to his father's war experiences because he did not share in them. Perhaps that is why we sense a certain gap between father and son at the close of the poem: 'I who brought peppermints and grapes only / Couldn't reach you through the oxygen tent'. The word 'only' suggests a sense of inadequacy on the poet's part. We sense that the gap between father and son is not only physical (they are separated by the oxygen tent) but also spiritual. The poet could not 'reach' or connect with his father because they were separated by a gap in age and experiences.

While there is an element of humour in this poem, it is also charged with emotion. Every detail of his father's death-bed scene is etched on the poet's memory. We can sense the younger man's feelings of love, sadness and inadequacy when he recalls his relationship with his father.

KEY POINTS

- Key theme is the father–son relationship.
- Unsentimental portrayal of the realities of war and of father–son relationship.
- Touches of humour, but a very moving poem that conveys a range of emotions.
- Language is generally simple, conversational.   *colloquial*
- Cigarette image unifies first and second parts of poem.

An Amish Rug

This is a love poem dedicated to the poet's wife. It is a poem rich in symbolism. The analogy drawn between the Amish way of life and this special love lies at the heart of this poem. The Amish rug, carefully crafted from strong, richly coloured threads, is symbolic not only of the Amish lifestyle, but also of the strength and richness of this mutual love.

In stanza one, the poet imagines himself, his wife and family as members of the Amish community. The references to a 'one-room schoolhouse' and black clothing and underclothes suggest a simple, severe lifestyle. The image of the children as 'silhouettes in a snowy field' evokes the black-and-white certainty of both the Amish lifestyle and the mutual love between the poet and his wife. The alliterative 's' sound conveys a sense of peace, while the assonant long 'o' sound evokes the serious nature of the Amish way of life. The simplicity of the Amish lifestyle – and, by extension, this love – is underlined by the image of 'a horse and buggy going to church'.

The patchwork quilt is aptly compared to the patchwork field pattern of a small farm where the poet imagines he has worked: 'I bring you this patchwork like a smallholding'. Work occupies a central place in the Amish world, and the poet describes himself as having 'served as the hired boy behind the harrow'.

The black and white colours of stanza one contrast with the richer, warmer, more sensuous colours of the rug: 'Its threads the colour of cantaloupe and cherry'. The richly coloured, strong threads (which are sufficiently strong to be used for 'securing hay bales') symbolise the richness and strength of the poet's love for his wife.

In the third stanza, the rug is compared to a cathedral window and a flowerbed. Both of these comparisons help to convey the idea of rich colour. The 'cathedral window' metaphor suggests the spiritual nature of this love, while the 'flowerbed' simile indicates its sensuous dimension. The public image of marital love and unity in stanza one ('Marriage a horse and buggy going to church') is juxtaposed with the private expression of that love in stanza three. The image of stepping over the rug 'as over a flowerbed' reflects the poet's reverential attitude towards this special love. The language throughout is simple, and the tone is one of tenderness and affection. In contrast to many of his other poems, which often convey the notion of conflict or tension, this poem conveys a sense of profound contentment. The poet appears to be deeply happy in his private life. It could be said that the poet's wife receives two gifts that are both carefully crafted: the rug and the poem itself.

KEY POINTS

- Key theme is the poet's love for his wife.
- An intensely personal poem.
- The poem is structured on an analogy between the Amish lifestyle and the poet's love for his wife.
- The strong, richly coloured threads of the rug are symbolic of the strength and richness of the poet's love for his wife.
- Effective use of imagery, metaphor, simile.
- The tone is one of tenderness and respect.

Wounds

[handwritten: Intimate relationship with father. Humanity / sympathy for helpless]

The title relates to the physical and psychological wounds of war. The poet conveys the obscenity and indignity of violence past and present through a series of graphic, disturbing images. While there are no direct statements about the horror of violence and war, the poet's precise descriptions evoke a sense of horror and outrage in the reader. In the first part of the poem he presents us with some of his father's memories of the First World War ('pictures from my father's head'). In the second section he presents us with some of his own memories of sectarian violence in Northern Ireland during The Troubles. This poem also provides us with an insight into the poet's relationship with his father.

The opening lines suggest that we are about to become privy to some images that the poet has, up to this point, kept 'like secrets'. What follows are memories of the First World War that the poet's father confided in him. Longley's father was an Englishman who somehow ended up in the London–Scottish Regiment. While his father was impressed by the bravery of the Ulster Division at the Somme ('Wilder than Gurkhas'), he was bewildered by the deep bigotry of their battle cries. The use of direct speech, including the shocking expletive, 'Fuck the Pope', adds to the poem's realism and impact, underlining the intensity of this sectarian hatred and bringing the scene in the trenches to life. The phrase 'a boy about to die' reminds us of the terrible loss of so many young lives in a conflict in which the number of dead and maimed was truly obscene.

The second picture from his father's head is of 'the London–Scottish padre' resetting the kilts of dead young soldiers 'with a stylish backhand and a prayer'. While this is a compassionate act intended to restore some dignity to the dead men, it seems that even the priest has become desensitised (hardened) to the horror of war. The image of 'a landscape of dead buttocks' powerfully captures the obscenity of a war that took the lives and dignity of so many soldiers. It was an image that haunted his father 'for fifty years.' He was 'a belated casualty' of this war because a war wound contributed to his final illness. There is a mocking humour in his dying father's observation: 'I am dying for King and Country, slowly.' The repetition of 'touched' in the closing line of the first section of the poem evokes the poet's love for his father: 'I touched his hand, his thin head I touched'. This is a tender, poignant image. The reference to his aged father's 'thin head' suggests his frailty..

The second section of this poem juxtaposes the violence of the First World War with the violence of The Troubles in Northern Ireland. The victims of this latter violence come from both sides of the religious divide as well as from the British Army, underlining the poet's unbiased, apolitical standpoint. In this section the poet draws on images that still linger in his own memory. Concrete, vivid images convey the full horror and ugliness of sectarian killings. What is especially shocking about the poet's portrayal of such violence is its invasion of the domestic world, its random nature, and the ordinariness of its victims. When the poet speaks metaphorically of burying 'three teenage soldiers' beside his father, it is clear that he is genuinely affected by their deaths. The image of 'bellies full of bullets and Irish beer, their flies undone' (the alliterative loud 'b' sound underscoring the harshness of their killing) is as vivid and as horrifying as the image of soldiers lying dead at the Somme, with their kilts awry. Once again the indignity of violent death is powerfully conveyed. The

Woodbines that the poet metaphorically throws into the grave are regularly associated with his father's wartime experiences. Again, in linking the soldiers' burial with that of his father, the poet reveals the impact of these killings on him personally.

The death of a Catholic child in his cot prompts the poet to suggest that the Sacred Heart of Jesus was 'paralysed as heavy guns put out the night-light in a nursery for ever'. This image seems to suggest that religious faith offers no protection against man-made violence, while the destruction of the night-light may symbolise the death of innocence.

The killing of a bus conductor is described in a typically graphic manner: 'shot through the head'. The references to 'his carpet slippers' and 'supper dishes' convey the man's ordinariness. Once again, there is a violent intrusion into everyday domestic life. While the poet presents us with the full horror of this scene, there are no words of condemnation; he describes without comment. Indeed his compassion for this victim of violence extends to the killer, who is simply described as 'a shivering boy'. The killer's casual, inadequate apology ('Sorry Missus') adds to the horror and realism of the scene, although it may be interpreted as a glimpse of humanity. Like the bus conductor's wife and his own father, the poet appears to be 'bewildered' by the sectarian hatred that prompts such callous, random killings.

KEY POINTS

- Key themes are the horror of violence past and present, and the poet's relationship with his father.
- Images of violence that are shocking in their vividness.
- The poet makes no moral judgements, he describes without comment or condemnation.
- The poet displays compassion for all victims of violence.
- Use of direct speech gives a sense of immediacy to the scenes described, and adds to the realism of the poem.
- Conversational language.

Wreaths

Humanity / Sympathy for the helpless.

In this poem (which is basically three poems in one) the poet commemorates twelve people who died violent deaths in Northern Ireland. He describes these atrocities in graphic detail, always emphasising the ordinariness of the victims and the human cost of sectarian violence. The fact that the dead are described in terms of their occupations underscores their ordinariness. These people posed no threat to anyone. As in *Wounds*, the poet does not express any political viewpoint on these killings, nor does he adopt any moral stance. However, while he never lectures the reader, his precise descriptions of the violent deaths of innocent people evoke a sense of horror and outrage within us. Also, while the tone is unemotional and factual, there is no doubting the poet's compassion for the victims of violence and their families. The poem is written in conversational language to make it more direct and matter-of-fact. The poet's

attention to detail, neutral tone and conversational language allow the reader a clear view of the realities of sectarian violence.

The Civil Servant

This poem was written in memory of Martin McBirney, a lawyer and magistrate killed by the IRA. In the poem we see how violence invades the heart of domestic life, the kitchen. The ordinariness of the victim is stressed: 'He was preparing an Ulster fry for breakfast / When someone walked into the kitchen and shot him'. The poet's coldly precise description of the murder conveys its brutal nature: 'A bullet entered his mouth and pierced his skull'. A rich and varied life is brought to a horrifyingly abrupt end: 'The books he had read, the music he could play'. The impersonal, factual tone is evident in the poet's use of 'He', 'someone', 'his' and 'they'. The poet is the objective observer who reports accurately, without judging or commenting.

The reference to the victim's 'dressing gown and pyjamas' reminds us that he was an ordinary person. The police seem to be inured (hardened) to such atrocities. The body lies there while they clinically analyse the crime scene: 'With notebooks, cameras and measuring tapes'. The poet's description of the victim being rolled up 'like a red blanket' underlines this sense of indifference. The image of 'a bullet hole in the cutlery drawer' powerfully conveys the idea of a domestic world that has been invaded, and will forever remain disrupted by violence. The unsettling image of the victim's widow destroying the piano with a hammer and chisel tells of a woman deranged by grief. It is an image that

brings the human cost of sectarian violence into sharp focus.

The poet next remembers Jim Gibson, a Catholic greengrocer murdered by the UVF, apparently because his business was in a Protestant area. It is ironic that this friendly, hard-working man was murdered as he served his killers ('death-dealers'). It is particularly ironic that he was killed at Christmas, the so-called season of goodwill. The contrast between the celebratory holly wreaths and the mourning wreaths, suggested by the title, adds to the poignancy of his death.

In the second stanza the poet offers an element of hope as he imaginatively considers the possibility of 'three wise men' searching for a modern-day saviour 'up the Shankill or the Falls'. The possibility of a Protestant or Catholic Christ child being born in present-day Northern Ireland evokes a sense of hope, and is a reminder that the poet does not take sides in the sectarian conflict. His suggestion that the three wise men 'should pause on their way to buy gifts at Jim Gibson's shop' is an imaginative tribute to that man's basic decency – it would be appropriate that gifts for a modern-day saviour should be bought at his shop. However, reference to the story of Christmas may also be viewed as ironic or satiric since this murder flies in the face of the Christian beliefs that both sides of this divided community profess to share.

The Linen Workers

This poem was inspired by the deaths of ten linen workers who were killed on their way home from work. By focusing on a variety of victims of sectarian violence, the poet suggests how both sides of the community have needlessly suffered. The ordinariness of the victims is conveyed by the references to their personal items scattered on the road after the massacre: 'spectacles, wallets, small change, and a set of dentures'. These everyday details also have the effect of making these deaths more immediate and real. The savagery of their killers is suggested by the verb 'massacred'.

It seems that the image of one of the victims' dentures lying on the road played on the poet's mind, leading to the surreal image of the resurrected Christ 'fastened for ever by his exposed canines to a wintry sky'. While this is an image of suffering, the Resurrection suggests hope. The reference to 'the bread, the wine' is another religious image, perhaps symbolising self-sacrifice and eternal life.

This atrocity also sets the poet thinking about his own dead father, and he pictures his false teeth 'brimming in their tumbler'. This poem is written in the first person, and is the most personal of the three poems since the poet views these deaths in terms of his own personal sense of loss. As in *Wounds*, the linking of his father to the victims of Northern violence suggests that the poet is personally affected by their deaths. It seems that with every new atrocity in Northern Ireland, the poet feels that he is burying his father all over again. The acts described in the final stanza ('I must polish the spectacles, balance them upon his nose . . . And into his dead mouth slip the set of teeth') suggests the idea of preparing his father, and the dead linen workers, for burial and for a new life after death.

KEY POINTS

- Key theme is the human cost of sectarian violence.
- The ordinariness of the victims is emphasised.
- The ubiquitous (present everywhere) nature of violence is highlighted – victims are killed in their own homes, in their places of work, and on the roadside.
- Atrocities reawaken the poet's personal memory of his own father's death.
- Graphic portrayal of violence, vivid imagery, attention to detail.
- The imagery is surreal in places.
- The tone is unemotional, impersonal – the poet reports without judging.
- Compassion for victims of violence.

Ceasefire

This poem is inspired by an episode in Homer's *The Iliad*. It is very much a public poem, written with the bitter Northern conflict in mind. The title of the poem refers to the IRA ceasefire in 1994, and indeed the poem was published in *The Irish Times* to coincide with the announcement of that ceasefire. Priam, the aged king of Troy, goes to the Greek commander, Achilles, who had killed the king's son, Hector, to beg for Hector's body. This poem reminds us that forgiveness and compassion are necessary if enemies are to be reconciled, and in this sense has an obvious relevance for the Northern Ireland situation. It also reflects the poet's preoccupation with the father–son relationship, highlighting the extent to which a father will go to reclaim the body of his son.

This poem is written in sonnet form, with the three quatrains and the rhyming couplet forming four distinct parts. In the first quatrain we see how Achilles feels compassionate towards the old, heartbroken king because he reminds him of his own father: 'Put in mind of his own father and moved to tears'. Achilles is not initially amenable to Priam's request, pushing 'the old king gently away'. When Priam curls up at Achilles' feet, we see that he is willing to humiliate himself in order to retrieve his son's body. Moved by this gesture,

Achilles is filled with sadness, weeping with the old king 'until their sadness filled the building'. At this point the powerful young warrior is dominant over the frail old king.

In the second quatrain we see how hatred has given way to compassion when Achilles, having earlier desecrated Hector's body by dragging it behind his chariot around the walls of Troy, now tries to make amends by having Hector's body washed and laid out in uniform. The image of Hector's body 'wrapped like a present' is a painfully ironic one.

In the third quatrain, Priam and Achilles eat and converse together – this indicates a shift in the balance of power between the two men, who now regard each other as equals. They view each other in a new light, and seem to have achieved an extraordinary rapport: 'it pleased them both / To stare at each other's beauty as lovers might'.

The poet gives emphasis to Priam's self-abasement (self-humiliation) at the close of the poem. The king is willing to 'do what must be done' in order to achieve reconciliation, and so retrieve the body of his son. He is prepared to kiss Achilles' hand, 'the killer of my son'. Here we are reminded of Priam's great loss and of his remarkable capacity for forgiveness. Both men are seen to grow in terms of their moral standing in the course of this poignant poem.

KEY POINTS

- Key theme is the need to show forgiveness and compassion in the interests of achieving reconciliation – a theme of universal relevance.
- The father–son relationship is another theme – the depth of Priam's love for his dead son is very moving.
- Unusual imagery (Hector's body is 'wrapped up like a present', the two men look at each other 'as lovers might').
- The serious tone befits the poem's serious message.

Self-Heal (from Mayo Monologues)

This poem is written in the form of a monologue delivered by a young woman. It is concerned with the complex relationship between the woman and a boy who is mentally and physically handicapped. The opening lines convey the idea of a sensitive individual who is anxious to teach the boy the names of flowers. Her detailed knowledge of plants ('Self-heal and centaury . . . bog asphodel . . . cuckoo-pint') suggests her love of the natural world. It seems that she wants to introduce the boy to the wonders of his natural environment as a step in the process of his self-healing. The poet's use of blank verse combined with such colloquial expressions as 'gone . . . in the head' gives a conversational quality to the language. The speaker seems to be unsure about her feelings for this boy: 'And, as they say, was I leading him on?'

We learn of the boy's harsh, impoverished background in lines 6–9. He slept in a cot until he was twelve years old, either because of his 'babyish ways' or the family's poverty. While poverty was endemic in rural Ireland at this time, this family's poverty was exacerbated by the father's gambling: 'hadn't his father / Gambled away all but rushy pasture?'. The boy's physical deformity is described in violent terms: 'His skull seemed to be hammered like a wedge / Into his shoulders'. It is ironic that the boy's deformity is said to give him 'an almost scholarly air'. In reality, the boy could not retain the names of plants that the young woman had taught him. His mental disability is memorably suggested by an image of delicate natural beauty: 'But he couldn't remember the things I taught / Each name would hover above its flower / Like a butterfly unable to alight'.

The image of the cuckoo-pint being pulled apart 'to release giddy insects from their cell' has sexual connotations, and the action that follows evokes the idea of momentary freedom from sexual repression. The speaker describes how the boy 'gently . . . slipped his hand between my thighs'. The adverb 'gently' suggests a non-threatening act and there is no sense of shock or horror on the part of the woman; indeed she confesses that she 'wasn't frightened'. Again we see her confusion as she struggles to understand her own subsequent actions: 'and still I don't know why / But I ran from him in tears to tell them'. The punishment meted out to the boy by his family is completely disproportionate to his perceived sexual 'crime'. He is savagely beaten with a blackthorn stick every day for a week and 'tethered' like an animal in the hayfield. This is an extremely disturbing insight into the sexually repressed nature of rural society at that time. The retarded boy's sexual advance is 'gentle', but he is brutally punished by a world that frowns on any open expression of sexual feeling.

The closing lines are even more unsettling as we see the impact of this brutal punishment on the boy. We see how violence leads to more violence as the boy gains revenge by venting his fury and frustration on innocent animals. The speaker seems to feel a degree of responsibility for the boy's cruel punishment, and for his resultant acts of savage retribution: 'I might have been the cow / Whose tail he would later dock with a shears, /And he the ram tangled in barbed wire / That he stoned to death when they set him free'.

Far from enabling any form of self-healing to take place, the actions of the well-intentioned woman result in the boy being left more brutalised than ever by a society that is depicted as uncivilised, primitive and cruel.

KEY POINTS

- Key theme is the cruel mistreatment of an innocent, retarded boy.
- The poem provides us with unsettling insights into Irish rural society at that time.
- A sense of awful irony pervades the poem in that a well-intentioned act aimed at improving the retarded boy ends up leaving him more brutalised than before.
- The speaker is confused about her own actions ('still I don't know why').
- The tone is conversational.
- The imagery is memorable.

Poteen

The title evokes the idea of a secretive, anti-authoritarian rural world of hidden stills and poteen makers engaged in an endless battle of wits with revenue officers and police. While this poem is ostensibly concerned with the clandestine making of illegal poteen, it may also be read on a metaphorical level as a reflection on the violence that pervades Irish history.

The first stanza gives us a matter-of-fact description of the equipment and process involved in the making of poteen: 'Enough running water / To cool the copper worm'. It describes how the wrist ('The veins of the wrist') of the poteen maker is also cooled by the cold water. While 'vitriol' may suggest the burning effect of the poteen on the throat ('Vitriol to scorch the throat'), it may also be read as a reference to the deep-seated bitterness generated by years of violent conflict.

The 'brimming hogshead' suggests the idea of an abundant supply of this precious liquid. The poteen is taken from this vessel by the 'noggin'. One such noggin was traditionally 'sprinkled on the ground'. Soaking into the earth, it conjures up memories of 'souterrains, sunk workshops'. The reference to secret underground activity connects the poteen makers with generations of secret political organisations intent on the violent overthrow of English rule. The phrase 'the back of the mind' is suggestive of a lingering folk memory that remains very much part of the Irish identity. The metaphor 'The whole bog an outhouse' suggests an area perfectly suited to covert activity – be it that of the poteen maker or the rebel.

The closing stanza clearly associates poteen making with violence. The poteen is buried in the bog 'alongside cudgels / Guns, the informer's ear'. The informer was, of course, despised by the poteen maker and the rebel alike, and often ended up paying a high price for what was perceived to be collaborating with the authorities. The 'Blood-money' may refer to the informer's payment. The closing line ('Blood-money, treasure-trove') suggests both the dangers (arrest, fines, imprisonment) and rewards (money) of poteen making. The closing phrase connects the poteen maker's financial reward with the similarly illegal wealth of swashbuckling pirates.

Laertes

This poem is concerned with one of the major themes of Longley's work, i.e. the father–son relationship. It is based on an episode from *The Odyssey*, with Odysseus returning home after being away for twenty years. The poem consists of a single sentence, suggesting the idea of an unstoppable flow of emotion. Odysseus finds Laertes 'alone on the tiny terrace' tending to a vine. Laertes is described in vivid detail. His gardening attire is 'patched and grubby' and he wears 'leather gaiters . . . gloves as well'. The colloquial phrase 'in his gardening duds' suggests that Laertes might be the poet's own father, as does the use of Belfast dialect in the phrase 'a goatskin ducher' (a flat cap worn by shipyard workers). Laertes is visibly dejected, the alliterative 'd' in 'deep depression' underscoring his despondency. He is worn down by age and grief, believing that his great warrior son is long dead. Odysseus is deeply moved by the sight of the sad, shabbily-dressed old man and 'sobbed in the shade of a pear tree for his father'. The lines that follow are highly emotive, touching the reader who can readily identify with the poet's feelings: 'So old and pathetic that all he wanted there and then / Was to kiss him and hug him and blurt out the whole story'.

Odysseus hesitates when he considers that his story would take so long to recount: 'But the whole story is one catalogue and then another'. When he approaches Laertes, he does not immediately identify himself. Instead he gradually reveals details of his childhood, which enables Laertes to recognise him: 'the thirteen pear-trees / Ten apple trees, forty fig-trees, the fifty rows of vines'. The images are of richness and abundance, suggesting a happy and contented childhood. The image of the young Odysseus 'traipsing after his father / And asking for everything he saw' touches an emotional chord within us all, underscoring this poem's universal appeal.

When Laertes recognises his son, he is overwhelmed with shock and joy, feeling 'weak at the knees' (a colloquial expression that further accentuates this poem's timeless, quality) and 'dizzy'. The image of the frail old man flinging his arms around the neck of his great and powerful son is deeply moving, as is the image of Odysseus drawing his aged father 'fainting to his breast' and holding him there. There is a sense of role reversal in the final touching simile: 'And cradled like driftwood the bones of his dwindling father'. This tender image conveys Odysseus' love and concern for his father as well as Laertes' fragility and closeness to death. It is appropriate that the final word in this poem is 'father'.

KEY POINTS

- Key theme is the father–son relationship.
- The passing of time and its impact is a secondary theme.
- The poem is replete with images that are deeply moving, with the closing image being particularly touching.
- Colloquial expressions give this extract from the Homeric epic a contemporary feel.
- A poem with a timeless, universal appeal.

Sample Answer

Discuss the aspects of Michael Longley's poetry that most appeal to you.

What most appeals to me about the poetry of Michael Longley is his consistently honest, unsentimental portrayal of the beauty and harshness of the world. In colloquial terms, the poet 'tells it as it is'. Violence past and present is described in all of its inhuman horror. The world of nature is never depicted in a romantic manner, but is instead described with typical realism. Also, he never sentimentalises the father–son relationship that was so important to him – his verse describes both tender and problematic moments in that relationship. He describes his love for his wife with similar honesty. The poet's detailed descriptions and vivid imagery are other aspects of his poetry that appeal to me. Finally, I particularly like the way he describes situations without commenting on them, allowing the reader to reach his/her own conclusions.

While romantic poets such as Wordsworth idealise nature, Longley portrays both the beauty and harshness of the natural world. A key feature of his nature poetry is his portrayal of man as an intruder in the natural world. *Carrigskeewaun* presents us with a series of contrasting snapshots of the rural landscape. *The Mountain* suggests the poet's sense of isolation and loneliness. He feels out-of-place here: 'This is ravens' territory'. The loud alliterative 'b' sound underscores the harshness of the terrain, while the assonant long 'o' sound helps to convey the lonely mood: 'bones . . . boulders'. The poet's description of his voice echoing around the locality is particularly memorable: 'My voice filling the district as I call their names'. *The Path* suggests how man often has a disruptive effect on the natural world – the poet describes how he 'dislodges' the mallards and 'nudges' the swans. Sensing the swans' 'gradual disdain', the poet sees himself as a barely tolerated visitor in the natural world. We see his sharply observant eye and his ability to describe a scene precisely in his image of the 'kittiwakes scrap(ing) the waves'. In *The Strand* the poet suggests how man is relatively insignificant compared to the overwhelming power of the sea, which is capable of 'reducing to sand the dry shells, the toe and fingernail parings of the sea' – a particularly memorable metaphor. While the poet conveys the harshness and power of nature, he is also very appreciative of its beauty as we see in *The Lake*: 'For a few minutes every evening its surface seems tilted to receive the sun perfectly'. Here the sibilant 's' sound helps to convey a sense of stillness and perfect peace. The harmony of the natural world and the poet's reverential attitude towards its creatures are memorably conveyed in the closing lines – the mare and her foal visiting the lake are described as 'special visitors'. While Longley, unlike Wordsworth, does not always achieve a sense of perfect inner peace in the natural world, the variety of emotions that nature evokes in him is closer to our own response to nature's many faces.

Badger is another poem that highlights the poet's ability to describe the natural world in a detached, precise manner. A well-chosen metaphor suggests the badger's strength and determination: 'Pushing the wedge of his body'. Sibilance is again used to good effect to suggest the tranquillity of nature: 'Night's silence around his shoulders'. As in *Carrigskeewaun*, the poet reminds us that nature belongs to nature's creatures – just as the ravens 'supervise' the mountain, the badger 'manages the earth'. The badger's death is described without comment: 'His limbs dragging after them, so many stones turned over'. An aspect of this poem that I found particularly memorable is the poet's use of the language and imagery of birth to describe the badger's death: 'For the digger, the earth-dog, it is a difficult delivery once the tongs take hold'. In a cruel irony, the burrow that was once a place of life now becomes a place of death. A series of verbs capture the badger's desperate struggle to survive: 'His limbs dragging . . . stones turned over . . . trees they tilted'. The poet's impersonal tone initially intrigued me. However, I soon perceived that it was not that the poet lacked compassion for the badger or felt no anger at man's violent intrusion into the badger's world, it is simply that he allows us to make up our own minds on the subject. In fact his vivid description of the badger inevitably evokes our sympathy for this gentle creature.

Violence past and present is similarly described in a detached, precise manner in *Wounds*, where imagery and dialogue bring the trench warfare of the First World War to life. We can hear the terrified young soldiers 'psyching' themselves up with their sectarian battle cries: 'Fuck the Pope!', 'No surrender!' A grim image captures the horror and indignity of violent death: 'a landscape of dead buttocks'. The extent to which we can become desensitised to the horror of war is suggested by the image of the padre resettling the kilts of the dead men 'with a stylish backhand and a prayer'. The deaths of three young soldiers in modern day Northern Ireland are vividly described: 'bellies full of bullets and Irish beer'. The repeated loud 'b' sound accentuates the harshness of their deaths. While the poet remains the detached observer, his coldly precise descriptions convey the obscenity and indignity of violent death. The violence in this poem occurs on the battlefield and, more disturbingly, in a domestic setting. It is shocking when the home that is normally a sanctuary is invaded by violence. The image of the night-light in a nursery being put out 'for ever' is especially grim, suggesting the terrible finality of an infant's death. Also, one could not but be moved by the poet's description of the killing of a bus conductor in front of his family: 'He collapsed beside his carpet slippers'. The poet never apportions blame or moralises, instead his verse vividly highlights the terrible human cost of violence.

Wreaths is one of Longley's most powerful poems because it also effectively highlights the obscenity and the awful human cost of violence. The poet reminds us of the flesh and blood people behind the cold statistics and impersonal news stories. Again, the reader is never sermonised – the poet's clinically precise descriptions leave us in no doubt as to how he feels. In *The Civil Servant* we are again appalled by the violent disruption of the domestic world. The death of the civil servant is described in horrifying, clinical detail: 'A bullet entered his mouth and pierced his skull'. The idea of a rich and varied life being brought to a cruelly abrupt end is effectively conveyed: 'The books he had read, the music he could play'. The widow's grief is described without comment: 'Later his widow took a hammer and chisel and removed the black keys from his piano'. Jim Gibson, the greengrocer was killed 'serving even the death dealers who found him busy as usual behind the counter'. The grim irony of this ordinary, hardworking man (who posed no threat to anyone) being killed in the so-called season of goodwill is not lost on the reader. The poet's description of the deaths of the linen workers again underlines their ordinariness: 'There fell on the road beside them spectacles, wallets, small change, and a set of dentures'. Without ever delivering any kind of a moral lecture, the poet sets us thinking about the horrific violence that for so long blighted life on this island.

Longley describes his relationship with his father in a typically honest, unsentimental manner. In *Last Requests* we see the communication gap between father and son. The poet thought that his dying father was blowing him a kiss, when in reality he was gesturing for a cigarette. The image of the oxygen tent is particularly effective in suggesting the gap between father and son. The tent separates them in a physical sense, while also suggesting how they are separated by an unbridgeable gap in experience: 'I who brought peppermints and grapes only / Couldn't reach you through the oxygen tent'. However, the poet also describes tender, loving moments between himself and his father. One such moment is depicted in *Wounds* where we see him at his father's death bed: 'I touched his hand, his thin head I touched'. The repetition of 'I touched' effectively evokes the poet's deep love for his father.

An Amish Rug expresses the poet's love for his wife with the honesty and lack of sentimentality that characterises his verse. The strong, richly coloured threads of the rug he gives his wife ('Its threads the colour of cantaloupe and cherry, securing hay bales, corn cobs, tobacco leaves') memorably symbolise the strength and richness of their shared love. I like the way the poet suggests both the spiritual and sensuous aspects of the love that he shares with his wife. The metaphor of the cathedral window aptly conveys the spiritual dimension to their love, while the image of the flowerbed evokes its sensuous quality: 'whenever we undress for sleep or love / We shall step over it as over a flowerbed'.

To sum up, Longley's poetry has a great appeal for the reader because of the range of his themes, his unflinching honesty and the power of his imagery.

Eavan Boland

Biographical Note

Eavan Boland was born in Dublin in 1944. Her father's career as a diplomat saw the family living in both London and New York before she returned to Dublin, aged 15, and completed her secondary education. Boland went on to attend Trinity College, graduating with a first class degree. Her peers at Trinity included other gifted poets such as Michael Longley, Brendan Kennelly and Derek Mahon. Boland lectured for some years at Trinity before devoting herself fulltime to her writing. She got married in her mid-twenties and her subsequent move to the suburbs had a major impact on her poetic development.

Though removed from Dublin's vibrant literary scene, Boland found inspiration in her experience of the suburban world. After much travelling, she appreciated the stability that married life in the suburbs brought. Realising that a predominantly male poetic tradition did not regard motherhood and the life of a housewife as 'fit material for poetry', Boland drew on her own experience as mother and housewife to give a voice to the thousands of women living in housing estates in the suburbs. Love, marriage, motherhood and the suburban experience now became her central poetic preoccupations. On the international stage, such poets as Sylvia Plath and Adrienne Rich were also using their experience of marriage and motherhood as subject matter for their poetry. Boland also explores such themes as Irish identity, the nature of the Irish historical experience and the role of the female poet in society.

The War Horse

This poem was inspired by a commonplace incident that occurred in the suburban estate in which the poet lived. Image and sound combine to draw the reader into the poem. It is a 'dry night' and a horse is wandering around the estate in which Boland lives. The horse has escaped from 'the tinker camp on the Enniskerry Road'. Onomatopoeia enables the reader to hear the 'clip, clop / Casual iron of his shoes', 'his breath hissing, his snuffling head'. The horse is regarded as a threatening, destructive presence 'as he stamps death / Like a mint on the innocent coinage of earth'. When Boland surveys the damage done after the horse has passed her home, she is relieved to see that 'no great harm is done'.

The poem becomes more interesting when

Boland uses the language and imagery of war to describe the damage done by the wandering horse. A torn leaf is described as 'a maimed limb'. A destroyed rose is depicted as a 'mere line of defence', and as a 'volunteer' that is 'expendable'. The connection between the damaged plants and the human victims of violence is very clear in the following image: 'a crocus, its bulbous head / Blown from growth'. The long 'o' sound helps to evoke a solemn mood. The crocus is depicted as 'one of the screamless dead'.

Boland's use of the terminology of war to portray the destruction wrought by the horse suggests that this suburban incident has prompted her to reflect on broader issues relating to our attitudes towards the threat and violence of war. When this poem was written in the mid 1970s, the violence in Northern Ireland was threatening to spill over into the Republic. When the threat of destruction has passed, the poet's feeling is one of relief, 'But we, we are safe'. The repetition of 'we' suggests the insular (inward-looking), self-absorbed mentality that prevails in this suburban estate. As the 'huge, threatening horse' ambles on, neighbours hide behind curtains. The destruction done by the horse may be seen as a symbol of the violence in Northern Ireland, while the refusal of Boland and her neighbours to confront the threat of the horse suggests the unwillingness of people in the south of Ireland to confront the violence that was blighting life in the North at this time. A rhetorical question sets readers thinking about our attitudes towards violence, especially the violence on our own doorstep: 'why should we care / If a rose, a hedge, a crocus are uprooted / Like corpses, remote, crushed, mutilated?' The adjectives 'distant' and 'remote' imply that we in the Republic of Ireland regard the Northern problem as being very far removed from us. Selfishly indifferent, we lack the 'fierce commitment' necessary to involve ourselves in a potentially dangerous situation.

The poem ends with Boland feeling a connection with her ancestors, who faced threatening, violent situations in earlier times, 'And for a second only my blood is still / With atavism . . . /recalling days of burned countryside'.

KEY POINTS

- Key theme is outsiders' detached, insular attitude towards the violence in Northern Ireland.
- An unremarkable incident that occurs in Boland's suburban estate prompts her to reflect on our attitude towards violence and war.
- The poem is written in a series of rhyming couplets.
- The language and imagery of war indicates that the poem is not just about the minor damage done by a wandering horse.
- Repeated use of 'our' and 'we' underscore our insular attitudes ('our laurel hedge', 'our house', 'our short street', 'we, we are safe').
- Other sound effects include internal rhyme and assonance ('hock and fetlock', 'blown from growth').
- Use of onomatopoeia enables us to hear the horse ('clip clop casual iron of his shoes . . . hissing breath . . . snuffling head).
- Rhetorical question prompts the reader to reflect on our attitude towards violence and war, particularly the violence on our own island ('why should we care if . . . ?').

Child of Our Time

This poem was inspired by the harrowing image of a dead child being carried from the rubble following a bomb explosion in Dublin in 1974. The title of the poem suggests that this innocent child was a victim of the times in which we live. This poem is both elegy (lament) and lullaby. A series of antitheses (contrasting ideas) in the opening stanza suggests how the tone of the poem alternates between tenderness and outrage. The antithetical style contributes towards the creation of a balanced tone. The opening stanza reflects Boland's desire to create some sort of order and harmony from the terrible chaos and 'discord' of the child's death, 'This song, which takes from your final cry / Its tune, from your unreasoned end its reason / Its rhythm from the discord of your murder'. Boland underlines the tragedy and terrible finality of the child's death, 'your final cry . . . your murder . . . the fact you cannot listen'.

In the second stanza the poet reflects on the failings of the adult world that contributed to the death of the child. The collective 'we' suggests a sense of collective responsibility, 'We who should have known'. The world of childhood is evoked by references to rhymes, soft toys and legends. Our duty was to create a safe environment in which this child could grow and learn. Ironically, the adult world must now learn from the dead child, 'We . . . must learn from you dead'.

The final stanza holds out the hope that we might learn from the child's death and rebuild around the child's 'broken image'. Boland attributes the child's death to our inability to communicate with each other ('our idle talk') and exhorts (encourages) us to find 'a new language'. Images and language ('idiom') relate to our culture, values and attitudes. The adult world stands accused, 'Child / Of our time, our times have robbed your cradle'. The final line has a prayer-like tone, expressing the hope that the death of the child – who may be taken to represent all innocent victims of violence – will awaken the world to the need for change, 'Sleep in a world your final sleep has woken'.

KEY POINTS

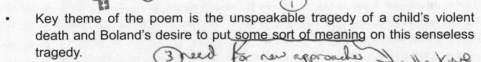

- Key theme of the poem is the unspeakable tragedy of a child's violent death and Boland's desire to put some sort of meaning on this senseless tragedy.   ①
- The poem's long lines reflect the sad, solemn mood.   ③ *need for new approaches*   ② *collective responsibility*
- The poet involves the reader in the poem in stanzas 2–3 ('We . . . our').
- Although the tragedy had its origins in the Northern conflict, politics do not enter into this poem, and names and places are not mentioned. In this way Boland highlights the universality of this tragedy.

The Famine Road

In this poem Boland reflects on the famine, the darkest and most traumatic period in Irish history and on the theme of colonial injustice. What is particularly unusual about this poem is the analogy that Boland draws between the suffering of the famine victims and the anguish of a barren woman. This is a dramatic poem with specific settings, 'characters', different voices and an element of conflict and tension.

The poem opens with Colonel Jones, an English official in Ireland, reading a letter from Lord Trevelyan. In a classic example of racist stereotyping, Trevelyan arrogantly dismisses the entire Irish nation as being 'as idle as trout in light'. He rejects the idea of giving the starving people any kind of charity, suggesting that both their bodies and weak characters would benefit from hard work. The 'toil' he has in mind is road building. These public works schemes were the government's response to the desperate plight of a famine-stricken nation. The infamous 'famine roads' rarely served any purpose other than sapping the little energy the starving people had, 'roads to force / from nowhere, going nowhere of course'. The image of the blood red seal on the letter suggests the callous indifference of the English administration.

The repeated harsh 'k' sound ('fork, stick . . . rock, suck') also suggests the harshness of these officials, who are happy that starving people 'suck April hailstones for water and for food'. An image suggestive of cannibalism underlines the desperation of the starving people, 'each eyed – / as if at a corner butcher – the other's buttock'.

Disease was as great a killer as starvation. Boland highlights the misery of a typhoid victim who becomes an outcast ('a typhoid pariah') because of others' fear of contracting the highly contagious, deadly disease. The extent to which people are dehumanised by starvation is powerfully conveyed when Boland describes how the unfortunate man is left to die alone, with no one to say even a prayer, 'No more than snow / attends its own flakes where they settle / and melt, will they pray by his death rattle'.

Jones' letter to Trevelyan is smug in tone. The public works programme went better than they expected because the famine victims were too exhausted to even contemplate any kind of rebellion, 'sedition, idleness, cured / In one . . . / the wretches work till they are quite worn'. The image of corn being marched to the ships when people were starving to death dramatically highlights the theme of colonial injustice. The image of Jones coldly viewing the bones of famine victims from the comfort of his carriage underscores the heartless detachment of these officials.

Intertwined with the dramatic portrayal of the suffering of the famine victims is the depiction of the suffering of a barren woman. In the italicised verses the woman is addressed by a doctor who unfeelingly quotes statistics when discussing her infertile state, 'one out of every ten and then / another third of those again'. The voice becomes even more insensitive and upsetting, 'You never will, never you know'. The repetition of 'never' is particularly hurtful and the advice he offers ('grow / your garden, keep house') hollow and meaningless to the devastated woman. The unfeeling voice of the doctor reminds us of the callous tones of the English officials. The famine road is a symbol of the futility of the lives of both the famine victims and the barren woman. The poem reminds us that those in positions of authority are often lacking in humanity and compassion.

KEY POINTS

- Theme is the suffering of famine victims and the callousness of the English administration.
- Boland draws an analogy between the suffering of the famine victims and the anguish of a barren woman.
- The famine road symbolises the futility of the lives of both the famine victims and the infertile woman.
- A dramatic poem with specific settings, 'characters', different voices and an element of conflict and tension.
- The adjectives 'sick, directionless' aptly describe the plight of the starving people.
- The image of the blood-red seal suggests the cruelty of the English administration.
- Repetition of harsh 'k' sound evokes the harshness of the ruling regime ('fork, stick . . . rock, suck').

The Black Lace Fan My Mother Gave Me

Similar to most poets, Boland writes regularly on the themes of love and relationships. This poem was inspired by a black fan given to Boland by her mother. This fan had originally been given as a gift to her mother by the man who later became her husband. It was in fact the first gift that Boland's father gave her mother and is seen as a symbol of their love. Typical of Boland, she does not attempt to idealise or sentimentalise her parents' relationship. She describes their love in an honest, realistic manner. The fan represents the joy and stability of their love, but also its imperfection.

The opening line gives a sense of personal history being recollected, 'It was the first gift he ever gave her'. Its importance is underlined by the fact that its exact cost ('five francs') and the place where it was purchased ('the Galeries') are clearly remembered. Sensuous imagery evokes the atmosphere of pre-war

Paris, 'It was stifling. A starless drought made the nights stormy'. A few crisp sentences give us a glimpse of their individual personalities, 'They met in cafés. She was always early. / He was late'. This particular evening, his purchase of the fan meant that he was even later than normal. Detailed description helps us to picture Boland's impatient mother looking down Boulevard des Capucines, before ordering more coffee and standing up as if to leave. Boland imaginatively recreates the scene, using sensuous imagery, 'The streets were emptying. The heat was killing. / She thought the distance smelled of rain and lightning'. The reference to the threatening weather may suggest that the relationship was problematical in some way or that the woman had doubts or worries in relation to the future of the relationship.

Stanza three gives us a vivid image of the fan. It is appropriately decorated with roses, the traditional flowers of love. The skilled craftsmanship that went into its creation is suggested by verbs and adverbs, 'darkly picked, stitched boldly, quickly'. While Boland appreciates the delicate beauty and elegance of the tortoise-shell, she is aware of the 'violation' of the tortoise that facilitated the creation of this love token. The description of the tortoise-shell as 'a worn-out gold bullion' suggests the rich, enduring nature of her parents' love. However, the following lines recall the dark hints of the opening stanza, 'The lace is overcast as if the weather / it opened for and offset had entered it'. The fan represents the beauty, longevity and imperfection of her parents' love. Put simply, it is a symbol not just of the romance of their early romantic days together, but of the real lifelong relationship – complete with all its ups and downs – that they have shared.

Stanza five returns to the scene of that stifling Parisian night. Thunder is in the 'airless dusk' – again, perhaps hinting at a stormy relationship. There is a sense of drama and anticipation, 'A man running. / And no way now to know what happened then – / none at all – unless, of course, you improvise'. Boland knows the history of the fan, but the story of her parents' love is incomplete, known only to her parents themselves. All we can do is 'improvise' or imagine how her parents got on through their years of marriage.

The final stanza is dominated by the image of a blackbird – the bird is another traditional symbol of love. The image of the blackbird is highly evocative. While the fan is beautiful, it has been affected by the ravages of time ('worn out'). It is, of course, also an inanimate object. In contrast, the blackbird is, like her parents' love, vibrant and alive. This closing image means that the poem ends on a triumphant, celebratory note, 'Suddenly she puts out her wing – / the whole, full, flirtatious span of it'. Her parents' love has weathered various emotional storms and survived. The adjectives 'whole, full' suggest a love that is balanced and complete, while the adjective 'flirtatious' suggests that the romance in their relationship remains intact. Sound effects (the alliterative 'full, flirtatious' and the sibilant 'flirtatious span') contribute to the upbeat mood at the close of the poem.

KEY POINTS

- Key theme is the nature of Boland's parents' relationship and love.
- The fan is a symbol of their love, as is the blackbird later in the poem.
- Sensuous images evoke the atmosphere in pre-war Paris.
- The story of her parents' early love is told in a clear, crisp manner (stanzas 1–2).

The Shadow Doll

In this poem Boland reflects on the nature and meaning of marriage. The poem was inspired by a Victorian porcelain doll that the poet viewed in a museum. The doll, a miniature bride, would have been sent by a dressmaker to a bride to help her decide on the design of her dress. As in *The Black Lace Fan My Mother Gave Me*, a concrete object prompts Boland to reflect on a range of issues associated with the particular object. The view of marriage expressed in this poem is very dark. Basically, marriage is perceived to be a form of imprisonment that confines, constrains and silences women.

In lines 1–9 the doll is described in a series of concrete images. The detailed description suggests the special, delicate beauty of the dress, 'They stitched blooms from the ivory tulle / to hem the oyster gleam of the veil'. However, the language used in relation to the doll evokes a sense of repression and containment, 'stitched', 'neatly sown', 'airless glamour', 'under glass, under wraps'. The doll would have been kept by the married woman and would have witnessed her unfolding life, complete with its 'visits, fevers, quickenings and lusts' (suggestive of sex, pregnancy and childbirth). Boland personifies the inanimate doll when she describes it as 'discreet'. Here she may be suggesting that women remain silent about their personal lives.

Lines 10–15 focus on the Victorian bride herself. As the bride-to-be views the doll in all its artificial perfection ('the shell-tone spray of seed pearls, / the bisque features'), she has a vision of herself in the place of the porcelain doll, 'she could see herself / inside it all'. Here she seems to gain a frightening insight into the restrictive nature of marriage.

The poem's final section (lines 16–21) switches focus from the Victorian bride-to-be contemplating her shadow doll to Boland on the night before her own marriage. Her endless repetition of her vows suggests her feelings of apprehension. A list of various items ('cards and wedding gifts – / the coffee pots and the clocks') suggests the typical pre-wedding clutter. Significantly, the closing image is one of confinement, 'the battered tan case full of cotton / lace and tissue paper, pressing down, then / pressing down again'. The repetition of 'pressing down' suggests a growing sense of claustrophobia at the prospect of the confinement of marriage. All of the suggestions of oppression and imprisonment culminate in the poem's final three words, which are set apart for emphasis, 'And then locks'. The clear implication of these words is that, where women and marriage are concerned, little has changed since Victorian times.

KEY POINTS

- Key theme is the way in which marriage represses and confines women.
- It is in examining a concrete object (the porcelain doll) that Boland is prompted to meditate on the nature of marriage from Victorian times to the present.
- Various images of imprisonment: the 'airless' glass dome that houses the doll, the locked suitcase, etc.

- Much of the poem's language has connotations of confinement: 'stitched', 'under wraps', etc.
- Repetition is used for emphasis ('pressing down, then / Pressing down again').

White Hawthorn in the West of Ireland

This poem describes a journey that Boland makes from her suburban Dublin home to the West of Ireland. This personal experience leads to the poet reflecting on the contrast between the confinement and boredom of the suburban world and the vastness and magic of the natural world. While Boland is a poet who regards life in the suburbs as suitable material for her poetry, her portrayal of the suburban world in this poem is distinctively negative.

The conversational tone of the opening lines draws the reader into the poem, 'I drove west / in the season between seasons. / I left behind suburban gardens./ Lawnmowers. Small talk'. This imagery evokes a dull, restricted, monotonous world. The regular full stops underscore the confinement and rigid order of the suburbs.

The contrast between Boland's normal humdrum environment and the wild landscape of the West is sharply drawn. The image of 'splashes of coltsfoot' with its sibilant 's' sounds suggests the beauty and tranquillity of nature. The oxymoron 'the hard shyness of Atlantic light' suggests the mysterious, indefinable nature of the light in the West of Ireland. (An oxymoron is a figure of speech which involves contradictory terms being used in conjunction with each other). The phrase 'the superstitious aura of hawthorn' suggests that there is

something mysterious about hawthorn. Boland has a longing to fill her arms with the hawthorn's 'sharp flowers'. She yearns to embrace the hawthorn and become one with the natural world, 'be part of that ivory downhill rush'. This image sharply contrasts with the images of confinement in the first stanza.

However, the poet's knowledge of the folklore relating to hawthorn causes her to pause and hold back from embracing the plant. In Irish folklore many superstitions surround hawthorn. Linked with the world of the fairies, hawthorn is associated with death and bad luck, 'the custom was / not to touch the hawthorn / . . . a child might die, perhaps'.

So the poet leaves the hawthorn 'stirring on those hills / with a fluency / only water has'. Here the hawthorn is seen as a mysterious, living entity. An energetic life force, it has the ability 'to re-define land'. Visitors are struck by the abundance of hawthorn in the western landscape. Boland states that 'for anglers and for travellers', it is 'the only language spoken in these parts'. The hawthorn now assumes a symbolic significance, representing the unique culture of the West of Ireland. Just like the other visitors, Boland cannot become part of this world, no matter how much she is drawn to the idea.

KEY POINTS

- This poem celebrates the unique beauty of the West of Ireland.
- Repetition of 'I' underscores the deeply personal nature of the experience at the heart of the poem.
- Poem contrasts the confinement of the suburbs with the freedom of nature.
- While regular full stops suggest the enclosed world of the suburbs, run-on lines evoke the unrestricted western landscape.
- Use of memorable visual imagery ('splashes of coltsfoot', 'that ivory downhill rush').
- Sound effects: – the sibilant 's' sound suggests the peacefulness of the West ('Under low skies, past splashes of coltsfoot').

Outside History

The theme of this poem is history's exclusion of the voiceless. In writing this poem, Boland remembers and honours those forgotten people who have remained 'outside history'. The poem opens with a factual statement, 'There are outsiders, always'. The natural image that follows depicts the stars ('those iron inklings of an Irish January') as being far removed from the reality of human life. They 'have always been / outside history'. The stars may be seen as symbols of myth – the idealised versions of Irish history. Under the stars real human history in all its pain and darkness unfolds, 'Under them remains / a place where you found / you were human, and / a landscape in which you knew you were mortal'. Boland sees history in a very negative light, describing it as an 'ordeal'.

Faced with the choice of myth or the real, painful world of history, Boland chooses the latter. It seems that she is 'only now' becoming aware of the 'darkness' of history. The image of 'roads clotted as / firmaments with the dead' suggests the devastation of the Great Famine. The image of people slowly dying underlines the terrible suffering that people endured throughout our history. The poet's compassionate nature is highlighted when she imagines us kneeling beside these dying people and whispering in their ear. The closing line reminds us that while we may remember and honour the forgotten victims of history, we cannot change or undo the wrong that was done to them. The closing line points to our collective responsibility for their suffering, 'And we are too late. We are always too late'. The repetition of 'too late' underscores the regretful tone. It seems that we are always too late in learning the lessons of history.

KEY POINTS

- Key theme is the forgotten lives of the voiceless.
- Effective use of imagery ('roads clotted as firmaments with the dead')
- Repetition of 'too late' conveys regretful tone
- Key words express the poet's deeply negative view of history, 'pain', 'ordeal', 'darkness'.

This Moment

This poem celebrates a special moment in everyday life. While *White Hawthorn in the West of Ireland* presents suburban life in a negative light, this poem suggests that everyday life in the suburbs has its moments of beauty. The opening lines set the scene, 'A neighbourhood /At dusk'. The mood is peaceful. There is a sense of anticipation, 'Things are getting ready / to happen / out of sight'. The natural world seems to wait in expectation, 'Stars and moths./ And rinds slanting around fruit'. The stars will shortly rise, the moths flutter and the apples sweeten. However, for the moment, everything in the natural world seems to pause 'But not yet'. The sense of anticipation intensifies. The next image is beautifully simple and vivid, 'One tree is black. One window is yellow as butter'. This domestic simile is very apt.

The moment at the heart of the poem occurs when a child runs into the arms of his mother, 'A woman leans down to catch a child / who has run into her arms / this moment'. By referring to 'a neighbourhood', 'a mother' and 'a child', Boland suggests the universality of this special moment. The natural world seems to respond to and celebrate the moment when mother and child are re-united, 'Stars rise. / Moths flutter./ Apples sweeten in the dark'. The sibilant 's' sound that dominates the poem conveys a sense of perfect peace. The natural imagery evokes a sense of universal harmony. The short lines and regular full stops encourage the reader to read through the poem slowly, and to reflect on the special beauty of a commonplace event.

KEY POINTS

- Key theme is the beauty of the mother–child relationship.
- Vivid images.
- Economic style.
- Use of simple, everyday language.
- Effective use of sound.
- Mood is quiet and reflective.

Love

This is a deeply personal poem, the theme of which is the changing nature of love. It was prompted by a visit to a 'mid-western town' in Iowa in the United States where Boland and her husband lived in the early years of their marriage. The reference to myths suggests the extraordinary, magical nature of their love at this time. The reference to the bridge 'the hero crossed on his way to hell' derives from a tale in Virgil's *Aeneid* that describes Aeneas' crossing the bridge into hell to see his dead comrades. In this instance Aeneas may be seen as a symbol for Boland's husband who often crossed this bridge over the River Iowa to visit their seriously ill infant daughter in hospital. That period in the family's life might certainly be described as hellish – Boland states that her infant daughter was 'touched by death'.

The family's old apartment is described in detail, 'We had a kitchen and an Amish table./ We had a view'. The language here is simple and crisp. A memorable metaphor suggests the strength and gentleness of the love that Boland and her husband shared at this time, 'And we discovered there / love had the feather and muscle of wings'. The wings image further suggests the power of love to elevate and inspire. The poet suggests the powerful, elemental force of their love when she personifies it as 'a brother of fire and air'.

Boland remembers how her ill daughter was 'spared'. When the poet again refers to the myth of Aeneas, she describes how, when his comrades hailed him, 'their mouths opened and their voices failed' – an image suggesting the impossibility of expressing intense emotion. This mythical allusion implies that Boland was unable to articulate the depth of love that she felt at this special time in her life.

Just as nostalgia for his previous life spurred Aeneas on to visit his former comrades in hell, Boland is filled with longing to return to the earlier life that she and her husband shared.

Boland now reflects on the present state of their love, 'I am your wife./ It was years ago. / . . . We love each other still'. The latter line clearly implies that their love is not the same as it was during that traumatic period in their lives, although it continues to survive, 'Across our day-to-day and ordinary distances / we speak plainly'. Boland longs to return to that earlier time to once again experience that uniquely intense love, 'And yet I want to return to you / on the bridge of the Iowa river as you were with snow on the shoulders of your coat and a car passing with its headlights on'. This romantic image has a cinematic quality. At that time the poet saw her husband 'as a hero in a text'. Now she longs to 'cry out the epic question' and ask him if they will 'ever live so intensely again'. Boland uses an apt adjective to sum up the strength of this special love, describing it as 'formidable'. Drawing again on Greek mythology the poet depicts love as a male god, 'it offered us ascension / even to look at him'. The use of the religious term 'ascension' suggests the spiritual quality of their powerful love – this image connects with the earlier 'wings' metaphor, underlining the idea that love has the power to elevate and inspire, enabling Boland and her husband to transcend the problems of everyday life.

The closing lines underline the impossibility of the poet returning to that earlier time in her life or articulating the uniquely intense love that she and her husband once shared, 'But the words are shadows and you cannot hear me. / You walk away and I cannot follow'.

The Pomegranate

The theme of this poem is the mother-daughter relationship and the manner in which it inevitably changes over time. Boland draws on the myth of Ceres and Persephone to underline the universal relevance of her own personal experience. The poem is written in blank verse which is similar to a natural speaking voice. This is appropriate for a poem in which Boland is clearly speaking from the heart.

The legend of Ceres and her Persephone tells of the abduction of young Persephone by Pluto, god of the underworld, who wanted her to be his wife. Devastated by the loss of her daughter, Ceres searched everywhere for her. As goddess of vegetation, Ceres threatened to interrupt all growth in the world until Celeus, the King of Eleusis, identified Persephone's abductor. Ceres went to reclaim her daughter from the underworld, only to discover that, having eaten some pomegranate seeds, Persephone would be forced to spend half of each year in the underworld. When Persephone is with Ceres, everything grows, but as soon as she returns to the underworld everything starts to wither and die.

As a child, Boland was drawn to this legend ('The only legend I ever loved') because, as a child in exile in London ('a city of fogs and strange consonants'), she could relate to

Persephone's exile in the underworld. Later, as an adult and mother, she could relate to the feelings of Ceres when she had to go out on a summer's evening searching for her own daughter at bed-time, 'When she came running I was ready / to make any bargain to keep her'. However, Boland realises that the special relationship between mother and daughter inevitably changes over time, 'But I was Ceres then and I knew / winter was in store for every leaf / on every tree on that road'. Boland is keenly aware of the universal, inexorable nature of the ageing process. Time would inevitably change the nature of her relationship with her daughter – this was an 'inescapable' reality.

Line 24 marks a turning point in the poem, with the movement from the past to the present. This section of the poem has a dramatic quality. The scene is set: it is winter, a starless night and Boland climbs the stairs. As she watches her teenage daughter sleeping, she is filled with conflicting emotions. The teen magazine and can of coke are typical of a teenage bedroom. It is symbolically significant that her daughter also has a plate of uncut fruit because this represents the pomegranate. In the context of this poem, eating the fruit symbolises leaving the world of childhood behind and entering the world of adulthood. The idea of eating the fruit also has obvious biblical connotations involving the loss of innocence. Boland now considers how things might have turned out if Persephone had not eaten the pomegranate, 'She could have come home and been safe / and ended the story and all / our heart-broken searching'. The use of 'our' indicates that Boland is speaking for Ceres, for herself, and for all mothers. However, she knows that the relationship between mother and daughter must inevitably change. Just as Persephone 'reached out a hand and plucked a pomegranate', so will Boland's own daughter inevitably enter the world of adulthood and so change their relationship forever.

Aware of the kind of experiences awaiting her daughter in adulthood, Boland wonders what she should do, 'I could warn her'. While the poet recognises that the suburban world in which they live is far removed from the world of Greek legend ('It is another world'), she knows that even this world can be harsh, 'The rain is cold. The road is flint-coloured'. However, if she postpones the grief, she 'will diminish the gift' – perhaps a reference to the freedom to live her own life that she will grant her daughter. Every world has its share of pain and sorrow and, while Boland would like to insulate her daughter from the harsher aspects of life, she accepts that she too must live her life and learn through personal experience the things that Boland herself now knows, 'The legend will be hers as well as mine. / She will enter it. As I have'. These lines suggest an unending, universal, natural process. When her daughter wakes in the morning, she will put the pomegranate to her lips. The poet resolves to 'say nothing'.

KEY POINTS

- Key theme is the changing nature of the mother–daughter relationship.
- A personal poem to which every parent and child can relate.
- Mythical allusions suggest the universality of the poet's experience and feelings.
- The harshness of the modern world is evoked in vivid, dark images ('The rain is cold. The road is flint-coloured').

Sample Answer

Write out the text of a talk that you would deliver to your class, outlining your response to the poetry of Eavan Boland.

Good afternoon classmates,

I found Eavan Boland's poetry to be original and thought-provoking. While female readers in particular appreciate Boland's poems on marriage, motherhood and the place of women in society, her work also has a wide appeal. She writes about history, violence, love and suburban life in a way that is fresh and interesting. I like the way she often uses a personal experience to reflect on an issue of universal importance. I admire her obvious compassion for all victims of violence and oppression and her anger at those who visit suffering and misery on innocent people. She has great powers of description and her verse has an appealing visual quality. Her use of sound effects to evoke particular moods is also very effective. I especially like her use of everyday, conversational language – Boland deals with issues that matter in language that we can understand.

I would first like to talk about *This Moment*, a poem of wonderful simplicity which conveys the magic of an everyday event. We could all relate to the heartwarming image at the heart of the poem: 'A woman leans down to catch a child / who has run into her arms / this moment'. Boland cleverly underlines the universality of this moment by writing of 'A neighbourhood . . . a woman . . . a child'. The poem's short lines and regular full stops create a sense of anticipation, while encouraging us to pause and reflect on the power and beauty of this moment. This poem contains one of my favourite images: 'One tree is black./ One window is yellow as butter'. This is a wonderfully simple, vivid image. I liked Boland's repeated use of the sibilant 's' sound to convey a sense of perfect peace. The way nature seems to respond to and celebrate the meeting of mother and child ('Stars rise. / Moths flutter. / Apples sweeten in the dark') underscores the naturalness of this special moment. There is a lovely sense of universal harmony in this poem.

I enjoyed reading the poem *Love* because it set me thinking about the way love changes over time. Again, the theme of this poem is both personal and universal. I admire the honest way Boland writes about her relationship with her husband. She seems to confide in the reader. She describes how her love for her husband was intensified by the traumatic experience of nearly losing her sick child. Simple details of her life in Iowa draw us into her domestic world: 'We had a kitchen and an Amish table./ We had a view'. I really like the image that she employs to suggest the beauty and strength of their shared love, 'And we discovered there /

Handwritten margin notes:

Paragraph
Layout
Poem name
↓
Theme
↓
Poetic Dev
+ = e
Your respons
to them
+
poem

love had the feather and muscle of wings'. Her description of their mutual love as elemental ('a brother of fire and air') was memorable. I think you will agree that, as a class, we found the reference to an episode from Virgil's *Aeneid* quite challenging. However, when we teased it out, we discovered that by employing this mythical allusion, Boland was suggesting how it can sometimes be impossible to express intense emotion. Like Aeneas' comrades in hell, her feelings were too intense to be expressed: 'their mouths opened and their voices failed.' While the mythical allusions mean that this poem has its share of metaphorical language, more of the language has a lovely simplicity and conversational flow: 'I am your wife./ It was years ago. / . . . We love each other still.' Here Boland reminds us that love can grow and change over time. This poem contains another memorable visual image – that of her husband crossing the bridge with snow on the shoulders of his coat 'and a car passing with its headlights on'. I could almost picture this image on a big cinema screen. Many of us can relate to the idea of idealising a person you love: 'I see you as a hero in a text – / the image blazing and the edges gilded.' I think 'formidable' is an apt adjective to describe a really powerful type of love. Boland offers us some words of wisdom at the close of the poem when she suggests the impossibility of returning to the past: 'You walk away and I cannot follow.'

One of the reasons Boland appeals to so many readers is that she writes about life in the increasingly populated suburbs. In *White Hawthorn in the West of Ireland*, she highlights the contrast between the suburban and rural worlds. A few well-chosen words suggest how the suburbs are both physically confined and spiritually stifling: 'I left behind suburban gardens./ Lawnmowers. Small talk.' I love the way Boland combines visual imagery and the sibilant 's' sound to suggest the freedom, wildness and tranquillity of the western landscape, 'Under low skies, past splashes of coltsfoot'. I can see why she longs to become one with nature, 'be part of / that ivory downhill rush'. Boland's use of punctuation in this poem is very effective. Regular full stops underscore the confinement of the suburbs, while run-on lines suggest the unconfined freedom of nature. I like the way she portrays the West as a special, magical place where one cannot but be aware of 'the superstitious aura of hawthorn'. I noticed how she draws a sharp contrast between the fixed, orderly suburban gardens and the seemingly fluid, shifting landscape of the West where the hawthorn is 'stirring' on the hills and has 'a fluency only water has'. I was struck by the way she presented the hawthorn as a symbol both of the West's wild beauty and unique culture, 'the only language spoken in these parts'. I like the way she celebrates all that is special about the West, while at the same time, setting us thinking about the quality of modern day suburban life.

Boland is again critical of the suburban mentality in *The War Horse*. Again, I admire her ability to use a personal experience to reflect on an issue of wider importance. I like the visual and aural imagery that draws us into the scene: 'the clip, clop casual / iron of his shoes / . . . his breath hissing, his snuffling head.' An original simile captures the damage that the wandering horse does to a manicured suburban garden: 'he stamps death / like a mint on the innocent coinage of earth.' This poem becomes more interesting as Boland uses the language and imagery of war to describe the destruction done by this frightening invader – a damaged leaf is compared to 'a maimed limb', while an uprooted crocus is 'one of the screamless dead'. The destruction done by the horse becomes a symbol of the violence in the North, while the image of Boland's neighbours hiding behind curtains suggests our insular, uncaring attitude towards the violence in our own country. The use of repetition effectively underscores our selfish indifference: 'But we, we are safe'.

Classmates, most of us share Boland's interest in our past. I admire the compassionate way she writes about the famine, the worst catastrophe in Irish history in *The Famine Road*. Her use of dialogue really brings home the indifference and harshness of the English regime. We can almost hear the arrogant Lord Trevelyan casually dismissing an entire nation as worthless, 'Idle as trout in light'. Boland makes effective use of sound, with the repeated harsh 'k' sound ('fork, stick . . . rock, suck') accentuating the harshness of the officials responsible for 'managing' the famine. Boland's use of a familiar image to suggest the horror of cannibalism is particularly disturbing: 'cunning as housewives, each eyed – as if at a corner butcher – the other's buttock.' The image of the typhoid victim dying alone is also very shocking, suggesting how the famine dehumanised its victims, draining them of any sympathy for others. Our entire class was outraged at Jones' callously pragmatic view of the famine as a cure for Irish rebelliousness. One of the most interesting features of this poem is the way Boland compares the suffering and oppression of the famine victims with the pain and humiliation of an infertile woman. The doctor who coldly quotes statistics and glibly suggests that this unfortunate woman look after her house and garden is as arrogant and as unfeeling as Jones and Trevelyan. Boland reminds us that those in positions of power and authority are often lacking in humanity and compassion. The famine road metaphor effectively suggests how the lives of the famine victims and the infertile woman are similarly futile, 'what is your body now if not a famine road?'

Child of our Time is similarly powerful and thought-provoking. This is a poem that really sets us thinking about the violence in our own country and about our responsibility for that violence. Boland was inspired to write this poem by the harrowing image of a dead child being carried from the scene of a bomb explosion in Dublin. I admire Boland's desire to create some sense of order and harmony from the chaos and 'discord' of the child's death. I was struck by the irony of the adult world learning from a child: 'We who should have known how to instruct . . . / . . . must learn from you dead.' Boland rightly encourages us to 'learn' from and 'rebuild' around the child's 'broken image'. She points to our collective guilt for this tragedy when she refers to our inability to communicate ('our idle talk'). Classmates, we should respond to Boland's exhortation to develop 'a new language' of reconciliation. We all share the hope expressed in the poem's poignant closing line that tragedies such as this will wake us up to the need for change: 'Sleep in a world your final sleep has woken'.

In conclusion, my overall response to Boland's poetry is very positive. She addresses issues that are relevant and important to the modern reader, giving us much food for thought. Memorable images, conversational language and effective use of sound add to the appeal of her verse. Thank you for your attention.

Conclusion
↓
feeling
↓
Thought on theme
↓
Thought on features.

Guidelines for Answering Exam Questions

Type of Questions

Leaving Certificate Higher Level Poetry questions tend to be general in nature. Questions essentially look for a candidate's personal response to a poet's work. Personal engagement with the text must be supported by detailed textual knowledge.

Examples:
(a) Write a personal response to the poetry of Adrienne Rich.
(b) Write an introduction to the poetry of Philip Larkin.
(c) Account for the popularity of Michael Longley's poetry.
(d) Explain what you liked and / or disliked about the poetry of Elizabeth Bishop. Etc., etc.

If a question is slightly more specific, the terms of the question must be addressed and kept in focus. However, at the heart of all poetry questions is the idea of personal engagement with the text.

The following are examples of slightly more specific poetry questions:

1. Write an article for a school magazine introducing the poetry of John Montague, to Leaving Certificate students. Tell them what he wrote about and explain what you liked in his writing, suggesting some poems that you think they would enjoy reading.
2. What impact did the poetry of John Keats make on you as a reader? Your answer should deal with the following: (a) Your overall sense of the personality of the poet, (b) The poet's use of language/imagery.

What does personal engagement with the text involve?

* Comment on themes, subject matter.
* Comment on the relevance of a poet's themes.
* Explain why a particular poem is worth reading.
* Say why you can relate to or 'connect' with certain themes.
* Discuss how particular poems had a particular impact on you.
* Explain why a personal poem has a universal appeal.
* Say which poems you most enjoyed.
* Comment on aspects of a poet's style:
* Language: accessible? simple/complex? etc.
* Imagery: vivid? precise? unusual? etc.
* Sound effects: alliteration, assonance, onomatopoeia, rhyme, etc.

Note: Your personal response must be grounded in the text – support your points by appropriate reference to and/or quotation from the poems on your course.

EXAMPLES OF THE LANGUAGE OF PERSONAL ENGAGEMENT

- *I can relate to this poem because . . .*
- *This poem remains relevant because . . .*
- *I enjoyed this poem because . . .*
- *What I liked / disliked about this poem was . . .*
- *This is my favourite poem because . . .*
- *This poem opened my eyes to . . .*
- *This poem helped me to understand . . .*
- *This poem had a profound impact on me because . . .*
- *This poem offers interesting insights into . . .*
- *This poem set me thinking about / made me aware of . . .*
- *I particularly like the image of . . .*
- *The image of . . . effectively conveys the idea of . . .*
- *The image of . . . is particularly striking.*
- *The vivid imagery fires my imagination . . .*
- *I like the way the poet compares . . .*
- *The poet employs a powerful metaphor to . . .*
- *This unusual simile is effective because . . .*
- *The poet's use of sound is particularly effective here because . . .*
- *The use of everyday, conversational language made the poem very accessible . . .*
- *I love the poet's wonderful use of detail . . .*
- *The poet's eye for detail brings the character / scene to life . . . etc. etc.*
- It is also important to write in the appropriate form and to employ the appropriate register (type of language).
- For example, you may be asked to write your response to a poet's work in the form of a letter in which you speak directly to the poet.
- If your response takes the form of a speech/talk, use conversational language / employ a chatty tone, etc, etc.

STRUCTURE YOUR ANSWER

- Brief introduction, addressing the question and outlining your response to it.
- One point (for example, a poet's use of imagery) or one poem per paragraph. Brief conclusion, referring back to the question.

Remember:

- Avoid summarising poems – remain focused on your key points. Aim to be analytical / discursive in responding to a poet's work.
- The emphasis throughout your response should be on personal engagement grounded in the text. Regularly quote from and refer to text to support points made.

- You do not have to discuss a fixed number of poems, but it is difficult to produce an impressive response discussing fewer than three poems.

RESPONDING TO THE UNSEEN POEM

In responding to this question, you must display an ability to personally 'connect' with the poem and the poet. You are expected to make intelligent use of the text to support your interpretation.

Look at the shape of the poem. Is it organised in stanzas? Is it written in sonnet form? Are any lines set apart from the rest of the poem? For example, the final line in Heaney's *Mid-Term Break* stands alone to emphasise the tragic nature of his young brother's death ('A four foot box, a foot for every year')

Note the title of the poem – it has not been chosen at random. What does the title suggest? Does the poem fulfil the expectations suggested by the title? For example, the title of Rosita Boland's poem *Butterflies* suggests that what follows will be a beautiful nature poem, whereas this poem is in fact concerned with the terrible destruction caused by landmines – the title is therefore ironic. In contrast, when we read *The Daffodils* by William Wordsworth, we expect – and get – a poem about the beauty of nature.

It is important to remember that a poet chooses his/her words very carefully to express his/her feelings. Words may be used literally or metaphorically ('I turned to ice', etc). They may be selected for their connotations / associations ('The waters of the canal pouring redemption for me' suggests the idea of an experience that is almost religious, etc.). Words may also be selected for their sounds.

Make a note of your first impression which will, naturally, be general in nature. What did you think of the poem's opening and closing? Did anything in particular strike you? A word? A phrase? An image? Were certain words suggestive of a particular mood or idea? Did the poet make use of repetition? Was the imagery primarily visual or did it appeal to a range of different senses? Are there any colours in the poem? If so, what feelings do you associate with these colours? Does the poem make use of contrast?

Your second reading of the poem will need to be more focused. Try to identify the dominant feeling in the poem and make a note of the key words and images that convey this feeling.

How would you describe the language? Is it formal or colloquial / chatty? Modern poets use the language of the modern age, ensuring that their poems are readily accessible. Is there any unusual use of language? For example, in Longley's poem *The Badger*, the poet uses the language of birth ('delivery . . . tongs') to describe the death of the badger. In his poem

The Tollund Man, Heaney uses the language of religion ('consecrate . . . pray') when writing about a long dead pagan. Does the poet invent any new words, and if so, how effective are they? For example, in *Lines Written on a Seat on the Grand Canal, Dublin*, Kavanagh describes the water pouring from the lock as roaring 'niagarously'.

Discuss the poet's use of imagery. Are certain images particularly effective? An image is basically a word-picture which may consist of a single word or a number of lines. Similes and metaphors are types of images. Does the poet make use of comparisons and, if so, are they effective in conveying a particular idea?

Consider the poet's use of punctuation. For example, regular full stops can serve different purposes. In her poem, *This Moment*, Eavan Boland makes regular use of full stops to create a sense of expectation. Regular full stops also help to create a reflective mood. A full stop at the end of a poem suggests a sense of closure, while its absence suggests the idea of something unresolved. Emily Dickinson often ends a poem with a dash or a question mark. Regular question marks suggest uncertainty.

What happens between the beginning and end of the poem? How do the poet's thoughts and feelings develop? Does he/she achieve some insight as the poem develops?

Consider the poet's use of sound (alliteration, assonance, onomatopoeia, rhyme, etc). Different sounds help to suggest different moods. For example, an alliterative 'b' sound can suggest a noisy atmosphere, a repeated 'd' sound a gloomy one and a repeated 's' sound a sense of peace. Are certain vowel sounds repeated and, if so, to what effect? For example, the repetition of broad vowel sounds helps to convey a serious, sad or lonely mood ('Alone, alone, all alone', 'staring face to face', etc.)

KEY POINTS – MENTION THE FOLLOWING:
- Title of poem.
- Key theme.
- Shape.
- Opening.
- Key words / phrases / images.
- Way in which ideas develop.
- Use of sound.
- Conclusion.

REMEMBER:
- Your response to the poem must be supported by intelligent use of the text.
- Show an awareness of literary terms in your response.

Key Literary Terms

ALLEGORY – A piece of writing that has both a surface meaning and another, deeper meaning. The purpose of an allegory is often to illustrate a moral or truth. *Example:* On the surface George Orwell's *Animal Farm* is a simple tale of animals taking over and running the farm on which they live. On a deeper level, this tale highlights the corrupting effects of total power. (Orwell had the old Soviet Union in mind when he wrote this novel.)

ALLITERATION – A run of words (usually consonants) starting with the same letter. *Examples:* 'Billy Brennan's barn' – Patrick Kavanagh.
'In the sun the slagheap slept' – Philip Larkin.

ALLUSION – This occurs when a writer refers to a well-known character, event, historical happening or work of literature. *Examples:* In *The Pomegranate* Boland alludes to the myth of Ceres and Peresphone. In *The Cage*, Montague refers to Homer's poem *The Iliad*, ' . . . for when / weary Odysseus returns / Telemachus should leave'. In *September 1913* Yeats refers to Irish history, 'Was it for this the wild geese spread / The grey wing upon every tide?'

AMBIGUITY – This occurs when a word, phrase or sentence is open to more than one interpretation. *Example:* 'I am king of banks and stones and every blooming thing' – Patrick Kavanagh.

ANALOGY – A comparison made to show how two things are similar. Similes and metaphors are based on analogy.

Example: 'Hope is the thing with feathers / That perches in the soul' – Emily Dickinson.

ANTITHESIS – This refers to the juxtaposition of contrasting phrases or ideas. *Example:* 'My words fly up, my thoughts remain below.'

ARCHAISM – This refers to a writer's use of old-fashioned (archaic) language.

ASSONANCE – This occurs when a vowel sound is repeated in words close to each other. *Example:* 'But ranged as infantry / and staring face to face' – Thomas Hardy.

BLANK VERSE – This is unrhymed iambic pentameter (each line consisting of ten syllables). *Example:* 'Your batman thought you were buried alive / Left you for dead and stole your pocket watch' – Michael Longley.

CLICHÉ – This refers to a well-worn, overused expression or phrase. *Examples:* 'Tomorrow is another day', 'raining cats and dogs', 'a crying shame'.

CLIMAX – This refers to a moment of great intensity in a play or dramatic poem. *Example:* Having reflected deeply on the plan to murder Duncan, Macbeth decides not to go ahead with it. However, Lady Macbeth intervenes and Macbeth succumbs to her powers of persuasion. At the close of a very tense scene, Macbeth declares: 'I am settled and bend up each corporal agent to this terrible feat.'

CONCEIT – This is an unusual metaphor or comparison used especially by metaphysical poets such as John Donne. *Example:* Donne compares his lover and himself to the two legs of a mathematical compass to suggest how they will never be separated, even when he embarks on his travels, 'As stiff twin compasses are two, / Thy soul the fixed foot, makes no show / To move, but doth, if th'other do'.

COUPLET – This refers to two successive lines of verse, usually rhymed and of the same metre. *Example:* 'I lift the window, watch the ambling feather / Of hock and fetlock, loosed from its daily tether' – Eavan Boland.

DIALECT – This refers to a form of language spoken in a particular geographical area, which contains words and expressions not found in the standard language.

DRAMATIC IRONY – This occurs in a play when the audience knows more than a particular character. It is very ironic that having been betrayed by the Thane of Cawdor, Duncan then bestows this title on Macbeth, little knowing that his apparently loyal and trustworthy kinsman plans to murder him.

ELEGY – This is a poem of lamentation, a poem mourning the dead.

EMOTIVE LANGUAGE – This is language that evokes an emotional response in the reader. *Example:* 'I touched his head, his thin head I touched' – Michael Longley.

EPIGRAM – This is a concise (short) and witty saying. *Examples:* 'But wild ambition loves to slide, not stand / And fortune's ice prefers to vertue's land' – John Dryden.

EPIPHANY – This refers to a moment of insight / understanding, such as Elizabeth Bishop achieves in the closing lines of *The Fish*.

EUPHEMISM – This is a gentle or indirect way of expressing something drastic, offensive or unpleasant.

Example: He passed away.

FIGURATIVE LANGUAGE – This refers to language which makes use of simile and metaphor to express an idea. To speak figuratively is to speak metaphorically.

FREE VERSE – This is verse that is unrhymed and unmetered. It is widely used by modern poets. *Example:* 'I caught a tremendous fish / and held him beside the boat / half out of the water, with my hook / fast in the corner of his mouth'. – Elizabeth Bishop.

HYPERBOLE – This refers to the deliberate use of exaggeration or overstatement to emphasise a point. *Example:* 'Ten thousand saw I at a glance / Tossing their heads in a sprightly dance' – Wordsworth.

IMAGERY – This is a general term which embraces similes, metaphors, symbols. Basically, it refers to any type of word-picture.

IRONY – Verbal irony occurs when one thing is said, while the opposite is meant. *Example:* 'For men were born to pray and save' – Yeats. Irony of

288

situation occurs when a situation is very different from what the protagonist believes it to be.

LYRIC – This refers to any short poem which directly expresses personal feeling.

METAPHOR – This is a type of image that directly compares two things, without using 'like', 'as' or 'than'. *Examples:* 'I turned to ice' – Derek Mahon.
'a leaping tongue of bloom' – Robert Frost.

MOTIF – This refers to a recurring theme or feature in a writer's work.

ONOMATOPOEIA – This occurs when the sound of the word suggests the sound being described. *Examples:* hissing, sizzled, clanging.

PARADOX – This refers to a statement that appears to be, but is not, a contradiction. *Example:* The freezing ice burnt my hand.

PATHOS – This refers to a quality in literature that evokes a deep, sympathetic feeling in the reader.

PERSONA – This refers to the voice or speaker in a poem. The persona is usually – but not always – the poet.

PERSONIFICATION – This is a technique whereby a writer attributes human qualities to an animal, object or idea. *Example:* The happy sun smiled down on us.

PETRARCHAN SONNET – This refers to a sonnet which consists of an octave/octet (set of eight lines) and a sestet (set of six lines). The octave presents us with a situation or problem which is resolved in the sestet.

QUATRAIN – This is a four-line unit of verse.

RHYTHM – This refers to the movement or flow of words.

SHAKESPEARIAN SONNET – This consists of three quatrains and a rhyming couplet.

SIBILANCE – This is a whispering/ hissing 's' sound. *Example:* 'Its surface seems tilted / To receive the sun perfectly' – Longley.

SIMILE – This is a type of image which compares two things using the words 'like', 'as' or 'than'. *Example:* 'One window is yellow as butter' – Eavan Boland.

STYLE – This refers to a writer's individual way of expressing his/her ideas.

SYMBOL – This is a word or phrase which represents something real and concrete, but also represents something other than itself. *Examples:* A dove is a symbol of peace, a flower a symbol of beauty.

THEME – This refers to a key idea in a piece of writing. (There may be more than one theme.)

TONE – This is the attitude of the writer towards his/her subject. A tone may be joyful, angry, bitter, self-pitying, etc. etc.

NEW ENGLISH KEY NOTES

Leaving Certificate 2009 – Higher Level
Series Editor: Tony Lake

The **exam-focused** approach of these comprehensive notes offers **practical advice** to students preparing for Leaving Certificate Higher Level English – Paper 2. The notes are presented in a **clear accessible layout** and explain and analyse the three elements of the literature syllabus for 2009, as well as **Key Literary Terms**.

Single Text: *Macbeth*

- Scene-by-Scene Summary and Commentary
- Characters and their Key Adjectives
- Key Points after each scene
- Exam Guidelines and Exam Topics

Comparative Study

- Texts: *Philadelphia Here I Come / Cinema Paradiso / My Oedipus Complex*
- Comparative modes: A. Theme or Issue B. Cultural Context C. General Vision and Viewpoint
- Analysis and Commentary / Key Points
- Guidelines for Answering Exam Questions and Sample Answers

Poetry

- Analysis and Commentary / Key Points
- Guidelines for Answering Exam Questions and Sample Answers